BRESCIA UNIVERSITY
COLLEGE LIBRARY

Manhood Impossible

BRESCIA UNIVERSITY
COLLEGE LIBRARY

Manhood Impossible

Men's Struggles to Control and
Transform Their Bodies and Work

SCOTT MELZER

Rutgers University Press

New Brunswick, Camden, and Newark, New Jersey, and London

BRESCIA UNIVERSITY
COLLEGE LIBRARY

Library of Congress Cataloging-in-Publication Data

Names: Melzer, Scott, author.
Title: Manhood impossible : men's struggles to control and transform their bodies and work / Scott Melzer.
Description: New Brunswick : Rutgers University Press, [2018] | Includes bibliographical references and index.
Identifiers: LCCN 2017056007 | ISBN 9780813584904 (cloth : alk. paper) | ISBN 9780813584898 (pbk. : alk. paper)
Subjects: LCSH: Men—Identity. | Masculinity. | Sex role. | Body image.
Classification: LCC HQ1090 .M4195 2018 | DDC 155.3/32—dc23
LC record available at https://lccn.loc.gov/2017056007

A British Cataloging-in-Publication record for this book is available from the British Library.

Copyright © 2018 by Scott Melzer
All rights reserved
No part of this book may be reproduced or utilized in any form or by any means, electronic or mechanical, or by any information storage and retrieval system, without written permission from the publisher. Please contact Rutgers University Press, 106 Somerset Street, New Brunswick, NJ 08901. The only exception to this prohibition is "fair use" as defined by U.S. copyright law.

∞ The paper used in this publication meets the requirements of the American National Standard for Information Sciences—Permanence of Paper for Printed Library Materials, ANSI Z39.48-1992.

www.rutgersuniversitypress.org

Manufactured in the United States of America

Contents

Manhood Impossible

Introduction

The Manhood Dilemma

"Do not cripple your friends. Do not bring them to tears," says the organizer. "If it's your first time at fight club," he adds, turning to face me, "you fight first." He hands me a rounded nine-inch training knife, padded gloves, and a fencing mask. My opponent, Mike, has a knife, too. Unfortunately for me, Mike actually knows how to use his. I have no fight training or experience, and it's about to be painfully evident.[1]

I try not to think about the language in the release form I just signed: "I the participant, am knowingly risking injury, which typically includes bruises, bumps and scrapes but can include serious injury and death from either fighting or watching." Bruises. Bumps. Scrapes. *Death?* It's unlikely anybody will come close to dying today—at least not of anything more than humiliation.

Mike and I are fighting under the auspices of the Gentlemen's Fighting Club, a San Francisco Bay Area group formed in the late 1990s. In GFC's history, there have been few serious injuries. This fact, along with the thickly padded gloves and sturdy mask, alleviates most of my concerns. Still, I am tempted to repeat the prefight instructions to Mike: *Please do not cripple me or bring me to tears*.

"Fighters ready?" the timekeeper asks. I tighten my fingers around the handle of the training knife and square off with my opponent. "Fight!"

It is Fight the Professor Day at GFC, a onetime gathering organized at my request. It's a comforting sign of the GFC "bring you up, not beat you down" philosophy that my original title—Punch the Professor—was rejected. Suddenly it doesn't sound as funny as it did when I first suggested it. While typical GFC novices fight in a suburban garage, today we're on a concrete patio and

1

grass in a fenced-in backyard. Despite my lack of fighting ability and the jarring reality of staring at a knife-wielding opponent of greater skill and experience, I'm not gripped with fear. I have watched enough GFC fight footage to have some sense of what to expect. I know that fights usually end after 60 seconds, when fatigue overwhelms most amateurs. I'm hoping a lifetime of competitive sports and good reflexes will offset some of my disadvantages.

Also, I did a lot of sandbagging to get my opponents to underestimate me. This was not difficult. I doubt they worried that the longhaired, 5'9" professor with no fight training or experience might discover and unleash his inner Bruce Lee. To ensure as much, I sent messages beforehand noting my chronic back injury, and on the day of the fights, I complain of jet lag and lack of sleep (all true). As we boil mouthpieces and wait for all the fighters to arrive, I add a healthy amount of self-deprecating humor. I've done everything except have my mother place a pleading phone call to Mike right before our knife fight. My strategy works. I find out later that the consensus was I would last only one fight.

The last of the day's participants arrive, and we head outside to the backyard. Everything is in place, including the generously supplied athletic cup. It's time to fight.

My brother, whom I persuade to drive with me to the event and be an observer, is assigned the role of timekeeper. This responsibility is accompanied by two others. First, depending on the extent of my dismemberment, he will either rush me to the hospital or just drop me off at the hotel. Second, he will have to make a convincing argument to our family that he was an unwilling participant forced to attend the event—a hostage, really—who tried to talk me out of it, failed to do so, and despite his strong reservations about my choosing to fight, felt obligated to watch over his younger brother.

His story is mostly true. "You're an idiot!" he admonished when I told him about my plans to fight. He added a well-placed expletive to avoid any subtlety. Proving him right, I aggravated my balky back several days before the event. A physical therapist friend realigned my rotated sacrum and manipulated my vertebrae back to their proper positions. She was surprisingly nonjudgmental about my upcoming foray into fighting. Other reactions ran the full gamut. One friend got teary eyed at the thought of me fighting. I suspected she lacked confidence in my abilities. Another friend questioned my sanity, but he sent a supportive text the day of the fights: "Good luck today you crazy s.o.b."

At dinner one night, a couple friends were skeptical and gave me some gentle ribbing when they find out about my research topic. ("I know you can't talk about it, but if you're in a fight club, put your thumb on the table.") Several others questioned me about the risk of injury and expressed curiosity, excitement, and enthusiasm. I considered inviting a linebacker-sized friend to help me with prefight "body conditioning"—a fighting euphemism for getting punched and kicked during training to acclimate the body to getting hit—but later changed my mind. When I finally told him about my now-abandoned idea soon before my fights, he replied, "There's still four days left!"

My then-partner may have been the most enthusiastic, which means our families later questioned her thought process as much as they did mine. Shortly after "Fight the Professor" was confirmed, it came up during a casual conversation at home. She asked me why I wanted to fight. Unjustifiably defensive, I questioned her motives for asking. Effortlessly, casually, she peeled back the layers of my psyche that I naively thought were hidden. "I just want to know the truth," she said nonchalantly, as she turned the page in the magazine she was skimming. I stumbled through a response about my responsibilities as a researcher. She has a degree in anthropology and sociology, yet I heard myself delivering a SOC 101 lecture about best practices when studying human behavior, about the importance of *participant* observation, of not really being able to understand the fighters and their experiences unless I've experienced it myself. All of it is true and half-true.

"I have no delusions," I told her, finally directly addressing what was unspoken. "I know that I have no training and no fighting experience, and I'll probably get my ass kicked." I sensed that she was waiting for a "but," yet she said nothing, and the conversation ended. The qualifier I suspect she awaited lingers in my mind. Why *am* I fighting? Is it for some of the same reasons the other GFC fighters do—to test their skills and toughness, to conquer their fears, and in some cases, to try to restore a sense of masculinity and control they lost during experiences of boyhood emasculation? Shouldn't being married and having a good job offset or eliminate these boyhood anxieties?

I'd like to think these guys are different than me. I was not picked on or bullied as a child. I live, work, and go out in areas that seem safe. I rarely think about having to defend myself and have no desire to take martial arts training. And I have been studying, reflecting upon, and trying to free myself from many of the burdensome and destructive aspects of masculinity for years—the expectation to be tough and capably violent chief among them.

But here I am. Knife in hand. Curious how I will do against more experienced and trained fighters, wondering if I have more than an amateur's 60 seconds' worth of fight in me. Sure, participant observation will benefit my research in ways that interviews and mere observation cannot. But even during interviews with GFC fighters many months ago, well before I decided to fight, I occasionally thought, or perhaps fantasized, about what it would be like to fight some of them. Why *am* I here?

Body and Breadwinner Failure

As with the men who fight at GFC, an honest answer requires an exploration of a lifetime's worth of experiences. Although I was not a target of bullying, I do recall feeling insecure and fearing violence from other boys throughout my childhood. These were due to being small; my parents didn't exactly hand me a winning genetic lottery ticket. Worse, I entered puberty painfully late, seemingly after every other boy in my grade. Eventually I arrived at about average size for an American man but only after suffering daily frustration and embarrassment over many formative years. I hated exposing my small, hairless body while changing in middle and high school locker rooms.

I avoided confrontations and sometimes even interactions with boys who used shoving and punching as their two primary forms of communication. I feared the violence that was so prevalent between boys, even acquaintances and friends. I watched teammates put on muscle, run faster, and jump higher, while my athletic exploits were developmentally stunted. Dating and girlfriends were alien concepts. All these experiences left me with an overwhelming desire to get bigger and stronger. I wanted to—felt like I *had* to—fix what I saw as broken. I did not have a word for it at the time, but I felt emasculated.

All that changed, though, when my body did. I turned 17 and turned the corner. A year later, in college, I looked and felt age appropriate for the first time since elementary school. I was determined to transform my body into a source of pride rather than shame, to go from feeling imprisoned within it to fulfilling what suddenly felt like its untapped and unconstrained potential. I committed myself to weight lifting even though I didn't enjoy it. What I did enjoy was how I looked and felt as my body developed. Steroids never appealed to me, but I knew plenty of guys who used them and recognized in them the same insecurities and desire for change. My anxiety-fueled workout routine produced 15 added pounds of muscle my freshman year of college.

I finally felt like a man instead of a boy. My confidence was growing. My athletic abilities were peaking. I still mostly avoided confrontations and did not get in fights, but I was not as intimidated by others. If my friends and I played a friendly game of tackle football, I expected to do and did just fine. I welcomed taking my shirt off at the pool rather than fearing having to do so. Dating became, well, at least a little less of an alien concept.

My physical peak was short-lived, though. I was overdoing my weight lifting and exercising, even for a teenager. The result was a severe lower back strain, which repeatedly left me unable to move for hours on end. A range of initial treatments proved worthless. I was 19 years old, and my body was disappointing and failing me. Again.

In an obsessive effort to repair what felt broken as a boy, I permanently injured myself as a young man. It could have been much worse, though; years of physical therapy has allowed me to stay active. But my back still affects how I sleep, sit, stand, work out, and live on a daily basis and will continue to do so for the rest of my life. My injury is a relatively mild example of the "costs of masculinity," or the downside of the pursuit of and access to power and privilege: "The promise of public status and masculine privilege comes with a price tag: Often, men pay with poor health, shorter lives, emotionally shallow relationships, and less time spent with loved ones."[2]

My injury has also helped shape my research interests. In a narrow sense, my motivations for fighting at GFC are quite different than the other members'. Broadly, though, we arrived here for the same reasons. Our interests, choices, aspirations, insecurities, identities, relationships—our lives—are defined and sometimes plagued by what American boys and men are expected to be and do and, perhaps more important, how we respond when we do not meet (or just think we don't meet) those expectations. These in turn are shaped by our race, ethnicity, social class, sexuality, and much more.

The list of expectations is long. I argue that the two primary ones placed on men revolve around their bodies and work. Men must demonstrate mastery and control over their bodies and achieve a sense of status and identity from their work to stake a claim to American manhood. Failing at either generates a range of powerful, mostly toxic emotions and responses.

This book examines four groups of men who grapple with body and breadwinner ideals: members of a fight club and an online penis health club that attracts men who seek to improve their size and sexual performance, and unemployed men and stay-at-home dads. The body and breadwinner ideals men are expected to fulfill lie mostly beyond their reach. Whether men pursue and partially obtain or fall far short of these ideals, the results are destructive for everyone. Manhood must be reimagined and redefined in such a way as to make it achievable for men and healthy for all.

Is it possible that being a man could be defined and practiced in a way that is much less toxic, even antisexist? Maybe a new ideal manhood marked by disinterest in power and control, nonviolence, and intensive parenting could become the new most celebrated, ideal version. Or will this merely produce a kinder, gentler patriarchy? Should we instead pursue a world where those arbitrary social constructions of "femininity" and "masculinity" are eradicated, entirely disconnected from female and male bodies? If so, how will we get from our current patriarchal system to a gender-free one? I take up these questions in more detail at the end of the book. For now, whichever objective we might pursue, I propose the starting point for gender reform or revolution must be a fundamental change to men's body and breadwinner ideals.

Controlling Bodies and Work

Control, and especially men's fears of being dominated and controlled by others, is the central feature of what it means to be a man.[3] This imperative was amplified and peaked first at the turn of the 20th century and again in the second half of that century. Both times, native-born white men's statuses and identities were threatened by sweeping structural and cultural transformations. In the early 1900s, industrialization and capitalism were making obsolete the agricultural and artisanship-based work that had long sustained native-born white men and their families. These men were thrust into the new marketplace where hard work alone was no longer enough to guarantee security. They were forced to migrate to cities to enter the paid labor force and compete with other men (and women and children), many of whom were new arrivals to the country or recently unshackled from the institution of slavery, in the case of many African Americans. In a massive wave of immigration from 1881 to 1920, 23 million people emigrated to the United States, most of them from Europe.[4] Prior to this era, manhood was contrasted with boyhood. It implied an inner quality that, although not preordained, could be fairly easily achieved and maintained by demonstrating maturity, responsibility, and autonomy. In the unpredictable new economy, manhood was replaced with masculinity—something to be worn for all to see and constantly proven—and it was contrasted with femininity. Industrialization and capitalism stripped away many men's firm control over their ability to work and provide for their families.

Native-born white men reclaimed some of this control by limiting and excluding women and other men from newly defined masculine arenas such as organized sports and fraternal organizations, and most notably the workforce.[5] Doing paid work, and especially being successful enough at it to support a family without financial contributions from wives, became the middle-class standard against which all men were judged. Being a breadwinner and earning a family wage was the primary and ultimate manhood ideal.[6] An unintended consequence of this arrangement was that boys were around men less. This produced in many men a fear of boys' feminization and a desire to segregate and differentiate boys from girls and women. It is this time in U.S. history when many of today's gendered differences in dress, play, and activities were created or greatly expanded. Boys—mostly privileged and white—were removed whenever possible from the perceived soft, civilizing clutches of women and cities. They were sent to the newly formed Boy Scouts or the Boone and Crockett Club, or the YMCA with its new emphasis on physical activity. Later, they attended gender-segregated colleges. Men also began worrying more about their bodies during this time, with an eye toward controlling them. Strength, appearance, and performance were important in a competitive marketplace. Exercise, escape from urban areas, proper diet, and resisting masturbation were all seen and sold as ways for boys and men to be masculine and successful. The new emerging breadwinner ideal was elusive, but at least men could attempt to maintain some sense of control by gaining command over their bodies and by excluding women.[7] The Allied Forces' World War II victory was a collective win for American manhood, too. War has long served in literature, lore, mythology, and cross-cultural history the role of ritual proving ground for men. American GIs returned to a hero's welcome and a booming New Deal economy, both temporarily cooling off many men's status anxieties.

Another series of sweeping structural and cultural changes began unfolding in the 1970s and continues today. These changes have made American men's chances of being sole or merely primary breadwinners more remote, thus placing manhood under even greater threat. They include deindustrialization, declining wages, a series of economic recessions and spikes in unemployment, the concentration of wealth in fewer and fewer hands, the flood of women entering the paid labor force, the necessity of dual-earner families, and women's own breadwinner desires and successes. Breadwinning men are becoming anachronisms. This is especially so among blue-collar, working-class men. The structure and ideology of capitalism and an open class system leave all men anxious and unfulfilled, including those whom others might see as successful. After all, there is no ceiling on income or wealth. There is always another man who earns more and has more—or is about to. A race without a finish line is a competition with no true winner.

Shaky job markets and invisible finish lines are part of the bigger picture of contemporary life for everyone, not just men. Our world is filled with uncertainty and unpredictability due to rapid social change, technological advancements, migration, media, and more.[8] This is the cultural milieu that propels us to turn inward, to focus on and manipulate our bodies in an attempt to maintain some feeling or semblance of control. For men, as the breadwinner ideal has become less obtainable and women have enjoyed more access and power in the workforce and other social arenas, body ideals have become more important, ubiquitous, and complicated. Men are increasingly judged on the basis of their bodies, and their bodies are increasingly judged on both appearance and performance. Women, conversely, have been judged much longer and more harshly based on their appearance, and these expectations continue despite women becoming breadwinners.[9]

The breadwinner ideal persists as the most significant and meaningful measure of manhood, but men's body ideals are a close second. As men's breadwinner options have deteriorated and women's labor force participation has expanded, men have focused more on improving and differentiating their bodies and appearances from women's. This is far from a new practice (think corsets and codpieces), especially among privileged men, who in the past wore

luxurious clothing, jewelry, powdered wigs, and skin-lightening creams to sig-
nal class and racial differences. But more recent shrinking social differences
have led men to expand their long practice of creating greater physical differences between themselves and women.

Charles Atlas's pitches to transform "97-pound weaklings" into strong and
tough men telegraphed a new era of gendered bodies and American manhood.
Fifty years later, in the 1980s, Arnold Schwarzenegger and Sylvester Stallone
conspicuously revealed men's new expectation to be conspicuous physical
specimens. Their bodies were celebrated for how they looked and how they
performed—the latter as weapons used to dominate and control other men.
The fitness craze that launched in the 1970s continues apace. Weight lifting
and bodybuilding; supplements, steroids, and other performance-enhancing
drugs; and mixed martial arts and fight culture are primarily, albeit not exclu-
sively, men's realms.

Contemporary younger men are particularly attuned to body pressures.
They do not yet have access to the breadwinner ideal, and their generation
has always faced these body pressures. Today, men who are not strong, tough,
and sexually active and skilled—men who are not in complete control of their
bodies—are not fulfilling this manhood ideal. Like men who do not fulfill the
breadwinner ideal, they are liable to feel like and be told they are failures.

The Manhood Impossible Study

When I began this project in 2011, I set out to study only the phenomenon
of men compensating for their masculinity failures. I sought to identify and
pursue data where the stakes for men are highest: in their work and in their
bodies. The Great Recession of 2008–2009 piggybacked on the long-term
breadwinner-undermining social changes outlined previously. It deeply under-
cut many men's breadwinner aspirations, providing a tragically ideal context
for my research. The more elusive breadwinning becomes, the more essential
it is for men to control their bodies. These acute and chronic social changes
implore researchers to better understand how men attempt to establish masculine identities in times of uncertainty and flux. I heed the long-standing
call to study men's responses to structural threats to their masculine status
and identity.[10]

Both body and breadwinner ideals are positioned beyond most men's grasp,
leaving men "unable or unwilling" to fulfill these ideals.[11] If we set men up to
fail, I ask, what are the consequences for them, their families and communities, and our society as a whole when men inevitably find manhood impossible? What do men do under these circumstances? I quickly discovered that
yes, they sometimes compensate, but they also respond in several other ways.

I selected four groups of men for my study, two for each ideal. For the dual key body ideals of physical and sexual competence, I interviewed and studied a group of men trying to test their toughness and mettle at a fight club, along with online members of what I call the Penis Health Club (PHC), who are focused on improving their size and sexual performance.[12] For the breadwinner ideal, I interviewed and studied involuntarily unemployed men and stay-at-home dads.[13] In total, I interviewed a diverse group of 55 men, collected field notes via participant and nonparticipant observation (at the fighting club and multiple job fairs), and analyzed a wealth of documents, namely online forum posts by PHC members and blogs authored by unemployed men and stay-at-home dads.

GFC members and stay-at-home dads tended to be in their 40s or younger. The Penis Health Club was composed of a disproportionate number of younger members, but plenty of older men joined as well. Unemployed men varied considerably, but my sample mirrored the bulk of the U.S. unemployed: men mostly in their 20s–50s.[14] The 14 PHC members, 13 unemployed men, and 16 GFC fighters I interviewed occupied various relationship statuses: single, partnered, married. Gathering data on participants' social class was more complicated. Nearly all of the unemployed men were in highly fluid situations. So were some of the stay-at-home dads, though they tended to be more stable, usually middle class. PHC members varied considerably in their socioeconomic statuses, with a wide range of educational backgrounds, occupations, and income levels. The GFC fighters I interviewed were disproportionately likely to have college or graduate degrees and be working in technology, reflecting their Bay Area location and social networks among the mostly tech workers who comprised the group's core. However, several of these men did not have college degrees, reflecting the group's diversity. GFC members lived all over the Bay Area, but more were concentrated near Silicon Valley, where fights were held. (See the appendix for more on this study.)

By definition, unemployed men and stay-at-home dads do not fulfill the breadwinner ideal. Some men who participated in the fighting club and online penis club joined these groups simply because they were doing what is expected of them—trying to be physically and sexually capable, not because they were motivated by a sense of failure. This kind of gender conformity explains plenty of men's behaviors, and it is crucial for identifying and understanding what the social norms are. However, my primary focus is on how men respond when they cannot or choose not to conform. What do men do when they fail to perform gender appropriately?

Four Responses to Body and Breadwinner Failures

Building on earlier research, I find that men respond the following four ways when they are unwilling or unable to fulfill body and breadwinner ideals: (1) *internalize* their perceived failure, (2) attempt to *repair* the failure, (3) *compensate* for the failure, reasserting their masculine selves elsewhere, or (4) *reject and redefine* what it means to be a man. These four responses do not represent four types of men ("Internalizers" or "Repairers").[15] Men from each of the groups I study exhibit all four responses. Many wrestle with whether they should follow cultural ideals, sometimes internalizing and trying to repair what they see as their own failures, and other times deciding the ideal is flawed and in need of rejection and redefinition. In short, these four responses are how men do masculinity after experiencing what they or others judge to be gender failure.

Internalizing

The term *internalizing* comes from developmental and clinical psychology. It is usually joined by the word *disorder* to describe problem-based feelings and behaviors kept to oneself, such as withdrawal, isolation, and feelings of worthlessness.[16] I borrow this term but use it more broadly to encompass any behaviors that are directed inward rather than outward (as a "disorder" or otherwise). Some of the men I study experience emasculation, anxiety, low self-esteem, weight fluctuation, decreased libido, disinterest in hygiene, depression, and suicidal thoughts in response to physical or sexual inadequacies or feeling like failed breadwinners. In the most severe cases, they are trapped in a negative cognitive and behavioral loop, getting slowly devoured by their perceived shortcomings.

And that's just what they are: perceptions. Symbolic interactionism explains that our social realities are far from objectively true or real. A shared understanding of reality is a production, dependent upon people assigning similar meanings to objects, groups, and actions.[17] Human bodies exist, but cultures and individuals determine what bodies are attractive or unattractive, normal or disordered, useful or a burden. Bodies have no inherent meaning. Perception is what guides men's interpretations of their bodies and work. Many men with average or above-average penis sizes and a biography free of humiliating sexual performances remain convinced they are inadequate. When a global recession kicks millions of men out of the paid labor force, most will view their own job loss as a personal failure. Our deeply held beliefs swat away contradictory facts like a hockey goaltender's pads deflect opponents' shots. In another culture or another time, men wouldn't be so emasculated by having an average-sized penis or losing breadwinner status.

The four responses I identify do not represent a linear stage progression of responses. An internalizing response may coexist or be succeeded by one or more of the three others, or it may be the only one men experience. For each of the last three responses, though, internalizing is a preceding step. Our cultural configurations ensure virtually every American man experiences some sense of internalized failure and feels badly about it, at some point during his life.

Repairing

Wherever possible, men seek to restore their masculine selves by directly *repairing* what they believe to be broken. Some members of the Gentlemen's Fighting Club join the group to restore what they lost when intimidated and bullied as kids. Fighting as adults helps them exorcise their boyhood fears by directly confronting their perceived flaws: physical weakness, passivity, and loss of control over their bodies. Of course, this repair work may be fleeting, reflecting the tenuous nature of manhood itself. Men flock to the online Penis Health Club to learn about stretches, workouts, and devices purported to improve what many of these men see as fatal flaws in their penis size and sexual performance. Members log countless hours trying to address these, regardless of whether they are small, average, or even above-average in size, or how gratifying or embarrassing their sexual histories are. And for failed breadwinners, there is a single avenue of repair: returning to a good job in the paid labor force.

Compensating

Restoring a sense of a masculine identity via repair is not always possible; what's broken cannot always be fixed. Physical limitations or economic recessions can block repair work. In response, men sometimes assert a masculine self in one area to *compensate* for their failures in another.[18] Unemployed men seek to control other parts of their selves, including their bodies, or are quick to use anger to control a situation. Some GFC fighters restore a sense of lost power and control by fantasizing about using their fighting skills to dominate other men in a barroom brawl or, more commonly, playing superhero to victims of distress. The popularity of fantasy sports and violent video games, television shows, and movies suggests that the realm of fantasy allows many men to restore their lost sense of control in reality. In more extreme cases, mass shooters such as Elliot Rodger and George Sodini play out these fantasies, using murderous violence against women and other men in response to their inability to gain women's sexual interest. Their homicidal violence is the most abhorrent reassertion of control. Such violence is a response to "the fear of shame and ridicule, and the overbearing need to prevent others from laughing at oneself by making them weep instead."[19] The initial internalization of failure, experienced as shame and ridicule, is supplanted by an externalizing response: compensatory violence, used to restore a sense of self.

Repairing and compensating are both attempts to restore one's lost manhood—which is often mostly illusory—and thus they reproduce and reinforce men's domination and control.[20] Internalizing does not reproduce gender inequality, but neither does it challenge the gender order. These three types of responses illustrate the many personal, relational, and social problems that can be traced to men's struggles to meet current body and breadwinner ideals.

Redefining

There are contradictions and tensions, though, as new ideals compete with older models of manhood. Some men reject restrictive manhood ideals in favor of less destructive and more attainable ones. They discard the expectations placed upon them, instead choosing to define manhood in ways that clash with hegemonic standards and practices. In the process, they begin to *redefine* what it means to be a man. Men in the Penis Health Club, especially its older members, encourage men to abandon unattainable, pornography-driven penis size and sexual performance ideals, revealing them as fabrications. Instead, they preach body diversity and acceptance. Some stay-at-home dads define their unpaid work as fathers as the ultimate demonstration of manhood. The most ideologically committed ones are bolstered by supportive partners, families, and peer groups and enjoy more financial stability. Some stay-at-home dads chose to leave the paid labor force, while others were pushed into their new roles. Regardless, they conclude that ego and selfishness (not a desire to be a provider) is what motivates men to be breadwinners, whereas leaving their careers to raise their kids is the most responsible and manly thing to do. Their embrace of feminine-marked, low-status, unpaid work is one of the missing pieces of stalled gender equality. Women have flooded into domains previously dominated by men, but the reverse has not occurred. Perhaps more men doing carework will lead to less devaluation of women and femininity.[21]

Extrapolating the Four Responses

Some of my case study groups may appear unique or exotic, which could suggest my research is confined to these exceptional men. I argue that men's experiences of emasculation are near universal, as are the various kinds of internalizing, repairing, and compensating responses. True, not every physically emasculated man joins a fight club or tries to enlarge his penis, and not all unemployed men become psychologically paralyzed. No human experience is universal. However, a common thread unites American men's experiences. The importance of the dominant culture's body and breadwinner ideals colors the experiences of men in every corner of American society. A suburban fighting club is uncommon, but asserting masculine identities via fight culture is not (as seen in boyhood fighting culture, gang and prison cultures, bar fights, and the practice and popularity of boxing and mixed martial arts). An online penis enlargement club is unusual, but men's deep concerns about their size and sexual performance are not (as seen in erectile dysfunction sufferers and a booming ED drug industry, a continuous stream of ads for these drugs and various enlargement products and devices, and extensive discussion of these issues in popular books and magazines).

Perhaps the group of non-breadwinning men in this book appear less exceptional given the common experience of unemployment. There are an increasing number of stay-at-home dads, but they remain a small minority. Today's new fathers, though, are more interested and active participants in childrearing than previous generations. Engaged fatherhood is becoming the norm, so more and more American men are faced with the now separate, competing demands of being good breadwinners and good dads. This book does not examine all American men's responses to not fulfilling body and breadwinner ideals. No qualitative study can do so. But my sample includes diversity in terms of race, ethnicity, sexuality, class, and age, allowing me to identify processes and experiences that generate common responses across a wide range of groups and contexts. The broadest context, the one that all these men share, is accountability to American manhood ideals.

Gender Accountability and Inequality

To understand manhood, we must first understand sex and gender. *Sex* refers to the biological characteristics that are used to distinguish females, males, and intersex people: genes, hormones, genitalia, and internal reproductive anatomy.[22] Conversely, gender lies outside of biology. *Gender* is a social construct, a set of arbitrary meanings and expectations mapped onto the biological categories female and male. We enact femininity and masculinity in our interactions; they are performances that are fluid, ones that vary from one situation and context to another. Neither femininities nor masculinities are identical in prisons, offices, parties, and funerals; the 1820s, 1920s, and 2020s; or the United States, Zambia, India, and Chile. Boys holding hands or men controlling family finances are actions that are interpreted differently by context. And we as individuals will behave in culturally defined ways that are both feminine and masculine over the course of our lives—if not each day. None of us succeeds (if it is our goal) in being 100% masculine or feminine, especially given that these are moving targets, as social norms shift over time. Gender is associated with sex, but not determined by or dependent on it.

Gender is not innate or static; it is a performance and accomplishment rooted in social interaction. It is not something we are born with but rather something we do.[23] Briefly, if a person looks and acts more or less like we expect a man should (i.e., if they appear cisgender), we assume that person is male. They might not possess all (or any!) of the biological characteristics of a male, but if they put on a good performance, then based on their appearance and behavior, we somewhat unconsciously place that person in the social category *man*. We then interact with this person accordingly.

Just because our gender differences are not biological or predetermined doesn't make them less real or consequential. We are always accountable to gender norms. We are always displaying ourselves for judgment and evaluation, self-regulating our performances, and judging others' performances against cultural criteria. Conforming to cultural prescriptions serves to reinforce what is "gender-appropriate." Violations of these socially constructed gender norms reveal how we are gender accountable. Doing gender *in*appropriately—to be a feminine man, or openly and proudly intersex, or transgender—may lead to being ostracized and marginalized, challenged, bullied, and even violently victimized: "If we do gender appropriately, we simultaneously sustain, reproduce, and render legitimate the institutional arrangements that are based on sex category. If we fail to do gender appropriately, we as individuals—not the institutional arrangements—may be called to account (for our character, motives, and predispositions)."[24]

Even if we reject the norms, we know what they are, we usually feel compelled to follow them, and (most) others will expect us to conform. Cultures take the broad spectrum of gender diversity and reduce and confine this array to two categories, or sometimes three (e.g., the *hijra* in India, or the *kathoey* in Thailand).[25] Through gendered socialization, interaction, and rewards and punishments, girls and boys and women and men are expected to (and often do) behave differently enough to make these normative differences seem natural. Doing gender appropriately reinforces gender inequality because it makes gender differences—men's domination and women's deference—seem normal and inevitable. We see gender and assume we are observing sex.[26]

A performance is something that is done with an audience in mind. In interaction, performances convey to others the most public aspect of our selves—our identities—or who or what one is according to oneself and others.[27] Gendered performances are attempts to communicate to others a gender identity—and therefore most typically one's status as a competent (American) woman or man. Identities that are salient in almost all situations and interactions, such as a gender identity, are deeply meaningful, core parts of our selves.[28] People who do gender inappropriately—who put on a bad performance—often place their gender identity at risk. Research reveals that men commonly try to "correct" behaviors that undermine claims to masculine identities, at times going to extreme lengths to do so.[29] In some cases, they may try to display the specific behavior judged lacking (repair), such as getting in a fight after being called soft. In other cases they may find an alternative way of laying claim to a masculine identity (compensation), like bragging about their penis size after getting beat in a competition.

Without question, how we perform gender matters. Our clothing, hair, bodies, mannerisms, speech, and actions often reproduce patterns of difference and inequality. Doing masculinity appropriately brings many rewards: social approval, sexual and romantic access to women, status and respect, power and resources, and much more. It is no wonder most men attempt to conform, even if they only access some of these rewards. When they do gender inappropriately, they are likely to lose all access. Yet many people intentionally do gender inappropriately. They attempt to redo gender in a way that challenges cisgender expectations. These performances can be both subversive—fostering changing beliefs about gendered norms and altering the accountability structure—and subject to overt, even violent "corrective" responses.[30]

Gender's reach extends well beyond interaction and identities. Gender is also built into our society. Groups, organizations, institutions, culture, and social structure are gendered.[31] That is, they are organized around gendered expectations, unwritten and written rules and policies, and ultimately, inequalities. Our opportunities and choices are influenced and constrained by the gendered worlds given to us. Children are born into families with gendered and unequal caretaking, housework, and paid labor roles. They graduate from babies to girls or boys by demonstrating not only greater cognitive and emotional development but gender competence. Outside of their homes, they are confronted by a gender-segregated and unequal world: scouting groups, toy aisles, bathrooms, sports teams, dress codes, and later, body products, magazines, college dorms, sex norms, jobs, and workplaces. Their bosses and their boss's bosses are more likely to be men. So are their legislative representatives. Workplace policies and cultures privilege and reward those who do not bear or rear children and are more likely to marginalize, derail, or jettison those who do. State and federal policies—such as the United States' minimal and unpaid family leave, lack of free or affordable childcare, a weak social safety net compared to similar nations, and a large proportion of the federal budget allocated to national defense—reinforce gender inequality and devalue much of the unpaid work that (mostly) women do. Gendered socialization, organizations, and institutions place women at a disadvantage in a competitive, capitalist society. Greater economic and social power is conferred to men because their gendered behaviors, expectations, and responsibilities are what our society rewards most. As I discuss throughout this book, social norms, practices, and policies further divide and disadvantage groups by sexuality, social class, race, ethnicity, age, and more.

Men's Power Paradox

Doing masculinity appropriately requires the devaluation of femininity and women. Cultural ideals and patriarchal gender relations reveal a hierarchical and complementary relationship between masculinity and femininity; masculinity is enacted and institutionalized at the expense of and on the backs of women.[32] Women disproportionately suffer from sexual harassment and various forms of intimate violence, including homicide, sexual assault, and rape.[33] Women work jobs that pay less, and they are paid less for doing the same work as men. They encounter glass ceilings in work and politics and lack political representation.[34] Women's lesser social, economic, and political power is exacerbated by their continued primary caretaking responsibilities, which produce more part-time women workers or burden them with the bulk of the second shift—childcare and housework duties upon returning home from a full-time job.[35]

As a group, men enjoy privileges that women experience as discrimination and oppression. But not all men enjoy them equally. Critical feminist theorists introduced the concept of intersectionality to sharpen our understanding of the multiplicative of identities and statuses we possess—categories that we may have viewed as disconnected or discrete.[36] For example, the gendered experiences of a resource-poor immigrant man from Guatemala doing seasonal farm work will be pretty dissimilar to that of a U.S.-born African American man who is CEO of a Fortune 500 company. Borrowing this intersectional approach, masculinities scholars have highlighted how men who are poor, queer, undocumented, disabled, and/or of color enjoy fewer or few gender privileges.

Ironically, most men often feel powerless despite their relative position of privilege and influence. Author Michael Kaufman explains,

> The very ways that men have constructed our social and individual power is, paradoxically, the source of enormous fear, isolation, and pain for men ourselves. If power is constructed as a capacity to dominate and control, if the capacity to act in "powerful" ways requires the construction of a personal suit of armor and a fearful distance from others, if the very world of power and privilege removes us from the world of child-rearing and nurturance, then we are creating men whose own experience of power is fraught with crippling problems. This is particularly so because the internalized expectations of masculinity are themselves impossible to satisfy or attain.[37]

Men have created the rules that provide them with social privileges, but the consequences of pursuing and actually obtaining social power causes them pain and alienates them from others. These costs arise from the spoils of being the dominant group, but men experience them as costs nonetheless. Men's expectations to compete, show no weakness, and to control themselves and others, leave them emotionally and socially disconnected from others, especially other men. Men are more likely to be both perpetrators and victims of violence (mostly as strangers), suffer the health effects of breadwinner pressure and the expectation to bottle up their emotions, be more emotionally stunted and socially isolated, and ultimately die younger than women.[38]

Just as the privileges of patriarchal gender relations are not equally shared among all men, neither are the costs. Not only do working-class white men and men of color enjoy fewer resources than middle-class white men, but the former groups also suffer from worse health, higher rates of violence, and shorter life spans.[39] All of these problems may arise from gender conformity but are more likely to occur following gender failure. Unmet body and breadwinner ideals cause men tointernalize a sense of failure and often redouble their efforts by trying to fix or compensate for their perceived shortcomings. This pursuit of manhood creates countless individual and social problems. Today's version of ideal manhood is impossible to sustain, and as I argue, it is ultimately destructive for everyone. It is not inevitable, though. As the stay-at-home dads I interview reveal, men can reject the breadwinner ideal and begin redefining manhood away from power and control.

Masculinity and Manhood

The terms *masculinity* and *manhood* are often used interchangeably, but they are not equivalent. *Masculinity* is a performance, something that is done. As with all performances, it is fleeting, tenuous, and influenced by past performances. It comes and goes. Anyone—males, females, intersex people, women, men, transgender people—can do masculinity, but their performances are tied to their social categories. Girls and women, for example, are not accountable to masculinity as are boys and men.[40] Girls and women may enjoy some of the privileges of masculinity, such as status and respect for their athleticism, or money and power for their workplace accomplishments, but their gender identities are not undermined by *not* doing masculinity. Quite the opposite, as women who act "too masculine" often have their gender or sexuality called into question; when they do masculinity, it challenges the hierarchical and complementary gendered expectations and patterns of American society.[41]

Boys and men are highly accountable to masculinity. If they do not do masculinity appropriately, they or others may question their manhood. The term *manhood* suggests an overarching sense of self that arises from the accumulation of credible masculine performances.[42] Doing masculinity appropriately over and over again may lead to a sense of manhood. However, manhood is elusive because boys' and men's gender accountability is more restrictive as compared to girls' and women's. Early in their lives, boys learn that they have to fit their behaviors into the narrow confines of the "act-like-a-man" box or others will force them back into it.[43] "Man up!" they'll say, perhaps teasingly, even affectionately. More often it is used as a challenge or as a put-down or attack.

There are three key reasons manhood is so inflexible compared to womanhood—that is, why girls and women have more freedom to do masculinity than boys and men have to do femininity. First, manhood is constructed in opposition to womanhood but less so is the reverse true. Second, manhood must constantly be proved. Third, our society offers more and greater rewards for masculine-marked behaviors, tasks, careers, and so forth.

Being a man is more restrictive first because it usually means convincing others that you are *not* being a woman—or more precisely, that you do not say, think, feel, or do anything that is associated with femininity. How do boys insult and demean other boys? They call them "girls," "crybabies," "wimps," and "sissies." When they are older, they use "gay," "fag," "bitch," and "pussy," equating who their targets are and what they do with derogatory terms associated with women, femininity, and being perceived as effeminate.[44] They are called a "pussy" when they are dominated by other boys or men and "pussy-whipped" when accused of being controlled by women. Men are admonished to "Man up!" or, in some locations, "Cowboy up!" The more provocative and confrontational insults use male genitalia as symbols of social manhood, such as when men's "testicular fortitude" is questioned and they are told to "grow a pair" and "sack up" or "nut up." Language is powerful. It both reflects and shapes our behaviors. These kinds of challenges to manhood are endemic in men's interactions, revealing and reinforcing men's power over women; they are attempts to assert power over each other, usually due to fear of being on the receiving end of such attacks.[45]

It is important to point out that the reverse mostly is not true. Women don't tell each other "Woman up!" or "Ovary up!" when they aren't being feminine enough. Challenges to women who are perceived as too masculine are more circuitous. Women get called "sluts" (not "men") for wanting and having "too much" sex. They may get lesbian-baited if they are deemed too muscular or athletic, fight for equal rights, or aren't dependent on men. Or they may be called a "bitch" if they are perceived as noncompliant or "bossy".[46] These stigmatizing labels—mostly but not solely wielded by men—are used to attack women who embody the masculine-marked qualities that help sustain men's dominance.[47] They are enough to discourage some girls and women from doing what they otherwise would choose to do. And women often alter their behavior to prevent or end this kind of labeling, by doing femininity in other ways such as emphasizing their heterosexuality and enacting more "feminine" styles of leadership. Still, significant numbers and in some cases majorities of women pursue casual sex, build muscle and compete as athletes, and seek economic and political power. In other words, an increasing number of girls enthusiastically embrace being a stud, tomboy, and boss.[48] The rewards for these identities, behaviors, and statuses, as well as their greater social acceptance compared to just a generation ago, often outweigh any negative consequences. Women don't flee from masculinity quite as fast and far as men do from femininity. The fears and insecurities that haunt women do so for different reasons.

The second reason manhood is more restrictive is that it is highly precarious—regularly subject to threat and capable of being undermined. There is a long list of possible sources of emasculation for boys and men, a seemingly endless inventory of manhood. Failing to be big, tough, strong, athletic, heterosexually active, stoic, independent, aggressive, competitive, successful, and in control—or simply thinking one is not living up to these standards—invites masculine anxiety. So does walking, standing, sitting, running, talking, eating, dressing, greeting others, flirting, checking yourself out in the mirror, petting a cute dog, doing handiwork, and literally, I argue, every conceivable behavior, if it is done in a way that could be judged feminine. Everything men do has the potential to discredit their masculine selves. Doing masculinity appropriately, or at least not femininely, may bring rewards. Or it may fly under the radar—just the daily routine of a guy doing what guys are supposed to do. Men don't always have to give an award-winning masculine performance, but they better not give one that audiences see as too feminine. (Conversely, masculine anxiety is not provoked by failing at empathy, kindness, patience, expressions of love, and so forth. Men, though, could be held accountable for doing these things too skillfully.)

Not all behaviors and expectations are equally important across all locations and situations. Men who are not handy, do not follow sports, are not outdoorsy, know nothing about cars, have some body fat, don't know how to grill food, or can't tie a tie may occasionally feel a fleeting sense of shame or embarrassment, but these masculine-marked expectations are not core concerns of manhood. Research suggests that physical, sexual, and economic competence and accomplishments are those to which men feel most accountable.[49] Notably, a single perceived failure on these—getting beat up or publicly humiliated by another boy, experiencing erectile dysfunction, losing a job or breadwinner status—is often enough to threaten one's manhood identity and status. People police themselves so harshly—they are so fearful and vigilant—that they often see shortcomings in themselves that others do not. This helps explain why many men whom others would view as manly (because of their physical or economic status) may see themselves as impostors, unworthy in some way.

Today's masculine failures, whether called out by others or conjured internally, lay waste to yesterday's accomplishments and claims to manhood. Manhood must be constantly proved.

Third and last, our patriarchal society provides most of the material and symbolic rewards to men and masculinities, thus further restricting manhood. Political and economic power is concentrated among men, especially men who fulfill masculine ideals. Jobs and activities associated with women and femininity, such as paid and unpaid carework, are devalued.[50] Breadwinning is rewarded more than caretaking, accomplishments are respected more than appearance, competition yields more rewards than cooperation. Men who do femininity relinquish not only some semblance of their masculine identities but also material rewards and social power. The societal pressure on girls to focus on caretaking and appearance is intense beginning in childhood, as they are expected to express interest in dolls, hair, makeup, jewelry, and generally, being pretty.[51] And even when girls and women do masculine-typed things, they aren't rewarded as much or are punished for doing so, because they are behaving gender inappropriately. The tough, assertive, career-oriented, accomplished woman is too often labeled a cold, ballbusting bitch and a terrible mother. This is changing somewhat, certainly more rapidly than are men's norms. But women are expected to find an elusive balance between feminine and masculine characteristics and behaviors: simultaneously caring moms and career-oriented professionals. Womanhood impossible!

Doing Dominance

If gender norms and arrangements are arbitrary, though, how did those of the United States come to be the way they are today? Anthropologists have documented a range of manhood ideals across cultures.[52] Why is U.S. femininity the antithesis of masculinity? Why is manhood so tenuous—and thus virtually unobtainable? Why are men and masculinity privileged at the expense of women and femininity? Sociologist R. W. Connell's concept of *hegemonic masculinity* provides answers.[53] It borrows from an early analysis and critique of capitalism that deployed the concept of cultural hegemony.[54] According to cultural hegemony, the ruling class maintains power not simply through economic or political coercion, or force and violence, but through cultural coercion. The dominant group maintains its power and legitimacy by imposing its ideology. The ways of the dominant group become normative and are embedded in organizational practices and institutional policies. These arrangements and beliefs are so pervasive that even those who suffer from them (the resource poor and working class) usually are complicit in following them. Subordinate groups adopt the ideology of the dominant group because everything associated with the latter group is held up as the cultural ideal. The ideal becomes so prevalent that it appears natural and inevitable. For example, the American political and economic system is deeply tilted toward the privileged and severely limits class mobility. However, most people continue to accept the entrenched ideology of rugged individualism in our capitalist, pull-yourself-up-by-the-bootstraps American culture. It is so accepted that it's often used to shame others (or oneself) for lack of success.

With hegemonic masculinity, gender substitutes for social class. The ideology and practices of the dominant social group—men—are upheld by processes of not only domination and control but coercion and complicity. All men are expected to adopt the ideology and practices of hegemonic masculinity, even if almost none of them can hope to fulfill its ideals. Women are similarly expected to uphold the status quo, even though it ensures their secondary status. For example, women are expected to and often do slut-shame other women and view non-breadwinning men as less desirable. As it was originally formulated, hegemonic masculinity was explained as "the currently most honored way of being a man[;] it required all other men to position themselves in relation to it, and it ideologically legitimated the global subordination of women to men."[55] It is normative, if not the norm. Women mostly conform even though doing so translates to having less material and symbolic power. They, too, are accountable to gendered ideals. Women and men must do gender appropriately because their "competence as members of society is hostage to its production."[56] Being appropriately feminine may validate women's identities and provide some material benefits. Deviating can be costly. Women's complicity is key to hegemonic gender relations; the subordinate group must somewhat buy into and uphold the institutional arrangements that oppress them. Yet women, gay men, and others also often resist and challenge these oppressive gender relations; it is a process.

Two key insights from Connell's work are well supported by years of research: there is a plurality of masculinities, and they are arranged hierarchically. The ideal type, *hegemonic masculinity*, sits at the top. Men who enact *complicit masculinity* conform to the ideal type as best they can but do not fulfill it and therefore do not enjoy many of its privileges. Still, their ideology and actions help ensure a hierarchical and complementary relationship between masculinity and femininity. The term *marginalized masculinity* is used to explain how resource-poor men or men of color may benefit from gender privilege but suffer discrimination and oppression from their other lower-status social categories. *Subordinated masculinity* lies at the bottom of the masculinity hierarchy. It represents failed masculinity; men who are subordinated are equated with women and thus subject to discrimination, violence, and oppression. Gay men and associated stereotypical behaviors are the most subordinated in American culture because they are typecast as feminine and passive—the opposite of hegemonic masculinity. Subordinated men lie near the bottom of the hierarchy because of their *extra*men identities and statuses. That is, gay men are subordinated because our heterosexist society discriminates against their sexuality. Overall, women are very likely to enjoy lower statuses and fewer resources than similarly situated men.

As influential as this concept has been, it suffers from some shortcomings and contradictions and therefore has its critics.[57] Some wonder why we should use the term *masculinity* at all given that anyone—biological females, social women, transgender people—can do masculinity. Sociologist Michael Schwalbe thinks researchers should focus on any and all of men's actions—individually and collectively—that subordinate women, as well as other men.[58] He proposes we focus on manhood acts, which are "aimed at claiming privilege, eliciting deference, and resisting exploitation," and thus reproduce inequality and preserve patriarchal gender relations.[59]

In these ways, manhood acts are the realm of men because their purpose is to maintain men's power over women. For example, men who feel threatened economically, or who perceive their woman partners as not sufficiently submissive are more likely to use violence against them to reassert a sense of masculine authority.[60] Boys and young men who feel as though they are not fully in control of their bodies sometimes assert their masculine identities by stigmatizing other men with the label "fag," drinking heavily, physically and sexually victimizing younger peers, and sexually harassing women.[61] In short, when men do masculinity appropriately—when they make a claim to manhood—what they are doing is attempting to align themselves with the dominant group (men as a gender class) at the expense of the subordinate group (the gender class of women).

Of course, not all men are situated equally. They have access to different kinds of manhood acts depending on their education level, social class, race and ethnicity, sexuality, age, and more. They are subject to the gender binary, but they use the tools they have available. For non-breadwinning men (younger, poorer), bodies become a more likely site of manhood acts. They may use their bodies to resist others' control (e.g., not doing "women's work" around the house) or to control others, such as through intimate violence. Presenting oneself and being labeled a man is not a difficult accomplishment. Manhood acts are what enable men to access a high-status identity and its accompanying benefits.[62]

The idea of doing masculinity is still a useful concept insofar as it speaks to how our embodied displays of gender are always accountable. We are evaluated based on our performance as well as our social categories. Masculine behaviors are not determined by biology, but they are differentially performed, experienced, judged, and responded to when they are done by women, men, or transgender people.[63] Masculine performances are situated—that is, they are determined and judged based on the characteristics of the person, the audience the situation, and locally prevailing masculine ideals. Southern, rural, white masculinity is not identical to East Coast, urban, Latino masculinity. Further, individual men in either context will assert their masculinity in numerous ways. This is why some question whether there is a monolithic cultural standard against which all men are measured. It is true that tremendous variation exists. But we must guard against being too reductionist. We mustn't ignore the commonalities among local versions that comprise the cultural ideals, which are what ensure systemic inequality.[64]

Redefining and Reimagining Gender

Focusing solely on inequality-reproducing manhood acts reduces multiple masculinities to a binary and seems to negate the possibility that an inclusive, egalitarian (or any other) masculinity ideal could emerge to challenge current patriarchal ideals and arrangements.[65] Let's remember that gender and gender arrangements are arbitrary artifacts of culture. The concept of doing gender was so revolutionary because it bridged micro and macro levels of analysis by deftly accounting for individual agency, social structure, and social change.[66] People might choose to do gender inappropriately, but they face social consequences for doing so. However, gender accountability shifts in response to changing historical and structural conditions as well as people challenging gender norms both individually and collectively. Cultures categorize and do sex, gender, and sexuality quite differently.[67]

Based on my interviews with stay-at-home dads, countless conversations with college-aged youth, and the emergence of more alternative, inclusive masculinities among younger men, I think widespread social change is possible, if far from imminent.[68] Whatever optimism one may have is likely tempered by how deeply entrenched are current American hegemonic ideals and gender arrangements. At the heart of this inequality is the importance of control for masculinity.[69] I argue that boys' and men's bodies and breadwinner status/ identity are the two primary sites for their expression of control. Controlling selves and others and resisting being dominated and controlled is most connected to men's bodies and work.

Reading Manhood Impossible

Part 1 of this book, "The Body Dilemma," examines the manhood ideals that boys first encounter: the expectation to control and master their bodies by proving their toughness and displaying heterosexual competence. Chapter 1 discusses how the Gentlemen's Fighting Club uses the manhood ritual of interpersonal combat to afford adult men the opportunity to confront their fears and test their fighting skills and selves. Fighting culture arises due to the absence of rites of passage for American men, along with conformity to body ideals. In chapter 2, I examine GFC members' internalizing, repairing, and redefining responses to not fulfilling body ideals. A subset of men who were physically controlled and dominated as boys internalized a sense of failure. GFC provides fight therapy—it allows these men to directly repair their earlier losses of physical control and sense of emasculation by fighting as adults. They restore a sense of control, paradoxically, by choosing to give up control and place themselves at risk. Even when they lose a fight, they demonstrate their ability to withstand violence and thereby begin repairing their damaged masculinity. Yet responsible adult men are not supposed to fight. Some GFC fighters see others' negative reactions as evidence of a society gone astray, one that threatens not only fight culture but men's natural predispositions. They blame the civilizing forces of modernization and urbanization or feminists for undermining ideals of physical toughness. Fighting becomes GFC men's expression of both personal and political manhood, a primal, tribal act in opposition to contemporary society.

Chapter 3 examines men who have joined the Penis Health Club in hopes of improving their penis size and sexual performance. Anxiety-producing locker room experiences, devastating comments by peers and sexual partners, racial stereotypes, inconsistent sexual performances, and distorted images from pornography produce in many boys and men an internalized sense of body failure. They conceal their bodies, avoid sex and relationships, and in some cases suffer from depression and suicidal thoughts. The Club provides size and performance therapy, and an opportunity to repair broken manhood both by helping men change their negative perceptions about their penises and actually improving their size and performance. They feel empowered by the mere possibility that they can change something they previously thought was static. (Re)claiming a sense of control over their bodies begins to repair some of the damage of internalized inadequacy.

Compensatory responses by both GFC and PHC members are the focus of chapter 4, along with high-profile cases of extreme compensatory masculine violence. GFC members sometimes slip into seemingly harmless fighting and superhero fantasies to compensate for their all-too-normal and mortal bodies. Younger PHC Club members lash out at women they derisively label "size queens" for desiring large penises, thereby causing men to feel small and incompetent. Sculpting and building the rest of their bodies helps some men offset some of their anxieties about their below-average or merely average penis size and sexual skills. The most serious and consequential cases of compensatory manhood acts include men who commit various acts of intimate violence and violence toward strangers.

Part 2 of the book, "The Breadwinner Dilemma," examines the manhood ideal to which adult men are most accountable: their ability to provide for themselves and their families. Chapter 5 introduces the unemployed men and stay-at-home dads who are the focus of this second half of the book. Men's status as breadwinners has been slowly eroding for decades and has always been more tenuous for men of color and working-class men. Despite sweeping changes to gendered work-family arrangements, the expectation for men to maintain breadwinner statuses and identities largely persists. In the midst and aftermath of the Great Recession, many men were forced out of or left the paid labor force. My job fair observations and conversations capture the structural obstacles that unemployed men (and others) often experience as personal failures: too many job-seekers, not enough jobs. A number of these men involuntarily became stay-at-home dads, while others chose to because they and their partners determined this is the best arrangement for their families.

Chapter 6 discusses the internalizing and compensating responses of unemployed men. Joblessness most affects men who are forced into unemployment, fail to live up to their own and their partner's expectations, have little support, and are struggling financially. Many of these men internalize their struggles, suffering from severe depression, insomnia, physical deterioration, withdrawal, and ultimately, a sense of emasculation. Others externalize their feelings of being failed breadwinners, expressing anger and aggression and asserting themselves more in attempts to control others and situations. Some milder forms of compensatory masculinity include behaviors that would be perceived as positive, such as getting in shape, acquiring higher levels of education, and trying to satisfy a partner's needs. I return to high-profile cases of violence, namely, mass shooters and terrorists, to illustrate more extreme, costly examples of compensatory manhood acts in response to being a failed breadwinner.

In chapter 7, I examine men who have embraced their status and identity as stay-at-home dads. They reject and redefine the expectation that men must be financial providers for their families, instead defining themselves as responsible providers because they prioritize their children's well-being over family income or their own ego or careers. Transcending the breadwinner ideal is a constant challenge, though. These men struggle with a sense of loss of status and identity, feeling unappreciated and, when finances get tight, guilty. They also face negative reactions in a culture that has not fully embraced men as primary caretakers—or for gay stay-at-home dads, same-sex parents in general.

The concluding chapter assesses how body and breadwinner ideals have been transformed over the last several decades and predicts the pace and prospects for continued change. Men from all four groups overwhelmingly reject a separation of spheres for women and men. They hope that American culture will purge some of the unattainable expectations that plague and emasculate men, oppress women, and contribute to countless social problems. Still, many men continue to believe that to "man up" requires them to be leaders, protectors, and breadwinners—and ultimately, not women. I argue that demographic trends (younger Americans are more likely to embrace gender equality), an economy that will continue to require multiple incomes, and the possible introduction of more progressive work-family laws and policies (to counter the neoliberal dismantling of many family and social support systems) will foster continued change. Finally, advocates and agents of change—feminists and profeminists, antiviolence activists, gender benders, breadwinning moms, stay-at-home dads, and many others—will also help American society redefine what it means to be a man, making manhood less violent and destructive, and the achievement of it more possible.

Part I
The Body Dilemma

1

Ritual Violence in a Two-Car Garage

The Gentlemen's Fighting Club

Fight the Professor

"Fighters ready?" I tighten my fingers around the handle of the training knife and square off with my opponent. We gently tap weapons to acknowledge we are ready, and I hope, to communicate to each other and the other fighters that we will fight without malice; no one will be brought to tears or crippled today. "Fight!"

My opponent, Mike, is in good shape, athletic and wiry-strong. Our fight begins cautiously. All the other fighters know each other's styles and tendencies. My only advantage is that I'm a wild card. No one knows what I'm going to do, including me. Mike and I exchange attacks and counterattacks, trying to strike each other with our training knives while maintaining our footing on the wet turf. Twice he sticks me in my mask, attacks that would be disabling and possibly fatal if we were street combatants using real knives. I land a couple of uninspiring kicks to Mike's torso as well as one or two stabs with my knife. Time expires. I survive unscathed, thanks to my headgear.

The 60 seconds is an eternity, yet it ends before I have time to process anything that happens. Fighting is an "in the moment" activity; my mind does not wander to writing deadlines or to-do lists. The event organizer and Gentlemen's Fighting Club cofounder, Rick, peppers me with questions immediately after the fight while his brother continues filming; all GFC fights are recorded and watched afterward. Rick asks me what went through my mind during my first knife fight. Camera shy and mostly unfazed by the experience, my response is brief and perhaps unsatisfactory. "Longest 60 seconds of your life, huh?" he says before moving to Mike. "How was it fighting the professor?" Rick asks. "It was nice. I've got a little ring rust," Mike says, referencing not having fought in a while. He notes an ankle injury slowed him down and limited his aggression but generously observes, "He actually got some good shots. Got me on my fingertips, I think an open shot on my elbow, so that let me know he was serious."

My bad back holds up well, I have no visible bruises, my energy isn't sapped, and I don't vomit. I feel good!

Another pair of fighters readies themselves. Six of us will continue to rotate through in paired fights. I have about 10 minutes to recover before my next one. As I watch the other fights, I'm struck by the ferocity and degree of violence between the experienced fighters. Their level of aggression is something I feel unprepared to match. My feelings are not atypical. Many GFC fighters struggle with being the aggressor. They share self-criticisms during interviews, revealing to me that inflicting violence is less enjoyable than dodging or even withstanding it. They derive satisfaction from avoiding or weathering big blows, not from clobbering their opponents. However, not all GFC fighters share this apprehension. A couple report that they relish landing big shots.

I recall the advice and pep talk emailed to me several days before the event. A GFC member unable to attend wrote,

KICK ASS AND TAKE NAMES!
You were **BORN** for violence my fellow MAN.
Take up that stick knowing in your heart of hearts that every fiber of your
    being
has either evolved through fighting and death
or was simply created
. . . to do . . .
THIS.

He and several other GFC fighters think men have a killer instinct—literally, not metaphorically. Fighting, they explain to me, is a primal act, one that men's bodies have evolved to do. They believe it needs to be freed from the suppressing forces of civilized society. If true, if interpersonal violence is in males' DNA, fighters shouldn't struggle so much with using violence. And there should be a line of men down the street hoping to join GFC. Neither are true. Violence isn't an essential feature of maleness. One reason "caveman masculinity" and pop-Darwinism evolutionary psychology resonate so strongly today is men's feelings of powerlessness in the face of their declining bread-winner status and diminishing cultural hegemony.[1] In other words, the rise in popularity of caveman masculinity as a lay explanation for men's more brut-ish behaviors is a collective compensatory manhood act, an attempt to justify and restore men's dominant position, because they believe it to be threatened or lost.

I feel personally powerless as I watch the other fighters and take mental notes on attack tactics, hoping to summon a greater level of aggression for my next fight.

Was I was born to do this?

Feeling well rested, I volunteer to lead off the second round of matches. Another fighter, Kay, does, too. Kay is not an intimidating presence: under-sized and gregarious, he has a sharp mind, a good sense of humor, and slightly disheveled hair and is prone to screaming when he receives a hard blow. I know better than to underestimate him, though. His physical appearance belies his superior skills and technique, which match or exceed most of his oppo-nents. Kay is among the many participants who view their fighting club expe-riences as self-defense training. They see GFC as a way to prepare themselves for unexpected confrontations that could happen walking down the street or socializing at a bar.

In this vein he suggests a "knife versus jacket" fight, where one of us has a knife and the other is armed only with the windbreaker he would be wearing walking around chilly San Francisco. "I'll take the knife!" I shout. Only my brother laughs. When the fight is delayed due to Rick fiddling with the camera settings, my brother and I huddle up and jokingly exchange a series of hypo-thetical, escalating asymmetric fight scenarios inspired by "knife versus jacket": "Uzi versus pen!" "Flamethrower versus thimble!" "Tank versus paper clip!" With the intensity level of the previous two fights fresh in our minds and my escape from harm seeming less likely, we find temporary refuge in humor. I suspect this fear and anxiety, ironically coupled with the somewhat controlled nature of GFC fights, is what sets its audience experience apart from watch-ing cage fighting, wrestling, or even dog- or cockfighting. The GFC audience and participants are one and the same; anyone may later end up on the receiv-ing end of a strike they now cheer. The costuming and occasional playfulness, along with padding and an array of skill levels, also alters the experience. It seems as if the strongest source of bonding is self-deprecation rather than cele-brating fighters' skills. Sure, an impressive move receives an audience response, but collectively and individually, fighters seem most connected laughing at their own and others' klutzy moves and failed attacks, whether in the moment or later on video.

I wear pad-free mesh gloves to grip the short knife I'm given to fight Kay. We both wear fencing masks. Kay begins our fight by unexpectedly going on the offensive and whipping me with his thin jacket. I had anticipated he would try to use it to wrap my wrist and disarm me. Instead he's using it to maintain distance from my hypothetically deadly weapon. After three stinging whips to my upper body, I am both impressed and annoyed. I grab the jacket the next time he tries to hit me and rip it out of his hands. The small crowd cheers my surprisingly effective countermove. The underdog has captured the crowd's heart. My lack of training exposes me, though, as I meekly hit Kay with his jacket using my off hand. Eventually I figure out that the jacket is a hindrance so I toss it into a bush. Now it's knife versus nothing.

A knife in my hands proves just as nonlethal as the jacket. Kay lunges forward and delivers a mighty punch to my head. I rock back a step and a half from the force of the blow, then quickly process two key pieces of information. First, despite being several inches shorter and many pounds lighter than me, Kay could easily knock me out if I wasn't wearing a helmet. Second, I *am* wearing a helmet. It absorbs virtually all of the force, and although temporarily surprised and knocked back by the punch, I am fine. I am better than fine. Feeling energized by the protection of my safety equipment, I go on the offensive. I return a punch to his headgear with my now jacketless left hand. The punch leaves my knuckles sore and stinging after the fight, but delivering a successful strike feels good in the moment. It feels like an accomplishment.

Even better, Kay is treating my training knife like it is real, testing his skills to see if he can avoid any contact from my blade. He could simply bull-rush me, get in close, and pummel me, ignoring whatever fake knife slashes I might deliver. Instead he chooses to engage in the academic exercise of avoiding a potentially lethal knife wound. Or rather, the real exercise of fighting a knife-wielding academic.

Near the end of our fight, he moves in to attack me but slips on a muddy patch of grass. A vision flashes in my mind: Kay on the ground, unarmed, pinned under me as I repeatedly stab and hit him. Before that violent thought is complete, I find myself on the wrong end of it. Kay pulls me down with him and suddenly I am on my back, disarmed, and ineffectually trying to use my hands, arms, knees, and legs to block the haymakers Kay is raining down on my mask. "Time!" my brother screams, mercifully and more emphatically than any of his other fight-ending yells. Damn. I don't feel so good.

The other fighters rotate through, and I get more rest. One fighter has his toe knifed or stepped on (it's unclear) and is likely going to lose a toenail. Another, Patrick, probably broke a finger. He did not wear gloves during his stick fight with Rick, or "the War Chief," as one member half-jokingly, half-affectionately calls him. Rick is intent on doing a stick fight with me as well. He checks with me to see how many more fights I can handle. I still have a lot of energy, and the only bad blows I've taken have been to my headgear, so I tell him I can do two more. I am saving the worst for last—my ceremonial beating at the hands of my host.

Lived and Bled with Us

Thinking about it now, agreeing to fight Rick is akin to my punching back against some of those high school boys who symbolically and physically dominated me. Rather than avoiding them in the hallway, this is me slugging them on the arm first and inviting a return blow. It is conquering fear and bonding through violence, thereby gaining full entry into the privileged dominant group. And unlike high school boys, GFC participants want nothing more than to bring me into the fold.

Hearing I am willing to participate in two more fights, Andrew extends an invitation. I accept, and we discuss our weapons options. We agree on the foot-long, hollow rubber hoses. Terrible choice. I pick one up and discover it isn't the flexible, jiggly rubber I was expecting. It bends a little, but not much. It's a hard, dangerous weapon. I instinctively held my hands up to deflect knife attacks and punches during the first two fights. Remembering this, I put on a heavily padded glove and smack myself on the back of the hand for a preview of what's to come. It hurts. A lot. I strap on a much sturdier kendo mask, which is heavily padded all around the head and neck, save for a series of bars protecting the face. "Fighters ready?"

I feel as disconnected as ever from my ancient human ancestors. I was *not* born to do this.

Andrew has a distinct size advantage over me and has a decade of martial arts training and fighting experience. Some of that experience includes rubber hose fights. I am quicker, though, so I plan to use my speed to get in and out, negating his greater size while avoiding getting into a grappling match. If I stay too far away, I expose myself to his reach advantage, but if I get too close he can grab me and eliminate my speed advantage. Who am I kidding? I'm armed with a rubber hose I just picked up for the first time in my life, and I have no training, experience, or technique. I'm in trouble no matter what I do.

Andrew confirms as much soon into our match. He lands a huge blow to my inner thigh, which will result in a multicolored bruise that will last the next couple of weeks. I use my padded glove to deflect a couple of Andrew's strikes, but it offers only so much protection against the sturdy hose. Caught up in the moment, though, the pain doesn't fully register. I fake an attack to Andrew's upper body and then swing my weapon at his legs, nailing him with a shot on his quadriceps that matches the one he gave me. I feel good. Another exchange nearly ends with my grabbing and taking away his weapon, but I fail to do so. Then with about 15 seconds left, I lose my weapon (again) in a scuffle. I retreat and hear my brother announce, "Ten seconds!" The rational part of my brain formulates a plan: run away and do not let Andrew come anywhere near me. The yard is plenty big enough to take evasive maneuvers for 10 seconds. However, that would violate the spirit of the fight club and probably leave me with a deeper bruise than anything Andrew can deliver with the hose.

I fake retreat and then try to get close enough to him that he can't effectively swing his weapon but far enough away that I won't get caught in a wrestling match. In other words, I try to exist in a space-time dimension I just invented. The first attempt fails and he smacks me on the top of my grilled mask. It jolts me and makes an echoing dinging noise when the rubber hits the metal. I know the ringing is in my headgear, not my head, so I make another attempt to move in closer. This time we lock arms. We methodically spin in a clockwise rotation, him looking for opportunities to strike me in my torso with his knee and me trying to keep him off balance so he can't do so. Fatigue sets in after a couple spins. I know I just need to hold on for a second or two more. Mercifully, again, the timer buzzes, signaling the fight's end.

"Keep going," Rick says from the sideline. It seems demonic in the moment, but at GFC, it is not unusual to extend the time if neither fighter is hurt and they have enough energy to continue. I already mentally checked out, though, and am physically exhausted as well. Dutifully following Rick's forceful suggestion, Andrew and I continue our orbital dance. His significant size and mass advantage allows him to expend less energy. He tries to knee me in my stomach several times. Each time I raise my knee to block his and keep us spinning to deflect the blows. I'm spent, running on fumes. Finally, unable to protect myself any longer, I let my guard down and Andrew knees me in my solar plexus. I audibly groan and bend over in pain as the air rushes out of me. The strike disables and disorients me. Thankfully, even though I fail to officially tap out of the fight, Andrew stops attacking me because he sees I'm incapacitated. A gentlemen's fighting club indeed.

Rick tells me to take a 15-second rest and then keep fighting. If I could breathe or speak I would curse at him. I stay bent over for a few seconds. A small part of me actually briefly considers his horrific idea before I realize I'm unable to continue. I mumble through my mouthpiece, "I'm done," hoping to convey every possible meaning of that phrase. I nearly vomited when Andrew's knee struck me, and the feeling isn't subsiding. Still, Rick subjects me to the postfight interview, which also includes a close-up examination of my welts and bruises. In what feels like a depraved sports physical, he gleefully and exhaustively probes my wounds, commenting on each. I feel awful.

I sit down, force myself to take a few sips of an energy drink, and try to recuperate. The next fight happens, but I barely notice. It ends, and the camera is unwelcomingly in my face again: "How are you recovering from the fight?" I answer truthfully: "I don't feel like I am." Everybody laughs. It looks like my stick fighting career will end before it starts. Meanwhile, Patrick and Andrew agree to a weapons-free fight. No weapons means no headgear is worn, so they follow what GFC calls "yuppie rules"—no shots to the head. The social class implications are clear: middle-class men insulate themselves from the dangers and consequences of street violence. They can't show up to their jobs or return to their families and communities with bruised and battered faces.

Earlier, Patrick broke a finger and briefly blacked out during a double-stick fight with Rick, who accidentally hit Patrick on a tiny unprotected area on the crown of his head where the helmet straps meet. Patrick and Andrew's helmetless fistfight is a marathon, a full five minutes. Both fighters are dog-tired at the end. This buys me enough time to recover, the pain and nausea finally subsiding. Rick checks to see how I'm doing but really to see if I will be able to fight one more time. I know I have to do so. Given how indebted I am to him for providing such extensive access to GFC, I mostly willingly accept his invitation to stick fight.

We follow our plan to do a single stick fight, using sticks about two and a half feet in length and an inch in diameter. "Just 30 seconds," he says, so I can get a taste of stick fighting. Rick is built like a linebacker. He is a skilled fighter with a reputation that extends beyond GFC to a broader fighting community. Once again, he promises to "bring me up" rather than "beat me down." Mike helps me strap on my kendo helmet and offers some advice on how to swing my weapon with greater force and how to most effectively attack Rick. I thank him but promptly forget his suggestions as soon as the sticks start flying.

Rick has me do one last prefight interview: "So you're going into your first stick fight here. What's running through your mind?" he asks. "What's running through my mind is that you've been incredibly helpful," I tell him, "and that I owe you a lot and I'm about to pay it back right now, because I'm dead tired. I just took a big shot, and I'm feeling like my tank is empty." I look into the camera, resigned to my fate: "But I've got to square off with this guy at least once, so . . ." Rick, buoyant now, shares his own preliminary thoughts with the camera: "All right. So I'm preparing myself to go up against the professor. You never know. You always learn the most from the new guy."

One last time: "Fighters ready?" We tap sticks. Rick motions for me to attack him, and I comply. His counterattacks are controlled, unaccompanied by kicks. Having watched his earlier double-stick fight with Andrew, I recognize (and appreciate) that Rick is holding back with me. This is what more experienced fighters do with less experienced ones, whether at GFC or when sparring in a boxing gym.[2] We have a series of exchanges before the 30-second timer buzzes. "Keep it going?" he asks. I feel OK so I nod to confirm. "Keep it going," he says joyfully, and the clock is reset for another 30 seconds. Rick strikes me on my noisy kendo grill a few times. He also hits me on my forearm, tricep, and outer thigh with his stick, all of which leave nasty-looking marks.

Still, I find that I am able to deflect many of his blows when there is some distance between us. I mimic his earlier move of starting a swing high and then
crouching low and striking a leg. I nail him on his inner thigh. "Good," he tells
me as I attack him. The timer buzzes again, and we lower our sticks. I take
off my helmet and spit out my mouth guard, happy that I don't have to fight
again. Rick asks me how I felt during the fight and then has the camera comb
over me like a full-body scanner again, searching for bruises and the conspicuous marks left from the rattan stick.

"All right, professor," he says, giving me a postfight hug. I observe at GFC
what I have seen countless times on ball fields and courts: competition, contact, and violence forge masculine bonding, intimacy, and friendship. I thank
him for the fight, the last of the day, and for setting up today's event. "Lived
and bled with us," he beams. My silver shorts do have several blood stains on
them, but fortunately, none came from me. Rick bloodied a finger in an earlier fight and likely reopened it during our stick fight. I am bruised but not
bloodied, hurting a little but not injured, and happily upright and walking. I
feel good.

Talking about Gentlemen's Fighting Club

Little is known about the number or nature of U.S. fight clubs and their participants. As I began writing this book, I did not locate any scholarly research
on actual fight clubs. There are, of course, panicky media stories about teenage
fight clubs. These fights are staged for fun, for gambling, and sometimes to
create homemade movies that are sold for profit. They have little in common
with the handful of adult fight clubs I discovered during my research. With
the exception of GFC, the adult clubs were either no longer active or deeply
underground, and they mostly mirrored increasingly popular and main-
streamed mixed martial arts events. GFC is the only club I located that uses
weapons and holds regular fight nights.

This fight club predates the popular film and did not gain inspiration from
the 1996 novel the film was based on. The first GFC participants were dissatisfied with the heavily padded, controlled sparring sessions their martial arts
instructors allowed. They wanted to see if their training and skills would translate in a real fight, so they created the best simulations they could while minimizing the risk of serious injury.

The GFC event I attended is similar to most of the ones they held during
the club's peak several years ago. The two-car garage they previously fought
in is no longer available, and the gatherings are more infrequent due to the
burdens of careers, family responsibilities, and aging bodies. First-timers and
longtime members alike fight in a rotation of 5 to 10 people, usually friends

and acquaintances, almost always only men. Approximately 300 people have fought at GFC, most just a few times or less, just to say they did it. Only a few dozen were regular participants at the club's peak, when they fought biweekly. These fighters are distinct in the camaraderie they enjoyed and in their desire to improve their fighting skills and be part of something unique.

Almost all the men have a martial arts or fighting background, but none are amateur or professional mixed martial arts (MMA) fighters. Sanctioned, refereed MMA fights are short, violent exchanges that typically end with a knockout or forced submission. GFC provides a more authentic combat experience than martial arts sparring and less risk of injury than MMA, as well as an especially varied and creative array of weapons. In addition to the grappling and hitting that are part of MMA and the training knives and rattan sticks found in other martial arts, GFC uses brass rods rolled up in magazines, unopened soda cans or soap bars wrapped in pillowcases, small purses filled with buckshot, toilet seats and plungers, folding chairs, cookie sheets, racquetball rackets, computer keyboards, and even metal chains.

Fighters can wear just about any protective gear they choose or none at all. They are gently encouraged to shed what is viewed as excessive protection (like hockey pads) as they gain experience. Bruises, cuts, blood, and pain are routine. Broken fingers happen. The stakes are higher than a schoolyard fight, but only rarely does someone get badly injured. They have to go home to their families and to work the next day, and they want their friends and foes to leave intact so they can return to fight another day. Law enforcement is uninterested in (and might not have authority over) these types of activities as long as they take place on private property and between consenting adults and nobody gets seriously injured.

GFC is a democratic institution. Race, ethnicity, occupation, and social class aren't used as filters for entry. Although members joke about excluding prospective fighters interested in "yuppie punching" and, conversely, the "gentlemen" moniker harkens to upper-class British pugilists, no interested fighter has been turned away. Landscapers, computer programmers, marketers, police officers, community organizers, students, and even a couple gang members have fought at GFC. In the fights, social class and status disappear behind the headgear and weapons. Gender is the most salient feature of their experience.

The media has portrayed the club as a collection of geeks, mostly software engineers and computer programmers, trying to escape their cubicles and their soft existence as nonworking-class men.[3] GFC's high proportion of middle- and upper-middle-class tech professionals reflects the Bay Area location, the founders (who came from those fields), and the members' own social and professional networks. More than their occupation or economic status, it is a background in martial arts—and some frustration with the limits of their training—that draws men to GFC. As Rick jokes, "This is a diverse group of people that get together, with backgrounds from all around the world, and beat each other up."

Darren, a 42-year-old GFC veteran, was the only fighter who agreed with the media's "geek fight club" narrative: "Oh, that's *so* accurate," he says. "I feel, sitting at a desk all day, physically underutilized. So absolutely, when you get out of there, you just want to go do something physical." It's possible other members feel similarly but don't tell me because they want to distance themselves from the stigmatizing narrative. Ronnie, a 24-year-old regular, was bothered by it because he and most of the other non-tech-sector fighters were made invisible by the narrative; it was incomplete, distorted. Some of the core members, who are longtime skilled martial artists or accomplished high school wrestlers, persuasively claim that their "nerd" and office worker statuses are unrelated to their desire to fight. "I don't feel particularly put upon in my cubicle life," thirtysomething GFC regular Jason says.

Even if they aren't drawn to GFC to compensate for being "soft" cubicle jockeys and all are welcome to fight, the group and the fights are situated in a particular context that is classed and raced. It's noteworthy that the violence and danger at GFC are controlled. Some members might view it as preparation for a street fight, but only a few grew up or currently live in locations where the odds aren't astronomically against their having to put their skills to serious test. Compared to the everyday street violence that confronts so many young people, particularly resource-poor young men of color, GFC is a space of the privileged. Fighting for these men is a source of bonding, not a means of survival. As a group, their bodies and memories aren't riddled with scars from old knife or bullet wounds.

The fighters I chose to interview are a racially and ethnically diverse group in their 20s, 30s, and 40s, single or with children, and mostly college educated.[4] Each fighter brings a different biography and life experience to the club. But they share a similar cultural upbringing: longtime American attitudes that value men's violence and combat. In some ways, these transcend divisions of class and race. In so many others—stereotypes about criminality, a culture of fear, discriminatory policing, mass incarceration, and much more—the experiences of different groups of men vis-à-vis violence couldn't be more dissimilar.

Fighting as Manhood Ritual

What motivates middle-aged men who have mostly met and exceeded educational, economic, career, and familial expectations to fight? A wide range of men use their bodies to demonstrate manhood. They use their bodies as weapons or tools to attack and control others (physically or sexually), to engage in competition and violence, to prove they can take it—whether *it* is other's violence, bodily injury, or unhealthy quantities of food and alcohol—and that they can do all of these with rock-like stoicism.[5] Many men are motivated to fight at GFC because they've arrived at adulthood without evidence (at least for themselves) that they've passed the "test." They feel accountable to the expectation that they maintain control of their bodies. They want to know if their own strength and training would hold up in a real fight, if they have the courage to face an armed attacker. Can they overcome a sometimes paralyzing fear of injury and protect themselves and their families—maybe even kick a little ass if they have to?

One subset of this group (discussed in detail in the next chapter) wants to exorcise particularly painful memories of fear, humiliation, and defeat that continue to haunt them. Several men I interview have met many of society's expectations for what men should be and do. Their college degrees, successful careers, and families offset some of the insecurities that arose from their physical shortcomings as boys, and they aren't conquering their childhood demons by committing acts of violence in the streets or using alcohol and drugs to escape their memories. Their class privileges and ages make these somewhat less likely. Yet they continue to define themselves in part by those boyhood experiences; old wounds don't always heal, even for men whose statuses are healthy. GFC gives them a chance to repair their broken masculine identities, to try to restore their manhood.

The prevalence of and expectation for boys' and men's violence isn't uniquely American, but the United States is distinctly violent among industrialized nations. Early 20th-century industrialization and urbanization sparked fear among male politicians, psychologists, educators, and many other men, who warned that modern machinery and other benefits of modernization found in cities would make boys soft and turn men weak. Worse, they argued, with men working outside the home in the newly constructed breadwinner role, boys were under the tutelage of women (whether at home or at school) for most of the day. Critics proposed solutions such as getting urban boys back to nature (e.g., via the Boy Scouts), creating fraternal organizations, and excluding girls and women from many social, political, and economic activities and organizations. Also, they thought boys should fight.[6] Boys embraced this so much so that up until the 1940s, some "actually carried little chips of wood on their shoulders daring others to knock it off so that they might have a fight. It is astonishing to think that 'carrying a chip on your shoulder' is literally true—a test of manhood for adolescent boys."[7]

The 1970s ushered in U.S. deindustrialization, and a virtual closing of the well-worn path to the middle class relied upon by high school–educated, blue-collar workers. The overpowering forces of technology, international trade agreements, recessions, and shifting labor markets made achieving breadwinner status and manhood via work, well, unworkable for many men.

Wherever good jobs are sparse, within and across countries and cultures, the expectation for young men to demonstrate toughness and use violence can be found.[8] Women's cultural, political, and economic gains following the 1960s feminist movement also reduced the significance of men's breadwinner identities. Bodies became a more important site of manhood because bodies are more easily controlled than work. Men might not be able to lift their families into the middle class, but they can lift weights to feel as if they are in control of their bodies, to feel manly. Of course, American culture's greater emphasis on bodies and control over them also applies to women and reflects a broader postmodern cultural turn.[9]

Today, U.S. culture simultaneously expects, celebrates, and punishes violence in boys and men depending on the context, target, and severity of that violence. Despite the complicated, sometimes conflicting messages and without a formal rite of passage from boyhood to manhood as found in cultures throughout the world, our society produces the unofficial, nearly universal boyhood ritual of fighting.[10] Unlike formal rituals elsewhere, which are led by adult men and conclude with public recognition that a boy has passed the test, there is no official marking of passage into American manhood.[11] A teenage boy may prove himself in a fight one day, temporarily demonstrating manhood, only to feel emasculated the next when he fails to fight or falls short on some other arbitrary test. Why should we expect men to stop fighting as boys do when manhood is so tenuous and unobtainable?

The messages boys receive about fighting and violence, though, are contradictory. In one ear are American educators, parents, and law-enforcement authorities. Most now discourage fighting, violence, and bullying (including both physical and verbal intimidation) among boys. In the other ear are older and same-age peers, and some adults (including parents and coaches), who teach and reward boys' violence. Real-life fighting continues to be the way most boys prove themselves physically, testing themselves and one another. For some men, GFC is simply an extension of their lifelong fascination with fighting—from vicariously experienced cartoon violence to actual schoolyard clashes and martial arts training. As boys they enjoyed the benefits of taking on the challenge of a fight, of controlling their own and others' bodies. As adults, GFC is the only outlet for them to enjoy similar benefits. Other potential tests, such as rock climbing or martial arts training, don't offer such an intoxicating masculine mixture of dangerous, carnal interpersonal violence.

Fighting is a distinctly masculine practice. It signifies toughness, fearlessness, and control. Girls and women fight, though much less frequently, and when they do so it is often viewed as a reflection of something unique and often perverse about their individuality, not evidence of biological forces inherent to their gender.[12] "Girls will be girls" isn't dismissively used to explain why they fight. And if girls fail to fight when provoked, they're much less likely to experience shame and humiliation than boys and men. As always, there are exceptions to these patterns. Girls growing up in resource-poor communities, disproportionately black and Latina, are likely to face more violence. Like the boys there, these girls have to be prepared to respond in kind.[13] When they fight, though, it is not seen by others as an expression of their essential femaleness. To fight is to do masculinity.

Just as economic success reflects ideal manhood and brings social power, so does enacting the physical ideals of masculinity. Economic and physical accomplishments are rewarded. The better men do at both, the higher up the masculinity hierarchy they climb. This is less true for women. Although women certainly enjoy many rewards from economic success and are increasingly enjoying those from physical accomplishments, a cultural gender gap persists. American measures of success and control are decidedly masculine. When men achieve them, they reap the full benefits of privilege and power. Men who reject manhood ideals of toughness and physical control relinquish some of that power and privilege. This is why many men fight. Women are still judged by and held accountable to other expectations, such as beauty and motherhood, at least in addition to (if not more so than) economic and (certainly) physical power.

A couple of GFC fighters eagerly speak of physically dominating their opponents, using aggression and overwhelming force. But being a man isn't really about pursuing domination over others—it's about controlling one's fears and other emotions and avoiding being dominated and controlled.[14] Reaching the top of the pyramid isn't really possible, but fighting to avoid being at the bottom is mandatory. For many GFC fighters, it's gratifying just to participate, to put oneself at risk and survive, to experiment with losing and establishing control. All this is to say, asserting masculinity isn't necessarily about inflicting damage. It's about controlling others and controlling one's own reactions and emotions—especially fear. Although some GFC fighters are animated by a sense of failure and in turn respond by internalizing, repairing, or compensating for that perceived failure, many are simply conforming to the hegemonic ideal that boys and men should be able to protect and defend themselves and others. For most fighters, gender conformity explains why they gravitated to wrestling and martial arts as boys and continue to pursue those interests at GFC as adults.

Confronting Fears

Expressing emotions is part of the human experience. Managing emotions—smiling at customers, showing empathy for patients, suppressing anger with loved ones—is a distinctly gendered cultural phenomenon. There are different feeling rules for girls and boys, and women and men.[15] Conforming to these

BRESCIA UNIVERSITY COLLEGE LIBRARY

norms brings rewards, while being unable or unwilling to do so brings consequences. Of all the expectations placed on boys and men, the emotional management of fear is as unobtainable as any. Americans, especially young men, are bombarded with images and messages of fearlessness. From professional athletes revered for playing through pain and injury to the increasing popularity of extreme sports and risk-taking activities to advertising campaigns that appeal to this emotion ("No Fear" or "Just Do It"). *Be in control*, these messages convey. Mixed martial artists signify their masculinity by controlling their own fears while trying to evoke fear in their opponents.[16] If they can suppress or at least manage their own fears of being humiliated, injured, or worse and create these kinds of emotions in their opponents by intimidating them beforehand, they will have taken control of the fight before it begins.

Fear permeates the GFC garage. As the fighters arrive and assemble for a gathering, anxiety masking itself as nervous energy fills the room. Fear is a slow-building, disembodied force at first, ushering in contradictory feelings of dread and excitement. It morphs into something sharper just moments before the first fight. It pierces central nervous systems, revealing itself as a racing heart, a tingling spine, and sweaty palms. "Fighters ready?" Just as a feeling of angst envelops the garage and seems on the verge of crescendo—"Fight!"—it disappears. A flood of adrenaline carries fighters into and through the action. Their fear is displaced by intense concentration, an immersion in the moment. The erratic yet rhythmic exchanges between combatants bring some measure of calm to spectators as well. These fighters in waiting are temporarily reassured, if not placated, by the familiarity of pedestrian swings and kicks and punches. They study the combatants dispassionately, coolly planning moves to try in their own fights.

Then *boom*! A massive blow is landed, generating a shockwave throughout the garage. Fear has materialized again, this time as a lightning bolt of energy electrifying fighters and spectators alike.

Experienced fighters are able to suppress some of these manifestations of fear, or at least prevent them from escalating to become debilitating. Veteran fighters can control fear rather than let it control them. For many first-timers, though, fear visits them one last time after their first fight. If they manage, they make it to the backyard before throwing up.

This is not to say that fear is a constant, crushing presence in the garage. Sometimes the mood at GFC is light, such as when they do "novelty fights" with toilet plungers or handheld minivacuums. "If you actually need to fight for your life," Kay tells me, laughing, "don't use a Dustbuster. It's useless." Other times, though, fighters use potentially deadly weapons such as chains and wood chairs. Rick says the chairs themselves aren't that dangerous until they break. Then "it's like you're watching a vampire movie. That stuff is really on the edge of almost killing somebody." The fights aren't stopped when the cheap wood folding chairs inevitably splinter and crack. "You have to really be careful with that," Rick says, explaining that he and other onlookers remind the fighters to take precautions after the chairs break.

The less lethal weapons GFC typically uses—sticks, training knives, fists, and feet—still generate plenty of fear. Onetime GFC participant Barry has taken on numerous physical challenges in his life, putting his body and even life at risk. He was blissfully calm—"I didn't really think about it at all"—until moments before his first fight. Suddenly, he realized "'Oh, that's right, I'm going to have to fight somebody.' And that's when I got a little . . . I did freak out. I didn't do anything about it, but that's when everything hit." His inexperience and unfamiliarity with his opponent was an overwhelming feeling: "It was intense. And it was also kind of fucking exhausting."

Another participant, 28-year-old Stuart, entered the garage expecting his first fight would be with his fraternal twin brother, as they had planned. He figured the couple of "schoolyard brawls" from his youth were insufficient preparation for any other opponents. However, because he and another person were both first-timers, they had to fight each other. He briefly pleaded his case with the organizers but soon relented. He wasn't going to fight his brother. "It was just kind of the courage of the crowd," he says, explaining why he gave in. The only other option, which wasn't really an option at all, was to leave without fighting, to choose fear and experience humiliation in front of his brother and a group of other men. He didn't know his opponent, who had some martial arts experience. That, he says, "freaked me, pardon my French, the fuck out."

An exhaustive training and fighting history prior to GFC didn't allay Ronnie's fears before his first garage fight: "I was really nervous. Like, 'Oh, my God, what's going to happen? I can break a bone. I could get knocked out. I could get my ass whupped. What if I can't drive home?'" He battled those fears initially, but later on, he was able to control them and concentrate on the fight, which also allowed him to control his opponent. His new approach focused on trying to make new moves work, "try to evade as much as possible and try to connect as much as I can and stay relaxed, stay cool, and destroy the person." Ronnie confronted his fears, but he readily admits he has not conquered them. The skill level of opponents and the possibility of injury prevent him and other experienced fighters from allowing their confidence to become cockiness.

Darren acknowledges he gets "a lot of butterflies and fear" before every fight. His fears are heightened when he squares off with some of the bigger, better fighters at GFC: "You know you're just going to get your butt kicked. And that's a hard thing to deal with, and it kind of grows exponentially" as a fight approaches. He starts thinking about the fights a day beforehand, "and then it's an hour before, it's just excruciating for me. I would literally get, you know, almost nauseous sometimes. Which is crazy for a one- or two-minute fight, you know. It's like, it's going to be over in a minute or two."

Uncertainty, doubt, and fear imply lack of control over the situation and outcome. Fighters who lose control of their emotions are more likely to lose control of the fight, thereby losing control over their bodies. Fear, then, undermines manhood because it exposes men to being physically dominated and controlled by other men. Trying to conquer those fears is a key motivation.

Forty-year-old GFC enthusiast Freddy says he manages his fears better now than he did before: "I'm calm up until the moment where there's no backing out. Then it's like I feel the acceleration into the chute. And then, hands up, start swinging." However, there have been times when he has turned down invitations to fight, citing fear.

> FREDDY: In the garage, there are, not challenges, but [there are] offers that get made, and I've backed down from them. [Another fighter] has said, "Let's do a shirtless double-stick [fight]," and I literally choose fear. I'm like, "I'm not feeling that right now."
>
> SM: And that person's not going to call you out because you didn't accept?
>
> FREDDY: No way. Not between the brothers. No, it's cool. You know, sometimes I'm done, and sometimes I'm just scared of getting hurt. You know, it's totally legitimate; it's so real. We fight as hard as possible. I don't want a guy to pull any punch, I want him to, you know, rail me, you know, knock me over or whatever, because then it's for real. If you half-ass it, then you don't want it.

Freddy is able to "choose fear" without suffering any abuse from his peers because they have seen him accept countless challenges before, and they, too, know that feeling mentally or physically unable to fight increases the possibility of being seriously injured. GFC helps them confront their fears. Opponents fight hard using dangerous weapons, but the "brothers" aren't trying to break anyone's spirit. Quite the opposite—they fight hard to raise each other's skills and confidence, not to beat down and demoralize each other. Fighters' physical limits are pushed, but they are not expected to reach a breaking point before stopping. This isn't a street brawl.

Veteran fighters have a greater awareness of both their own breaking points and what their opponents are capable of doing. They may enter their first fights thinking they are putting their lives at risk, but they learn that the average amateur fighter is unable to cause serious damage. It may turn out bad, but probably not too bad, and fighters learn how to protect themselves and prevent the worst-case scenarios they initially imagined. Years of experience haven't erased George's fears, but they allow him to control his emotions in anticipation of a fight. "Oh, there's always the fear. There's butterflies in the stomach. You don't know how it's going to turn out," he says. "But there's a confidence in the end [that] you'll be all right. How bad can it be? It cannot possibly be worse than that one time. And so you have these past experiences where it was really bad." George says he has reached a point in his life "where if I lose a tooth, that's OK. If I get a scar, that's OK. If I really can't use my left hand as well as I could before, that's OK, too. I just don't need it. I don't have that fear of bodily injury."

GFC reinforces these men's belief that overcoming fears of bodily injury is more important than avoiding serious injuries. The risks are outweighed by the masculine reward: demonstrating fearlessness. At age 30, Jackson says, "I really didn't go into [GFC] with some idea that I was going to grow as a person and I was going to conquer my fears and things like that." He feels that he has, though: "Fears, challenges, you know, insecurities. Yeah, all those things." Before he joined GFC, Jackson was jumped by a couple of guys outside of a movie theater: "I remember feeling how unprepared I was for that. And I mention this because it really was like fear. Things turned out OK, but it really was fear, and now after spending so much time in the garage, if someone bucks up to me, it's almost comical to me. Like, I have no fear of getting into little altercations and things like that. It's just like, 'Really?' Not only do I not have to fight, but I'm more than capable of defending myself, which gives me less of a reason to fight people now." His newfound feeling of fearlessness spills over into risk-taking hobbies he enjoys, such as rock climbing: "I'll reach an obstacle, and I just have that little hint of fear. And after fighting, a lot of the things I used to not be able to do, they're less [of a] concern to me now. Because I'm like, 'What's the worst that could happen? I could land on my head?' Whoop-de-doo, I've done that before." He enjoys a body awareness and "overall confidence [in] just about everything" he does after fighting at GFC.

These men believe the only way to conquer their fears of getting injured is to be tested, to be exposed to the possibility of injury. Failure, injury, and "getting your ass whupped" all pale in comparison to succumbing to fear. Like boys who comply with the powerful cultural norm that they should accept rather than back down from a playground fight, the physical beating many fighters endure is worth it to them. Fearlessness bears social and psychological fruit in the form of respect and admiration from peers. Conforming to the masculine ideal of physical toughness brings social and psychological rewards.

"If you go to fight club, nobody's a pussy there. You know what I mean?" says Sean, an otherwise laid-back 28-year-old. "There's no fuckin' . . . there [are] no losers. We're all here. Ain't nobody else here doing it." He thinks GFC fighters are tested and proven, unlike the "losers" and "pussies" who do not risk themselves in the garage. Sean uses the widely uttered sexist epithet *pussy*, which labels the target as cowardly, weak, fearful, and effeminate and is often used to embarrass, motivate, or provoke men. His words insulate GFC fighters from attacks, implicitly bonding them via the well-worn masculine paths of misogyny and implied homophobia.

Interestingly, women are sometimes called pussies in a similar context, even by other women. The impact is less devastating, though, because the label doesn't convey gender failure for women. They can enjoy some of the same benefits (perhaps less frequently and with less enthusiasm) of being considered brave, tough, and fearless. Why? Because these masculine traits are highly and broadly regarded and rewarded in American culture, unlike, say, being gentle or caring.[17] If stereotypically feminine traits were similarly regarded and rewarded, we would expect men to display them more frequently and more confidently. Manhood wouldn't be defined and measured so narrowly.

Testing Skills, Testing Selves

Contemporary martial arts schools and styles descend from cultures around the world. The rise of mixed martial arts, which blends styles across geographic and cultural divides, is the rare case where globalization produces an actual melting pot. GFC fighters reflect this trend. They train in various combinations of karate, tae kwon do, aikido, Muay Thai, Eskrima, judo, Brazilian jujitsu, Wing Chun, kickboxing, wrestling, and more. No matter how diverse or extensive their training, GFC participants crave something more.

Simulations allow people to approximate an event in a safer context, one that allows for play and experimentation while reducing physical and emotional risks. Simulations are especially useful for activities like boxing or fighting, where the risks and consequences are great.[18] Martial arts training helps students learn how to defend themselves, disarm attackers, subdue threats, stay calm, and formulate a plan. What it does not offer is a test of these skills at full speed using full contact. This is what GFC provides. The garage gives fighters an arena to confront their fears and doubts and to test their training and skills. Here, they can approximate an unpredictable street fight while minimizing the risk of injury. It is a more realistic and risky simulation but still a simulation nonetheless.

On a cool, beautiful autumn day in the Bay Area, I sit down with Kay, Rick, and Patrick in the same backyard where we would fight months later. Over beers, we discuss GFC and their experiences. Kay recalls when he was first invited to a fight night. "I thought, 'Well, maybe I should come here and show them how to properly fight,'" he says as Rick and Patrick erupt into laughter. "I mean, to be honest, that was my first thought," Kay says sincerely, as the others continue laughing.

Absentmindedly fiddling with one of the training knives, Kay tells me he was attracted to GFC because it provides him with a way to test himself. It allows him to apply his extensive martial arts training to uncontrolled fights.

Like many other GFC fighters, he was dissatisfied with the guarded sparring sessions in classes. He says, as "nice, law-abiding citizens" the martial arts students aren't getting in fights, "So you're not sure if it's real or not. [Instructors] say, 'Oh, you do this move. You do that move. Then it will have this effect.'" But Kay sees the drills as kind of fake:

> So you have to test it somehow. And the best way to test it is when people don't give a shit about your training or your technique. So, for example, in my first fight I [tried] to throw this punch, or throw this kick. You try your best. But then you also try to control it, right, thinking you may hurt this guy. But here's the thing. You kick him, it doesn't hurt. [*Rick and Patrick laugh.*] So then you get a little bit desperate. So you say, "Now I'll go 50%." So I give 50%. Fucking... the guy still doesn't feel shit [*more laughing*]. So I said, "Fuck it." Right? And I just go all in. 100%. The guy still does not fall [down]. Then what are you going to do? You gonna do 120%? I think this is the telltale sign. If you go [all-in] and the guy still doesn't feel it, then you know there's something fucking wrong with this skill. The reality is, 90% of the time you try your best [and] that still doesn't get it done.

Kay quickly discovered that he could fight as hard as possible without endangering his opponents. They test their own and each other's skills by fighting all out. What they do not do is gouge each other's eyes, target vulnerable joints, use crippling holds, or enter a bout with "malicious intentions," as the release form describes it.

Protective headgear is also essential. It allows the use of weapons that could be deadly in a street fight. Fighters experiment with different styles, attempt to string together combinations of moves, battle opponents of all sizes and skill levels, practice disarming someone with a knife without getting touched, and ultimately discover just how dangerous it would be to fight an armed attacker.

Jackson has suffered a few injuries in the garage, but so long as his body will allow, he will continue to fight. "Yeah, you could put me in a dojo all day, just punch, kick, punch, block. And until it's applied to real-world events," he says, "or at the very least, studied and practiced [with] someone else, it's not the same. And honestly, it's pretty boring." Self-defense is not the sole or even primary goal for many martial arts instructors. They seek to instill discipline and teach students to clear their minds of distractions. Learning these lessons requires countless hours of drills. Like young athletes, some martial arts students find drills tedious and monotonous. They want to scrimmage, to test their skills in a more enjoyable and challenging way.

"I was always looking for an upgrade," Jackson says. "The risk factor, I guess, [is what] I'm really into. Because what's the point of doing anything if it's just going to be safe and controlled? You know, that's not a way to live—for me, anyway." By embracing activities that place him at risk, Jackson asserts that he is in control of, or at least able to manage, his fears. His actions and thoughts about what he does and why he does them communicate to others that he's a "real man." At his first fight, Jackson was immediately disabused of his concern that GFC garage fights might be the same as his sanitized dojo sparring sessions: "Once you get tagged, [you're] like, 'Oh, oh, OK. I see this is real. This knife is real. This stick is real. This pain is real.' And you know, you realize, OK, that guy didn't hold back. This isn't some little tea party or something like that. These guys are actually swinging at you." Thirty-four-year-old Asher echoes Jackson's thoughts. "That's kind of part of it," he says, "[you] put yourself at risk just to see how you handle it."

Early on in GFC's history, some of the founders visited local martial arts classes to recruit new fighters. They were shocked that almost none were interested. Only a few women and a tiny fraction of men share the same desire to test their skills in a full-speed, full-contact setting. They prefer safe, controlled, and heavily padded sparring over GFC's risk factor. Chris always wanted more "practical" training. He "never really liked doing any of the formulaic martial arts." At GFC, he says, "It's not really whether you win or you lose, because there's always somebody bigger, faster, or younger or stronger who has more technical skill than you. Mainly, you're not fighting against somebody else. You're fighting against yourself. Will you put yourself through the events? Will you do the best you can? If you do the best you can, you think you have success."

Like Chris and many other fighters, Freddy has an impressive training résumé. He downplays the value of that training compared to GFC. "I feel like a guy in [our] fight club has, I don't know, the equivalent of 10 years in a dojo," he says. He figures he has been in more fistfights in two years at GFC than in all of his previous training and scuffles combined. Whereas martial arts training prepares students for violent confrontations, GFC plays out those scenarios in real time. "Well, we test each other," Freddy observes. The tests bring bruises, bloodshed, knockdowns, and only rarely, a knockout. All are acknowledged as possibilities but dismissed as side effects of their ritual test. "Us in the garage, we're all friends," Jackson says. "And everybody wants to see everyone go home at the end of the night. But we also want to test each other. So I'm going to test him, but I want him to come back. I don't want to hurt anyone that bad."

For some fighters, the stakes go well beyond testing their skills. They are testing a lifetime's worth of training and commitment and sometimes even their familial upbringing and cultural heritage, as is true with Ronnie. He has fought many times at GFC. He practices and teaches martial arts because of his Thai ancestry and what he finds are the positive impacts it makes on his community. Fighting at GFC is a test of his and his forefathers' skills:

My family is from Thailand, and learning about history and the martial arts aspects of it, they really wanted me to understand and apply what I learned and know. And so [I] just want[ed] to know that I'm not being taught lies or bullshit that won't really work in a real situation. I mean, that's what kind of got me interested in fighting... martial arts is a very big part of who I am. I want to see if I can do what people teach me, and if I can't, I'm going to find a way to try to make it work. And I would never teach anyone anything that I can't do myself. What I get [from fighting at GFC] is the truth. And to know that my martial arts works and that I can apply it and utilize it and know [whether], in a real-life situation, as real as you could get, will it work and can you make it work and can you come out as unscathed as possible, you know?

Ronnie says "a lot of people fold" during confrontations; they back down and offer excuses: "And I don't want to be that person. I want to know that if it happens, I could do it. That I could turn the switch on and fight for my life, fight another person and know that I'm using some kind of art, some kind of controlled theory." He explains,

I [fought] for the art. I did it to see if I could prove myself against any other discipline—that I could hold my own in real time, in a real situation with real weapons. I put myself in situations where I'm facing a person that's bigger, heavier and has more experience than me, and I'm not afraid. I'm not afraid to do that because I know that wherever I am in my life, this might happen and I have to prove myself. So what happens is a mental toughness and a mental diligence that surpasses the physical body, you know. What pushes you to your limits and [takes] you to places you could never go normally, or recreationally, it's how much you want it with your mind. And what you commit to. What you say you're going to do, and you do it. I love martial arts. I love what it's done for me. I love how it builds the community. I love how it's trained me physically and mentally and challenged me to push my limits and stretch myself and my growth process of being a person.

Ronnie pushes his physical limits as a ritual test of his skills and his heritage. His body is the medium through which he practices his culture. Like his ancestors, he believes he must hone his skills in case a situation arises where he has to defend himself.

Confidence in the Streets

Most of the men I speak with had stories of fighting when they were younger; several recounted recent experiences of street violence. Only a few, though, feel there's a chance of facing a violent confrontation outside of GFC. Most live comfortable suburban lives and occupy spaces that pose few risks, whether due to the comforts of a middle-class existence or because they have outgrown their riskier youthful ways. For the Asian American and white men—especially those in their 30s and 40s—they are unlikely to be perceived as threats, further decreasing the odds of their experiencing street violence. GFC gives them insight into how they might respond in the unlikely event they do face an attacker.

Sean says the club tested his courage and bravery, comparing it to tackle football games he played with friends when he was younger. He spends time in areas of San Francisco that require him to be alert: "Living in the city, sometimes someone will try to fuck with you, rob you or punk you or something—well, my situation was a couple times they tried to rob me—where if you can't resolve it with words and can't run, that's when you have to defend yourself. In the fight club, it was like, you have a very limited time, so you really had to attack once in a while. Yeah, it really did change me. With fight club, you actually did it. You approached it as if it's a real situation."

Even though most GFC members face almost no possibility of getting in a street fight, they repeatedly cite the confidence their fighting experience gives them if they are ever physically confronted. "I find that thrilling, to be able to walk in a room and say, 'It doesn't matter, I can fight any of these guys and take it,'" George says. Darren joined the group years ago because he wanted to get in shape and do something physical. He also wanted "a feeling like, you know, you can take care of yourself in a fight. I don't want to sound like I'm making the case for some practicality of it because I don't believe that, not in a second. But it still nonetheless feels good to be able to have the physical wherewithal to take care of yourself if there was a physical altercation." He feels tested, prepared for the unexpected, and in greater control of his body.

As with most but not all of the GFC members who have multiple college degrees and upwardly mobile professional lives, Darren lives in a low-crime Bay Area neighborhood. These upper-middle-class members are motivated to fight for the same reasons that motivate working-class GFC members. Social class is not a good predictor of who gravitates to GFC, why they do, or how well they fight. Neither is race or ethnicity. Boxing is the fighting sport where these statuses and identities are more visible and important. The ubiquity of martial arts classes in public and private recreation centers, universities, and urban and suburban communities speaks to their broad appeal. The garage is perhaps the ultimate example of how amateur sports approach the ideal of pure meritocracies. Group statuses and identities shape people's lives, but those histories and experiences are meaningless when a basketball is tossed in the air or punches fly. If you can play, you can play. And for GFC, if you're willing to fight, you can stay. The GFC members living in areas perceived to be dangerous are less likely to have advanced degrees and high-status careers. They are a little more likely to encounter possible confrontations on the street. Few GFC members do, though. If not wealthy enough to avoid those situations, they are old enough and wise enough to do so. Fighting is such a universal boyhood experience and proving toughness such a fundamental feature of masculinity that all of the in-group differences that otherwise divide the men matter less.

Stuart fought only twice at GFC, but he too gained confidence in his physical abilities after enjoying some success there: "It's nice to feel [that] in an aggressive situation, you will be able to take care of yourself and also those around you. [GFC was] just an attempt to fulfill that kind of a need, where you need to test yourself and challenge one another, and we do that as kids, but we don't do it as adults." This ritual test of manhood is, in Stuart's mind, "more about validating your own self-worth [than trying to hurt anyone]. And for me, it was actually very validating to win [fights]. But to more of an extent, it was having the courage to do that in a public forum."

For some, this sense of empowerment spreads to other aspects of their lives. They are more relaxed, at ease as they walk the city streets or participate in other risk-taking activities they enjoy. They feel as though nothing they will encounter will test them more than the larger, skilled opponents they've fought at GFC.

Ronnie's many fights provide him with peace of mind and confidence, knowing he could protect himself. "There's a level of beauty in your life when you know you can apply martial arts in your life or martial arts has worked for you," he says. Fighting experience and the confidence it breeds have their limits. They don't make these men feel invincible, and they don't predispose them to being more confrontational elsewhere. Quite the opposite. They learn that weapons are dangerous, possibly deadly, and how strangers look and present themselves doesn't fully convey the threat they may pose.

Ronnie says, "I know that if I have to, I can [fight], and if I had the opportunity to, I wouldn't, because it's not worth it, you know. Anything could happen in those kinds of fights, you know, especially in [knife] fights." He has learned it's nearly impossible to avoid getting touched during training knife fights at GFC: "Each touch could be a slice and each slice could be a vein and each vein could be a tendon and, you know, each placement could be your life." He loves everything martial arts and GFC have done for him. "It's not your bulletproof vest, though," he cautions, "and it's not your ticket out of jail either."

Although GFC has given Jason a sense of confidence, he claims that this fighting knowledge and skill simply means he is "less likely to be in that situation in the first place." He says, "I don't have anything to prove at all. I think maybe sometimes guys get in fights in bars and other situations like that because they want to prove something, and I've got nothing to prove. I'd probably be more inclined to back down, walk away, and say, 'It's not worth hurting anybody about. Let's just go our own way.'" Sean has a lifetime's worth of experiences, enough to know that a confrontation can quickly spiral out of control: "In real life you never know what's gonna happen. People got guns. On the street, it's fight or flight. I'd run away first instead of confronting someone. I don't want to hurt anybody, and I don't want to get hurt. I don't want to get my shit taken [*laughs*]. [But] what do you gotta prove for $20? Or if someone is looking at you funny? Fight club was just for fun. Martial artists have their code, their form of respect, but people on the street have no respect."

The unpredictably of a street fight exceeds GFC fighters' desire to confront their fears and test their skills. Sammy says he would gladly hand over his wallet if someone with a knife confronted him: "It's not like [by] handing over money instead of fighting that I'm showing my weakness. I'm just saying, 'This is not worth the fight.' But if shit happens, the guy still wants to kill me after that, I mean, what can I do, right?" They are not compelled to risk their lives to prove their manhood. They feel as if they have already passed the test countless times in the garage. Also, virtually all of the people who fight at GFC have careers, families, homes, and community ties, the kinds of conventional attachments, commitments, involvements, and beliefs that keep them connected to mainstream society and reduce deviant or criminal behavior.[19] There are no gray areas or blurred lines to decipher: Inside the garage, you take on all comers, confront your fears, fight like hell, and gain confidence in your skills. Outside the garage, you avoid conflicts that might take you away from the people you love, jeopardize the life you built, or risk your life itself.

2

Fighting Back

The Gentlemen's Fighting Club helps men face physical tests and conquer their fears, engendering a sense of confidence in their ability to protect themselves and their loved ones. The garage is a place of contradictions, though. It is a source of both therapy and ridicule. It is a space where men who were bullied as boys can repair and restore a sense of masculine identity. Yet fighting is not acceptable for adult men, especially those with families and careers, men who are unlikely to need these kinds of skills. To many outsiders, the garage is a symbol of arrested development, of men who need to grow up.

Some GFC members frame their involvement as a rejection of contemporary society, with what they see as its contempt for fighting, risk-taking, and ultimately, visceral masculinity. We have become soft, fearful, feminine, they believe. Fighting is their act of political protest. Their need to embody masculinity, to literally feel and enact it physically, is not unique. Researchers have found men embracing these kinds of corporeal-protest masculinities everywhere from construction worksites to men's movements.[1] Feeling masculine brings physical and psychological pleasure, whether from the rigors and muscled rewards of blue-collar work or from all-men retreats where participants do ritual dances meant to symbolize animalistic spirits. Whether explicitly or implicitly, individually or collectively, many men respond to what they see as a feminized culture by doing visceral masculinity. Fighting makes some GFC participants feel connected to real or imagined men of the past, whether tough guys from American history or the proverbial caveman from which we evolved. Adult men shouldn't be ashamed of fighting, they say. They should celebrate it, collectively, via ritual celebrations of primal (fighting) man.

The contradictions of GFC and the garage are reflections of broader cultural incongruities. We send mixed messages about violence to boys and men. Violence, sometimes even the same act in the same context, might be celebrated, rewarded, justified, accepted, tolerated, dismissed, ignored, derided, or punished. Violence is omnipresent. It is the pornography served up nightly by local news, a weapon used by the state, the focal point of much media entertainment, integral to many individual and team sports, and though largely in steep decline in recent decades, still too prevalent in families and communities.

We expect young men to follow Cold War protocols when deciding if and when to use their bodies for violence: Bodies should have the capacity to perform like dangerous weapons but should be used only to deter others' aggression or, as a last resort, for self-defense. Otherwise, they should exist mostly for show and as a source of pride. Using bodies to initiate violence is unacceptable (excluding sports).[2] But soldiers are trained for war, not simulations or exercises, and certainly not diplomacy. Cold wars heat up. Fight culture produces fighting. Boys and men who fail to fulfill this embodied manhood ideal internalize a sense of failure and/or attempt to repair that failure, restoring their masculine identities. GFC can provide collective repair against perceived threats to fight culture.

Internalizing: Losing Control

Most of the GFC fighters I speak with have always enjoyed watching and participating in fight culture, from *Teenage Mutant Ninja Turtles* and *Kung-Fu Theatre* as kids to schoolyard fights and contact sports as teens to martial arts training and Gentlemen's Fighting Club as adults. Some of the GFC participants attribute their interest in fighting to a rather unremarkable continued expression of manhood. Nearly all of them shared stories of getting into conflicts and fights during their youth, in many cases due to being targeted as a racial or ethnic minority at school or in their neighborhood. Several got into fights after entering adulthood. In almost every case, they say they did not initiate the violence but rather were placed in the position of deciding whether to act defensively. In that regard, their experiences mirror most boys' and men's.[3]

Several GFC fighters, though, relayed incidents that were poignant and formative, marked by fear, humiliation, and loss of control. They were picked on, bullied, harassed, and beat up. In short, they were dominated and emasculated. Their response was to seek ways to address their inability to fight and try to overcome their perceived shortcomings as well as their fears. Those who did not take action soon after being bullied or controlled were plagued by feelings of low self-confidence and weakness or issues with control. Victims of bullying exhibit lower levels of self-esteem and poorer academic achievement, as well as higher rates of anxiety, depression, and antisocial behaviors, among other negative consequences.[4] If boys are expected to be able (or at least try) to defend themselves but are unable or unwilling to do so, they are likely to feel emasculated and humiliated. Eventually those suppressed emotions will bubble over, whether as raging violence directed at others or self-directed abuse and dangerous, self-destructive behavior.

Fighting-filled memoirs and rich ethnographies provide a window into boy codes in tough neighborhoods.[5] Boys, even very young ones, have to be prepared to fight other boys, even those who are older and bigger, to prove they aren't afraid. The consequences of getting beat up aren't nearly as severe as are crying, showing fear, or backing down from a fight. Failing to fight back marks a boy as passive, making him more likely to be targeted by other boys.[6] These "codes of the street" are more prolific in distressed and disadvantaged pockets within communities populated largely by African American and Latinx residents. Fighting for boys in these contexts provides them with access to respect and dignity in the face of poverty, racism, and racial profiling.[7] Still, the codes precede and reach far beyond poor urban ghettoes to communities and boys of all types.[8] GFC fighter Stuart's "courage of the crowd" is an example of how masculinity and violence norms appear in a suburban setting among adult men.

I argue that boyhood experiences of backing down—of choosing not to fight—become gendered humiliations that compel men to try to repair their wounded masculine selves. They do so by trying to correct the perceived failure directly instead of reasserting themselves elsewhere (such as excelling at work or using violence against intimate partners) to reclaim their masculine identities. When they were younger, they lost control of their bodies to other boys and men. As adults, they place themselves in a similar situation to try to reclaim and restore control.

Other GFC members such as George and Sean redressed their negative experiences by conforming to boyhood norms: they lifted weights, learned how to fight, or simply chose to fight back in the moment, saving face and buoying their sense of self. They behaved gender appropriately, confronting their bullies and fears, and gained confidence and fighting experience. Clearly, that option is not always available, effective, or appropriate for victims of bullying. Some research has found that boys who use reactive aggression in response to being victimized are more likely to be victimized again.[9] Fighting back could be met with escalating and even more dangerous levels of violence.

Also, boys fight to establish themselves in the pecking order, learning how to use violence and suppress emotions when called for, and these behaviors occur "within a nurturing environment of violence: the organization and demands of patriarchal or male dominant societies."[10] In extreme cases, boys' violent responses to being victimized may turn lethal. Boys who kill have often suffered from a constellation of abuse and neglect at home, in schools and their communities, and at the hands of law enforcement and the mental health system.[11] Some kids who are victimized—who are subject to shame and ridicule and who feel abandoned and rejected—lash out immediately instead of bottling up these feelings. This doesn't preclude them from later acts of violence. Toxic shame accumulates: "Hurt little boys become aggressive big boys."[12] They experience what they rightly feel is an injustice: that they are treated as though they are worth nothing and are nothing. A mortified self and wounded soul can bring forth restorative violence.[13]

I am not suggesting that victims of bullying who don't fight back are responsible for their continued bullying. Instead, I merely note that boys' gender conformity (i.e., fighting back) can give them a sense of empowerment, regardless of any potential short- or long-term negative consequences, individually or collectively. GFC members report that family, friends, and older boys or men in the neighborhood often encouraged or facilitated their boyhood fighting, whether through verbal guidance or challenges, training, or enrolling them in martial arts courses. Whatever confidence they gained from childhood fights or martial arts training is far exceeded by what they now get out of GFC.

Asher—mid-30s, married, and a father—has a lucrative career in the technology sector. Like several of the men I meet, he was bullied and beaten up as a boy and considers those experiences formative. When I ask him what led to his interest in martial arts and GFC, he says, "I was kind of picked on in high school, a little bit when I was younger. In college, I was kind of a skinny, not [a] very active or strong or athletic guy. I don't know—but I mean there was more than that. I think it was kind of something I always wanted to do. I wanted to know how to fight." After graduating from college, Asher committed himself to martial arts training. A friend recommended he train with a skilled fighter named Lars: "[He] was saying, 'If you do martial arts stuff, you should get together with Lars. Like that guy really knows his stuff and he'll just fucking kill you.' I think I wanted people to say that about me—not that I wanted to be like a bully or that I wanted to fight people at work or be a jerk about it, or like start fights with people—[but] that was how I wanted to be thought of." I ask him why he wants that feeling, and he explains, "Because I guess I always—I don't know, I felt like a weakling most of my life and I don't know, it's . . . haven't you ever been beat up or bullied when you were a kid?" Asher's father enrolled him in martial arts classes, but he quickly quit and has long regretted not being better at "standing up for myself when I was younger."

GFC fighter Sammy, married and in his mid-40s, is slight of stature, which, not surprisingly, exposed him to more bullying as a child and teen in the occasionally violent and gang-ridden neighborhoods where he grew up. When

threatened by gang members, he says, all of his options felt emasculating: crying for help (dependence), begging for mercy (submission), or suffering the
pain and failure of being beaten (lack of control). He chose submission to
avoid the physical pain. "Saying, 'Sorry, sorry,' many times definitely hurts your
ego," he tells me, laughing ruefully. Even while finding humor in the memory,
he recognizes its importance. The physical peace he secured by apologizing
and submitting to the other boys came with a social psychological price. It was
"powerful," he says, "because I was all cocky when I was young and then, 'Oh,
fuck.' A few guys come [at] you, and then you're nobody. Definitely, this had
something to do with getting me to try to practice [martial arts] and prove my
manhood."

Sammy's experiences illustrate the need for men to constantly prove themselves; despite feeling as though he won his earliest childhood fights and, as
an adult, becoming a skilled martial artist, the times he failed to act continue
to bother him years later. Much like Asher, Sammy's professional and family
life is settled, and he does not fear what he sees as his safe surroundings. Still,
his childhood experiences influence his adult choices, behaviors, and identity.
He spent years training in martial arts, but GFC afforded him an opportunity
to test his training, obtain a degree of confidence in his ability to fight, and
reclaim the physical aspect of his manhood.

Freddy, one of the longtime GFC regulars, says he got into grappling and
wrestling to get the feeling that he could control his own body and others'.
Once, when he was in elementary school, two older neighbors pinned him
down, stripped him of his clothes, and ran away, leaving him to try to sneak
back into the house, naked, in front of some older women relatives. "I seem
to recall them mocking me and making fun of me," he says of the older boys.
"So that's kind of a formative situation. Where I would never want to be in a
situation where I was out of control of myself again." Freddy not only lost control of his body but was exposed, literally and figuratively. He also attributes
his previous strong homophobia to this humiliating incident.

Freddy's combustible mix of angst about being dominated and virulent
homophobia led to a violent reaction in college when some friends tried to
pull a similar stunt, grabbing him and attempting to strip him naked in a
dorm hallway:

> I was like, I ain't down with that. And that was during the time that I had that
> homophobia. . . . I went through the doorway, and they grabbed me, and I
> kneed the first guy in the balls; I turned around and grabbed the other guy by
> the throat and threw him down. And I looked over in the closet, and there was a
> two-by-four, and I grabbed it, and I raced over; he's yelling, and he was like, "No,
> no!" and I just dropped it and walked away.

Freddy's violent reaction stemmed from what happened to him as a young child. However, it must also be understood in cultural context: "To be fully, appropriately masculine, [a man] must exhibit physical control of his space and be able to act on objects and bodies in it."[14] These expectations exacerbate Freddy's lost sense of control and desire to reclaim it. It would seem to make sense that GFC would attract some men who've been bullied for being gay or getting gay-baited. Sexuality is not used as a filter to participate, but all of the men I interview identify as straight, and none suggest that homophobic taunts led to their fighting.

Repairing: Fight Therapy

Social science research reveals that men who are prevented from fulfilling one measure of manhood often find other outlets to compensate for their perceived shortcomings.[15] Young men living in poverty and denied access to good jobs may assert themselves through sports, sexual conquests, or risk-taking activities like crime. Adult men who fail as breadwinners are more likely to abuse their wives or girlfriends.[16] Men with physical disabilities may highlight their decision-making skills and authority to offset their inability to live up to men's body ideals.[17] In these cases, men's economic or physical circumstances block them from directly fixing what they and others often view as failed manhood. Their manhood acts are adaptations; they use the resources and skills available to them.[18] GFC offers one group of men—those physically emasculated as boys but otherwise physically capable of fighting—a way to directly repair and bolster their masculine identities. They don't have to compensate elsewhere. They can fight, as adults, and (at least attempt to) restore their lost manhood. This may help explain why these men don't reject masculine ideals of physical toughness and control or embrace a different definition of manhood. They aren't forced to rework it.

Violence often arises from shame and ridicule. Boys and men can use violence to restore and repair their masculine identities and their lost sense of self due to previous experiences of humiliation, whether physical or otherwise. One study found that boys who were victims of bullying, physical violence, and sexual violence attempted to reassert control over their bodies and selves by identifying younger and weaker targets. Their efforts to reestablish a sense of control and power were short-lived, though, when older and bigger peers (or family members) continued to target them. This may help explain why some of these boys engage in severe acts of physical and sexual violence against younger and weaker victims, repeatedly and fruitlessly trying to reclaim control.[19] No GFC members report experiencing severe bullying and physical violence or any sexual violence as boys. They are able to reassert control over their bodies without preying on others, whether as adults at GFC or as boys getting into fights with peers.

For Asher, Sammy, and Freddy, GFC offers an opportunity to replace the psychological scars of bullying and submission with physical scars they can wear as badges of manhood. Fighting is therapeutic. It brings more than insight. The fighters can confront their feelings of failure *directly*, as adults. And they restore control over their bodies, paradoxically, by choosing to give it up, placing themselves at risk. Even when they lose a fight, they are reestablishing their masculine identities by demonstrating the ability to withstand violence.

Asher's long journey toward repairing began the way it does for many young men: by trying to get bigger and stronger. He started lifting weights, eating more, and "[got] to the point where I looked, I guess, intimidating enough that people wouldn't just assume I was a wuss." Still, he says, "[What] I found was that even though I looked stronger, you know, certainly felt better and more confident—I still do—I still was never really sure I could do it, you know? I was really never sure I could fight somebody and not just lose my cool during the fight and panic and then end up getting beaten up or . . . It was like some of the martial arts and getting in shape wasn't enough. I needed to know I could really do it." It wasn't until he found some success fighting at GFC that he restored a sense of control over his body. He found it crucial to not just spar but participate in a fight because it's "a situation where you just don't know what's going to happen." Fighting is not about eliminating fear, he says, "but knowing you're not a coward." I ask him if he has gained enough confidence in his fighting abilities to overcome his boyhood experiences. He tells me, "Uh, yeah. I mean that's not to say—certainly not to say I'm the best fighter there ever was or even particularly good, necessarily—but I know what I can do, and I know that if I'm in a fight, I'm not going to lose my cool. I can, you know, I know I can compose my thoughts and come up with a plan."

One key source of his renewed confidence is his friendship with sparring partner Lars. Lars is a highly trained, skilled fighter who is passionate about teaching and learning how to fight. Asher's efforts to repair his broken manhood were initially undermined by a series of what he experienced as dignity-crushing sparring sessions with Lars: "I have spent a lot of time getting my ass kicked by him. I think there came a time, like a couple of years ago, where you know I was sparring or grappling or whatever and I just felt like . . . I just felt like he was like trying to humiliate me or something." Asher discussed it with his therapist, who encouraged him to talk to Lars, which he did:

So I was like, "You know I kind of felt like the other day, when we were sparring, as I was working really hard trying to get up I kind of got this feeling like you were trying to humiliate me or something." And he says, "Oh, no, I was never trying to do that. [Just] always trying this new stuff or stuff I haven't worked with before and just kind of seeing what it does. But you're my friend, and I would never try to humiliate you or try to break your spirit or anything." And he apologized, you know, for what he had been doing.

The conversation and apology left Asher feeling "more free to say what I was feeling, to express myself while we were training," which made it more fun and the fighting feedback more helpful: "At times when—if I was getting over-whelmed and just getting beaten up—Lars would just stop and [say], 'Oh, gosh, I'm only attacking you that much because you're not hitting me back. The real solution here is for you to just attack me more. Like if you attack me enough, I'm not going to be able to respond like that.'" Asher began reinter-preting Lars's physical domination: "I saw that he wasn't trying to break me down or humiliate me or make me feel like a wimp. He was actually trying to help me get better. And that he was willing to work with me on my particular issues, psychological issues about all this stuff—I think it made me a better fighter and made us better friends." Once Asher was able to redefine the situa-tion as a source of training and growth, and with Lars's help, recognize that Asher could use his offensive fighting skills to impose some of his will on a big-ger and better opponent, he no longer felt controlled and humiliated.

Sammy has enjoyed professional successes, but they do not offset his sense of boyhood emasculation. He does not view his work as being particularly important for his masculine identity. Sammy says the ability to fight is "basi-cally your real confidence. Let me put it this way. It's almost like the test of your manhood, or a test of your superiority in terms of handling things. I think that has something to do with [why I fight]. A sense of power and control, right?" Whereas he avoided being hit as a child as an act of self-preservation, today he happily subjects himself to such violence. "After I got punched enough times [at GFC]," Sammy says, "I understand that I can definitely take a [big] punch, and then I'll nail you [with one]." He doesn't expect to be bullied by gang members now that he's an adult, but if he finds himself in that situation, Sammy now has the confidence to deal with it.

Freddy began reclaiming a sense of control over his body when his parents enrolled him in wrestling. He later trained in martial arts, eventually landing at GFC, which he calls a life-altering experience. Freddy's extensive GFC expe-rience has translated to an acute self-awareness and sense of control. "Now I think of myself as a hard target. I don't feel like a mark," he says. "Only I kill me." With the skills and confidence he has developed, he believes it's only his own mistakes that expose him to painful or theoretically dangerous blows.

Other GFC members also share stories of being bullied and picked on as boys but appear to have short-circuited the most negative social psychological consequences by asserting themselves in the moment or soon after. American culture celebrates and rewards masculine violence (especially when it's considered justifiable); expects boys and men to be tough, aggressive, and in control; sends kids to schools that are only now beginning to institutionalize antibullying programs and practices; and lacks strong antibullying peer cultures of support to resist or offset the bullying. Thus it is not surprising that the GFC members who tell me they fought back against boyhood bullying enjoyed increased confidence and self-esteem and came away less psychically scarred.

George, one of the bigger fighters at GFC, was skinny and experienced some bullying and got into fights as a young child. After he lost his first fight to a boy at school, George "really wanted to lift weights," thinking, "I must fortify myself." He tried doing so, but without the benefit of puberty and no one to instruct him, the weights had little impact on his body. He recalls deciding to fight back in a later incident at school, in fourth grade, when he and his classmates were learning a dance:

> It's a small group of kids, and you see the same kids for over a decade. So there's this built-in hierarchy. It's a small class. They gang up. They pick on you. They're physically bigger . . . They just kept doing all kinds of stuff: tripping me, kick[ing] you in the shins and they laugh, and all that sort of stuff. I didn't want to take it anymore. [As we're going around the circle dancing,] I caught [one boy with a punch to] the elbow. Well, he hurt his elbow real bad. And of course it broke my finger. And he stopped. That was it after that.

George had a few minor incidents in the years that followed, but eventually his body filled out. The earlier incidents had little long-term negative impact and probably little influence on his interest in fighting, as he later enrolled in martial arts training mostly by chance.

Sean's uncle taught him martial arts when he was in middle school. He did so because Sean "used to always get picked on as a kid," even by an older cousin. Sean was small and skinny and grew up in tough neighborhoods, often as one of the only kids of Asian descent, all of which led to him being targeted by other boys. "A lot of the kids in the neighborhood, yeah, they would outright just see me and beat me up," he says, laughing as he shares this memory. Sean seems less damaged from getting picked on because he quickly learned to fight back effectively. As a kid, he had little interest in fighting, "'Cause like, I'm pretty much a nice guy." He was mystified to discover that fighting was the best way to prevent others from trying to fight or bully him: "A lot of the older cats in the neighborhood were like, 'You gotta fight back. You've got to defend yourself. You can't always just run.' That's one thing that really confused me as a kid. It's like, OK, if I hit this guy, he's going to leave me alone? What the fuck?" Sean reluctantly learned to defend himself. He explains, "Growing up, a lot of the kids, a lot of the gangs, that stuff, they'll call you like, 'You soft. You square.' Maybe something like that, and if you don't react to it, they [go after you] relentlessly. They just see you every day, they pick on you. There was a [bigger] guy in high school [messing with me] for three or four months . . . and I just couldn't take it no more, and we got in a fight, right in front of the teacher and everything. I hit him with a computer monitor." Sean fought older and bigger boys to successfully avoid being viewed as someone who could be picked on. He learned "the code of the street," which says you have to be prepared to use violence to avoid being a target of violence.[20] All boys face the expectation to be physically tough and in control, but boys in distressed and disadvantaged neighborhoods—mostly resource-poor young men of color—are likely to live under its crushing weight anytime they leave their homes. The stakes, too, are amplified.

Boys who fought back and men who later learned to fight and tested their skills at GFC found some peace of mind. Even after proving themselves repeatedly in the GFC garage, though, they were motivated to continue fighting. They cite many reasons and many benefits of doing so, but one likely reason is how manhood is constructed. Boys and men must constantly prove themselves over and over again. This helps explain why men who have exorcised their boyhood demons continue to test themselves, even though our society tells them that they should abandon the youthful activity of fighting. Even after proving their courage, toughness, and ability repeatedly at GFC, some fighters return again and again, for months or even years. The ritual binds them.

Collective Repair: Fighting Modernity

"Fuck it, man, if I want to fight, I'm going to fight until I can't do it anymore," 42-year-old GFC fighter George says. "I don't really care if people think I'm violent. Just look at me: no criminal record, career man, family, kids. And you know what? fighting is fun. I want to make a statement: Fighting is fun. This is what we do for fun." George is responding to what he and many other fighters see as a perverse trend in our society: the domestication of men. Modern society, they believe, fears and frowns upon violent combat. They attribute this mostly to an economy, culture, and lifestyle that rely less and less on physical strength and toughness.

A couple GFC members also blame feminists. They do so because of feminism's critiques of orthodox masculinity and its challenges to biological explanations of women's and men's differences. If sex differences don't explain gender inequality, sexism does. George is the most vocal critic of feminism and the social changes it has helped produce. He says it is no coincidence that a book and film about a fight club, and GFC itself, appeared and captivated people's interest when they did; they are pushbacks against the rise of metrosexuals and men's increased concern with their appearance. From George's perspective, modernization and feminism have led American men astray. Interest in fight culture is a natural corrective: "I'm a child of the late '60s, early '70s, where we were told we were all the same. No, we're not. We're not. I mean, men have these big bodies. I have these physical urges to be active. I can't just sit there. I don't know if fighting is exactly it, but it has to be something strong. There's some physical urge to really just [*makes gesture and noise indicating pounding someone*]."

He sees other contradictions in American culture. Capitalism requires masculine-marked characteristics, but feminist-inspired curricula discourage these behaviors in boys and men, he says:

> It's a tough, progressive, competitive society, and you have to compete. Competition, aggression—those are traditional male attributes. Not physical violence but social, and not quite the way women do it either. You basically have . . . if you win, you're honored. And I think modern-day boy culture doesn't prepare you for that at all. There's an undervaluation of what men have or a male teaching style in all of our education, K–12. And I'm not sure why that has occurred, but I think there's a certain social force that innately women believe that they are superior beings because they have these attributes such as cooperation, lack of aggression, able to follow directions more often, and a preference for social versus physical outlets . . . elimination of recess, all these things. And maybe it'll turn back the other way or even out, but right now it seems like there's a certain bias. There's a bias against boys and for girls. Physical fitness tests—they don't have those anymore. Getting rid of dodgeball. Sports are designed so that both girls and boys can play equally. I heard that even at my school. Touch football and they told us, "Don't run as fast." Don't run as fast? Why? Why would anybody say that? Why not run as fast as you can? . . . Yeah, I feel the physical outlets and the physical expression are indeed suppressed to the point of oppression. Where [there is] zero tolerance for fistfights in school. It's squelching [for boys]. Who does that select against? If you're biologically driven, it's discriminatory to throw one person out for something that they do and not for the other, which is like, for a girl, an example would be complete social alienation, telling everybody not to talk to this person. It's a little harder to prove damage from one versus the other.

Instead of the Boone and Crockett Club from a century earlier, George might have boys be segregated in junior fighting clubs to stave off what he sees as their feminization. Men fight off fears of feminization everywhere, including schools, churches, on dance floors, at salons, and more.[21] A fighting club is seen by a few GFC men as a collective response to threats to men's essential natures. In this context, GFC is not being used to repair individual men's loss of power and control but rather to address their sense that *all* men have lost something, and that an essential manhood needs to be restored. Their solution of reinstating a more physical, perhaps violent version of manhood is best understood as a collective effort to restore what it used to mean to be a man.

Adult men who fight, much to George's dismay, are now often labeled criminal, crazy, or if they are lucky, merely juvenile. His and others' desire would be to restore dying and displaced models of manhood. Threads of these older versions of manhood, which expect and celebrate men's violence, continue to exist. Yet these are arenas for young men. Today's hegemonic ideal requires family men to focus mostly on providing and being responsible. Yes, they are still expected to be able to protect themselves and especially their families. And it's fine to watch boxing, mixed martial arts, or football or to play video games to scratch that violent itch vicariously. What is not acceptable for adult men is to actually get in fights, even relatively safe ones such as those at GFC.

Reactions to GFC

GFC teeters on the edges of legality and deviance. What makes its members feel and what makes the group itself exceptional is the same thing that generates criticism and illustrates their defiance of social norms. Members commonly share their fighting exploits with others and enjoy their appearances in local and national media. Telling people you are a member of a fighting club is quite the conversation starter; curiosity and adulation often follow. When Sammy's close friends introduce him to others and say he is from Silicon Valley, he says he is met with yawns—until his friends add, "And he fights, too.' Then people's eyes start lighting up." Many of the fighters' spouses, friends, and coworkers enthusiastically solicit blow-by-blow highlights from the latest gathering in the garage.

Over time, though, particularly as the core members have grown older, they have learned that some of the interest is due not to admiration but morbid curiosity, like rubberneckers slowing down near an accident. Participation in GFC also generates a lot of harsh and negative reactions. A sizeable proportion of family, friends, bosses, coworkers, and public critics express disdain for GFC, viewing the violence as repugnant and fighters' participation as objectionable. Media attention has been a double-edged sword. Sammy acknowledges the downside of being known as the guy from Silicon Valley who fights: "They probably think you're just weird. They'll just think you're immature. The way the media image was projected and the way people perceive it is [that] fighting is immature. It's only kids' stuff."

Asher notices the connections detractors draw between violence and immaturity: "From the outside, it's easy for a lot of people to look in and say, 'Oh, this is working out their aggression and working out their anger.'" He admits that there are times he wants to fight at GFC because he is "frustrated and pissed . . . but it's not because I want to let out my anger on somebody. It's because I just want to forget about all that other stuff for a while and concentrate on something that's immediate."

Jackson compares it to any other form of stress relief after work: "You know, everyone has their outlet, after their eight-hour day—even if they're not working, everyone has their outlet where they go take a jog, or they skydive, or bungee jump, cycling. And this is my outlet. This is my physical test. And I'd liken this to almost the same as just going to the gym. Some people get it out at the gym, and I get more of it out at the fight club." Despite their protests, members recognize that their participation falls outside of social boundaries of acceptable adult behavior. When Jason's bruises and cuts draw attention, he chooses to obfuscate to deflect attention: "If it's not a good friend, I'll usually say it's martial arts training, that I was sparring with somebody, or something like that without getting into the whole, 'Yes, it really is a fight club' sort of thing." I ask him why and he says, "Because it does sound kind of crazy. It does sound crazy. I think for people who aren't exposed to it, it sounds like somebody who goes there must be inherently violent, and unstable, aggressive, out to hurt other people, and that sort of thing. Without a long explanation . . . you wouldn't want to get into it." When Jason and I discuss women fighting at GFC, he assumes one reason so few participate is gendered social stigma. "Whatever strange looks I get when I tell people about it," he says, "I'm sure it would be 10 times more for a woman saying that she was in a fight club. That probably would raise a lot of eyebrows."

It is revealing that fighters consistently conceal their participation from strangers and acquaintances alike. Several, including one who declined to do an interview with me for fear of professional repercussions, expressed concern about their employers' reactions to GFC. One GFC member was admonished by a boss and avoided by some coworkers after soliciting participants in a posting at work, thinking it was no different than the frequent recruitments for company softball and soccer teams, lunchtime Ultimate Frisbee, or self-defense courses.

Another indicator of the social inappropriateness of an adult fighting club is the overwhelming disinterest among men recruited to fight, even in the martial arts community. George estimates 99 out of 100 men declined his invitation. He blames what he sees as our feminized culture. "I call it domesticated feminist society," he says, arguing that it "forces masculinity underground. If it weren't for this, [more men would] be doing this for fun. Why does it have to be underground, in the garage, where nobody hears about it?" George is incredulous that contemporary American culture deems fighting as taboo.

Primal, Fighting Man

George implies that fighting is intrinsic to being male. He thinks we are trapped in a contemporary American culture that socializes boys and men away from their primal natures. Jason doesn't articulate the same critique, but he nonetheless has discovered that few men share what he experiences as a natural urge to fight. "I was initially inclined to think that it was totally to do with maleness," he says, but "the majority [of men I told] just had zero interest in it." This was surprising to Jason because fighting feels so instinctual to him:

> It's just an unconscious, "Of course this is right." Unquestionably, this is what I love to do. Sometimes I feel like I'm meant to do this. Not in any hocus-pocus sense, but this is what, as a human being, I'm built for. I've talked to other people about this when people say, "What the hell are you doing?" Sometimes I describe it like discovering that I had an appendage that I never even knew was there. It just totally felt natural and right.

Fellow longtime GFC member Jackson says fighting is analogous to breathing; both are integral to his state of being. In a follow-up email exchange after having some time to reflect more on our interview, Sammy writes, "The more I think about it, the more I feel it is an innate need to feel in touch with individual (maybe just male) power at the more primal form, without [hiding] behind any societal decorations. In short, I need to feel the 'gut.'"

Instinctual. Innate. Inborn. Natural. Pop culture, propped up by some evolutionary psychology arguments, deploys a simple, one-size-fits-all model of women's and men's behavior: biology is destiny.[22] Leadership styles are attributed to testosterone levels, talent for math or language is due to our being left- or right-brained, job attribute preferences reflect maternal and reproductive instincts, assertive versus affiliative relationship styles date to our hunter-gatherer ancestors, and on and on.

Evolutionary psychologists argue that today's gender differences are the result of different evolutionary pressures faced by females and males, mostly revolving around reproduction.[23] Humans, like other animals, are driven to reproduce. Our ancestors evolved based on how they were best able to adapt to their physical environments. Males faced paternity uncertainty, and females had to survive during pregnancy and while raising very dependent offspring. Males could impregnate many females. Females enjoyed fewer reproductive opportunities. These different pressures, so it goes, caused females to seek males who were able to provide more resources, while males sought females who would not mate with other males. Yesterday's hunter becomes today's breadwinner. Likewise, according to evolutionary psychology, widespread cross-cultural practices such as valuing women's virginity or women being "slut-shamed" for their actual or perceived sexual desires can be explained by sexual selection pressures faced by our early *Homo sapien* ancestors tens of thousands of years ago.

Innumerous social characteristics and behaviors presumed to be categorically different between women and men are attributed to our evolutionary past. It matters little that the vast majority of psychological variables reveal no or very small gender differences[24] or that the small differences that do exist, along with the handful of moderate and large ones, are easily and perhaps better explained by cultural factors. Anthropologists and sociologists, bolstered by decades of empirical evidence, would point out that gender differences are not observed universally, as would be true if biology was the sole or primary predictor of women's and men's characteristics and behaviors.[25] Instead, we find variation within individuals over their life course, within American culture (and others) over time, among subcultures and groups, and across cultures and societies around the world. The evidence is overwhelming. It demands that our models recognize the subtlety and complexity of social behavior and, at minimum, highlight the interaction between culture and biology, if not argue for the primacy of gender over sex.

Freddy and I discuss at length his views on the nature of men. We meet after dinner outside of a coffee shop in Palo Alto, California, near Stanford University and an array of Silicon Valley companies that give Palo Alto a healthy economy and high profile.

Freddy has had his ups and downs throughout his life, including his longtime struggles with being and fearing being physically dominated by others. GFC has helped him address those fears and establish a life philosophy that, in his mind, is an expression of men's essential nature. "I used to be fat and unhappy, but that man's dead, and I'm in his place," he says. He is evangelical about fighting in general and GFC in particular. Freddy believes he has figured out how men should live: they should fight, compete, and try to excel and win at everything but do so in ways that enable them to bond with each other. They also should be supportive, loving, and engaged partners and fathers. He wants other men to enjoy life as much as he does, and he believes fighting is the key. We have a long conversation about caveman masculinity and contemporary manhood while sipping our coffees on a bench outside of a quiet, upscale strip mall.

"I really think the definition [of manhood] is stronger, more visceral for me," he says, adding, "When you ask what it means to be a man, I almost want to say, 'To fight.' And maybe metaphorically and literally. I think we're just built for it. I really think we're built to fight." Freddy and I discuss an interaction he had at a bar and how it epitomizes his beliefs about the biological basis of men's behavior.

FREDDY: A guy stands in front of me, blocking my view of the TV screen. I look him up and down, and he turns around and looks at me, and this is a guy that's pretty big, you know. He looks at me and goes, "Oh, sorry." And he moves out of the way. And I don't thank him. I really feel like I moved him by aura. Like, he looked back, and he could just see that, you know … and maybe that was because [the next night] I was going to do my first night [SCUBA] dive, and I was already in full courage mode. But also, it's totally because of fight club.

SM: You're carrying yourself differently since joining the fight club?

FREDDY: Yeah, right. And in two different ways: Since being in [GFC] I haven't had to get into any altercations [because he has found happiness and no longer has a chip on his shoulder]. I haven't been in any street fights. And then, the other branch of that isn't the happy branch, it's the yeah, like, "Fuck you, dude, let's do this!" It's that kind of comfort. Like, I've been hit in the head with all kinds of stuff [at GFC]. You know, I like to say I have a head full of cement.

SM: So that moment, where you felt like you moved that guy, how did that feel?

FREDDY: It felt great. Oh, yeah.

SM: Can you describe the feeling? Was it like a sense of control?

FREDDY: Dominance, yeah. A guy that big. I mean, he was a big dude, he could handle people in that bar, but he looked back, and he looked at me, and … that's the other thing, I lock eyes with guys, now, in public, and I wait for them to look away. I never used to do anything like that. Not this coffee shop, but I had been to another coffee shop [recently], I did that.

SM: Do you do that consciously? Are you kind of testing them?

FREDDY: Totally. I'm testing them, and I'm testing what I'm doing. I will look at somebody until they look away. And when they look away, I win. That's sort of mandingo.

SM: [*joking*] I do that with my dog.

FREDDY: [*Grunts several times, half-jokingly, both of us laughing.*] I'm not a prick at all [*laughing*]. You know?

SM: Yeah, I've known you for 20 minutes, and I've heard about you [from other fighters], you kind of seem like a nice, sweet guy—

FREDDY: Totally. Totally.

SM: —I gotta be honest, so, how do you kind of reconcile that?

FREDDY: [*laughing*] I don't. You know, it's all one—it's a pillowcase full of shit. And you know, here we are, talking on a bench. Yeah, a paradox. It's part of our nature. But I feel evolved. I feel … before, I felt manly; now [after fighting at GFC], I feel *man*. There's that kind of projection of aura—you know, masculinity and strength—that I use, and then I have no problem putting my body into something where, you know, I'll force somebody out of the way. I used to not do that.

SM: An outsider would say, "Oh, it's like a pissing contest." You know, like who can make the other person move.

FREDDY: Or, the staring in the eyes, and the . . . one or the other looks away.

SM: Sure.

FREDDY: That's completely, yeah, at one level, that's ridiculous, honestly. But on another level, it's very primal.

SM: I'm looking around, we're in a pretty nice place, it seems like a fairly safe place.

FREDDY: It's Palo Alto!

SM: It sounds like you're highly unlikely to get in these confrontations, right? It's pretty damn unlikely, but yet, you still kind of live your life in such a way that you're thinking about this all the time, and you're preparing for this stuff, and you're asking, "Why don't more men do this?" And so maybe you've kind of answered the question, because we are in a situation where we mostly don't have to face those kinds of fears. You're escalating every confrontation or the possibility of there being a serious confrontation, so if all guys are walking around with this training, and with this kind of caveman attitude—

FREDDY: We would be so polite, and nobody would . . . nobody . . . I would hold the door for another man, because we would really know—I already know that any of us could kill each other—that any of us . . . there's a bunch of guys over there sitting on a park bench, hey, those guys could kill me. That's just the way it is. You know, an armed society is a polite society. I used to carry a knife all the time, I don't anymore, because I feel like, if I would ever pull it out in a situation where I couldn't prove, in a court of law, that I really needed it, that I would do time. So I'd rather fist and kick and, you know, punch my way out of something, and then run my ass off. I'm going to run. Dear God, make no mistake, courage . . . courage is to jog away from doing an eight-year bid. That's courage, running away from that.

SM: Your first inclination would be to get the hell out?

FREDDY: Oh, I'm out. I'm out. Hell, we're sitting here—again, in Palo Alto—but if something happened, or let's say they get in our face or there's nowhere to turn, Scott, you and me, we're fighting out of it because we have to. But then once we're out of there, I'm like, "Dude, let's beat feet and call the police." But yeah, the primal thing, I really believe in it.

. . . I just, I want more men to [try fighting]. I want more men to run, fight, I want them to have great sex, I want them to just . . . all of that. I just wish men were stronger, you know? I talk about that a lot. Are men lost nowadays? If men were strong, I think women wouldn't be bitchy, you know? And I'm not saying this role or that role—each marriage, figure it out. Every marriage is completely its own. I just wish [men] were stronger. Stronger as fathers, stand-up guys . . . you know, not that they're not "good guys."

SM: I get the sense that you are always pushing yourself, at work and at play.
FREDDY: Always.
SM: Is there an ego part to that?
FREDDY: Definitely. You're pegging me right, man. Scott's understanding me.
   Yeah, I feel like the day is won when I, let's say if I have a really good fight
   night—it's great, right? I mean, you feel . . . I feel alive, I feel happy, I've
   rebonded with the brothers, right? You know, with the tribe. I feel like
   I'm renewed as a man, as a male *Homo sapien*, you know what I mean? As
   a human animal, I've . . . because, you know . . . this concrete sidewalk's
   bullshit, these manicured trees on this road next to us—it's all BS. [We sit]
   under fluorescent lights on soft cushy chairs. I don't worry about where my
   next 100 meals are coming from, so there's sort of that disconnect there.
   But you know, after a fight night, I really feel like I'm, you know, back to
   the original man. [When I'm older,] I'll be able to look back . . . you know I
   really lived. I've really lived. And that's why I try to get guys who aren't fighters to come to the garage once, man. Just come once. Fight just once.
   We're not built to live how we live now. It's definitely comfortable, and I
   wouldn't choose to be a caveman, but physically, we're built to be cavemen,
   right? And I use the term *cavemen* in a, you know, not, duh, rock, you know,
   club guy. Not the Flintstones, but more like the mobile hunter-gatherer.
   That's . . . our bodies are built for that. Male bodies are built to last, you
   know, 30 years, maybe, of hunting and running and spearing. So for me, personally, running and fighting go very well together, I believe. We're built for
   three physical things: violence or hunting, running, and making more of us.
   We are really, really good at those three things. We are excellent at making
   babies, we are excellent at fighting each other and hunting animals, and we
   are built to run. Built to run, so I think we're built to fight.

Despite the cultural resonance of evolutionary psych models of women's
and men's behaviors, caveman masculinity is not a socially suitable justifi-
cation for adult men's participation in a fight club. GFC members' asser-
tions that fighting is a natural expression of maleness—a biological state of
being—challenges the cultures' elaborate antiviolence social mechanisms.
Adult fighting clubs are taboo. To fight in one is to participate in a subculture
mainstream society sees as deviant.

Tribal and Fraternal Bonds
Since the late 19th century, American men have created organizations to
separate themselves from women. Sports teams, unions, and fraternal organizations (such as the Elks and Moose Lodges) are examples. Men carved out
more of these homosocial spaces as women gained greater economic power

and social access.[26] Although not entirely exclusive to men, the Gentlemen's Fighting Club serves as a fraternal organization for many of its core members. They describe GFC fights and the group itself as a noncompetitive, tribal-like bonding experience. One of their mottos is "You don't know a guy until you fight him."

Fighters are not judged, ranked, or humiliated. Camaraderie replaces competition. Winning and losing are irrelevant. No one scores the fights or keeps track of the number of strikes landed. There's almost a team spirit, despite the one-on-one nature of combat. The fighters have an interest in helping each other build their skills, but they show no interest in ranking each other, playing out anger, or humiliating anyone. They certainly deliver painful blows and occasionally cause injuries to opponents, but there's no intent to cause serious harm. In one of my fights, my stronger opponent skillfully delivered painful strikes using rattan sticks, but he didn't bull-rush or grab me, pin me down, or pummel me. Stronger and more skilled fighters use various weapons to expand their own and their opponents' skills. They gain nothing by overwhelming smaller, less experienced fighters with brute strength. Winning is supplanted by skill development.

New fighters may feel as if they are undergoing a controlled hazing ritual, but the regulars help create the best of a fraternal atmosphere—camaraderie and bonding—without fear of being judged by other men. The bond is evident in the postfight hug, an authentic embrace of appreciation and respect. My afternoon of fighting ended, as they all do, with beer and laughter while watching recordings of the fights. (No copies of the videos are made or distributed.)

GFC may be unique in the way it cultivates the most visceral element of American manhood. Unlike mixed martial arts competitors, these garage fighters don't attempt to injure each other to win. And unlike middle school bullies, they don't try to physically humiliate each other. They push and challenge each other, encouraging everyone to grow as a fighter—and as a person. As one veteran explained as I prepared for my first fight, your fellow fighters are "there to bring you up, not beat you down."

Manhood is elusive and tenuous, always capable of being undermined by a single failure. GFC gives men a venue where they can prove themselves physically, shielding them from the burden of trying to dominate others—and the fear of being dominated. The garage serves as a protective membrane from the outside world. GFC offers therapy to those men seeking to heal their wounded masculinity and often feelings of powerlessness. Not all men participate for that reason, but those who do enjoy an experience similar to the men's retreats that peaked in the 1980s and continue in smaller numbers today. (The politics of those groups ran from liberal feminist to antifeminist backlash.[27])

GFC has no explicit masculinity politics or agenda, but its ritual violence and fraternal atmosphere share characteristics of men's retreats. Outsiders' negative reactions to GFC reinforce an "us-against-them" collective identity and bond. "For me," Freddy says, "It's about the brotherhood. It's tribal. We're all warriors, we're all in the tribe." Whoever fights earns Freddy's respect. When new fighters show up, he is quick to integrate them into the group and alleviate their anxieties. Conversely, MMA fighters seek to intimidate each other before fights to increase their chances of controlling and dominating their opponents.[28] Freddy explains, "I'm completely inclusive, you know, not quite a 'Thanks for coming,' more like a 'Hey, how are you doing, my name's Freddy.' I try to quell any fears a new . . . you know, a young buck has." Freddy will say to new fighters, "'Oh, yeah, man this is going to be great! I can't wait. Maybe we should do a keyboard fight. You ever fought with a keyboard?' [My approach is] ha ha, make some jokes."

Other fighters, including longtime core participants, dismiss the tribal or fraternal aspects of GFC. Jason says the camaraderie part is "not a big deal" for him. He just enjoys fighting. Most fighters show up for fight nights, enjoy the evening's experience and leave. They may return many times, but it does not produce lifelong friendships or bonding. Fighters with extensive childhood histories of getting into fights seem least likely to experience GFC as a fraternity or fighting as a tribal ritual. A few who come from fighting cultures dismiss as fake other fighters' claims that GFC offers a tribal atmosphere. One fighter, Barry, felt like the ritual became sadistic over the course of his several experiences. He was pushed too far and hard in his fights, leaving him alienated from the group: "I'm all in favor of sadism, but you've got to find somebody who wants to be beaten up. That wasn't what I was there for."

George has arrived at the conclusion that one of GFC's most important functions is its fraternal atmosphere. He supports women training in self-defense and once saw GFC as a potential source of that training. Over the years, he found that almost no women were interested in fighting, and he lost interest in their participation. He folds this information into his negative views of feminism and women:

I believe in a fraternity. I like a fraternity. I like a place where you can go and you can speak as a man would. I mean, we don't demean women, or we don't talk about bad things about our wives and girls. In fact, strangely enough, in most fraternities, those conversations are nearly absent. And it would be only fair and equal for men to malign women the same way that women malign men. They get together, and the bulk of their conversations really are about how inadequate their provider is or how he doesn't measure up against the sum of the next 10 guys. So the conversations are different. But I do like the fraternal aspect of it.

And I do think one woman showing up changes the conversation. I think it's the same in the workplace as well. It's the same thing.

The combination of homosociality and what fighters describe as the pure honesty of this kind of physical exchange leaves many feeling deeply connected. Some describe their fights as a form of art, as a tribal ritual, an expression of respect, and the source of some of the strongest bonds they share with other human beings.

Yet there have been some women who have fought at GFC. However, only one, Beth, was a regular. She was respected and viewed as a serious fighter. Beth's presence did not alter Freddy's view of GFC as a fraternity and brotherhood: "She's the only female I've ever fought. She's great with the blade. She carved me up. I give her some back, some knees, elbows, you know, bang it out. I don't hold back. She's tough." Freddy says he has no problem with women and men fighting but knows others do: "Some guys don't want women to fight at [GFC]. I really don't care."

"You treat them just like anybody else," Darren says, while expressing enthusiasm for women fighting. A few of the much larger and highly trained GFC participants, such as Ronnie, report holding back some when fighting Beth. They did the same with other fighters who were at a size or skill disadvantage, in all cases with the goal of fostering growth and building confidence; bringing your sister up rather than beating her down. Jackson also fought Beth at GFC, and he, too, welcomes women fighters. Recalling his fights with Beth, he says,

> That chick fucked me up! That chick kicked my ass. I remember she had me on the ground, and she was taking shots at me and stuff. Or, no, she was trying to submit me. And I just . . . You know, it clicked, like, "Oh, my God, this chick's going to kick my ass." And at first I kind of went easy on her, and then I realized, OK, she's not playing. And I remember I was on my back, and I just reared up, and I decked her in the face, like as hard as I could, and it was like an instinct. And the guys were like, "Hey, no face, no face," and she just shrugged it off, like, "Really? Is that all you have?" And every time I fought Beth after that, I did not underestimate her. She's quite versed in stick fighting, and she's a tough girl.

Jackson's minimizing terminology ("chick" and "girl") for Beth contrasts with his view of her as a skilled, tough fighter—one who nearly emasculated him when she was controlling and dominating him.

Fighting is no longer solely men's terrain. Women have long been practicing the "manly art" of boxing, competing in 2012 for the first time as Olympic athletes.[29] Women's MMA has gained popularity, drawing huge audiences during Ronda Rousey's 2012–2015 rise and reign. Rousey's judo skills, which earlier won her an Olympic medal, translated to her dominating opponents for several years. She is also girl-next-door pretty, which helped launch a modeling and acting career and landed her on various "most attractive women" lists. She does gender in both the most conventional and the most unconventional ways possible, reflecting in part the rewards women can enjoy for doing masculine-marked things, especially if they conform to heteronormative beauty ideals.

Rousey's reign as champion was so prolific and respected that many admirers wondered aloud whether she could defeat professional men fighters in her weight class. Rousey's self-confidence was balanced by her understanding that fighting a man would have broader implications than even Billy Jean King's 1973 "Battle of the Sexes" tennis match versus Bobby Riggs. In a 2015 interview, Rousey said, "I don't think it's a great idea to have a man hitting a woman on television. I'll never say that I'll lose, but you *could* have a girl getting totally beat up on TV by a guy—which is a bad image to put across" given recent high-profile cases of violence against women by professional football players.[30]

The stakes are much lower when GFC fighter Beth arms herself with a training knife and squares off with a man in the garage. Still, several men say they would not fight a woman at GFC. Barry captures the sentiment of a couple of them when he explains, "The main reason I wouldn't is there's no way to win that. So if you win the fight, you beat up a girl, and if you lose the fight, you got beat up by a girl. You're not coming out on top there." Sean knew Beth fought at GFC and "thought it was real cool," but he says he would not spar with her because, "I still have that thing—'You don't put your hands on no woman.'" The reasons for not doing so run from chauvinistic and patronizing to ideological opposition to violence against women. Beth had plenty of takers, but some men were unwilling to treat her equally. Gender politics are messy in a fighting club.

Beth was exceptional and her participation was temporary. Most of GFC's history is men fighting and bonding with other men. Freddy explains why he has become such close friends with two other fighters. He says,

> I've hit both of them as hard as I possibly could, I've belted [one of them] with a stick, after the buzzer, or whatever, and just kneeing him, kneeing him, kneeing him, and he kind of just calmly afterwards, [says] "So are we done?" You know? And that's that moment of bonding. I'm like, "Sorry, bro." And he's like, "Whatever, don't worry about it, it's all good." You know, and that's a guy you can depend on, that's a guy who would stand tall with you, that's, you know, that's that bond, right? Because, well, I guess in a sense, I have tested all of them myself.

Pushing and testing each other is a sign of respect. Holding back too much does not foster growth and might be perceived as condescending and insulting.

Conversely, demolishing a novice fighter also stunts their growth; that form of humiliation is unwelcome in the tribe. The bond develops as fighters push and get to know each other in ways that starkly contrast with everyday interactions. Rick explains, "At some point, you end up pushing somebody and they push you back. You really know them on a deeper level. And rather than what beer they like or what cheese they eat or where they work or where they were born—I mean, I guess it's OK. I don't really care where they were born [*laughing*]—I mean, that comes afterwards, right?" Jackson's years of fighting at GFC have fostered deep connections. He says, "I know if I ever got like in some real, real shit, they're some of the first people I'd want to go to."

As with many fraternities, sophomoric and other humor helps solidify brothers' bonds. Fighters often wear flashy or goofy clothing, target each other's groins and love handles, and choose nonlethal weapons merely for entertainment, including Dustbusters and toilet plungers. (The latter they occasionally use to plunge a bowl before arming unsuspecting participants and quickly launching their fight.)

Fights are recorded, watched, and when something funny happens, cued up and watched over and over again. "Watching videos constitutes 50% of the fun," Kay says, "because you do this and then you watch yourself. You look more ridiculous than anything. It's just funny." There are countless sources of self-mocking, good-natured teasing, and laughter. Excessive screams of pain, unexpected in-fight dialog ("Gotta dig deep!"), clumsy and failed moves, and in one incident during Fight the Professor, two fighters' simultaneously kneeing each other in the groin, all bring howls of laughter when replayed. Unlike groups of men gathering to watch MMA fights or football games, watching their own fights isn't a vicarious manhood act. Neither is it parallel to young men's practices of watching porn together or going out to "hit on" women and bond. From what I observed and heard, the fighters bonded watching their videos—but they did so because of their comedic value rather than as a celebration of violence or men's physical dominance. (The organizer's wife is a regular viewer and also finds the videos funny.) Kay jokes that he is a very shallow guy, that he does not practice martial arts for spiritual reasons. Rick laughs and suggests that fighting has "no higher purpose," that GFC's original rationale did not extend beyond "My Fist. Your Face."

When American men have isolated themselves, gathering separately from women, they have mostly done so as a means of escape. The humor GFC fighters sometimes use to poke fun at modern society—jokingly inquiring if their opponent would prefer "cucumber lime" or "revitalizing pomegranate and mango" for the soap bar they will wrap inside a towel and use to pummel each other—has clear implications for gender relations. Take, for example, when fighters use magazines rolled around a heavy, solid object such as a brass rod. When they choose Martha Stewart's magazine, *Living*, the threat posed by the weapon extends from physical to symbolic. Fighters are in danger of not only getting bruised and battered but emasculated. One fighter joked, "Yeah, getting beat down by popular feminine culture. I mean, come on, I don't wanna get hit with Martha—she's done time."[31] A short prison sentence for obstruction of justice isn't what makes *Living* magazine's editor-in-chief such an overtly gendered choice, though. Martha Stewart is a symbol of feminine domesticity: an imaginative and skilled cook, interior decorator, and gardener. Her name conjures images of 1950s housewives—or at least it does to the guys who use her magazine to beat up their friends in a garage. It's not CEO Martha or multimillionaire Martha and not even "ex-con" Martha that makes her such an appealing weapon. The fighter who gets pounded by a brass rod encased in Martha gets the message loud and clear: you just got your ass kicked by a woman—and not just any woman, but an icon of femininity. What kind of a man are you? Not one at all. Of course, the magazine is used in a joking manner, not unlike men's countless other homosocial hazing rituals.

Feeling Pain, Feeling Alive

GFC fighters object to the idea that their club is too dangerous, an unnecessary risk to one's health. Their objections are often unpersuasive; they are left balancing their desire to fight with society's general disapproval of it. Bruises, scars, and other more visible markers of fighting invite conversations and the possibility of being harshly judged. *Why would a father so selfishly put himself before his kids? How could you risk breaking your fingers when you need them for work? What do you have to prove?*

Risking and enduring pain and injury are rites of passage in youth sports. Boys and young men are respected and celebrated for suffering without tears or complaint, all the more so if they can persevere and keep playing: "Suck it up!" "Walk it off." "You gotta take a licking and keep on ticking." Adult men are eventually told to settle down, listen to their bodies, stop viewing overcoming pain as a competition or manhood act, and prioritize their families and careers over adrenaline-fueled gambles with their physical well-being.

GFC members protest that fighting is no riskier, and usually safer, than many other activities that they and plenty of other adults do, such as snowboarding, mountain biking, and rock climbing, to name just a few. All occasionally produce an array of acute injuries resulting in emergency room visits and short- and long-term disabilities. Weekend warriors who break a leg skiing or trail riding are much more likely than GFC participants to receive sympathy and admiration, perhaps to even have their dangerous pursuits romanticized in such a way that others vicariously enjoy the thrill. Pushing your body to its limits in a test against nature receives a qualitatively different reaction than doing so in a fight.

There are other grounds on which fighters can and do protest the disparagement they receive for participating in a fight club. Beyond what they see as the hypocrisy of stigmatizing one risk-taking activity while accepting another, they point to the cumulative effects of years of participating in otherwise safe sports such as tennis, golf, and running. The wear and tear often lead to surgeries and joint replacements, which are not met with righteous indignation. Tennis elbow, shredded knee cartilage and tendons, and bulging discs are not visible to the naked eye, lessening the moral outrage levied against even much older participants who are injured. I would add that our jobs often pose the greatest risks. Stress, repetitive motion injuries, overuse or underuse of our bodies, and other job-related threats to our health abound. Recent research suggests the more time we spend sitting, whether on couches watching TV all night or at office desks all day, the likelier we are to die sooner.[32]

Is there really that much difference between wrecking our bodies one way versus another? Is fighting really that different than other risk-taking activities and sports? Yes and no. Fighting, like boxing or football, is a hitting sport. Basketball, by contrast, is a contact sport. Interpersonal contact is part of the game but not an end in itself. Tennis is a noncontact sport, although most tennis players' knees would beg to differ. Chronic injuries common to all physical activities seem less grotesque than acute injuries, especially those wrought by interpersonal violence. And whereas pain and injuries are unwelcome among most athletes, there are exceptions among fighting club participants.

As part of their fight against modernity, some GFC members embrace physical pain rather than try to eliminate it from their lives. Pain is euphemized as "feedback" from other fighters. Instead of retreating from it, many fighters invite pain as they would a friend to dinner. They ensure its arrival by being as welcoming to it as possible. They fight without pads and even shirts, use weapons that bruise and tear skin, and revel in (minor) damage to their own and others' bodies. They view injuries as teachable moments. Immediately after the injury, they examine what they did wrong that allowed it to occur. The weeks and months of healing and recovery, culminating with a return to fighting, are seen as a period of growth that reveals their character, determination, and courage. Fighters accept that if they spend enough time in the garage, they will experience broken fingers and toes, cracked ribs, and battered bodies. Injuries and wounds are things to "experience" rather than from which one "suffers." They are assumed to have been part of daily life for our ancestors. To fight through them is to confirm that one is merely hurt and not injured, that modern man hasn't fully succumbed to the assimilating forces of modernization.

Several fighters tell me they have experienced and fought through mild concussions. They talk about "getting dizzy," the "curtains falling" and the "lights going out" before their brains regroup and "check back in" so they can continue fighting. At Fight the Professor, Rick and Patrick's double-stick fight is halted when Patrick has his bell rung. Turning slightly sideways, Patrick exposes an unprotected spot on the back of his protective headgear during the fight. Rick's stick hits Patrick's head instead of the padding during that split-second move, and Patrick is visibly shaken. He wants to resume, but Rick stops the fight. In the postfight interview, Rick asks, "Why did you want to keep on going?" Patrick responds, "I feel good. I mean, I'm not tired." When we watch the video later, Kay says, "That's one psychopath right there!" Mocking Patrick, Kay continues, "'It feels good. I feel I almost passed out. I feel good. I feel I need to be punished. I need to be punished!'" We all laugh. Rick adds, "That's not the usual response [to getting hit in the head]." The labeling and sarcastic imitation Patrick receives are thinly veiled expressions of respect. The group uses humor to acknowledge his demonstration of toughness.

Jackson's one serious fighting injury initially made him angry, but eventually he became introspective before defiantly returning to the garage. He says,

> I remember I was like face down on my floor, just like in so much pain . . . [I was in pain] for like a month or a month and a half. I went through the gamut of emotions. I was like, "Man, [the guy he fought]'s a big guy. He's like twice my size, why would he hit me like that? He knows I'm smaller." But at the same time, it's like, yeah, you know, that's the risk. The guy's big, you know. And I started asking myself, "Well, why did you put yourself in that situation? You didn't have to. Like, come on, think about this, don't blame him. I came to [GFC to] build myself up. I came to challenge myself, and hey, I got dusted. I might have failed this little test, but there's a lot to learn from this." And I became a much better fighter after that incident. It was after that where I got a little bit more cautious, a little bit more serious. You know, it was like a growing point for me . . . When I came back, I was like, "Screw that, I'm no bitch. I can do this." You know, so there was a lot of ego and bravado in there. Like, "I'll show them. I'll come back even better." Yeah, that was absolutely going through my head at the time.

Dominating other fighters produces less satisfaction, self-esteem, and sense of accomplishment for most fighters than does overcoming adversity. Demonstrating resilience and courage are highly valued manhood acts. Weakness is for "bitches." It is, in Jackson's account, symbolically feminine, thereby reinforcing fighting, toughness, and dominance as features of maleness and manhood.

Sammy initially expected to reclaim his manhood by beating up his opponents. Instead he came to believe that the "true power" was being able to withstand a beating. Getting hit is, in many ways, more important than hitting. "So sometimes losing is winning?" I ask him. "Losing is *definitely* winning," he says. He now invites and even embraces fights with men at GFC who are stronger and may subject him to countless strikes. The same confidence has helped him handle nonviolent confrontations at work, he notes. Darren feels more robust after years of being "toughened up" at GFC. With experience, he says, "you figure out how to absorb the blows and how to endure past that. It feels really, really good. It's like you pick up your endurance level, feel like you're able to get through life a little better. I mean, let's face it, it's kind of like life, right? It's just a series of blows and getting through them; it's how you get through them. You know, get through them with a smile on your face and a positive attitude instead of just succumbing to them." Darren and like-minded GFC fighters believe they should literally be smiling through the pain. They smile not to ridicule opponents' ineffective blows but to dismiss contemporary society's frowning upon their fighting. They take pleasure in experiencing pain.

Of course, not all fighters enjoy getting hit or view pain or the scars of violence as badges of honor. On the contrary, some fighters see their bruises and cuts as sources of shame. These marks indicate failed technique. And, fighters note, it sucks to be in pain. Some of this subset of fighters takes pleasure in dominating and controlling fights, but not for sadistic reasons.

Ronnie says he wants to win the fight in the moment, "but in the end, it's really about the challenge and about the growth in it. So immediately, it's like 'Yeah, I don't want to lose you. I want to make sure I whip your ass as much as I can.' But in the end, for me, it's like a period of growth." He asks himself after every fight night, "How did I grow from the last time? How did I grow from the two times before that? How did I stretch myself into a place where I could become a better fighter, or feel more confident, or more fluid in my motion and actions?" Ronnie fights to improve his technique and to grow as a fighter, not to prove his manhood or as a form of protest against social norms.

Other fighters are less interested in dominating fights via violence than demonstrating their ability to avoid pain and injury. Sean attempts to deliver a blow and avoid preemptive or counterstrikes. He approaches fights as if they are simulations and each weapon as if it could be lethal. "If that was a [real machete] fight, that one good shot could kill you," Sean says. Barry fantasizes about exerting the least violent form of control over opponents and fights. He says,

> I don't mind getting hit, but I really like, if I could've waved a magic wand, I
> would want to be like a master of aikido. I would like to be able to dodge any-
> thing that someone throws at me and always come out on top—but always come

out on top where I'm using two fingers to put them in a hold that, if I went a little farther, I would break their arm, but at this point, I haven't hurt anything, and then they're going to say, "You win." I would have been happy with that. I didn't want to beat up anybody.

Fantasies aside, even Barry says he "probably took more pleasure in surviving a punch than anything."

It pays to be a winner, but given how manhood is constructed, it's more important to avoid being at the bottom than it is to be at the top. Boys and young men, including those who are badly beaten, obtain masculine capital when they attempt to fight; complying, however unsuccessfully, brings some reward. Those perceived as too fearful to even try to defend themselves are the ones who lie at the bottom of the hierarchy; they are the ones who are most subordinated. GFC affords men opportunities to repair their broken manhood or assert a primal version of it, whether individually or collectively, in response to perceived challenges to their status and identity. Individually, some men use GFC to repair and restore what they lost as boys. Collectively, some members view GFC as a way to restore a sense of fighting, primal man.

3

Seeking Growth

The Penis Health Club

> Look at those hands. Are they small
> hands? . . . If they are small, something
> else must be small. I guarantee you, there
> is no problem. I guarantee.
> —Donald Trump at a 2016 Republican
> presidential primary debate

Donald Trump's comment was a response to competing candidate Marco
Rubio's less-than-subtle taunt that Trump might have a small penis. The
exchange was a first because it took place during a live, televised debate and
not between middle school boys. Watching it later, though, I imagine millions of middle school boys (along with older boys and men) examining and
perhaps measuring their hands, or maybe jamming them into their pockets
if anyone was nearby. That Rubio would deliver the taunt and Trump would
respond speaks volumes about both men, but I will refrain from psychoanalyz-
ing either. More important, the exchange opens a window into our culture:
penis size and performance are inextricably tied to contemporary American
manhood. Trump sought to assure everyone he was, in essence, "dick proud,"
not ashamed, that he doesn't have any "problem" down there. This implies
that it would be a problem if he had a small penis. And it would be for a man
in general in our culture (and many others), and one running for the world's
most powerful office in particular. The argument that the phallus is a symbol

of power was never made so abundantly and publically clear. I briefly wondered if Trump could be goaded into tweeting a photo if his opponents or the media continued questioning him about his size.

Then I thought about the members of the online Penis Health Club in this study. They, too, are consumed by the possibility that they might have a problem and how to avoid situations that might confirm it. So many of these men, especially the younger ones, feel inadequate, regardless of how they actually measure up or perform. They fear exposing their bodies to men (in locker rooms or as sexual partners) and women alike. Some have been mocked, some bear the burden of racial stereotypes, and many compare themselves unfavorably to porn stars. Some internalize such a deep sense of failure they suffer from depression and even suicidal thoughts. They join the Penis Health Club for similar reasons as those that cause some men to gravitate to the Gentlemen's Fighting Club: to try to fix what they see as their broken bodies and broken manhood. There they find advice and workout routines to increase their size and improve their performance. This produces in some members a restored sense of control over their bodies and thus a source of manhood repair. They also are coached to free themselves of their distorted views about size, performance, and manhood.

Penises and Manhood

Gendered norms and the legacy of patriarchal relations have produced separate, unequal heterosexual expectations for women and men. Men are assigned the role of initiators (active, assertive, aggressive) and women the role of gatekeepers (reactive, passive, defensive).[1] Men are supposed to desire sex and always be ready to have sex. If they have sex with many women, they are mostly rewarded and celebrated by other men. Women's gatekeeper role has been altered since the introduction of the pill and the women's rights movement. Both challenged men's control over women's bodies and sexuality, making sex more a source of pleasure than shame for women. The results have been uneven. Women's pleasure, and especially women's orgasms—which *Saturday Night Live* once joked were first discovered around 1970—has led to men being more conscientious lovers—that is, they are expected to put on a good performance. Women certainly have much greater sexual freedom today than they did before the 1960s. They, too, are expected to be sexually skilled and initiate more. Women enjoy greater autonomy as well as some pressure to perform, less frequently serving as passive objects upon which men exercise their desires. Sexy, in-control women are a cultural phenomenon and force. However, women's sexual agency and demand for sexual pleasure have also led to a lot of flaccid penises.[2] Some men—expecting and used to being in control—have a hard time with women taking on the masculine-marked initiator role and demanding to be pleasured. And young men in particular have increasingly felt like they are competing with and losing against each other: "They worry that perhaps they're not doing it enough, or well enough, or they're not big enough, or hard enough."[3] Giving up some power and control has proven more than some men can handle.

Significant power differences remain. Girls and women are still widely sexually assaulted and raped. Data reveal that most of this sexual violence is committed by men who are their husbands, partners, boyfriends, friends, and acquaintances.[4] Women's gatekeeping role, their power to say no, is often trumped by men's coercive and controlling behaviors, physical and otherwise. Progress is also contradicted by the gatekeeper-based phenomenon of "slut-shaming." Women are still judged, chided, and ostracized for enjoying sex too much—certainly casual sex.

Not everyone buys into or complies with these gendered norms. The dichotomous roles do not even apply to people who do not identify as straight, or as women or men. These norms do exist, though, and they can be made shockingly clear when people violate them. Straight men who fail to pursue— or worse, turn down—sex with women have their manhood and sexuality questioned ("Is he a fag?"). Women get ostracized for the same actions that elevate men ("What a whore!" versus "What a pimp!"). Men brag about how big they are, how many women they've had, and how impressive their performances are. In school locker rooms, popular music, and fraternity houses, men's sexual bragging conjures images of domination (if not violence) and so often takes away women's humanity: "I had her screaming." "She was begging for more." "I put her ass to sleep."

We know that sex is a performance and a manhood act because impotence is so emasculating. *Impotence* is the inability to *achieve* or *sustain* an erection for the purpose of sex; a demonstration of incompetence. But being impotent is also alternatively defined as being powerless, helpless, weak, without force or effectiveness, or lacking vigor, power, strength, and ability. These secondary meanings read like a list of antonyms for manhood. To be impotent is to not be masculine.[5] Feminist philosopher Susan Bordo observes that we "define it as the inability to achieve an erection that is adequate for 'satisfactory sexual performance'! Not pleasure. Not feeling. *Performance*. Eighty-five-year-old men are having Viagra heart attacks trying to keep those power tools running."[6]

Men's pressure to perform during sex and their accountability to that performance causes them to view their penises as their manhood. Researchers have found that men have greater concerns about their penis size than their height or weight, this concern decreases little with age, and men's overall views about their bodies and appearances are influenced by whether they perceive themselves as having a larger or smaller penis.[7] Even though "impotence" has been replaced with "erectile dysfunction," many men still seem aware that their erection problems lie in their heads more than their physiologies. But now, instead of years of psychotherapy to identify and address their under-lying issues, men can just take a pill—a magic "masculinity pill."[8] Viagra led the booming industry of pills and devices that prey upon men's size and per-formance anxieties. Viagra's ad campaigns used several different appeals, one of which was that it would help men reclaim their masculine identities by reclaiming their youth, restoring their control over their bodies, and accessing sexual power and performance. The new medicalized "ED" problem framed men's bodies as machines (power tools) to be tweaked and optimized for per-formance. Viagra promised the ultimate in tool repair. When penises become tools—when they are wielded to acquire power and control—they lose their source of pleasure.[9] Beyond ads and spam email selling various ED- and penis size-related products, internet pornography further fuels men's anxieties. Por-nography's nonrepresentative and often camera-distorted bodies cause deflat-ing comparisons for men, too.

Unless and until we decouple manhood from size and sexual performance, men will continue to feel emasculated by every sexual encounter that does not go well and women will continue to be sexual objects—dehumanized con-quests used as proxy measures of manhood. If sex continues to be viewed by men as an accomplishment—a scoreboard for their masculinity—instead of a source of pleasure and intimacy, men will inevitably find that a perfect score is unattainable. They will internalize a sense of manhood failure and chastise themselves for it. Worse, they may literally project that anger onto others, usually women. What they most assuredly will continue to do is find ways to alleviate their size and performance anxieties. ED pills and penis exercises are Band-Aid solutions to the fundamental problem of how destructive body and general manhood ideals are.

The Club

The ubiquity and popularity of U.S. health clubs is one indicator of our body-obsessed culture. I studied a unique health club that targets all men over the age of 18, one that exists only online and focuses solely on penis exercises and health: the Penis Health Club.[10] Despite the broader emphasis on penis health, increasing size is most members' foremost concern.

The Penis Health Club (hereafter, PHC or the Club) mirrors a brick-and-mortar gym in many ways. New members join daily. Some stay for years, but many quickly become inactive. Others come and go over the years because of injuries, life changes, and guilt from inactivity. Cliques and friendships emerge based on shared exercise and personal interests. Conversations extend to dating and relationships, work, politics, music, sports, and more. Regular and longtime members establish close bonds, meet up (online) regularly, pro-vide advice and support, and hold each other accountable to their workouts.

"There's so much more to it than just pulling on your dick," one member told me.

Like most fitness centers, all stereotypical groups are represented at the Club: hardcore gym rats, extroverted greeters who welcome new members, well-sculpted exhibitionists. The insecure are rampant. Anxieties about imperfections are compounded by the sprinkling of ideal bodies on display (clothed and unclothed) as well as some men's belief that they alone suffer such body shame. There are even personal trainers: for a fee, they will assess members' individual concerns and perceived deficiencies, develop long-term goals and a workout regimen to achieve them, and provide feedback on form and technique.

Despite these many similarities, the Club isn't exactly your local YMCA. There are no membership dues. Voluntary donations are supplemented with ads for penis enlargement devices to keep the site running. The Club's unique topical focus makes it distinct and results in virtually all club members concealing their identities behind a pseudonym. (Whatever clever penis pun you can conjure has already been claimed as a user ID by a PHC member.) Member profiles allow users to share information such as their locations (usually country), join dates, site activity, measurements (beginning, current, and goals), groups they've joined (smaller, larger, older, too thin, erectile dysfunction, hangers, etc.), and for the bold few, photos. The Club has its own vernacular, highlighted by a military-like cluster of acronyms and slang terms like *growers* versus *showers* (for men with greater or lesser disparities in their flaccid versus erect penis sizes), and the derisive *size queens* (for women deemed unduly obsessive about penis size). Other than its distinctive content, PHC looks and behaves much the same as many other online forums.

It has tens of thousands of members from all over the world, although it caters primarily to English-speaking users, mostly Americans. Only a small fraction of members who have joined over the years continue to be active. Literally hundreds of thousands of posts are accessible, organized by topic and including conversation threads such as penis enlargement exercises and products, erectile dysfunction, size anxieties and studies, masturbation, foreskin restoration, curvature, pornography, multiple male orgasms, relationships, sex, politics, balding, and much more. An endless stream of new posts and threads appears each day. Volunteer site moderators and administrators welcome new members, provide advice, organize threads and posts, and keep the peace, which sometimes includes banning members who are rude or obvious trolls. The overall tone is one of support and community, not unlike the Gentlemen's Fighting Club.

Many men log onto the Club multiple times per day to read the latest posts, private message their friends, and see if anyone commented on their latest posts or pictures. It's their Facebook, or at least a second social networking site. It is both more intimate and less. Pseudonymously, men share with strangers and online friends their anxieties, humiliations, relationship struggles, battles with depression, life dreams, sexual fantasies, penis pictures, detailed logs of workout routines and gains, and an endless array of intimate thoughts and experiences, most of which they withhold from their offline friends and family—even their partners. This depth of intimacy is offset by the fact that almost no one reveals their actual identities and virtually all interactions are confined to the website. Anonymous forums like PHC allow men to safely navigate potentially dangerous terrain: they can share their insecurities and feelings with other men and cultivate close connections, but by doing so behind pseudonyms, they aren't, ahem, fully exposed. The vulnerability they demonstrate comes with the cloak of anonymity. Nobody can identify them, so nobody can exploit these men's perceived weaknesses in person.

The Club is a kind of bizarro world of straight men. Everyone sees, knows, and matter-of-factly comments on each other's genitals—"great starting numbers," "nice hang," "massive," "good wood," "same size as mine"—but has no idea what their clothed bodies or faces look like. Self-identified gay and bisexual men participate, too, as do a handful of women, often in conjunction with their male partners. They, too, sometimes comment on measurements and photos. These aren't pornographic "dick pics," though. Men are not undressing or posing provocatively, and the photographs are not taken with special lighting or in exotic locations. They are documentary. Even for people who are otherwise titillated by images of men's bodies and penises, the pictures and conversations lean more medical than erotic. Plenty of other websites better fulfill people's sexual desires.

Longtime members and moderators continuously stress to new members patience and safety. They attempt to disabuse (mostly younger) members of their bloated average size myths as well as the belief that size is synonymous with pleasure and performance, that making gains will suddenly transform their sex lives and relationships. New members are encouraged to follow a generic three-month stretching and conditioning program (45 minutes per day, five days per week) before attempting more advanced or strenuous activities or incorporating devices into their routines. Extenders, pumps, clamps, weights, and other devices, including do-it-yourself versions, complement an assortment of manual exercises (jelqs, kegels, edging). Creams are discussed. Enlargement pills are dismissed. Surgeries are discouraged. Workout routines are painstakingly documented, shared, studied, and tweaked. Time commitments vary but approximate those of fitness buffs of varying dedication. For example, novice hangers are discouraged from hanging weights from their penises more than 10 hours per week, whereas more experienced hangers may do 10 hours in a couple of days. Researching routines, exchanging suggestions, ordering or building devices, and carving out time to do the workouts (often during limited windows of privacy) all add up to a significant commitment. Reported gains vary, with many men seeing little to no changes.

My interests lie not in the efficacy of penis exercises but rather in men's motivations for doing them and why it is a collective process. Interviews and forum posts reveal that many men endure doubts and anxieties about their size and performance. These arise from comparisons with peers and porn stars, negative or humiliating comments directed at them or overheard, and problematic sexual experiences. Oftentimes (mis)perceptions are more powerful influences than objective truths about their penis size. Many Club members who self-report average to well-above-average measurements suffer from the same self-doubts and sense of emasculation that haunt men with smaller penises. They internalize their perceived size and performance failures, exhibiting anxiety; emotional, social, and sexual withdrawal; reduced self-esteem and confidence; and sometimes depression and even suicidal thoughts.

Some members report no negative experiences and appear quite comfortable with their bodies. Although not fueled by anxiety, they still tend to adhere to a "bigger is better" philosophy. Almost all continuously active members, and especially those who have internalized a sense of failure and inadequacy about their size and performance, enjoy modest to life-changing benefits from participating in the Club and penis exercising. PHC helps them reinterpret their penis size and performance concerns as normal and provides them with a road map to make improvements. Both contribute to the restoration of their sense of manhood by repairing what they had perceived as body failures. Five of the fourteen men I interview report starting below or just below average in penis size as adults, but only two of those five say they remain below average. The majority say they began at or above-average penis size before doing exercises, and many say they grew well above average. They also vary in their commitment level to the exercises and forums, from nonexercising lurkers to multiyear, deeply committed exercisers and forum moderators.

Internalizing: Not Measuring Up

When I asked PHC members to recall their earliest memories about their bodies and penises, most shared stories from late elementary school and middle school, as puberty approached and began to alter and distinguish their own and their peers' bodies. There were some earlier memories, including playing doctor with other kids and seeing older siblings naked.[11] Middle and high school locker rooms and showers, though, had the greatest impact during boyhood. Feeling and looking different heightened boys' awareness of their own bodies. Later, in high school and into their 20s, sexual play and partners began to wield more influence over young men's self-perceptions.

"Small-penis syndrome" or "locker-room syndrome" is attributed to men with average-sized flaccid penises whose anxieties about their size affect their emotions and behaviors in ways that seem to exceed what would be expected for their perceived flaw.[12] Men's anxieties and physicians' responses include both flaccid and erect size concerns. Small-penis syndrome tends to emerge during secondary school, along with puberty and greater scrutiny of one's own and others' bodies. When boys and men perceive themselves as small in size, it may reduce self-esteem and cause anxiety, and lead them to conceal their penises in public settings, avoid potential sexual encounters, and suffer from erectile dysfunction.

Men who have grown up in the digital age encounter not only this intense scrutiny of and cultural emphasis on their bodies but also countless images of men's bodies, penises, and sexual conquests in online pornography. Viewing pornography is like looking at bodies and sex through a carnival fun house mirror. With few exceptions, it provides a distorted, unrealistic view of what people actually look like, desire, and do. Of course, porn producers are not sex educators; they are motivated by profit. Conversely, what is supposed to be sex education is widely viewed by U.S. teens as warped in another way: a joke—uninformative and often ideological (e.g., abstinence only). The puritanical thread in American culture leaves schools and parents uncomfortable with and even fearful of discussing these issues with kids. The conversations are stilted, superficial, and ineffectual. Young people desire and need knowledge about their changing bodies and emerging sexuality to alleviate their anxieties. What will happen—what seemingly *always* happens—is they will acquire that knowledge somewhere else.

Today, porn and peers are the primary sources. Both are dubious. Our current cultural approach is analogous to gang life—when communities and families are unable to fulfill kids' basic needs, gangs composed of other young people fulfill that role. Our children are receiving the sex equivalent of street socialization, coupled with a heavy dose of unhealthy input from the porn industry.[13] What teenage boy could navigate such a cultural maelstrom and emerge intact, comfortable in his manhood and free of anxiety about his size and sexual competence? With few exceptions, the men I interview internalize body or penis size and performance flaws, whether real or, for the most part, perceived.

Comparing to Peers and Porn Stars

Middle and high school locker rooms and gym classes are usually the first places where boys begin sizing each other up, especially their penises. In the context of many years of gendered socialization, the comparisons feel more like competitions. PHC member Tomás, a 56-year-old Latino man with a wife and two children, has endured a lifelong series of bodily and sexual challenges. He grew up in a very conservative household, which contributed to his masculinity and sexuality struggles. Tomás describes himself as smaller, rounder, softer, less developed, less masculine, and less endowed than other boys and men, beginning in elementary school: "I just noticed that [my penis] seemed to be a little bit smaller, even at that time, and I just felt a little bit off." Admiring older boys in various states of undress, he recalls, "It just seemed like I wanted something else than what I had." He says that he does not have a *micropenis*, a medical term referring to rare cases of exceptionally small penises, approximately two to three inches erect. "I guess I'm just smaller than the average," he says.

The internet provides him with a sexual outlet that he believes allows his marriage and family to stay intact. The downside is that when he sees other men's erect penises in photos or on webcam masturbation sites, or women's desire for bigger men in online pornography, it "damages" him and reinforces his inadequacies. Tomás, though, really suffers from locker-room syndrome: dissatisfaction with his flaccid length: "I just notice when I'm not more erect or aroused, then it tends to be [comparatively] smaller in that situation."

Travis, a 40-year-old, straight white man, first thought about his flaccid penis size in high school, when he was on the water polo team. "We'd compete in Speedos," he says, so "[there] was not a lot to hide." Later, while showering during military training, he saw that his flaccid size was smaller than other guys' flaccid size, but his average erect size mostly alleviated his concerns. Kenneth, white, gay, and in his 50s, felt fine about his penis when it was erect, but he was uncomfortable in his high school locker room. "I'm a grower, not a shower," he says, "so basically, I feel uncomfortable in locker room settings or anything like that where I have to be exposed to other people because I don't have the flaccid hang that other men seem to have." He was showering in a fitness center a few years ago when a young man with a big flaccid penis entered the showers, "and the look on his face, I just felt like crawling into the locker. I mean I just felt so inadequate, or embarrassed."

The practice of comparing and ranking genitalia might strike some as a peculiar activity. Odder, still, seems to be doing so in a state of nonarousal. After all, we ogle and celebrate Olympic-champion sprinter Usain Bolt as he races ahead to the finish line, not when he's lounging trackside. But worrying about flaccid length and hang is similar to trying to look jacked 24-7, not simply during a workout or while flexing and posing. Even in relaxed physiological states, we are displaying our gendered bodies to others, receiving feedback, and evaluating and adjusting how we present ourselves. Boys and men's pursuit of dominance is amplified in the context of a homosocial setting like a middle school locker room, where boys' bodies are in flux and their masculine identities are at their most tenuous. It is in these pressure-cooker contexts that boys and men jostle for rank order and bond, all too often via homophobic taunts and by sexually objectifying and demeaning girls and women.[14] The primary, nearly sole, source of teenage masculine identity is the size and performance of their bodies. With such a limited cultural repertoire for establishing boys' identities, penis size—even flaccid penis size—is of great importance.

Brandon is a white, straight 24-year-old. He remembers making explicit, hierarchical comparisons between himself and his high school classmates: "I thought my size was OK, and then after high school, as far as like, relationship-wise, nobody really complained about my size. But then there were times when I felt like [my penis] wasn't big enough. As I got older, and then going to the gym, and then seeing the other guys shower, I was like, 'Holy shit, like, this dude has a huge dick!' So then I bought a pump." Brandon's self-reported initial penis size, before attempting penis enlargement, was just a shade below average.

His fellow Club member, Ed, began much smaller. At age 60 and straight, Ed's sources of knowledge about erect penis sizes were limited when he was growing up. Finally, shortly after high school, he bought an educational book on men's bodies and health. It provided visual representations of small-average, average, and large-average penises: "Well, I fell out of my chair. I said, 'Oh, shit!' I placed myself in the small-average." Ed's later exposure to porn also affected him. Pornographic images of men with perfect bodies are mono-lithic and pervasive: "That's all you see. So your perception is that everybody is well-endowed and you're the only one that isn't, which of course isn't true, but man, it's hard to break through that barrage." Prior to the at-your-fingertips availability of porn, most men (especially straight men) had to go out of their way to see another man's erect penis.

A recent medical study obtained a sample of more than 1,600 men (mostly 18- to 39-year-olds and disproportionately white) and provided them with the necessary instructions and materials to do self-measurements and submit their data. The reported average erect length was 5.6 inches and the average erect girth was 4.8 inches, which are consistent with the limited data available from previous studies.[15] A recent metastudy using health professionals' mea-surements resulted in even smaller averages.[16] These are *not* the average measure-ments of porn actors. Some research has found that men are so insecure that they tend to underestimate penis length in survey research.[17]

As boys become men and their careers, relationships, and families take on greater importance, their lives and identities are anchored less to their bodies. However, this source of masculine identity remains important. Club members often provide positive feedback and support on the forums, encouraging men to appreciate and not be ashamed of their bodies. However, the seemingly dis-proportionate number of Club members with above-average penises can have the opposite effect, exacerbating feelings of insecurity and anxiety that parallel overexposure to porn.

Disparaging and Intimidating Comments

Boys and men's awareness and anxieties about their penises come not only from visual comparisons but from others' bragging, teasing, mocking, and fantasizing about penis size and performance. A hurtful comment by a cousin still evokes an emotional response in Glenn nearly half a century after the incident. He and his younger cousin were changing in a van after a day at the beach when his cousin ridiculed Glenn's size.

I ask Glenn if he can recall how he felt in that moment, and he responds, "I do, still, very strongly. It's like, you know, 'fuck you.' I remember being embarrassed. You don't know it at the time, [but] it's like, it's genetic roulette. You don't know at that young of an age. You almost feel like you did something wrong or that [it] was your fault." Glenn internalized his cousin's mocking comment and felt embarrassment, despite never having thought or worried about his prepubescent body before then. A single criticism is a flashbulb memory of failure. Decades later, it still channels strong emotions. After that incident, Glenn never had a conversation with anyone about his penis size, including any of his boyfriends over the years.

Locker-room syndrome is triggered not only by comparisons but also by bragging, joking, and mocking. A couple of Club members have lucid memories of middle school friends who entered puberty early and whose penises were much bigger than average. One boy was known as "Big Dick Martinez," and another was "the Incredible Hulk" because he had a "hulk dick, giant compared to the rest." Twenty-two-year-old PHC member Stephen, who is white and straight, laughs at his earliest memory of middle school boys bragging about their penis sizes while hiding behind their towels. They would shout out fantastic numbers ("I have a 10-inch penis!"), so Stephen "decided to measure my junk."

A few of the older Club members share the painful school experience of jockstrap-fitting sessions. Glenn, observing that schools would never allow such a thing today, remembers the "humiliating moment for everybody" when he and his peers "would stand in a line in [our] underwear, and then the coach would come down and yell, 'large, medium, medium, small, large.'" Tomás went to a sporting goods store to purchase his gym class jockstrap. That memory set off a chain of painful recollections that spanned his high school and college years:

[The guy at the sporting goods store] says to me, "Really all you need is a rubber band and a peanut," or something like that, and I just remember those things as just cutting right through you, and being very hurtful. Yeah, it even got worse. As I got into junior high and high school, it was mandatory that you take group showers after PE. I really noticed the big difference, jumps in the guys—that more of the guys were getting hair, more of the guys were getting larger in their penis size and everything, and mine was still staying small. And again, having some people that would be next to you in gym, kind of teasing you, saying, "My God, what's wrong with you, you've got a little kid's penis." [And then in his college fraternity house] every once in a while, you would have some idiot that would come up, and make a comment [like], "I was walking around the shower, and I just saw you, and my God, you've got a . . . what's wrong with you? You need to have the doctor take a look at you," and, "You need hormones, you need this, you need that." And that would hurt. And sometimes [strangers] would call you names, so you'd get the "fag," "he's queer," "he's this or that," but you just live through it.

This "fag discourse" is less about Tomás's perceived sexuality (he was and is closeted) than his failed masculine performance.[18] Boys who do masculinity inadequately, due to their actions or bodies, are policed by other boys using fag discourse. In her research on high school boys, sociologist C. J. Pascoe found that their perceived incompetence (e.g., while doing repair work in auto shop class), lack of heterosexual prowess, and physical weakness attracted negative comments from other boys. Given stereotypical equations of gay men with femininity, fag discourse subordinates and emasculates its intended targets. Boys play a game of hot potato with the fag label, elevating themselves in the hierarchy by weighing down others with this stigma. Calling someone else a fag is both an offensive and a defensive manhood act.

As straight young men become sexually active, young women and prospective sexual partners wield more influence over men's self-perceptions about their size as well as their sexual performance. Club member *Dreamgirl* believes men's identities are as fragile as china. She writes, "Every man has an Achilles' heel, and it's sitting in his pants. Even the most skilled man in bed can be reduced to nothing if you tell him he has a small dick or he's a terrible lay." Travis agrees, saying, "The male ego may be the most fragile thing on the earth. For a woman to question whether you are a man would be stomping on a delicate flower." Women's belittling comments about a man's penis size can have far-reaching and long-lasting consequences, but so can women's mere mention of other men's larger penises. An ex-girlfriend's fleeting reference to another man's "big Polish sausage" made Ed "turn red in the face" and feel humiliated.

Colin overheard some young women talking about big penises, and he hasn't been the same since. He is a 22-year-old white college student who is currently single. He has had casual sex and sex in relationships and has never received a negative comment about his size; one girlfriend told him he was big. He was a multisport star athlete in high school, valedictorian of his class, and well-regarded and liked by peers, coaches, and teachers. His penis size, though, is just average. His accomplishments on the field and in the classroom and the significant sexual interest he attracts from women are undermined by his own perceived size inadequacy. Before he began doing penis enlargement exercises, Colin exhibited some symptoms consistent with small-penis syndrome. Being just average on this one, albeit crucial, measure of manhood was a crushing blow to his confidence.

Colin attributes some of his struggles to misrepresentations in pornography; his friends bragging and, he admits, likely exaggerating about their size; and most important, women's comments about desiring huge penises. When he was a high school freshman he was intimidated by the older, more developed boys. Not only were they stronger and presumably more well-endowed, but high school girls flocked to them. Even when Colin became that star athlete, though, he worried about what girls thought and said about boys' penis sizes:

> Maybe I hang out with the trashiest girls, but sometimes you'll hear them say something like, "Oh, yeah, I heard he's got a big dick," or something like that. And you know, it kind of is like, "Oh, man, I wish that was me." One time, a couple of girls were talking about it and then another one just blurts out, "Oh, I have to try *that*!" I mean, isn't it pretty much confirming your worst fears, right? If you're worried about size, the fact that it's like a conversation between them is worrisome. It definitely doesn't help.

I ask Colin if he's thought about men's frequent conversations about women's bodies. He acknowledges that men and the culture at large worship women with larger breasts, among other features. He does not buy into the widespread double standard that slut-shames women and strips them of their sexual agency, including attacking them for desiring particular physical traits in men, yet simultaneously places women's bodies under constant scrutiny and evaluation under the guise that men can't help but ogle women because of male wiring. Colin says, "I can't imagine that girls wouldn't enjoy seeing a large penis. It doesn't seem unreasonable that they would want that. It's hypocritical even for us to say that, 'Oh, you shouldn't want [a big penis],' when we're here, you know, having our wives get boob jobs or whatever. If a girl prefers large penises, who's to say that's any different from somebody that has a foot fetish or something? You could look at it like that. I don't think every girl is a size queen, though."

Although our culture's emphasis and pressure on men to improve their appearance and bodies have intensified and many women do publicly and privately comment on men's penises, the situations are not equivalent. Women's bodies continue to be exponentially more likely targets of evaluation and judgment. Following Colin's point, one might say there are a lot more "boob men" than "size queens." The latter is a decades-old term that appears to have originated in the gay community (thus, "queens"). Some gay men have used this label to describe men who desire sexual partners with big penises. As with the straight men who've adopted the term and deployed it against women, it is used as retaliation by prospective/rejected sexual partners with average or smaller-sized penises. When men use it to label women, the implications are clear: these women are shallow and slutty; maybe they desire big penises because they have a big vagina from having so much sex. The term reinforces the sexual double standard, undermining women's agency and power.

The comments that trip up Isaiah, a 20-year-old, sexually inactive but straight-identifying African American college student are about race. He says he regularly hears his mostly white peers and sees popular media discussing and debating widely held beliefs that black men "are gifted down there." In a separate conversation, fellow young Club member Brandon confirms Isaiah's worst fears. Brandon says, "I just wish that I had some black in me, so I could have had a bigger dick," because guys with big penises "are the ones that get more pussy than the rest of us." This stereotype dates to the end of slavery, when whites labeled freed blacks as more animalistic and sexual than whites and as sexual predators and a constant threat to white women. Framing black men as rapists reinforced the racial status quo and was used by Southern whites to justify their continued violence and discrimination against African Americans.[19]

One of the only other African American students at Isaiah's school was known to have a huge penis and brag about it along with his sexual exploits, which weighed heavily on Isaiah. When a friend raised the topic with him, he quickly dismissed the racial stereotype, until it became personal: "She asked me how big I was, and of course, I didn't feel comfortable explaining that fact, so that was the only time it really came up, ever, with a girl. I think I lied and I said that I was like around eight inches or something like that, just so I could get the heat off my back." Isaiah was quick to dispel the stereotype until he was held personally accountable to it. He likely ended up reinforcing it when he simultaneously claimed he had (what would objectively be) a huge penis, but black men are not bigger than other men. And he can't help but admire porn stars, whom, he points out, have the same size, sexual prowess, and ripped bodies that are celebrated among black athletes. "It just seems like the kind of thing that any guy would want," Isaiah says. All these pressures have prevented Isaiah from dating and having sex.

African American PHC member Andre says the racial stereotypes thrust upon him, combined with not having a porn star–sized penis, "[create] such a disgusted feeling . . . almost as if I let my race down." Some of his nonblack male friends take offense to the stereotype because of its implications for them, "but in my mind, they are lucky [because] those idiots don't have the expectations of being big and great in bed like we do." Cultural critic Wesley Morris observes, "There is no paradigmatic white penis. To each man his own. But there is a paradigmatic black one"[20]

There are many desperate-sounding forum posts by new Club members, overwhelmingly young and perhaps disproportionately black, who report average or above-average measurements but suffer from feelings of inadequacy. Eighteen-year-old Club poster *LittleP*, also African American, says his erect penis is 7″ long and 5″ in diameter, but he worries about his "small cock" after having his pants pulled down at school. He says he needs help fast—a red flag for veteran Club members preaching patience—because his classmates are relentlessly texting him small penis jokes: "Please help me ASAP! Life is not worth living right now."

Of all penis size comments overheard or received, the ones offered by sexual partners cut deepest. Men with average and slightly below-average penises share countless stories of mostly younger women cracking jokes, expressing dissatisfaction and disappointment, and terminating sexual encounters and relationships due to men's small penises. Shaken young men say women have seen their penises and had the following reactions: "I thought you were going to be bigger." "Yeah, you're small." "You shouldn't ever go streaking." "Are you a little kid?" In an extended, candid, and somewhat divisive forum discussion about the merits of trying to increase penis size versus obsessing over it, one poster, *PEfan1994*, says the decision is basically out of his hands. He was mockingly asked by a woman if he was a "baby" when he revealed his penis in an online sex forum. She saw it and immediately logged off. "Imagine the pain I felt when she said that to me. After that, who could possibly convince me to pretend that the size of my cock isn't important?" he asks. Other posters chime in with support and empathy, some sharing their own similar occurrences of being mocked and humiliated by sexual partners.

Repeated or, worse, consistent negative feedback on men's penis size multiplies the pain, but many young men say that a single comment can "mindfuck" them, causing them to completely reevaluate their feelings about their size and what is normal. A 10:1 ratio of effusive praise to negative comments is meaningless. The single emasculating remark calls into question their manhood. Some men are in loving relationships with partners who express tremendous sexual satisfaction, yet they are haunted by a former sex partner's nasty comment, even if it was delivered in spite at the culmination of a bad breakup.

Brandon is young, dates a lot, and is sexually active. He recently had sex with a young woman who told him he was her first sexual partner. Afterward, she expressed disappointment:

> She was like, "Well, I thought you were going to be bigger than that." I was like, "Wait, what? Nobody's ever complained. Nobody's said anything about my size. You're the first person to complain about it." I was like, ouch. Definitely that's

kind of... left a hole in me. Yeah, I have gotten good feedback [previously]. Nobody's really complained. [They said] it was a good size, my stamina, people didn't complain about how long it took. I've tried to let it go, but then it's like, it just sticks in my head; I can't let it go. I haven't had complaints after that, but you would think that [you'd] just brush that one off and then continue from there, but I mean, it is kind of hard to hear.

It is men, rarely women, who think much about, let alone obsess over, penis size. An unusually large but nonrepresentative online survey found that 96% of women thought their current partners had average or large penises.[21] One in seven women wished their partner had a larger penis, and a tiny fraction wanted their partner to be smaller. The (sizeable) minority of women who desire larger penises have a disproportionate impact on men's psyches. They are the "size queens" upon whom men project their fears and, sometimes, anger. Steeped in porn, men can't untangle size, performance, accomplishment and a warped sense of what women desire.

Worrying about Performance

A vocal majority of Club moderators and senior members take the position of "it's not what you have, it's what you do with it that matters." Alongside endless threads and posts offering a dizzying array of penis enlargement advice are discussions about sexual performance and ways to pleasure women (but not other men). Young men are advised to be conscientious lovers. They are coached on various techniques and counseled to consider the many reasons beyond penis size—such as emotions, familiarity, and love—that contribute to women's sexual desire and satisfaction. "Having a big dick doesn't mean you can be a big dick," Club member Travis says. Of course, cockiness and over-confidence are not what attracts men to the Club. Insecurity is the primary motivator.

Younger men's inexperience adds to their performance doubts. For older men, declining erection quality—they are literally becoming soft—and their partners' diminishing sex drives are more likely causes of concern. Older men simply aren't the same as their younger selves, but our culture doesn't accept that. Neither do they. All men's episodes of erectile dysfunction serve as reminders that their penises could fail them at any moment. Flaccid penises are feminizing. They convey weakness, inaction, an inability to perform.[22] Men's sexual performance—their *manhood*—is tenuous and not entirely under their control.

Anxiety, self-doubt, and performance problems are absent in pornography. So is rejection. Instead, porn targeting young, straight men consistently conveys the following mix of false and misogynist messages: women are sluts who secretly, or not so secretly, desire sex with men with huge penises; most men have huge penises and are always ready and able to perform; sex is aggressive and multiorgasmic, oftentimes involving multiple people. In other words, it's nothing like your or anyone else's actual sex life. The narrative of heterosexuality, amplified many times over in porn, does not align with men's experiences. They are left confused and melancholy by—or worse, respond violently to—the unkept promises of heteronormativity.[23]

Fifty-eight-year-old Paul is bisexual but chooses to conceal his same-sex interest and live straight in a committed marriage. He thinks younger men's consumption of porn is so distorting that it's ruining their sex lives: "They think that an average sexual encounter involves double or triple penetration, and all of the guys involved have 10-inch schlongs, and the women just . . . and it's just a 40-minute long orgasm. Then [young men] all think, you know, gosh [the woman I just had sex with] didn't scream and writhe in obvious passion, so I'm a failure." Twentysomething Andre is impervious to the numerous Club posts challenging men's size myths and obsession, and critiquing the negative effects of porn. He regularly compares himself to porn stars and, unsurprisingly, finds he doesn't measure up: "The issues have grown and grown to the point where I doubt my ability to give maximum pleasure due to my average or relatively thin girth."

Colin was motivated to try penis exercises because he thought his average size would underwhelm and disappoint young women. Size and satisfaction aren't one and the same, he says, but they are connected: "I don't think that instantly, you know, if you have a large penis that it's just like an orgasm producer for every girl, you know, without even trying. But I do think that it helps. I can't imagine it hurting, put it that way." None of the men I speak with has ever been told his penises is too small to provide pleasure. However, the Club is littered with stories of such exchanges. *MountainBiker* says his girlfriend confirmed for him that he had a small penis and, worse, told him he was only erratically satisfying her. He has "lost all hope" because of his tiny flaccid size and inconsistent performance.

Stephen committed a Penis Health Club cardinal sin when he, like many men in their teens and early 20s, asked his first girlfriend, Jenny, about her previous sexual partners. She told him about one guy, who Stephen knew, whose penis was so thick "that she described [it] as incredibly painful during sex." He adds, "But nonetheless, hearing that made me think, well, I guess I'm too thin if I don't feel like my penis is experiencing much pressure from her vagina during sex. My only comparison is my hand at that point, [so] I assume that it must not be good for her either. And I [didn't] express that to her, because I [felt] too bad about that. So it sort of was an inner turmoil. I bottled it up, and it festered." Jenny's description of "incredible pain" from an ex-boyfriend's thick penis isn't enough to dissuade Stephen from believing he needs to increase his girth. Stephen comes across as a sweet guy and a caring boyfriend and is a well-respected poster at the Club, but his masculine insecurities filter out his girlfriend's desires. He sees himself on the losing end of an imaginary competition with her ex-boyfriend. Stephen (mis)interprets Jenny's unpleasant sexual experience with a thicker penis as an indication that she may not desire him. His assumption about ideal size incites jealousy and is compounded by the couple's lack of communication. An opportunity for further intimacy is undermined by fear: "The more preoccupied with control men are, the more lovers recede as full people with feelings, thoughts, will, and soul and become vehicles for bolstering manhood and relieving anxiety."[24]

Sexually active gay men are more attuned to realistic distributions of penis sizes and, at least for themselves, how size correlates with attraction and pleasure. Still, though, there are some intracommunity stereotypes about gay men being well-endowed, Glenn says. Most of the guys he's dated "were blessed, you know—quite large." (As Club members point out, it's possible that men may perceive other men's penises as larger, even those of sexual partners, due to the perspective of looking down at their own penis). After visiting a gay bathhouse in his late 20s, he questioned why anybody would want him when there were so many other and bigger options: "You know, it was a veritable candy dish from what I could see."

Glenn wonders if his thinner body and smaller penis have determined his "bottom" status, and what he sees as his feminized, subordinate sexual standing in relationships. He explains,

> There can be negative connotations to being called a bottom as opposed to a top, and it seems with that body image of the more masculine [in the 1990s], that stuff sort of happened at the same time. It became really obvious that when I was dating people I was the bottom [*laughs*]. You know? And it was like, hmm . . . that made me wonder. I mean, it makes me wonder, does the size of your dick determine, you know, [being a top or bottom] during sex? It became really obvious that nobody was interested in oral sex with me. They were only interested in fucking me, you know, as a bottom. And I started wondering, well, what's up with that?

Being assigned a passive role removes Glenn's option of putting on a fully masculine performance; it threatens his manhood. His interpretation of penis size, gender, and sexual position reflects some patterns among men who have sex with men (MSM), but it's far from universal. Among MSM themselves, there is a correlation between feeling more masculine as well as having a bigger penis and being a top. But many men, especially younger men, reject these gender norms, instead adopting more gender fluidity and versatility in their sexual behavior.[25] U.S. prison culture and some Latino cultures make sharp gendered distinctions between tops and bottoms.[26] Tops are dominant, in control of the action, masculine. Bottoms are passive recipients, dominated and controlled, viewed and labeled as feminine ("queens," "punks") or essentially women. Even though American culture tends to label MSM as gay, regardless of whether they take on the (masculine-labeled) top role or (feminine-labeled) bottom role, these distinctions reflect patriarchal gender relations that expect and celebrate men's power over women, especially sexual power.

Explicit conversations about size and performance are more common in long-term relationships. Young people are having sex mostly without communicating about it. This is compounded by sexual inexperience and general lack of knowledge, leaving young men questioning their performances. Having sex for the first time is widely regarded as a stressful moment for everyone, but the added burden of revealing their erect size and being expected to perform well makes it even more of a ritual test of gender for men. Twenty-six-year-old Andre says, "While it felt good to lose your virginity, I still felt unsure of how good of a job I did. It took me a while to actually get erect, due to nervousness, and during the act, I was very concerned about her level of pleasure." Sex, here, is a two-step feat: first, get it, and second, be great at it. What's missing is *enjoying* it, and communicating with your partner to make sure they're enjoying it, too.

"What I see on the website is a lot of guys who have the same issue that I often had," Stephen says, explaining, "They relate penis size to manhood more because they relate penis size and sexual performance. They're worried they're not giving enough, and no matter how much they give, they want to give more. You know, they want to be able to be better, because it's not about having sex, and getting off and enjoying it. It's about being the girl's best sex they've ever had, kind of attitude. And it's the wrong attitude." Stephen says his first sexual encounter was marked by fear that he would "mess up" and do something wrong:

> I think it was a source of anxiety and concern to the extent that sex itself was a source of anxiety and concern. I felt awkward around women, and once I learned not to be awkward around women, I still felt awkward about sex, because I didn't have much experience with that, and I didn't know what to expect, and I was a perfectionist. So it was kind of like I saw it as a performance rather than a fun activity kind of thing. It took a long time to break those feelings and realize that it's not about making mistakes and stuff like that. It's about actually experimenting. So with that, penis size became a concern, the idea that, well, given the amount of importance I've been taught to put on it, it must have some importance in bed. Therefore, I worried about it, because at the end of the day, the thing I really worried about was being able to please whoever I ended up having sex with.

Travis has seen his marital sex life cool off in middle age. His wife is less interested in sex, which he thinks might be due to his declining performance. He asks himself, "What can I do to help her like it more than she does now?" and one conclusion he reaches is that she might be more interested if he was bigger. He is somewhat skeptical of her previous positive comments about his size because she's never had sex with another man: "I thought, like any other guy, bigger might be better, and I wanted to see if it was possible to make it bigger. So that's why I started doing [penis exercises]."

Older men are less worried about size than they are erection quality, erectile dysfunction, and a sense of lack of control. Performance encompasses size, firmness, and the ability to "get it up" as needed and to go all night (or at least long enough to provide satisfaction). Younger men flock to the Penis Health Club not only to increase their size but to increase control over their orgasms. They are frustrated and embarrassed by the unpredictability of how long they last—"anywhere between 15 seconds and 15 minutes." The randomness of each performance gnaws at them ("it's wrecking my life!"). Sometimes they feel like sexual rock stars. Other times the show is over before it gets started—or at least too soon after the audience arrives.

Rarely is anything "wrong" with them: their testosterone levels are fine, blood work returns normal, they get erections in the morning or at other times they aren't trying to have sex. They are in their own heads, especially if they have failed before. They don't understand how their sexual performance remains so elusive, while they can master and control other aspects of their bodies. Despite older Club members' best efforts, younger members struggle to see sex as anything other than a performance. Doing penis exercises to increase their size and improve that performance is essential to restoring and maintaining a sense of control over the bodies.

Ed's health, financial, and aging struggles all added up to a severe case of erectile dysfunction. He was a failing breadwinner, and his already poor body image was deteriorating. Ed was feeling bad about himself, dissatisfied with his body, and let down by his performance with his wife. "Our sex was almost nonexistent and very unsatisfactory. I could barely get it up, and it was all stress-related," he says.

A handful of retired Club members in their late 60s and 70s report experiencing similar problems. Older men, even the privileged wealthy and white, are often unable to fulfill the two most important hegemonic ideals: vibrant careers (breadwinner) and physical strength (body).[27] The antiaging industry preys on these men's insecurities by promoting their products' ability to help men exert greater control over their bodies. Atop the list are Viagra, Cialis, and other similar drugs, which equate restoring erections with restoring manhood and control.

Larry's sex life before and after getting married and having kids was also closely connected to his stress levels and accomplishments at work: "If everything else in my life was going great, [sex] wasn't a problem. If I was undergoing a difficult time in my career, or in my family relationships or other aspects of my life, then it tended to [accentuate] those difficulties." When he was much younger he saw sex as a last refuge, a place of emotional escape when life was difficult. With those personal troubles spilling over into the bedroom, sex started to become an "anxiety" and he was easily "distracted." His erections were "not as spectacular as they used to be," and he was having difficulty ejaculating. Although this might sound like nirvana to younger men who wish they could last longer, he observes, it was unpleasant for his wife, and her interest in sex deteriorated. She interpreted his inability to orgasm as a reflection of his lack of desire for her. Larry's less-than-ideal performance created a negative control loop: an inability to orgasm, his partner's insecurity, stress and anxiety about his performance and her feelings, less firm erections, and some fear-based avoidance.

The Consequences of Not Measuring Up

Men who mostly meet body-based manhood ideals enjoy many benefits, including greater status, attention, self-esteem, and even social and economic power. Conversely, men who fail to live up to cultural standards lose out on all of the powers and privileges, instead enduring shame and embarrassment. Cultural ideals are, by definition, virtually unattainable. Perfectly sculpted and performing penises are no exception. This nearly impossibly high cultural standard is made even worse by its relative importance. No man will always measure up, and these inevitable failures spark numerous problems for men and others. Some GFC fighters and PHC members share the inevitable experience of falling short of body ideals.

Severe consequences follow men who internalize their perceived or actual shortcomings as a sense of failure. All of us have at least fleeting moments where we question something about ourselves. A minority of us suffer from crippling emotional and behavioral disorders. I use the term *internalizing* here to include a range of men demonstrating everything from consistent self-doubt and feelings of inadequacy about their size or performance to suffering from debilitating anxiety, fears, phobias, and depression. The consequences are many, including masculine insecurity and identity problems; concealing, withdrawing, and isolating their bodies and selves from others; and depression and suicidal thoughts. As I discuss in the next chapter, the consequences for women and others can be even worse when men externalize their perceived body failures.

Masculine Insecurity and Identity Problems

Coupling penises and manhood while setting unrealistic expectations for both fosters men's insecurities. Club members illustrate this dynamic by writing and talking about their own and other men's size and performance issues, as well as the benefits of fulfilling body ideals.

> ANDRE: [I shouldn't have these thoughts], but I do have times where I feel less of a man because I am not swinging a big dick between my legs.
>
> BIGLOVE: There's nothing that will make you feel more secure about yourself than having a huge meat pipe dangling down to your knees. And when a woman sees that monster cock, I bet she thinks you have incredible confidence and power.
>
> OHIOBOYYY: My wife says I'm big, and she's totally satisfied in bed. I'm a man though so I want to add some size and the bragging rights that come with it.
>
> GOTTAGROWNOW: Of course guys like me who have small dicks feel so inadequate. These idiots with large dicks are insecure too!
>
> PLZGETBIGGER: I joined [the Club] because I couldn't get my dick hard and it is tormenting me. There's nothing more psychologically disturbing than a man with a broken dick. It's just like losing your soul.

Security, power, confidence, soul, ego, and manhood are inseparable from penis size and performance for these and many men. As Susan Bordo explains, unlike someone suffering from a headache or some other malady, we say that men *are* impotent rather than they *have, caught, were stricken with,* or *contracted* impotence. In this way, we attribute the problem to a character flaw, not external factors. She examines how penises are viewed globally, concluding, "The magnificently large penis . . . is an icon of cross-cultural potency. So it's not surprising that size matters very much to men."[28]

Kenneth says he is "kind of obsessed" with penis enlargement. He regularly examines and compares other men's clothed packages while walking around. I ask why he does this, and he says, "[Because] I'm gay, but also because I think [bigger penises are] really the masculine ideal—the measure of a man, so to speak." He equates feelings of gender inadequacy among less-endowed men like himself to women who have smaller breasts: "It just makes me feel less secure about myself. [Although it isn't paralyzing], it's just like an issue that's always in the back of my mind." He believes that penis size contributes to men's identities and their confidence levels:

> The way you conduct yourself, [present] yourself, or the way you do things, I think, is affected. Sometimes I'm more timid about things than I should be. [And I wonder], is that why, is it deep in my subconscious that [I feel] I'm less

masculine than [other men] are? Yeah, it plays with your head. [A guy I work with] is a very confident person. And voila, he's got a big dick. OK, are they related? I don't know. I'm sure there are plenty of men with little dicks running around that are very confident. Good for them. I just, it just is something that's in the back of my mind.

Speaking with Club members and reading the forums suggests there are actually very few men with even average-sized penises who have much confidence. Colin felt great about himself until he measured his penis. Unlike everything else that was important to him and at which he excelled, on this measure, he was "just average, mediocre, whatever term you want to put to it; it's a blow to your ego." High school student *Whatshisname* was so intimidated by his girlfriend's negative comments about the size of her ex-boyfriend (who seemed to be average) and her gossiping about it with her friends that he ended the relationship before they had sex. His confidence was undermined and his anxieties were fed. He feared what she would say about him if they slept together and later broke up: "I really wanted to lose my virginity but I had to protect my honor and be saved from humiliation." This teenager's dignity, identity, and penis size are inseparable.

As though not having a huge penis isn't stressful enough, Club members internalize their performance anxieties and failures as reflections on their manhood. Ed's lifelong body shame and adult erectile dysfunction have chipped away at his masculine identity, leaving him feeling powerless and not in control of his body. For Ed and many others, every other guy who has a bigger penis, lasts longer, or gives his partner multiple screaming orgasms is a source of comparative shame and failure. Masculinity is organized hierarchically: some men are winners, others losers. This is why, despite its intentions otherwise, the Club sometimes perpetuates feelings of inferiority among men. Members write about being inundated with unattainable measurements and intimidating photos. Combining this with the site's obsessive focus on increasing size proves toxic for a subset of men who already feel inadequate.

Concealing, Withdrawing, and Isolating

Boys and men suffering from locker-room syndrome, especially those with smaller-than-average penises, internalize their issues by finding ways to conceal their flaccid penises in intimate and public settings.[29] PHC members say they avoid changing in locker rooms, looking at themselves in mirrors, sleepovers, public showers and urinals—especially the pig trough–style urinals—and often other men with large flaccid penises. Skinny dipping, nude beaches, and sometimes just wearing shorts or swim trunks are nonstarters. They hide behind towels and lockers when forced to change in public, suffer from shy bladders at urinals (while standing at an angle to block others' view, with two hands covering their penises), stick a sock in their pants to look bigger, and quickly put on underwear after sex. One man posted that he aroused himself slightly before a doctor's examination. Several worry about postmortem judgments of their small penises as their bodies are prepared for burial. Attending his friend's wake made one man "more dedicated to penis exercises knowing the next funeral may be my own." Now *that* is an existential crisis. Size and performance fears also cause some men to alter their behavior and experiences. They date smaller women (who they presume will have smaller vaginas), avoid dating entirely, turn down opportunities for sex, stay out of long-term relationships, withdraw from conversations about size and sex, struggle to get and maintain erections, and socially isolate themselves, occasionally escaping via alcohol or drugs.

Stephen sees younger men like himself doing more concealing of their penises in public. Older men, he says, are less concerned about it. This may be due to their age, but probably is also a cohort effect, where older men are less ashamed because they grew up before fitness crazes and Schwarzenegger movies. Still, men of all ages say they did things like take gym showers at odd times and hide in corners of locker rooms to protect themselves from unwanted scrutiny, or bullying in school. Isaiah says he was late to practice sometimes because he waited until his teammates left the locker room before changing. When he was forced to change around others, he would hide behind his full-sized locker. When Ed was younger, he often skipped taking a shower at school.

The dating and social lives of young Club members Andre, Colin, and Isaiah reveal the internal conflict and anxiety they experience daily. Because of his race-fueled size insecurities, Andre introspectively acknowledges, "I am afraid to let my guard down and be vulnerable." He says his negative thoughts about his penis size don't affect his ability to have sex, but he assumes his partner won't enjoy it. "I get it with ease and can carry out the act as normal," he says, "[but] I mentally prepare myself for the worst sexually so that if she is not satisfied, it isn't a surprise." More important, he is "in fear of constantly being compared to past bigger lovers [so] I see every potential relationship as fleeting or short-term. I believe it's a defense mechanism." Hooking up instead of entering a relationship protects Andre from his fear that his size and performance doubts will be confirmed. Constantly on the move, he reduces the likelihood of having a conversation with women about his or their past lovers' sizes. (Recall that Andre's self-reported penis size is above average.)

Colin, too, has shied away from long-term relationships because of his size insecurities. Worse, though, in his mind, is that he has avoided hook-up opportunities, fearing that he "would have to reveal my average endowment." Throughout high school, it weighed on his mind every weekend and whenever he interacted with girls. I ask him how much anxiety this caused him during his high school years. He admits, "I would say a lot. And a lot more than it should have. I can tell you that I don't think I had a sexual encounter that I was not intoxicated for. I mean it's not like I was drinking to kill the pain, you know, you have to drink like a bottle of vodka, but a couple beers to get the liquid courage flowing." Colin, like so many of his teenage and twentysomething peers in hookup situations, uses alcohol because it disinhibits and reduces his stress level, lubricating his interaction and helping him escape his negative thoughts.[30] He is in college now and is thrilled with his now above-average sized penis, but he undergoes some similar internal conflicts in his dating life. He still sometimes hesitates to make the first move: "Lately, my issue hasn't been in the sack; it's getting there in the first place. It's like, you know, this ridiculous fear. It's like worrying about getting on a roller coaster, right. You're worried and you're scared while you're waiting in line. But once you get on, you wind up having a good time." Colin's bigger penis and pleasurable dating and sexual experiences do not engender enough self-esteem and confidence to allow him to completely escape his past. Although he appears to be on his way to repairing what he perceives as his "just average manhood," his actions continue to be colored by his damaged self-image.

For other men, it's much worse. Intimidating comments, pornographic images, and men's performance pressures to "show off, and impress, and do some sort of magic trick," as Stephen says, leads to a self-fulfilling prophecy. They doubt they are big enough or skilled enough or even able to get an erection when the time comes, and their body confirms it when they try. We define manhood so narrowly that many men view anything other than a rock-hard erection and a mind-blowing performance as a failure. And any single failure raises the possibility in men's minds that they are total failures. Avoiding being soft—physically, emotionally, or in this case physiologically—is avoiding being perceived as lacking some part of manhood.[31]

Many men's short-term solution to erectile dysfunction is complete avoidance. After experiencing a few humiliating sexual encounters that culminated with him being unable to stay erect, Club member JrPE'er has chosen to avoid one-night stands: "Sadly, I've found excuses to avoid sleeping with several girls because I fear the outcome. I can't bear their obvious disappointment when we try to have sex and it doesn't happen."

Isaiah is even further down the rabbit hole. He has retreated so far in his head that it manifests itself in social and physical isolation from others: "I've kind of like, turned into a hermit, almost." He either hangs out with his roommate or spends hours online, hiding out from everybody else. He eventually found the Club's website because he always clicks on penis enlargement website ads. Isaiah says that a few times, girls seemed interested in him, but "I couldn't pursue them. I just squandered [the opportunities]. I just squashed them and went back to my hermit ways. 'Cause in my mind, I'm still not where

I want to be in terms of how I view myself and my body size." He shies away from conversations and people altogether, because he expects that his white peers will project their racial and gender stereotypes and fantasies onto him, and he does not meet those expectations: "From what I had heard back when I was younger, a black male is someone who's confident, maybe a little cocky, knows what he wants, knows how to get it, and will get it at any cost. And I didn't really see myself as that, and I kind of put myself down for that." He isolates himself to avoid the possibility of having to confront others' expectations. Although young, he is wise enough to recognize that physical improvements will not be enough to repair the long-term damage to his sense of self:

> I do think that there is great responsibility put upon men throughout the world to put on a front for a lot of stuff. And no one really realizes it until that front cracks, and you see what's in the dam burst wide open, and you see what's really behind it.
>
> It's going to come out eventually, whether or not I make [penis size] gains, and whether or not my body becomes the way I want it to be. Because even if most of those things do happen—I mean, yes, I'll be more confident, yes, I'll be out of this phase that I'm in right now, but still, I'll have to confront the issues that I've let build up over the past years. I still have to confront them no matter what.

Size and performance anxieties flood men's psyches and often trump their ability to view sex as a pleasurable act or relationships as an opportunity for intimacy, empathy, experimentation, and growth. The pressure to impress and perform alienates men from their own bodies as well as their potential and actual sexual partners. They withdraw physically and emotionally to avoid potential shame. According to manhood ideals, vulnerability is weakness, and the weak are vulnerable.[32] In truth, these young men are following a script that makes them more vulnerable: isolation and lack of intimacy damage not only their relationships but their own health.

Depression and Suicidal Thoughts

The consequences of Isaiah's internalized manhood failures were the most severe of the men I interview. Other Club members, none of whom I have managed to speak with directly, post stories of more extreme consequences, including depression and thoughts of suicide. Isaiah's social withdrawal and isolation lie at one end of a spectrum of behaviors consistent with dysmorphophobia, otherwise known as body dysmorphic disorder (BDD). Individuals with BDD have "a fixation on an imaginary flaw in the physical appearance. In cases in which a minor defect truly exists, the individual with BDD has an inordinate degree of anguish." Isaiah isn't experiencing severe depression or thoughts of suicide, both of which mark sufferers of BDD, but for him and many other men at the Club, "there is embarrassment and fear of being scrutinized or mocked, which often causes these individuals to avoid social situations and intimate relationships."[33] PHC members who believe their only psychological escape is to increase their penis size are exhibiting BDD-like symptoms. Their happiness and mental health are contingent on repairing their perceived flaw.

Similar to Colin, 24-year-old *SlimJimmy* has avoided pursuing sex or relationships with women: "When I meet a girl I want to sleep with, the only thing I think about is her laughing at me when I'm naked." His body dissatisfaction has led to social isolation and depression. In an extended forum discussion about the negative effects of feeling inadequate, many posters share their struggles with what appear to be severe cases of BDD. *StayAnon* offers his fears and insecurities as a show of support for another Club member:

> You're not alone. I've been depressed and suicidal because of my small cock. I pass up chances to sleep with girls because I'm so small, which makes me look like I'm gay or just an asshole. I was so depressed about it that I stayed in my room for a year, bottomed out, and attempted suicide. I'm slowly recovering, but the anxiety isn't gone. [The Penis Health Club] is giving me hope reading about the possibility of increasing my size. Just the thought that it's possible to get bigger feels great! All I want is to be average, not huge. If I reach that goal, it will change my life and let me live again. Honestly, my entire future is riding on making my dick bigger.

These men's shame about their penises and sexual virility mixes dangerously with the broader cultural expectation that men should stifle emotions and keep others at arm's length. Their lack of emotional intimacy and inability to build relationships undermines more than just their manhood; it also prevents their accessing basic human emotional needs.

As with many psychological disorders, unfulfilled arbitrary social norms sow self-doubt and manifest themselves in self-destructive behaviors. If our culture didn't place such undue importance on men's size and performance and demand that men maintain control and establish dominance over others (or their own penises), fewer would suffer from BDD and other disorders. And fewer would project their disappointments and shame onto others, especially women.

Club member *DrSmith* regularly imagines how his size and performance compare with other men and believes he is lacking:

> I often think about suicide, mostly but not only because of my small size. I just don't see how I'll ever satisfy a girl the way other guys can when every other dude

is bigger and better than me. I just put my tail between my legs and walk away if another guy starts talking to a girl I'm interested in. Even if she likes me as a person, thinks I'm funny or whatever, it doesn't matter. Once we have sex, she'll be disappointed. When I feel really bad, I go in the basement and work out as hard as I can, hitting the heavy bag and beating up a wrestling dummy. I just imagine I'm pounding away at my insecurities until they're gone.

DrSmith and other men with smaller-than-average penises are more likely to suffer from BDD. Their perceptions are confirmed by the Club's widely read and frequently discussed summaries of research studies on average penis size. When average is deemed unacceptable and even inadequate, below average is devastating. When physicians, spouses, partners, and penis size studies fail to alleviate men's concerns—or, worse, exacerbate them—the Club's multitude of exercise regimens and recommended penis enlargement devices provide these men with hope of repairing what they see as their broken bodies—and manhood.

Repairing: Size and Performance Therapy

Many men never move beyond the process of internalizing feelings of inadequacy. They feel stuck, their negative emotions slowly consuming their confidence and sense of self. For other men, internalizing is merely the first step toward change; a motivator that forces them to seek ways to restore their lost manhood. The Penis Health Club offers men two ways to reduce and eliminate their perceived body failures and ultimately repair their manhood: changing their negative perceptions about their penises—mostly by showing them they aren't below average—and improving their size and performance. Neither provides the possibility of moving beyond arbitrary manhood ideals; instead, these repairs reinforce men's pursuit of power and control. Down that path lies no progress toward sustainable, collective, egalitarian definitions of manhood.

Cognitive Therapy and Positive Feedback

Trying to change men's negative perceptions about their bodies is a challenging task, but it reminds us that body ideals are arbitrary—that they *can* be changed. Depending on one's culture, community, family, era, beliefs, age, and situation, a penis might be perceived as average or otherwise, a threat to women's chastity, uncontrollable, a source of giving and receiving pleasure, something not to be touched by anyone until marriage, a source of income, a measure of manhood, and much more. The meanings we assign to penises can and do change. Of course, as difficult as it is for men as individuals to change their own perceptions, it is even harder to change cultural beliefs. The latter do change, but more slowly.

The Club tries to convince men that the world is not filled with eight-inch penises and sexual partners' nonstop screaming orgasms and that a man's own size and performance is likely just fine. Friends in school locker rooms brag and mislead about their size. The Club responds by sharing research studies summarizing average sizes. Pornography depicts and celebrates well-endowed men. The Club points out how camera angles and selective samples distort reality. Men hear some young women share their desire for large penises. Women members at the Club tell men that penis size is low on most women's list of desires, and if girlfriends and wives tell men their size and performance is good, they should be believed.

Travis says, "It's a very helpful site for men who may feel in some way inadequate or uncomfortable with themselves. And if they go on there and educate themselves, they would find out that they're not so bad of a guy after all." He implies what many men think and feel—their self-worth is attached to their size and performance.[34] Travis always felt comfortable with his size and was not in need of body image repair. Still, discovering on the Club site that his penis size is above average was like "stroking my ego." New member *Just-Joined* says, "I was surprised to find out that my dick isn't small but average. I started to get over my size insecurities almost immediately!" Stephen says the most important thing the Club has provided him with is not a bigger penis but a better level of comfort with himself.

Glenn, in his 50s, wishes that the Club was around during his teenage years because "a lot of time was wasted on wondering [about size]." Knowledge about average penis sizes, especially average erect size, simply hasn't been widely available or discussed in such detail before the internet. Upon finding out that average penis size is, well, average, one new Club member after another begins to overcome their size anxieties.

Urologists offer a number of suggestions to help treat patients with small-penis syndrome. These include not dismissing men's concerns about their size, normalizing their feelings, and offering reassurance, providing accurate information about average size and where men lie relative to others on a normal range of sizes, noting media and societal pressures as compared to the actual importance of size (especially for sexual partners), and pointing out men's potential biases and misperceptions about their own and others' size.[35] The Club does all these things. In some ways, it is playing the roles of both doctor and therapist for men. Tomás posted pictures of his penis, which he says was very difficult to do given his history of negative feedback and bullying, and his ongoing concerns about his masculinity and sexuality: "I thought, 'You know what, I've got to try this to at least get some type of feedback.' [And the feedback was] pretty good. I've got to say that most of the people are very kind." Nonsexual compliments are widespread at the Club, regardless of the size, shape, or any other characteristic of the penis that is up for discussion.

As Glenn observes, most straight guys don't sit around and talk about their penises with other men—at least not in a serious manner. The Club is different. Anonymity allows men to reveal their penises visually or through description, along with their anxieties, failures, and more. Ed's size and performance were lifelong sources of anguish, but he dealt with them alone before discovering PHC: "There's nobody I could talk to, I didn't really have any confidantes that [I] could talk to about that, you know? I guess one of the great things about the internet is you have these blogs, and opportunities where you can [anonymously] share your concerns and anxieties, and it provides some great feedback." Paul says he feels as close to some Club members as he does to his face-to-face friends, even though he has no idea who they are or what they look like. It allows him to "talk about stuff that I really never talked with anybody about," including human sexuality, forbidden fantasies, and his own belief that he is actually bisexual. The Club's message is the same that's conveyed to sufferers of addiction or scarcely discussed illnesses: "It's OK, you're not alone, what you're experiencing is completely normal and common, and you shouldn't feel badly about it."

Fixing Broken Bodies

Perceptions and beliefs are resilient, though. They take years to form and ossify over time. Abandoning them requires significant cognitive and sometimes behavioral changes. This is why, even when perceptions and beliefs appear unsustainable in the face of obvious contradictory evidence, they are slow and difficult to change. Some men find it easier to repair their sense of broken manhood by improving not their perceptions but their actual penis size and performance. For some GFC members, fighting is their fix; for some Club members, penis exercises are the source of healing.

Nine of the fourteen men I interview say they have enjoyed substantial size and performance improvements from penis exercises and devices.[36] Their improved self-perceptions are due to both acquiring more knowledge about average size and seeing firsthand how their size and performance can change. Several of these men's sexual partners provided further affirmation.

Club posters also frequently write about their reparative processes. After another poster gives *TrjnHrse* positive feedback about his penis size, he says his self-esteem issues are due to his sexual partners seemingly always having bigger penises, "but [the Club] and penis enlargement exercises are relieving those negative thoughts." Club member *BeachLife* is reluctant to admit that the size of his penis causes him insecurity, but he says, "Seeing my workouts lead to gains is such a massive boost to my ego!"

Brandon has made only minor gains, but he is pleased to have moved from just-below- to right-around-average length and girth. His longer flaccid penis and weight training make him more comfortable being naked. He frequently compares his body and penis to other men when he showers at the gym. Recently comparing himself to a guy with a good body, Brandon noticed the man's penis get erect while showering: "I felt good about myself because my flaccid [was] bigger than [his] hard." Glenn, older and single, has met and exceeded his goals. He has seen gains in his size, erection quality, stamina, control, and ejaculation force. He is "perfectly happy" with moving from slightly below to above average in erection size. At his age, he says, "I am beyond trying to impress anybody or thinking that, you know, if I get a bigger package I'll get more dates." A key reason he is so satisfied with his gains is that his goals were modest: "I didn't have any unrealistic expectations of having some sort of porno dick." His new personal ideal was just a little bigger than his previous size. Glenn's modest goals and lack of desire to set new ones are fairly unique.

Sixty-year-old Ed's transformation is emblematic of what the Club hopes to achieve. Ed's discovery that his penis was below average knocked him off-kilter when he was young. He felt humiliated and emasculated, avoided being nude in locker rooms, lacked confidence, was less likely to pursue potential dates, tried to date smaller women, and felt embarrassed hearing women's comments about other men's larger penises. He says that for much of his life, his body image and size concerns were a daily source of stress, anxiety, resentment, frustration, powerlessness, and lack of control. Worse, he suffered a major financial setback, and his health had deteriorated in the last 10 years, causing severe erectile dysfunction and eventually resulting in his having to be on dialysis and later get a kidney transplant. Today, though, he is a new man. His finances and health have greatly improved, and his penis size and performance are bigger and better. A combination of penis exercises (PE), penis enlargement devices, and Viagra have repaired his size and performance insecurities, sex life with his wife, and ultimately, his shattered manhood:

Yeah, I mean, it changed my life, you know. There [have] been two major changes in my life. One is [getting a new kidney and getting off dialysis]; that's a major life change. The second major life change has been my PEing and getting a bigger dick. I know that I'm now up [to] slightly above average, which makes me feel a whole lot better. I talked about that book I saw when I was in college, you know, my mind always goes back to that image, right. Instead of being on the small-average size, I'm now on the average-size, just slightly above-average size.

I ask Ed why he thinks he feels so much better now that his penis size has increased. He says, "There is so much emphasis on penis size and manhood that even though I reject a lot of that, there's still a sense of accomplishment, and satisfaction to know that I overcame an obstacle towards being a better man, so . . . yeah, it makes me feel like I have been able to add more to my manhood." I ask him if making size gains has caused him to embrace those masculine expectations a little more. "I suppose. Yeah, I suppose, to be brutally honest, yes," he acknowledges.

Ed's wife never complained about their sex life, but he says, "Since I've gone through PE, and gained substantially in length and girth, our sex is 100% better." Much of that, he says, is attributable to erection quality, which has improved both his performance and his pleasure. After several months of PE and taking Viagra, Ed beams: "[My wife, Judy, said] 'OK, you can take the Viagra, and you can keep doing the PE, because that was great!' So that of course affirms what I was doing made a difference," and it made him feel "great. Fantastic. Yeah, it was incredible." Ed also now enjoys greater sexual pleasure:

> Well, the quality is 100% better. It's hard to describe what a difference it makes. I mean, I have unbelievable orgasms, I mean, screaming orgasms, and I never had that before, ever. I mean, it is night and day. The quality is just unbelievable. And I last a lot longer, and it's just . . . It's amazing. I feel a lot better when I'm performing sex. And I don't know if it's totally physical, or whether it's mental as well because I feel better about myself and about my dick. I don't know, I haven't been able to resolve that. I have to say the physical probably weighs heavily in that equation.

Ed's physical gains are objectively substantial. His penis is larger and is able to do more—to *accomplish* more—than before. The physical and physiological changes from drugs and PE overlapped with his financial and health rebounds, all of which are inseparable from the social psychological gains he has enjoyed. Previously, he felt anger, frustration, and a lack of direction when he was dealing with financial difficulties: "As I got more and more work, I got better and better results with my PE. So they went hand in hand. And I also felt, I mean, once I got the ball rolling with the PE, I really didn't want to stop. I mean, it was a great feeling. It was a really good ego boost, self-esteem boost, and I just kept going with it." Ed is so pleased with his gains that he recently told his wife his flaccid hang is enough that he would not be humiliated going to a nude beach. I ask him what that would be like. "Liberating," he says. He would no longer feel "humiliated" or "out of place."

Ed's transformation is so profound because he has restored a sense of control over his body after feeling out of control for decades: "The fact that I know I can do something about my penis size, and actually it's happened, is overwhelming in terms of a sense of control . . . Yeah, I feel like I have more control of my life, and empowered."

Colin was feeling hopeless and distraught before he found the Club. He figured he was stuck with his average size for the rest of his life. Not even out of high school, he was distressed and overwhelmed at the thought of a life with an average penis. Then he found the Club: "I know it sounds very weird, but it almost was necessary for me to find, to have to take my life back. I think it's crazy how when it was really getting to me, that I was going to have an average penis for the rest of my life, that magically I found my way on to this website." Colin has made substantial size gains, but he argues that the appeal of PE and the Club is primarily the *idea* that men can change their size and performance: "Maybe the best thing about it is not the actual increase in size so much as the thought that you can change this aspect of your life. That you're actually not stuck with it. It's a very empowering thought, and I think that gives you the confidence in and of itself. Although of course seeing gains does definitely help." Despair and resignation are replaced by hope and empowerment. A sense of control is restored and the work of restorative manhood therapy begins.

What is the recipe that attracts men to strenuous and time-consuming PE workouts? It's simple: combine the cultural importance of penis size and performance with men's perceptions of their own inadequacies, add in a feeling of hope that change is possible, include a bunch of rewards for making those changes, and stir in the reality that the ceiling for possible improvements is limitless and thereby unattainable. It is an addictive cocktail, an intoxicating pursuit of manhood ideals, the sourness of failure too rarely balanced with the sweetness of redemption. Too few members are able to post "success stories" that are subsequently replicated by others. Results do vary.

At his peak, Glenn was doing PE 10–15 hours per week. His cousin's stinging size comment in early childhood, along with Glenn's size and performance gains, provide a window into his motivations for his multiyear workout commitment. Other Club members' routines are more intense, on par with those of bodybuilders. Glenn thinks nothing of his routine compared to others: "You read what some of these people go through in their regimens or how much time they are spending, it is a little overwhelming. I look at some of these people [thinking], 'Jesus, when do you work?'" Glenn finds that level of commitment surprising in the context of our immediate-gratification culture: "You know, we're such a microwave society, people stand by their microwave and go, 'Hurry up!' So the idea of starting a process of actually changing the tissue of your body, which takes years—most people don't have the patience for that."

Colin knows that his penis has grown to well above average in size and, once he gets over his anxiety about hooking up, he doesn't suffer any performance problems. His thirst for more gains feels unquenchable, though. He set an initial goal of a one-inch increase in length: "But now that my penis is actually that size, it doesn't seem that big to me. I'm used to it. And it's like I want some more now. It's almost an addiction. I totally recognize that I'm above average, but for some reason it is not enough." Surely the human body is limited in its ability to increase in size and performance. The gendered mind, though, sees no limits. Bryan says, "I know there's some guys who, their wives have said [about their penis enlargement], 'Stop, enough's enough.' But they're doing it for themselves, and they don't want to [stop]. Which is kind of sad. It's like, hey, you're going to limit your fun time here, if you're going to make someone sore."

Some men can't help but feel better about themselves after they see where they fall on the scale and after they make gains, even if they never really experienced self-doubt or emasculation. Paul had some "mild anxiety" about his body (but not penis size) when he was young. After doing PE and improving his physique, Paul sees his body comparing favorably to men 20 years younger: "I'm going, 'Yeah, I got it, I'm OK.' And not trying to be boastful, but I can look and genuinely, objectively say, 'Yeah, I'm good. Yeah, my penis is bigger than yours. Yeah, I look better than you do.'" He has also received helpful comments from Club members responding to his pictures and ego-boosting ones from his wife after he made gains: "[She] would be saying, 'Man, you're just too big for me. You have to slow down, you're too big.' I'm like, yeah, I'm loving that."

Travis invests two to five hours per day between doing PE and spending time on the Club website. Yet he says he has not had any negative experiences that stand out in his life. He has a lot of downtime in the military, but time alone doesn't explain why he is so committed to PE. I ask him to explain why, despite his obvious lack of perceived inadequacy, he's so invested. He says,

Can I be a bit crude? So the question, it's along the lines of, "Why did the dog lick his balls?" Right, it's because he can. So I PE for health. That's why I continue to PE, and I can do that in 30 minutes, and I could do it three times a week, and I would be able to maintain very firm erections and be able to maintain good control over my arousal and ejaculation, and I would be able to maintain a very short refractory period. And those are all very positive benefits to just general sexual health, I believe, which are great. And the reason I PE to try and get bigger is because I can. And I want to see if I can do it. And it's really, it's really nothing more than that, you know. People go to the gym to exercise, and if someone wants to set a goal to bench-press 300 pounds, it's not because they have a need to; it's just because they want to see if they can do it.

Travis's joke is revealing. *Of course* he, like any man, wants to grow his penis, regardless of its current size. Knowing he is above average in size and that he can continue to grow is "empowering" and has boosted Travis's self-confidence. The Penis Health Club has improved his self-perception and his size and performance, which help remind him that those "fleeting insecurities that might crop up are really out of place." A greater sense of control over his already good-sized and well-performing body attracts him to PE: "I think the thing that benefited me the most [was] when I realize[d] that you can do something to change your penis size." He felt liberated by the possibility that something he previously thought was static is actually malleable: "There's a feeling of, I would say helplessness [when you can't change something]. Some people might say hopelessness." Thanks to the Penis Health Club, he was able to move penis size from his list of things he thought could not be changed to ones that can. Increasing penis size and performance are accomplishments that restore and bolster masculine identities.

4

Compensating for Body Failures

Despite the Penis Health Club's best intentions and efforts, it is not always possible for men to restore their sense of manhood by repairing their perceived body failures. When men are wounded by their failure to fulfill arbitrary manhood ideals but are not able or willing to fix these via repair, they often reassert a masculine identity through other means; that is, they compensate.[1] This can be seen among men who commit violence against woman partners whom they deem unsatisfactorily submissive, gay men who participate in "bear" subcultures that celebrate beefier and hairier bodies, and working-class men's resistance to control by their bosses.[2] These men have experienced some decline in their status and identity, so they reassert their masculine selves by controlling their partners or bodies or by resisting being controlled by others. Some Club members mistakenly believe that if they make their penises big enough and perform well enough, their confidence will skyrocket and no one will ever laugh at them or reject them again. It's unlikely to be a permanent fix. Similarly, some Gentlemen's Fighting Club members find that their fighting experiences do not fully sate their desire to control their own and others' bodies. Faced with body failures that produce fear of rejection, humiliation, and loss of control, some men reassert their sense of self by trying to neutralize it with a masculine alternative. GFC members may slip into harmless superhero fantasies to compensate for their all-too-normal bodies. PHC members may turn to weight lifting and bodybuilding or lash out at "size queens" for ruining their lives. And in the most extreme cases, mass shooters like George Sodini and Elliot Rodger murder innocent women (and men) to compensate for failing to fulfill body ideals. Violence can restore a sense of control, at least temporarily, compensating for shortcomings elsewhere.

It is not always possible to simply repair what feels broken. Countless biological, psychological, and social forces can prevent or undermine men's efforts to fix what they and others see as broken masculinity. An alternative attempt to restore manhood is to compensate for the perceived shortcoming. To *compensate* is to counterbalance, to make up for something missing or defective, to offset or put back into equilibrium via a counterforce, to correct or neutralize something that is unpleasant. The human body regularly compensates for weaknesses or defects caused by injuries and illnesses. A sprained ankle induces a limp, which places more weight-bearing responsibility on the healthy leg. Loss of sight often results in more highly developed auditory and tactile sensory perception. Weak abdominal muscles create more strain on the lower back. In each case, rather than correcting the problem by repairing the malfunctioning part, a different part of the body compensates for what's missing.

Our minds are capable of performing similar feats when a perceived flaw threatens our identities. Compensating is often healthy, even essential. People with visual impairments can use a walking cane or echolocation to maintain mobility and autonomy while minimizing risks to safety. Similarly, children struggling with arithmetic can offset feeling unintelligent by focusing on and highlighting their exceptional creative abilities. We all have strengths and weaknesses. Who wants to agonize over their own shortcomings?

Well, the choice isn't entirely our own. A daily blizzard of social influences blasts us with images, messages, and an array of positive and negative reinforcements, sparking our emotions and affecting our sense of self and identity. Our gender statuses and identities are essential features of a core self, or an umbrella identity that impacts others. Threats to our core selves, especially repeated threats, can generate powerful responses. The general phenomenon of compensating in response to threats isn't unique to men and extends beyond gender. This book, however, examines threats to men's gendered identities and the particular dynamics that follow, focusing on threats to body ideals in this chapter and the breadwinner ideal in chapter six.

Compensatory Manhood Acts

Men's identities are contingent on fulfilling manhood ideals, yet these ideals are unattainable. Masculine identities, then, are fragile. Compensatory manhood acts are a defensive response to threats to men's gendered identities. They are attempts to stake claim to a masculine identity using compensation instead of repair or redefinition. Compensatory responses arise from insecurity and an array of accompanying negative emotions—fear, anxiety, humiliation, shame. These emotions suggest loss of control and are themselves marked as nonmasculine, thereby compounding the sense of manhood failure. Psychoanalytic theorists dating to Freud have suggested that men's compensatory behaviors are the foremost expression of their attempts to distance themselves from femininity.

Compensatory manhood acts take numerous forms, as they are contingent on the "masculine resources" available to men in any particular context.[3] They may appear fairly innocuous, such as escapist daydreams, youthful boasting, or conspicuous consumption. They may directly or indirectly endanger the well-being of the one doing the compensating in the cases of physical risk-taking, displays of toughness, or the suppression of human emotions. They also may target others—intimates and strangers alike—through verbal, emotional, physical, and sexual attacks. The unifying thread across compensatory manhood acts is a sense of lost power and control, which undermines boys' and men's identities. When they fall short of a particular body ideal, they attempt to resist being controlled as well as try to exert control over themselves and others. Compensatory efforts to restore power and control are attempts to reacquire masculine privilege, which reinforces gender inequality. Men's efforts to restore control are often done individually, but collectively, men's efforts to fulfill hegemonic ideals reinforce patriarchal relations.

Superhero Fantasies

Some men in GFC help restore a sense of lost power and control by fantasizing about using their fighting skills to dominate other men, or more commonly, playing superhero to victims in distress. These fantasies can offset childhood memories of humiliation or allow some to imagine their bodies wildly exceeding their all-too-normal mortal limits. Fantasies allow people to restore in their minds what they've lost in reality. Compensatory fantasizing was more common among the GFC men who were beat up and controlled as boys and less common among those more likely to face real violence. However, there were exceptions among both groups.

Freddy, whose childhood experiences left him with a strong desire to maintain control over his body, regularly daydreams about dominating and controlling others. He was out with two other GFC members at a brewery and drunkenly imagined the three of them fighting everyone there. "I looked around, and I was certain in my heart of hearts that the three of us could fuckin' clear that place," he says. "I mean, we would wreck this place. There would just be chairs everywhere, and . . . so that's the hyperbole, a sort of daydreamy, kind of, part of it for me." As Freddy and I sip our coffees on a strip mall bench, he invites me into his mind. He says he is imagining an altercation taking place in the parking lot in front of us and sees us having to intervene: "I can just kind of project myself into that." Freddy even fantasizes about physically dominating people when he's at work: "Sometimes I'll be walking through the hall at work, and like, a guy will be coming at me, and I'll think about just plowing him right over, in public."

Most GFC members' fantasizing is of the superhero variety. Jackson says he daydreams "all the time, daily" about being a superhero and has since he was an adolescent. After watching *Ironman*, Darren says, "I thought, oh, my God, this is like every person's fantasy." Sammy connects the superhero fantasy to GFC, explaining that the latter attracts those who want to learn fighting skills that will make them "superior to a normal man." Rhetorically, he asks me, "I mean, you fight . . . you're kind of like a superhero, right?" The blurred line between skilled fighter and superhero is most apparent in martial arts action films and their stars, like Jackie Chan and Jet Li. Using their finely tuned bodies and refined skills (rather than alien or mutant powers, or gadgets), Sammy observes, "they could just kick the ass out of like 10, 20 people. We know this is actually not a reality, mostly. But it's a good fantasy, right?" These fantasies attracted Sammy to martial arts when he was younger: "My thinking was, 'If I become a black belt, I'll be able to beat down people, and then I'll be able to save people.' I'd be able to beat down villains in the street, saving the beauty, or something like that, that fantasy stuff." He still has these fantasies, but they have diminished as he's aged.

Asher and I discuss whether he thinks he will have to use his GFC skills in a real-world situation, which leads him to hesitantly share his fighting fantasies:

> You know, it's kind of embarrassing to talk about. I mean a lot of it is like kind of the boilerplate stuff like you read in comic books. Especially if you just got dumped or you're jealous about some girl, it's always you fantaciz[ing] about kicking somebody's ass in front of whatever girl and how awesome they would think you were for doing that. I mean, I know this sounds completely silly and adolescent, but I think there are always certain elements of the fantasy when you're not just being a bully or the aggressor, like you were somehow pushed to it.

Asher and Sammy's fantasies *are* boilerplate. Comics, cartoons, movies, and other media have long celebrated the hero who uses violence to save women and girls from the villain. In this predictable scenario, an iteration of the "protection racket," women are passive, weak, and dependent, victims to be exploited or saved only by attaching themselves to men.[4] It makes women dependent upon men, not to mention it ignores the greater threat posed by intimates than strangers.[5] Men are at the center of the action, using violence for good ("the protector") or ill ("the bully"). In this sense, these superhero fantasies reproduce and reinforce the gender order. Boys and men, perhaps emasculated by losing their girlfriends or failing to stand up for themselves when a bigger man kicked sand in their face, use violence to defeat the bullies, get the girl, and ultimately restore their masculine selves. Of course, these compensatory daydreams are restorative only in passing.

Two GFC members, Sean and Ronnie, both of whom live and work in areas of the city that expose them to the possibility of violence, were dismissive of these kinds of fantasies. Sean says those thoughts require "a big-ass imagination, like a kid" and don't reflect reality. "I don't want to use my martial arts training to be Batman," he says, laughing, somewhat mocking the idea of fending off armed robbers with his bare hands. Ronnie says he has used his skills and especially the confidence they engender many times. He self-assuredly intervenes in public settings when someone makes an ignorant comment or he sees a man grope a woman:

> I don't [fantasize] about being a hero. I don't think about, like, saving an old lady from a robber, or whatever. But in real-life situations, people do say stupid shit, or say something ignorant, or grope a girl and I'll be like, "Hey, that's fucked up. Don't do it." [But] I don't fantasize about the one-in-a-million chance that, you know, you defeat three murderers after they've [killed] someone with a hammer, or whatever. But I do know being a hero is really just sticking up for somebody when they can't. And that's the best, biggest hero you could have, when you feel protected or supported [after] someone makes you feel terrible or small.

Ronnie's protective actions are scaled down from superhero to human. Neither he nor Sean are trying to restore something they lost as boys or escaping into a fantasy world. They do not enjoy the safe cocoon of class privileges; their everyday-grounded corporeal experiences eliminate any need for fantasizing.

Men's individual motivations for compensatory masculine fantasies are inseparable from their cultural context. Sweeping changes to the economy, challenges to gender arrangements, and other social forces gave rise to our current unattainable body and breadwinner ideals. These have left many men feeling powerless, as though they lack control. One compensatory response after the United States' failed war in Vietnam was American men slipping into "warrior dreams."[6] Vicarious fantasy outlets like action films, books, and video games grew in popularity, along with other avenues of reasserting a heroic, warrior masculinity such as Soldiers of Fortune conventions, paintball competitions, and elite combat shooting schools. These trends coincided with deindustrialization, a spike in women's labor force participation, and various feminist gains. Many men felt not only as if they had lost a war but as if they had lost their agency and efficacy, so they sought ways to compensate.

GFC member Barry says he fantasizes less about being a warrior or super-hero and just more generally about having "absolute power and control." He sees humans as ineffectual creatures, with only a few having any significant impact on the world: "When you think about the opposite of that, that's when you get those fantasies of, 'Well, I have power, I have control, I can make things happen. I can make people do what I want. I can make the world better, or worse, or at least make it something different than it is now.' And I don't think any of those things are really true in real life." Barry's and other men's desires are gendered masculine. Manhood requires being seen, heard, and felt, and it leaves a lasting footprint.

Nonviolent Compensation

In everyday interactions, boys and men commonly respond nonviolently when their masculinity is threatened. They compensate rhetorically through brag-ging, exaggeration, and denigration of others, and they compensate physically by exerting and resisting control over their own and others' bodies.[7]

Boys and young men's lack of access to breadwinner status magnifies the pressure on them to fulfill body ideals. The insular worlds of schools, youth peer culture, cliques, teams, clubs, and fraternities elicit an array of compen-satory behaviors. Strangers, acquaintances, friends, teammates, and even par-ents, coaches, and sexual partners may call out boys and young men for various physical failings. These are powerful generators of compensatory behavior, but they aren't always essential. Many boys and men will identify or misper-ceive their own bodily shortcomings and suffer the same effects, especially if they buy into the ideals. The possibilities for failure can seem endless. Boys and men are liable to feel or be told they are small, weak, wimpy, nonathletic, uncoordinated, sexually inexperienced or unskilled, not hung, and worst of all, gay or effeminate. Ironically, because there are so many ways to fail, there are an equivalent number of bodily options that can be used to reassert one's masculinity when it is threatened.

Verbal attempts to compensate are probably the most common. Get called out for one shortcoming? Brag about your dominance in something else. The partygoer who is mocked for not being able to hold his liquor brushes it off by bragging about getting laid. The teenager who is mercilessly teased for being a virgin says he can kick his tormentor's ass. The ridiculed loser of a video game competition announces he has the biggest dick in the room. And on and on. The formula for each of these responses is to implicitly attack and denigrate others while reasserting your own manhood.

The most common and effective counterattack is to call a guy a "fag." Despite notable shifts in public attitudes and significant legal momentum for lesbian and gay rights, gay men continue to be the most subordinated.[8] Boys and men may use this blunt weapon offensively, without first having their manhood challenged, but at the heart of this attack is defensiveness, the fear of being the target of that emasculating label. Boys sometimes respond to this epithet by using the usual reassertions, bragging about their sexual prowess, toughness, and so forth.

Boys and men may experience being called a fag or viewed as gay as a body failure for two reasons. First, gay men are widely stereotyped as feminine (soft, weak, dependent). The term *fag* implies masculine incompetence—being unable to control things, defend oneself, perform athletic or other feats, and so forth. Second, gay men are subordinated and emasculated because dominant culture places them in the same sexual role as women: the passive recipient, one who is receiving rather than doing. Gay masculinity is stereotyped as a penetrated masculinity, abdicating power and control—or, more accurately, the absence of masculinity. Perhaps that is why bragging about penis size is such a rote response to being called a fag.[9] The phallus, especially the mythical magnificently large one, represents power and agency.[10]

Homophobic teenage boys may be the most fearful of being stigmatized, but men's fear of feminization is widespread. Many self-identified, out-and-proud gay men compensate for their subordinated sexual status. Gay men often use their bodies to stake a claim to manhood. They distance themselves from feminine stereotypes through their gender performance, behaviors, and work. Some gay men enact a butch identity that conforms to hegemonic masculine ideals while simultaneously dismissing what they see as feminine, campy "queens."[11] They signify their masculine selves by playing competitive sports, highlighting their athletic abilities, doing physical and dangerous work, and celebrating bigger, hairy, strong bodies via "bear culture."[12]

Men with physical disabilities, such as spinal cord injuries, confront an embodied threat to their masculinity, not just one of their own or others' imaginings. They may be viewed, treated, and feel weak, passive, dependent, and even genderless. The culture's focus on men's bodies as a source of manhood can make physical limitations feel emasculating.[13] They adapt to their physical limitations and reclaim masculine identities in various ways, including compensatory behaviors. Some compensate for a loss of bodily control by finding ways to exert control over others. They equate their verbal instructions directing paid personal care assistants (i.e., employees) to the independence they enjoyed when they completed those tasks themselves. In another example, one paraplegic man focused on sexually pleasing and exhausting his partner—even at his own expense—to compensate for feeling vulnerable.[14] The desire to feel in control of one's body is not uniquely masculine. Girls and boys who are abused or shamed may "turn to their bodies in an attempt to establish a private domain in which a sense of control and self-esteem can be reestablished."[15] Girls are more likely to seek to thin their bodies and boys to build theirs, with contrasting diets, exercise regimes, and harmful consequences such as eating disorders and steroid use. (This binary has broken down some—more girls and women are strength training.) Self-injury such as cutting is another method used by kids to reclaim some control. Regulated physical pain allows them to cope with various kinds of overwhelming emotional distress.[16]

There are a handful of compensatory manhood clichés that circulate in pop culture. The middle-aged, balding man buying a red sports car, the short guy with the Napoleon complex trying to symbolically tower over other men, and the most mocked of all, the guy with the tiny penis doing any number of over-the-top actions to compensate. A well-worn story among a group of my college friends was the time one of them, Tommy, installed outrageously large tires on his SUV, elevating the truck to an impressive height. He visited our friend, Joe, to show it off. Joe's mom came outside, and in her usual scathing, deadpan humor, said, "Hey Tommy, nice truck. You know what they say: Big tires, small penis." Penis Health Club members and other men feeling ashamed of their size may find the joke tasteless and possibly true.

Addressing men's psychic and spiritual wounds, Greg Perry's essay "Hung like a Hamster" describes his reactions to imagining he has a small penis.[17] Despite never being told he was small by peers or sexual partners and even being informed by a doctor that he has a normal phallus, every other penis he saw seemed bigger than his own. He compared himself unfavorably to underwear ads and "felt inadequate, impotent, cheated." He avoided public nudity and found ways to compensate. He explains, "My lack of size below the belt was compensated for with obsessions of grand dimensions. At different times I've been addicted to good grades, good drugs, big money, and running. If I was accomplished in one small part of my life then no one could shame me about my other small part."[18]

Some members of PHC turn to sculpting and building their bodies to off-set their anxieties about their below-average or merely average penis size or sexual skills. Young member Colin thinks this might explain his own commitment to going to the gym. He says, "I wasn't saying to myself, 'Oh, I'm going to go and get big muscles to make up for having an average penis.' But it's very possible that that was subconsciously driving me to do that, to, you know, make my outward appearance more masculine. It's definitely possible." Colin was animated by embarrassment about his average penis size. He internalized his perceived shortcomings, tried to repair by doing Club-endorsed exercises, and compensated by building the rest of his body. Club forum poster *LittleRock98*'s small penis size contributes to his depression. He says he pushes his body to its limit with hard workouts to cope with his insecurity, which inhibits his ability to approach women and have sex.

For other members, embarrassment is eventually replaced by anger, most of it directed at women. Younger Club members sometimes lash out at women they derisively label "size queens" for desiring large penises and causing men to feel small and incompetent. When forum member *WalterIce* was in high school, he relied on alcohol and drugs to hook up with girls without worrying about his penis size. He thought that sleeping with and sexually satisfying many girls would make him feel like a real man and change his mind about his penis size. However, he calls the ones who did not have orgasms "whores," blaming them for having had sex with men with big penises or using large vibrators. In this way, he compensates by attacking the "size queens" who implicitly make him feel small and, he believes, caused his alcohol and drug addictions because he needed these to have sex. *WalterIce's* anxieties are reinforced by fellow Club poster *@Zenith*, who writes, "Now that I have a big dick, it's easy for me to talk to women and 'conquer' them. My big cock makes me feel powerful, and it scares women who want monogamous relationships. Women want men to be confident, and I've got it in spades thanks to my incredible dick. It's like my confidence is reaching out and slapping them." These kinds of control-as-violence metaphors are littered throughout men's descriptions of their sexual conquests of women. Men use words like destroy, demolish, smash, crush, slay, wreck, and kill in recounting or bragging about what they did to girls, women, and their bodies. These gendered metaphors, like all others, structure what we perceive in our social worlds, and how we perceive them.[19] There are clear parallels to fantasies of using violence to control and dominate other men. Sometimes men's compensatory violence is not metaphorical, rhetorical, or confined to fantasies.

Compensatory Masculine Violence

When author Margaret Atwood asked a friend of hers why men, given all their physical and socioeconomic advantages, feel threatened by women, he replied, "They're afraid women will laugh at them." Later, speaking with a group of women, she asked why women feel threatened by men. "They're afraid of being killed," they replied.[20] These two fears are inextricably linked. "The emotion of shame," Psychologist James Gilligan says, "is the primary or ultimate cause of all violence, whether toward others or toward the self."[21] Shame-fueled violence may take the form of repair, as is true for a subset of GFC members who were physically humiliated as boys. Oftentimes, though, boys' and men's violence is a compensatory response, such as when homophobic insults are met with physical retaliation. At home and in relationships, women are the most likely to be the targets of that violence. In bars and on the streets, it is mostly other men. Adult men are more likely to use compensatory masculine violence for being failed breadwinners, while body ideals are more important for boys and young men.

Gilligan says shame is a necessary but not sufficient cause of violence. Studying men incarcerated for murder, he concludes they are most likely to resort to violence when shame threatens their sense of self, they have no nonviolent recourse for staving off shame, and their ability to experience normative feelings and emotions that restrain violence is short-circuited (usually temporarily). He says that men feel ashamed of feeling ashamed, and these feelings are exacerbated because they possess them regularly and often over trivial matters. Shame must be closely guarded because it can cause loss of face or, worse, the death of the self. The threat of a symbolic death can arouse physical and even lethal violence, a self-defense with no legal backing. Without a viable career, social prestige, or some other face-saving status, shame is more likely to threaten the self and lead to violence. And a temporary flood of shame can overwhelm other emotions, making violence more likely. I would add that what also seems essential, at least in explaining boys' and men's lethal violence against others, is their acceptance of hegemonic masculine ideals. Their shame is reduced, but not eliminated, if others target them for failing to fulfill ideals that they themselves do not embrace. (Perhaps these individuals are more likely to internalize others' abuse, resorting to suicide instead of murder when they can no longer take it.) Violence is a visceral reclamation of power and control in response to the perceived injustice of being shamed.

Men's violence against women, other men, and themselves form a linked triad.[22] All three forms of violence are the inevitable result of requiring boys and men to bottle up their emotions, especially their fears and anxieties, to avoid being perceived as weak and feminine. As with any bottle under constant pressure, eventually, it's likely to explode. I focus on violence against women and other men, but there is an argument to be made that some forms of violence against the self (e.g., risk-taking activities like binge drinking, drunk driving, playing dangerous sports, and doing dangerous work) are compensatory in nature.

The pattern of bodily shame turning into violence typically begins in middle school and, based on what is currently known, is fairly consistent across racial and ethnic groups, regions, and social classes.[23] Boys' fragile masculine identities are tested in the anxiety-producing, pressure-cooker setting of schools. Threats abound. Being teased, mocked, or challenged for an array of actual or perceived body failings is the precursor to much of boys' and young men's violence. Schoolyard fights with other boys, physical and sexual violence against girls and women, and lethal violence, typically shootings at schools and in communities, often piggyback on feeling a loss of bodily control, of being dissed, punked, or bullied in physically emasculating ways. The fears of being considered soft or weak explain some youth gang crimes, violent and otherwise.[24] Instead of restoring their masculine selves rather innocuously via superhero fantasies, managing fantasy sports teams, or playing fantasy video games, a small but significant number do so via violence.

School shooters—mostly white, middle-class boys from suburban and rural areas—have garnered much attention and professional scrutiny since a spate of shootings in the 1990s. Almost all the school shooters targeted boys who bullied and gay-baited them, girls who rejected them, or both.[25] They did not appear to be gay but were labeled fags because they were different than the jocks and popular boys. They were low in status, academically oriented, could not live up to the hypermasculine expectations of their peer cultures, were mostly unsuccessful with girls, and not as wealthy as popular kids. Their violence was a reaction to "oppressive social hierarchies in their schools."[26] They were shamed and felt ashamed, and they experienced these as injustices—especially middle-class boys, who tend to enjoy a greater sense of entitlement:

> What transforms the aggrieved into mass murderers is also a sense of entitlement, a sense of using violence against others, making others hurt as you, yourself, might hurt. Aggrieved entitlement inspires revenge against those who have wronged you; it is the compensation for humiliation. Humiliation is emasculation: humiliate someone and you take away his manhood. For many men, humiliation must be avenged, or you cease to be a man. Aggrieved entitlement is a gendered emotion, a fusion of that humiliating loss of manhood and the moral obligation and entitlement to get it back. And its gender is masculine.[27]

Righteous violence in the face of perceived injustice is part of the American fabric. Our culture of revenge celebrates this narrative in comics, western and action films, and the practice of capital punishment. Far from being "crazy" (almost none would be adjudicated as such), school shooters are "overconformists" to gendered cultural expectations that boys use violence to control their own and others' bodies.[28] For many, their violence was preceded by withdrawal, isolation, depression, and escape, including the use of alcohol and drugs. They compensated first by fantasizing about exacting revenge, sometimes by playing first-person shooter video games, as was true of Columbine shooters Eric Harris and Dylan Klebold.[29] Eventually, school shooters acquire the weapons they intend to use, and the fantasy becomes more conceivable. They possess in their hands the tools to enact their revenge. Boys and young men are more likely to use compensatory mass violence when they experience body failures, but adult men are also capable of these kinds of shame-induced violence.

George Sodini

A man needs a woman for confidence. He gets a boost on the job, career, with other men, and everywhere else when he knows inside he has someone to spend the night with and who is also a friend. This type of life I see is a closed world with me specifically and totally excluded. Every other guy does this successfully to a degree. Flying solo for many years is a destroyer.

George Sodini was a systems analyst at a local law firm and a homeowner in the Pittsburgh, Pennsylvania, area. He had no close friends and did not appear to be close with his mother or siblings. He was single, never married, rarely went on a date, and at age 48, hadn't had a girlfriend for 25 years or sex for nearly 20 years. His sexual and emotional isolation caused him despair and pain. In his online diary, he wrote, "I know I will never enjoy life. This is an over 30 year trend. Some people are happy, some are miserable. It is difficult to live almost continuously feeling an undercurrent of fear, worry, discontentment and helplessness." His loneliness devolved to hopelessness, and he directed his anger at girls and women, 30 million of whom (his estimate of single, desirable women) had rejected him and chosen to sleep with other men. He called women "hoes" and "bitches," his resentment and frustration feeding each other, escalating and intensifying his sense of sexual and romantic failure.

In 2009, Sodini went to his gym in a local strip mall, entered a women's aerobics class, turned off the lights, pulled out two semiautomatic handguns and began shooting. He murdered three women and wounded nine others. Then he killed himself.

His diary, which he wrote for less than the last year of his life, began with the question we are left asking following each of the all-too-common mass shootings: Why? He wrote, "Why do this?? To young girls?" The second question confirmed his intended victims and revealed his single-minded resentment. Sodini's decades of unmet social and sexual needs persisted despite various attempts to improve his appearance and make himself more attractive to women. He had a good job and occasionally participated in social activities, both of which helped keep him tethered to society. But the culmination of so many years without change, without progress, made life seem futile. "Women just don't like me," he concluded. "The biggest problem of all is not [a lack of] relationships or friends, but not being able to achieve and acquire what I desire in those or many other areas. [Everything] stays the same regardless of the [effort] I put in. If I had control over my life then I would be happier. But for about the past 30 years, I have not." And he had no explanation for it. He couldn't find a reason women did not find him attractive and why nothing seemed to change.

Meanwhile, everyone else seemed to be having sex and enjoying relationships, something he thought he deserved. He jealously and contemptuously identified the culprits: Carefree couples in their twenties, black men having sex with white college girls ("Black dudes have their choice of best white hoez [*sic*]"), and even his fortysomething neighbor, whom Sodini assumed was sleeping with the college-aged "hot little hottie" who visited his neighbor's house. Sodini read online forums where teenage girls talked about their active sex lives: "One 16 year old does it usually three times a day with her boyfriend. So after a month of that, this little hoe has had more sex than ME in my LIFE, and I am 48. One more reason. Thanks for nada, bitches!" Life was unfair, he thought, and the future would be just as cruel and hopeless. He was tired of being ignored and disliked by women, of living a lonely life. "I don't have kids, close friends or anything. Just me here. If you have nothing," he wrote, "you have nothing to lose." Along with his fraying social ties, he disassociated from basic morality by interpreting his former pastor's teachings to mean that "you can commit mass murder [and] still go to heaven." Because Christ died for everyone's sins, Sodini believed, everyone was going to heaven regardless of their actions.

Sodini left limited information. His diary doesn't fully convey the anger he must have felt to justify his grotesque violence, nor does it go into detail about his earlier life. He complained about his father being merely a "useless sperm donor"; a mother he described as bossy, controlling, vindictive, and a my-way-or-the-highway type; and a brother who was a "useless bully." He was embittered because he said none of them or anyone else ever provided him with guidance or feedback: "There is something BLATANTLY wrong with me that NO goddam person will tell me what it is." He was conflicted because he did not think he was "ugly or too weird" and even wrote, "I actually look good. I dress good, am clean-shaven, bathe, touch of cologne—yet 30 million women rejected me—over an 18 or 25-year period."

As the months ticked by, he was surprised to survive multiple rounds of layoffs at his firm, which would have pushed him to initiate his "exit plan" sooner. His diary conveys the mixed emotions of taking his own life but does not reference taking the lives of others. He related to a radio talk show caller who "was describing the despair in certain black communities" and lack of quality of life, which left residents feeling life is cheap. The caller's main point resonated with Sodini: "If you know the past 40 years were crappy, why live another 30 crappy years, then die?" On the eve of the original date of his intended murder-suicide, seven months before the actual date, he reflected on his life: "Young women were brutal when I was younger, now they aren't as much, probably because they just see me just as another old man. Why should I continue another 20+ years alone? I will just work, come home, eat, maybe do something, then go to bed (alone) for the next day of the same thing. This is the Auschwitz Syndrome [*sic*], to be in serious pain so long one thinks it is normal. I cannot wait for tomorrow!"

He "chickened out" the next day, in his own words. In the coming months, he would feel a little better, but he sensed that he was delaying the inevitable: "The problem is I feel too good now to do this but too bad to enjoy life. I know I will never enjoy life." Hopelessness eventually set in again: "I made many big changes in the past two years but everything is still the same. Life is over." In the intervening months between his aborted and actual attack, he went on a date and was rewarded at work instead of getting laid off. Neither event moved the needle. Two weeks before his deadly actions, he wrote, "Everything still sucks. But I got a promotion and a raise, even in this shitty Obama economy. No more grunt programming. Go figure! New boss is great ... But that is NOT what I want in life. I guess some of us were simply meant to walk a lonely path. I have slept alone for over 20 years. Last time I slept all night with a girlfriend it was 1982. Proof I am a total malfunction. Girls and women don't even give me a second look ANYWHERE."

George Sodini's years of isolation, loneliness, frustration, and anger arose from his actual and perceived body failures. He felt powerless to change his circumstances, which he saw as unjust, especially given that so many other undeserving men were enjoying sex and relationships. Sodini's final act was to reassert control by ending and destroying the lives of those whom he felt stripped him of control and ruined his life: women. It was a horrific act of misogynistic compensatory masculine violence.

Elliot Rodger

All of my suffering on this world has been at the hands of humanity, particularly women ... All I ever wanted was to fit in and live a happy life amongst humanity, but I was cast out and rejected, forced to endure an existence of loneliness and insignificance, all because the females of the human species were incapable of seeing the value in me ... I will never have sex, never have love, never have children. I will never be a creator, but I could be a destroyer.

In May 2014, a damaged young man went on a murderous rampage near Santa Barbara, California. Twenty-two-year-old Elliot Rodger targeted his college-aged peers for causing him so much suffering. His killing spree, which he spent months planning, began when he stabbed to death three young men—his two roommates and their friend—in his apartment. He then drove his car to a specific sorority house he had targeted. Unable to gain entrance, he shot three young women nearby, two of whom died. He returned to his car and drove to a nearby delicatessen. There he shot and killed a young man before shooting others from his car and also striking pedestrians with his vehicle. He had planned to kill others, including his stepmother and young brother.

Mercifully, the carnage ended soon after he exchanged gunfire with police, was shot in the hip, and crashed into a parked car. He then shot himself in the head. Elliot Rodger's rampage cut short the lives of six young people. Fourteen others survived gunshot wounds or injuries from being hit by his car.

These acts of mass violence cause immeasurable suffering for the survivors and the loved ones of both the survivors and those killed. The emotional and psychological wounds never fully heal. Richard Martinez, the distraught father of slain son Christopher Ross Michaels-Martinez, was the most public face of that anguish in Santa Barbara, describing his family as lost and broken. Memorials quickly appeared all over the city where the violence took place. Funerals followed. Parents did the unimaginable, burying their children. The surviving victims convalesced in the weeks and months ahead. No one's lives were the same.

Rodger's motivations are found in his book-length accounting of his life, which he titled "My Twisted World," along with a series of videos he posted online. His words reveal a powder keg of humiliation, rejection, isolation, entitlement, anger, and delusions of grandeur. He lacked power and control but was determined to claim these. Rodger was depressed for a long time, appeared to be borderline suicidal on a couple of occasions, and saw various mental health professionals over the years. There is conflicting information about his actual mental health status.[30]

As long as he could remember, from his early years living in the U.K. to his childhood in Los Angeles, Rodger was always smaller, less athletic, and weaker than his peers. He couldn't keep up with the other boys. He took more notice of and was increasingly bothered by his small stature in elementary school. When Rodger was nine years old, he noticed that taller boys enjoyed more respect, causing him "the first feelings of inferiority." He was "physically weak compared to other boys" of both the same age and younger. In numerous ways, he didn't measure up to his peers, a perception that never changed: "Jealousy and envy . . . those are two feelings that would dominate my entire life and bring me immense pain." Rodger was also frustrated by his inability to excel at anything, including activities into which he put a lot of time. "Why did I fail at everything I tried?" he asked himself.

He was further marginalized because he lacked social skills. Rodger was socially awkward and outcast, bullied by the boys he envied and ignored by the girls he desired. He took note of the various social hierarchies and statuses in middle school and his own standing: he was not one of the cool kids, wealthy kids, jocks, or boys whom beautiful girls found attractive. He was low status, he wrote, because he was shy and had a dorky haircut and clothes. This lowered his self-esteem and heightened his sense of being different, due in no small part to his multiracial identity: "I am half White, half Asian, and this made me different from the normal fully-white kids that I was trying to fit in with."

Rodger's earliest embodied experiences and memories were marked by differ-ence, incompetence, and inadequacy.

His fear of girls and anxiety around them dated to middle school. A sum-mer camp experience proved formative and scarred him for life. A pretty girl whom he accidentally bumped into angrily cursed and pushed him, embar-rassing him in front of their peers. He happened to also have a crush on that same girl. He wrote,

> [The incident] made me feel like an insignificant, unworthy little mouse. I felt so small and vulnerable. I couldn't believe that this girl was so horrible to me, and I thought that it was because she *viewed me* as a loser. That was the first experi-ence of female cruelty I endured, and it traumatized me to no end. It made me even more nervous around girls, and I would be extremely weary and cautious of them from that point on.

Rodger's middle school status as the "shy kid" later evolved to the "weird kid," when he found that acting out and being made fun of was less painful than simply being ignored. "Infamy is better than total obscurity," he observed. Obscurity is passive invisibility, coded feminine. To be infamous is to force others to acknowledge your influence on the world, coded masculine.

His transition to high school brought even more marginalization and suf-fering. His already comparatively small body produced even more embarrass-ment and dissatisfaction when his peers entered puberty years ahead of him. Worse, high school peer culture was harsher, more hierarchical, more judg-mental, marked by more physical bullying. "They teased me because I was scared of girls, calling me names like 'faggot,'" he wrote. He was too little and weak to fight back and was often mocked because of it. He avoided bullies by hiding and taking circuitous routes around the school. But the bullying mounted and took a toll: "I became more shy and timid than I ever was in my life. I felt very small, weak, and above all, worthless. I cried by myself at school every day."

Reading his story, it was at this point, as he transitioned into high school, that I really began to wrestle with contradictory thoughts about Elliot Rodger. Before I learned more about his life, he possessed no identity to me other than "mass shooter Elliot Rodger." Like other distant observers, in my mind, I pref-aced each fact I discovered about him with the modifier that will forever pre-cede his name: "Mass shooter Elliot Rodger was hung up on social class and status." "Mass shooter Elliot Rodger was jealous of his peers." "Mass shooter Elliot Rodger hated women."

Rodger's childhood experiences, though, complicate his monolithic public identity as a cold, calculated killer. His own story and subsequent interviews with family, friends, and acquaintances tell of how he experienced long-term, painful social isolation as well as repeated social and physical bullying. Like most adolescents and teenagers, he simply wanted to fit in. He was never able to do so. Long before committing unthinkable violence, he was just a socially awkward kid; an undeserving target, lonely, insecure, depressed, and under the care of counselors. Staff at the alternative high school where he eventually found safety referred to him as "our Elliot" and recalled how many of his peers at that school also felt protective of him in the way that people feel protective of and want to insulate kids who lag behind physically, socially, or cognitively. They recognized in him what is true of so many similar kids who are vulnerable and unprepared to deal with the particular cruelties of peer culture.

If Rodger had not gone on his violent rampage, his earlier experiences might generate—perhaps necessitate—widespread sympathy and empathy. We might recall kids from our own childhoods who were marginalized. Some of us might have been one of those kids at some point or another. We might be able to, as I can now, remember the anguish of being rejected by at least some of our peers. We might try to imagine what it must have been like for socially isolated kids, ones who didn't have friends to counterbalance rejection from other peers and help maintain their self-esteem. With some guilt, we might recall how we quarantined ourselves from the social outcasts for fear of being contaminated. With white-hot shame, we might even, as I do now, recall occasionally making fun of these kids behind their backs, embarrassed by our youthful ignorance, insecurities, and lack of empathy. If we consciously consider any of these thoughts, we might also see "mass killer Elliot Rodger" as "bullying victim Elliot Rodger" or "awkward kid Elliot Rodger" or "marginalized, depressed Elliot Rodger." He might be "our Elliot" instead of "that maniac."

None of this excuses or justifies his violence. And it is not my place as a distant observer or my business as a sociologist to determine whether anyone should forgive Elliot Rodger. That is for the surviving victims to decide. We are collectively responsible, though, for attempting to understand and trying to address the circumstances that contribute to these tragic losses of life, assuming we choose to offer something more than simplistic, reactionary responses ("He needed to toughen up, everyone gets bullied," "It's the parents' fault," "He was a psychopath," "Violent video games made him do it," and so on).

We must confront many challenges: the unrealistic and narrow expectations we place on boys and men; our cultural devaluation of girls, women, and femininity, often in dehumanizing ways that precipitate misogynistic violence; widespread bullying among youth; and, as Richard Martinez has tirelessly advocated for since losing his son, keeping guns away from people who pose short- or long-term risks to their own or others' safety. There are more challenges, but these may be the most sweeping and difficult.

Rodger was physically bullied his first two years in high school, mocked for being wimpy and weird, haunted by other boys' sexual exploits and accompanying boasting, entrapped by his shortcomings in an unforgiving peer culture. About this time in his life, he wrote, "I still looked and sounded like a ten-year-old. Such a persona attracted zero attention from girls, of course, but it did attract bullies like moths to a flame. . . . The most meanest and depraved of men come out on top, and women flock to these men. Their evil acts are rewarded by women; while the good, decent men are laughed at. It is sick, twisted, and wrong in every way. I hated the girls even more than the bullies because of this." He fled two high schools, a private all-boys school, and a large public school, eventually settling in at the alternative high school that provided protection. Still, he continued to struggle under the weight of thwarted hopes, a sense of invisibility and insignificance, and isolation.

Years of rejection and isolation, and especially his status as an "Incel" (involuntary celibate), ate away at him. To cope with his sexual and social failings, Rodger often retreated to the fantasy world of video games, specifically MMORPGs—massively multiplayer online role-playing games. There he could escape his problems, finding peace and safety, and even success and friendships, in an alternate reality where he enjoyed some power and control. "Life would be impossible to handle without those temporary respites," he wrote. He sometimes played 14 hours per day.

For years before he carried out his self-described "Day of Retribution," he constructed elaborate fantasies to compensate for his real-world disempowerment. He alternately fantasized about becoming rich and desirable, great and powerful, preventing all others from enjoying what he saw as the barbarity of sex and pleasure, quarantining women and controlling human reproduction, and committing murderous revenge.

Rodger cycled through phases of envy and anger, followed by fantasy-fueled optimism, and which concluded with a crushing hopelessness when change eluded him. He rode this roller coaster many times during the last years of his life. The peaks were rare and fleeting. Feeling condemned to celibacy, he "developed extreme feelings of envy, hatred, and anger" toward those who weren't: "I saw them as the *enemy* . . . I felt inferior and undesirable." He describes a "major turning point" when he began turning the anger of "injustice" into strength. Rodger saw himself as exceptionally intelligent, destined for greatness, and anything but insignificant, despite his treatment. He fantasized about "[changing and shaping the world] into an image that suits me." Thoughts of injustice, revenge, destiny, and power consumed his 17-year-old mind. He began studying social and political history with omnipotence in mind: "My torment would continue, but I had something to live for. I felt empowered."

It didn't last: "As time progressed, I realized how hopeless everything in my life was. The chances that I will ever rise to power and right the wrongs of the world were extremely slim." He knew he was confined to fantasy. Down he went, "[twisting] even deeper into darkness and despair." Seeing other couples kissing and enjoying each other tormented him: "My life, if you can call it a life, was living hell." His descent accelerated until he realized he could jump off the ride. Unable to climb to the heights he desired, he sought to pull down the people whom he felt condemned him to his depths.

Rodger could not comprehend why he was marginalized, why he was subject to what he saw as a grave injustice. He reacted with entitlement-fueled defiance. The entitlement came in part from the insular wealthy world in which he sometimes traveled and always aspired (though his brand comes across as exceptionally shallow, even for his age). "Wealth," he wrote, "is one of the most important defining factors of self-worth and superiority." He felt entitled to women's bodies and affection, an opulent lifestyle, and a world that would bend to his will. He wanted beautiful girls to have on his arm (as mere objects), Hollywood-level recognition, wealth, and elite social status. These would prove to the world that he was a real man. He reveled in flying first class, eating at fine restaurants, and owning expensive clothing. His parents' divorce and their changing financial circumstances allowed him only occasional morsels of this level of conspicuous consumption. Wealthy peers sparked jealousy. He was embarrassed when his mom had to rent apartments or homes in "bad" (less wealthy) areas.

When his parents forced him to try to find a job, his social counselor got him the only one he thought Rodger was capable of: a custodian. He was indignant when he arrived for work: "To my horror and humiliation, the job turned out to be a menial custodial job . . . There was no way I would ever degrade myself to such a level." He quit after a couple hours. He refused even to do entry-level retail work. Rodger expected women to befall him as wealth should. Beautiful girls should have been approaching if not throwing themselves at him, he thought, due to his inherent magnificence. Rodger's aggrieved entitlement—his belief that he deserved everything he desired yet was unjustly denied—explains in part why he externalized his sense of manhood failure and engaged in compensatory violence against others (as opposed to solely internalizing his failures).

Sexual desire and failure occupied much of Rodger's thoughts through the end of high school and increasingly so after he graduated. He enrolled in some courses at local junior colleges at his mother's demand but also hoping life would improve after high school. He repeatedly dropped those courses due to anxiety around and anger directed at attractive girls who ignored him, flirted with other boys, or engaged in public displays of affection with what he saw as the same boys who undeservedly held high status in high school.

Despite years of what he experienced as the ultimate failure—never even kissing a girl, let alone having a girlfriend or losing his virginity—he did not attempt to take his own life or harm others because he enjoyed family, a few friends, video games, and moments or even periods of optimism and hope that he would eventually overcome his youthful struggles and failures. He remained tethered to society. His mother was uniquely attuned to his wants and needs, and she along with other family provided Rodger with love, care, patience and understanding, few expectations to take on adult responsibilities, life coaches and social counselors, and money and material resources to cushion his jealousy. He was periodically buoyed by new clothes, a new haircut, a new car, and attempts to work out and build his body.

Nothing fundamental changed, though. The lonely days and nights continued, repeatedly dashing his hopes after bouts of optimism. "My hope that I will one day have a beautiful girlfriend and live the life I desire slowly faded away," he wrote, recalling his night alone on New Year's Eve after graduating high school: "I was in the same dark and miserable place I had been a year previously; lonely, unwanted, miserable, and seething with rage at the world." A former friend with whom he was feuding told Rodger, "No girl in this whole world will ever want to fuck you." He was insulted and angry—mostly because it rang so true.

After refusing to work, withdrawing from most of his courses, and getting into regular and escalating conflicts with his father and stepmother, his parents told him his situation was unhealthy, that he needed a fresh start. He also suspected his mother was tired of him and wanted him out. They chose to enroll him at a junior college near the beautiful, upscale coastal city of Santa Barbara, California, populated by thousands of college students. Rodger felt OK about the plan, concluding, "If I can't get laid [by a beautiful girl] there . . ." This had become virtually his only concern. Every day that he failed to do so was like a straightjacket tightening around him. "The loneliness was *suffocating*," he later wrote. "I could barely breathe." He labeled this time in his "extraordinary and tragic life," before leaving for Santa Barbara, as "the era of Hope and Hopelessness." His flirtations with hope were always "shattered"; he was "suffering this lonely existence" while his peers "lived their happy lives of pleasure and sex." He wrote,

> I can never forgive such an injustice, and it was my bid to overcompensate for it in the future. I had to make up for all the years I lost in loneliness and isolation, through no fault of my own! It was society's fault for rejecting me. It was women's fault for refusing to have sex with me.

As with all his previous attempts at change, moving to Santa Barbara was no panacea. The same patterns persisted. He dropped courses because he could not handle seeing couples in class or the shame of not receiving girls' attention. He spent much of his time alone, and he cried a lot. His downward spiral accelerated. His resentment grew. So did his sense of entitlement, which at first shielded him from his harsh reality but eventually just fed his sense of injustice. It proved crucial in moving him from depressed loner to vengeful killer. He wrote, "I am an intelligent gentleman, and I deserve the love of girls more than the other obnoxious boys of my age, and yet they get girls and I don't. That is a crime that can never be forgotten, nor can it be forgiven." He saw his move to Santa Barbara as "a chance that I was giving to the world, not the other way around!" It was "one last chance to give me the life that I know I'm entitled to . . . the last straw" before his "vengeance" if nothing changed. If Rodger had not acted on his words, they would sound almost cartoonish, juvenile, cringeworthy, like those written by a petulant little boy who was not getting his way.

His sense of entitlement is inseparable from his struggles with his racial identity and his racist attitudes. "I always felt as if white girls thought less of me because I was half-Asian," Rodger wrote. He obsessed about blonde girls and took it as a personal insult when they were with men of color. His room-mates' African American friend bragged about losing his virginity to a blonde girl when he was 13. Insulted by the thought, Rodger retreated to his room and cried. He later wrote about the incident with incredulity, calling the visitor "ugly black scum" and "filth," and blaming women for their ridiculous taste: "How could an inferior, ugly black boy be able to get a white girl and not me? I am beautiful, and I am half white myself. I am descended from British aris-tocracy. *He* is descended from slaves. I deserve it more." When his father took him out to lunch one day, Rodger felt humiliated by the nearby presence of "a dark-skinned Mexican guy [with] a hot blonde white girl. I regarded it as a great insult to my dignity. How could an inferior Mexican guy be able to date a white blonde girl, while I was still suffering as a lonely virgin?" He assumed his father was ashamed of him.

Rodger's transition from vengeful fantasy to action first happened at a cof-fee shop. A couple kissing while waiting in line made him "livid with envious hatred." He followed them outside, splashed his coffee on them, and quickly drove away. He was filled with "rage-fueled excitement" when he fled, shaking and unable to contain his emotions: "I had never struck back at my enemies before, and I felt a small sense of spiteful gratification for doing so." He would repeat this act several other times, dousing a couple with iced tea, throwing coffee at two girls at a bus stop who didn't return his smile, and buying a large squirt gun and spraying couples with orange juice at a park. After the first inci-dent, he wrote,

> I wanted to do horrible things to that couple. I wanted to inflict pain on all young couples. It was around this point in my life that I realized I was capable of doing such things. I would happily do such things. I was capable of killing

them, and I wanted to. I wanted to kill them slowly, to strip the skins off their flesh. They deserve it. The males deserve it for taking the females away from me, and the females deserve it for choosing those males instead of me. . . . I had never been a violent person in nature, but after building up so much hatred over the years, I realized that I wouldn't hesitate to kill or even torture my hated enemies if I was given the opportunity.

These hated enemies were strangers, people with whom he had no interaction.

Over the years Rodger did many things in response to seeing happy young couples living the life he desired. He internalized his failures, feeling lonely, miserable, depressed, and crying to himself a lot. He tried to repair his short-comings by working on his body and appearance, and working with counsel-ors and coaches. And he compensated via consumption ("Delicious food was the only vice I was able to enjoy, since I was deprived of sex."), angry shouting to himself and rants to his one longtime friend, and escapist fantasy through video games and books or imagining being omnipotent and exacting revenge. Fantasy provided alternate realities where he could be someone else, someone powerful, even god-like—someone capable of controlling, dominating, and imposing his will on others.

Rodger made a few casual friends in Santa Barbara, but the relationships were marked by mutual disinterest. As had happened with previous friends, they would do things without inviting him. Besides, they didn't help him meet beautiful girls, so their friendships mattered little. He also had regu-lar conflicts with a series of roommates and their friends, highlighted by nearly fighting one who teased him about his virginity. Rodger interpreted one roommate having sex as an act of "insolence" and an obvious flaunting attempt at humiliation.

Living in Santa Barbara several semesters only heightened his anxieties and insecurities. He dropped all his courses and lost all hope. "I realized that I would be a virgin forever, condemned to suffer rejection and humiliation at the hands of women," he wrote. Dying seemed better than suffering: "I knew that if it came to that, I would exact my revenge upon the world in the most catastrophic way possible. At least then, I could die knowing that I fought back against the injustice that has been dealt to me . . . I will destroy all women because I can never have them. I will make them all suffer for rejecting me. I will arm myself with deadly weapons and wage a war against *all women and the men they are attracted to*. And I will slaughter them like the animals they are." Still, he harbored some hope he could get untracked and be happy, that he would enjoy a "peaceful revenge" filled with wealth, beautiful girls, and the comeuppance of lording these over his peers: "I didn't *want* to do it. I wanted to *live*. Thinking about the Day of Retribution made me feel trapped. I wanted a way out."

His entitlement interfered again. He lacked ideas or business skills that would quickly create wealth and preemptively aborted any plans requiring effort or time. Desperate, he repeatedly played the lottery, even driving through the night to Arizona for a large Powerball jackpot. He believed he would win, that he could will it to happen, that the lotto money was *his* money. He lost repeatedly, spending hundreds and perhaps thousands of dollars. Around this time Rodger also lost "the one friend I had in the whole world who truly understood me," leaving him "completely and utterly alone, in the darkest pit of despair." His planned retribution against humanity became more probable. He anticipated it elevating him, reigning over his victims like a god: "I imagined how sweet it would be to slaughter all of those evil, slutty bitches who rejected me, along with the fraternity jocks they throw themselves at. To see them all running from me in fear as I kill them left and right, that would be the ultimate retribution. Only then would I have all the power."

The powerlessness that motivated these feelings first manifested itself in a breakdown. He called his parents to tell them he was suffering loneliness and "had no hope of ever having a happy life," that they must be ashamed of him and he could no longer take being a social outcast: "People having a high opinion of me is what I've always wanted in life. It has always been of the utmost importance. This is why my life has been so miserable, because no one has ever had a high opinion of me." His parents had him see a psychiatrist, but Rodger refused to take the medication prescribed.

He purchased handguns, which gave him a sense of power. "*Who's the alpha male now, bitches?*" he wrote. Still, he hesitated going through with his plan. He felt trapped and lost after initially setting a date: "I didn't want to die. I fear death, but death is better than living such a miserable, insignificant life." Setting himself up for failure, he went out one final night thinking he was giving the world its last chance to fulfill his dreams. He got drunk and went to house parties in hopes of losing his virginity before he turned 22, but no one paid him any attention until he became verbally and physically aggressive. He "was filled with rage" at the sight of "this white girl at the party talking to a full-blooded Asian." He went outside and tried to push some girls off of a 10-foot ledge, only to be pushed off himself and have his leg broken. He returned to the house to find his expensive sunglasses, got called a "faggot" and a "pussy," took a swing at someone, and then got jumped by several boys: "I had never been beaten and humiliated that badly." He couldn't believe that no one helped him—even though he mentioned a group tried to do so before he went back to the house—and that no girl would comfort him or offer to sleep with him to make him feel better. He was devastated by the night's outcome but used it to fuel his horrific plan.

Waiting for his leg to heal, Rodger reflected upon his life, cemented his reactionary misogynist ideology, and formulated how his rampage would unfold. Near the end of his 100,000-plus word diary, he elaborated on his views of women and sex: "The ultimate evil behind sexuality is the human female. They are the main instigators of sex. They control which men get it and which men don't... Women have more power in human society than they deserve, all because of sex," he wrote. He viewed women as mentally flawed, animal-like, incapable of reason or thinking rationally, "controlled by their primal, depraved emotions and impulses." They are "beasts" attracted only to other beasts, "a plague that must be quarantined," he says. "Beasts should not be able to have any rights in a civilized society. If their wickedness is not contained, the whole of humanity will be held back from advancement to a more civilized state. Women should not have the right to choose who to mate with. That choice should be made for them by civilized men of intelligence." Rodger saw it as his duty to exact a ritual purification of women and society ("I am like a god, and my purpose is to exact ultimate Retribution"). His violence would avenge his own mistreatment and solve social ills.

Rodger's fantasy of cleansing the culture of savagery and civilizing the savages deploys the same "regeneration through violence" ideology that was the mythology used to justify Europeans' genocide of Native Americans.[31] Dehumanization fosters the mistreatment, assault, and even murder of other human beings. Violence in this context is revitalizing, a necessity for progress. Rodger's self-described "perfect ideology" revolved around killing and controlling women. He imagined quarantining women in concentration camps, starving most to death, to control their sexuality and human reproduction. In this he "would take great pleasure and satisfaction." He fantasized about breeding out sexuality and love to "purify the world" and raise humanity.

In the end, he knew he was engaging in fantasy to distract himself from his reality. "It is such a shameful pity that my ideal world cannot be created," he wrote, acknowledging that "there is no way I could possibly rise to such a level of power in my lifetime." He believed his life would continue to be one of rejection, isolation, and sexual frustration. He used rejection from women specifically and "the human race" in general to fuel a compensatory assertion of self, and his delusions of grandeur. He wrote,

I am more than human. I am superior to them all. I am Elliot Rodger... Magnificent, glorious, supreme, eminent... Divine! I am the closest thing there is to a living god. Humanity is a disgusting, depraved, and evil species. It is my purpose to punish them all. I will purify the world of everything that is wrong with it. On the Day of Retribution, I will truly be a powerful god, punishing everyone I deem to be impure and depraved... My Retribution will be so devastating that it will shake the very foundations of the world. Women's rejection of me is a declaration of war, and if it's war they want, then war they shall have. It will be a war that will result in their complete and utter annihilation. I will deliver a blow to my enemies that will be so catastrophic it will redefine the very essence of human nature.

#YesAllWomen to #MeToo

In the aftermath of Rodger's violent rampage, a debate played out in social and traditional media about the connections between Rodger's violence and the extent of misogyny in American culture. Some men used social media to protest being associated with these views, let alone Rodger's violence. They borrowed the hashtag #NotAllMen to argue that not all men are like that. A woman created the hashtag #YesAllWomen to explain that even though not all men are violent or misogynists, all women have experienced or know someone who has experienced men's entitlement to women's bodies in the form of sexual harassment, sexual assault, rape, stranger or partner violence, or murder. And recalling Margaret Atwood, all fear and have to live with the fear of these things, adjusting their daily behavior accordingly. Women of all backgrounds used the hashtag to flood social media with their stories. The deluge was so overwhelming it even drowned out the inevitable antifeminist backlash that always seems to accompany women's (and men's) mere mention of indisputable examples and patterns of sexism and misogyny. In 2017, the hashtag #MeToo caught fire in response to multiple women's sexual assault and rape allegations against movie mogul Harvey Weinstein. The immediate aftermath included a wave of men's firings and resignations in entertainment, journalism, politics, academia, and more. Just a few months on, the activism triggered by this social media-born organizing produced pressure for changes in workplace training and policy, schooling, and criminal law, and it has become a global movement.

George Sodini, Elliot Rodger, and many of the school shooters represent extreme cases of compensatory masculine violence in response to body failures. Mass shootings and mass violence are atypical, but these men's experiences of shame and anger are not. The attention-grabbing spectacle of mass shootings means the motivations of the perpetrators are researched and scrutinized. Countless other similarly motivated violent acts do not receive the same attention, but the consequences are no less severe. We must examine individual motivations for violence without ignoring the broader American cultural context that produces greater levels of violence than other comparable nations.

Part II
The Breadwinner Dilemma

5

Non-breadwinners

Unemployed Men and
Stay-at-Home Dads

It's a moderate Autumn day in Southeast Michigan, sunshine and comfortable temperatures concealing the long winter ahead. The sounds of Detroit-area radio fill my car as I travel east on I-96 toward a job fair. I scan the FM spectrum until it lands on a Motown station. Smokey Robinson is crying the "Tears of a Clown" for a lost love. I exit the highway onto Greenfield Road, having missed the expressway split that allows for local exits. This error takes me through the Fishkorn neighborhood of Detroit, a predominantly African American area struggling to survive years of tough times, like much of the city. No snow yet means it's still construction season. The middle lane is being resurfaced, but the harsh weather and what looks like years of neglect leaves the street pockmarked with potholes and generally unforgiving to the dutiful Motor City procession of American-brand cars. Rundown buildings house small businesses and chain fast-food restaurants. Auto repair, hair care, men's clothing, and tire and rim shops are nestled by gas stations, a dollar store, a county agency and low-cost apartments. Many of the businesses are closed, some permanently, and others only curiously so during business hours, as the weekday lunch hour approaches. Steel fencing and bars protect business windows from being smashed and imprison cars awaiting repair in auto shop lots. This section of the city looks like what I imagine most rustbelt areas of the country do: battered by decades of deindustrialization and disproportionately suffering from the lingering effects of the Great Recession.

Another scan of the radio and the tuner finds a station playing gospel music. Kirk Franklin sings "I Smile," dedicating his song to "recession, depression, and unemployment." He tries to lift the spirits of those in Fishkorn and everywhere else, sharing their struggles, singing of better days ahead, telling them to remember that God is working for them, encouraging them not to give up despite how difficult their lives seem. He asks them to smile even though they hurt.

Abruptly, without turning, I enter the city of Dearborn. The roads, buildings, and landscaping suddenly and dramatically improve. Well-maintained businesses flank the smooth streets. A right turn onto Ford Road opens up a newer and shinier world. Big-box stores and national chain restaurants accompany a shopping center that can compete with most upscale malls; their website offers the tagline "You have the right to remain fabulous." I envision Kirk Franklin smiling ironically.

I pull into the hotel parking lot where today's job fair is being held. Staring back at me across the highway is Ford Motor Company's sprawling headquarters, glistening in the sun, looming as a reminder of why Dearborn's streets and businesses contrast so starkly with Fishkorn's. But the imposing glass buildings emblazoned with the Ford emblem also tell another story. They are a reminder of the decline of the auto industry and U.S. manufacturing. For so many listening to Kirk Franklin (and, more so, their parents and grandparents), Ford's headquarters speak to a mostly bygone era when blue-collar workers entered the middle class en masse—no college degree required. That road to the American dream, though, like the one running through Fishkorn, is in permanent disrepair.

Job Fairs and Job Seeking

The recession is officially over, but its effects are visible all around. The large lobby in the hotel where the job fair is held is populated by several dozen jobseekers, along with other hotel guests and staff. Most attendees are African American, in their 30s–50s. Oversized leather chairs surround a flat-screen television in one corner of the lobby; candidates who have heeded the job fair flyer's request to "Dress for Success" are filling out applications and reviewing their résumés, ignoring news coverage of the latest panicky decision in Europe in response to the global recession. The indoor fountain drowns out the TV news anchor, who wasn't going to capture anyone's interest anyway. The afternoon session will begin in 30 minutes. I walk the lobby and overhear the usual chatter outside of a job fair: unsolicited advice shared by fellow job-seekers, a smattering of hopeful enthusiasm, and friendly confirmations of location and start time. A couple of people are muttering to themselves or sharing their struggles with other job-seekers they just met. One woman exits the hotel with another, either a friend she came with or just made. "Girl," she begins, drawing out the word in commiseration as they leave, presumably without the new jobs they were hoping to find at the morning session. This job fair, like every other in the aftermath of the recession, has too many job-seekers and too few jobs.

Near the TV, a half-dozen apparent strangers—three professionally dressed twentysomething African American women, two white men in their late '50s or early '60s who are dressed for what will likely be blue-collar opportunities, and a young African American man in a shirt and tie—share generic application forms to fill out before the afternoon session begins. Images of protestors on Wall Street fail to attract their attention. Three of them begin intently filling out applications. The atmosphere is supportive rather than competitive. Women outnumber men by a healthy majority, most outfitted in professional attire. Male attendees occasionally sport three-piece suits at one end of the spectrum or ball caps and jeans at the other, reflecting the range of advertised employers and job opportunities. Virtually everyone has a stack of résumés in hand and many have a look that suggests fatigue more than hope. Perhaps it's just the long wait until the doors open or the way we tend to downsize our outward emotions in the company of strangers.

The lunch hour ends, and the job fair doors open. Sixty of us politely fall into line and deliberately enter the fair, which takes place in a windowless conference room off the lobby. A few dozen employers, most in business casual attire, stand behind or in front of their tables. They are cheerful, quick to greet anyone hovering nearby to initiate a conversation. Display boards are designed to attract attendees as they would judges at a science fair. Sales jobs dominate—cable, cell phones, security, insurance—no experience necessary! Like every other, this misleadingly titled fair mostly offers jobs rather than careers. But there are some positions that require professional training and presumably compensate accordingly. Corporate-speak and business buzzwords litter employers' literature. Candidates are invited to take advantage of "the opportunity of a lifetime" to join a "success-oriented environment" in a "rapid growth" sector and become "part of our family." I feel fortunate to be doing my job instead of having to look for one.

"How interested are you on a scale of 1 to 10?" asks a prospective employer to a job-seeker inquiring about a sales job. "Full-time or part-time?" a job candidate asks of another employer a few tables away. U.S. Border Patrol agents in full attire are recruiting job seekers in one corner of the room. Educational opportunities in the medical, hospitality, and culinary arts fields are pitched to those who might be interested in obtaining specialized training. Representatives from the Unemployment Insurance Agency have a table that receives steady traffic, despite a recent spate of news coverage about employers notifying the unemployed they need not apply. Five minutes after the doors open, the conference room is packed and several dozen conversations fill the room. Résumé doctors providing free feedback attract a long line. Many more people filter in, making it difficult to walk around and look at display boards and flyers or make eye contact with employer representatives without bumping into someone. Too many job-seekers. Not enough jobs.

The dozen round tables in the lobby outside the conference room are intermittently occupied. People filter in and out of the job fair, sitting down in the lobby to fill out applications, make calls, regroup with friends, and gather their thoughts. After a couple hours, I have not seen anyone show any overt joy or excitement about a lead, although one woman tells someone on the other end of a cell phone call that she found an opening that is a perfect fit. Roger, an African American man in his 40s with a wisp of silver atop his full head of hair, is working on an application when I introduce myself. He is one of the long-term unemployed, out of the workforce more than a year because he has been taking care of an ill family member. Roger says he staves off depression by avoiding the news and its negativity, and he doesn't get his hopes too high about a job opportunity. He focuses on his kids and his faith. But he can't avoid explaining to me Detroit's problems, including corruption, white flight to the suburbs, and city politics. A few minutes later, I sit down and speak with another man in his mid-40s, Melvin, who is reviewing an application he completed. He quietly and somewhat skeptically listens to my introduction and spiel before we begin discussing the recession and the job market. Melvin's distrust quickly disappears, replaced by an openness and kindness that I imagine must be difficult for him to suppress, even for a few short seconds when approached by a stranger outside a job fair who looks like he's selling something. Melvin is wearing a button-down shirt and dress pants, black-rimmed glasses, and his hair in cornrows. He is looking for a guaranteed-income job after working a couple of sales commission jobs. Salaried jobs with benefits are scarce, here and everywhere else.

The same conversations and scenes are repeated at the five job fairs I attend in five cities and three states. Outside the fairs, in lines and waiting areas, attendees slouch in chairs and lean against walls; they joke and sympathize with each other (one woman says to another job-seeker, "To look for a job *is* a job."), enjoying informal conversations with others in their same situation. As they approach the entrance to the fair, they adjust themselves the way that one does before exiting a bathroom, fixing their hair and clothes before straightening their posture. When they exit the fair, many return to their earlier physical state, their posture and sometimes their hope deflated. Instead of jobs, nearly all leave the fair with free tote bags filled with the usual swag: cups, pens, and pads with company logos, and goodies such as tickets to a free movie screening or coupons for discounted meals.

Prospective employers also lurk outside of fairs, soliciting applicants while avoiding the steep fees to rent a job fair table. These parking lot pitches, often literally out of trunks of cars, are all commission sales jobs. Most are in financial services—life insurance, mortgages, investments. One such recruiter, a friendly, engaging man in his 30s with an accent that suggests he is from the Caribbean, says he is looking for people to train and help pass the certification exam so they can work part-time (no benefits). His company offers the 32 hours of classes for free and pays the exam fee. "People don't realize most of the good jobs are gone," he says. "You have to work for yourself now. But they still want the jobs with the benefits." His pitch generates slightly more interest than the two middle-age men armed with bottles of creams and seeking sales associates to join the "antiaging" industry.

My own solicitations for interviews are mostly met with similar disinterest. People want paychecks, not face cream sales jobs or unpaid opportunities to bare their souls to a stranger. At a fair in South Florida, I walk quickly to an adjacent parking lot to catch two young guys before they get in their car. They are recently graduated international students, from France and Albania, respectively. They are struggling to find work both because of their international status and their lack of work experience. I apologetically explain that my focus is on American men. The young man from France says, "Even you!"—referring to them being excluded yet again due to their citizenship status. He says it jokingly, and we all share a laugh, but our conversation suggests the rejections are piling up and taking a toll. At a West Coast fair, I meet an IT worker who is returning to India the next day after living and working in the States for a decade. He says there are no more jobs here for him, citing outsourcing and free trade agreements.

There are many commonalities across the fairs I attend. The most striking pattern is the disconnect and power dynamic between the job-seekers on the one hand and the employers and job fair organizers on the other. Employers are overwhelmed with applications. Job-seekers are underwhelmed with the available positions. Recruiters are *so* excited to share amazing opportunities with motivated, enthusiastic self-starters. Job-seekers want salaries and benefits, not commission-based sales jobs. Recruiters are disproportionately young, attractive, and enthusiastic. Job-seekers are diverse, many appear haggard from extended bouts of unemployment or underemployment, and they are sometimes unable to conceal their disappointment with a fair's offerings.

Job fair literature provides advice and long lists of "Do's" and "Don'ts" for before, during, and after the event. All candidates are encouraged to shower or bathe, wear little or no perfume or cologne, bring copies of résumés, make eye contact, remember and use names, and be genuine and positive. Women are told to wear simple makeup and dress conservatively—no hemlines above the knee or sheer fabrics. Men's guidelines have no don'ts; wear a suit or a jacket and tie is all. Advice extends to how to keep a job after landing one: show up on time, do not gossip, be honest, don't clock-watch, get along with others, don't steal. *Don't steal!*

At one fair there are a handful of motivational signs scattered about on easels. They are of the widely parodied and mocked variety that litter company hallways, often further disaffecting office workers. One sign is titled "Destiny" with a two-headed arrow pointing in opposite directions beneath it, followed by the words, "a matter of choice or a matter of chance." A second reads, "Goals" and "to get started, you must have a destination." A third sign includes the formula "$E = MC^2$," where "Excellence" equals "Motivation × Confidence^2." As we are ushered down a long hotel lobby, a job fair staff member tells us, "Throw away your gum. Put your cell phones on vibrate. Smile. The littlest thing can make a big difference." The condescending advice and platitudes feel like finger-pointing. The message seems to be, "Fix what's wrong with you or you won't get a job."

But no amount of individual effort, enthusiasm, or preparation—hygienic or otherwise—can turn few options to many, or lousy options to viable ones. The ratio of job seekers to available jobs is more than four to one when I attend these fairs in late 2011 and early 2012. Employment seems more a matter of chance than choice. The unemployed are well represented by highly motivated people with clear goals in mind, but multiple years of historically high unemployment has taken its toll on many people's confidence. Individual effort is no match for structural unemployment.

The Breadwinner Ideal

The second half of this book examines men's breadwinner expectations, the manhood ideal for adult men when they eclipse adolescence and youth. Bodies become a secondary source of masculine status and identity at this stage of life. Adult men's ability to maintain control over their own and their family's financial situation is their foremost expectation. Just as American body ideals are unattainable for boys and men, so is the breadwinner ideal. The breadwinner ideal is unattainable because of how it and the contemporary U.S. economy are structured. And despite men's breadwinner status being more myth than historical fact, despite it being more elusive today than in previous decades—and less desirable for many families, especially those with women who gladly join a decades-long influx into the labor market—the man-as-breadwinner ideal persists. This means that men who are unable to fulfill it, due to unemployment or low-paying jobs, and men who choose not to fulfill it, like voluntary stay-at-home dads, often bear the consequences of failure. Like men who don't meet body ideals, they often bring those consequences to bear upon others.

The breadwinner ideal arose due to an array of structural and cultural forces. The United States' shift from an agricultural to an industrialized society, peaking in the late 1800s and early 1900s, transformed work and family life. It resulted in massive immigration to the United States and internal migration to urban areas for factory work. Political, religious, scientific, educational, and economic leaders with the most power and influence were native-born white men. They excluded and marginalized women in all of these arenas. By actively attempting to exclude women from the public sphere and confining them to the private sphere, they masculinized work, feminized the home, and created the breadwinner and homemaker ideals. By actively excluding and marginalizing immigrant men, African American men, and other citizen men of color, they denied these men access to the breadwinner ideal and ensured that immigrant women, poorer women, and women of color were more likely to have to work in the paid labor force.[1]

A post–World War II economic boom, highlighted by the GI Bill and the growth of the suburbs and auto industry, allowed many men, including blue-collar workers without college degrees, to earn a "family wage" that supported an unemployed wife and kids. The 1950s father-as-breadwinner, mother-as-homemaker model was mythologized by popular television programs such as *Leave It to Beaver* and *Father Knows Best*. But this arrangement was never the majority. American families have always been more diverse than the two-parent, nuclear version, and women have always worked for pay (at jobs and inside the home via small businesses) at rates that further debunk the separate spheres myth.[2] Beginning in the 1970s, the U.S. economy shifted again, eventually resulting in widespread deindustrialization due to globalization, international trade agreements, and advances in technology. This coincided with second-wave feminism and its challenges to gender inequality. Together they enabled and demanded a spike in women's labor force participation.

Slightly more than 1 in 3 women ages 18–64 were in the labor force in 1950. By 2011, it was up to roughly 3 out of 4, with women comprising about 47% of the workforce. More than 7 in 10 moms with kids under 18 are working due to a mix of financial and ideological reasons.[3] In terms of the men-as-breadwinner ideal, what this now means is that only 1 out of 5 American households with children under 18 have working husbands and full-time, stay-at-home wives.[4] Of married moms, 15% earn more than their husbands, up from just 4% in 1960.[5] The transition from a General Motors to a Walmart economy for the majority of Americans without college degrees means few men earn enough to sustain a middle-class existence as sole breadwinners. Still, men's breadwinner ideal persists.

My research began as men confronted another undermining structural force: the Great Recession. The recession lasted fewer than two years, from the end of 2007 to the middle of 2009. But it was deep and wide (spreading across the globe), and the recovery slow and incomplete. It did not approach the devastation of the 1930s' Great Depression, but it was much worse than all other recessions. There were precipitous declines in GDP, the stock market, home prices, and families' and organizations' net worth, and steep rises in foreclosures, bankruptcy, and personal and national debt. The U.S. unemployment rate peaked at 10% in 2009, took two more years to fall below 9%, and very slowly declined to 5.5% by the middle of 2015.[6] Many discouraged workers eventually stopped looking, the older ones waiting out the clock to collect social security benefits and, if they are lucky, retirement funds. When workers stop looking, they are no longer counted as unemployed; therefore, the actual unemployment rate has been much higher than the official one. The "long-term unemployed" are those who have been out of work and looking for a job for at least 27 weeks, or about six months. During and after the recession, single people, people of color, those with disabilities, those in poverty, and construction workers were most likely to be unemployed long term.[7] The initial heavy loss of (and later recovery of many) blue-collar jobs generated a lot of coverage of men's unemployment, but this narrative is incomplete.[8] Throughout the slow recovery, women's rates of unemployment were lower, but African American and Hispanic women's rates were still higher than the overall average. African American men's rates were much higher, peaking at more than 16% and remaining about double the overall rate several years into the recovery.[9] The recession led to an increase in less desirable part-time jobs, not to mention poverty.

American culture, and even more so, American men, still cling to the breadwinner ideal, which is now more difficult than ever to achieve. Critics of capitalism point out its key contributions to the breadwinner dilemma. Boom and bust periods, regular changing workforce demands, and the rising concentration of wealth among those at the very top exclude many workers from breadwinner status. The economy is structured in such a way as to systematically disempower large swaths of workers, but the American Ethos says failure is the result of an individual lack of effort, intelligence, and ability to compete. With no upper limit on men's earnings, even those who enjoy middle-class incomes or better may ceaselessly feel as if they are not making enough. They look around and see so many others earning so much more. Critics argue that capitalism provides the economic and political circumstances that inevitably lead most men to perceive themselves as failures.[10] Market capitalism strips most workers of their sense of autonomy, control, satisfaction, and ultimately for men, breadwinner status and identity. In turn, this causes men to feel anxiety, shame, and frustration, which makes them more susceptible to being controlled and therefore to conform to hegemonic masculine ideals.

Perhaps what's most surprising about the breadwinner ideal is how it has endured despite the near equal presence and widespread acceptance of women in the workforce. Less than one-third of Americans think men should earn more than woman partners, though those whose education level maxes out at high school are twice as likely to think so.[11] Being the *sole* breadwinner is no longer the standard, but being *a* breadwinner remains the masculine ideal. Families' need for two incomes explains in part why few men have quit their jobs to become stay-at-home dads, but more so it is the feminization, stigmatization, and devaluation of childcare that prevents most men from considering doing this kind of work. Our society values and rewards paid work and does little to support parents or childrearing. Choosing to be a stay-at-home dad is to defy social norms and relinquish economic power. Estimates of this population vary widely, numbering anywhere from fewer than 200,000 to around two million, depending on who gets counted.[12]

Feminist progress toward eliminating gender inequality at work and home is unfinished and stalled.[13] Many more men (younger men in particular) ideologically embrace shared parenting and dual careers.[14] However, there is a gap between their attitudes and practices. "Forces of change" such as men's declining breadwinner status, women's economic gains, and new fathering and relationship ideals are up against "forces of resistance" such as the persistence of the "ideal worker" ethic, increasing time demands of workplaces, and market measurement of "marriageable" (breadwinning) men. These institutional contradictions produce stressed-out dual-earner couples and cause many men to remain single longer or adopt a neotraditional model that still prioritizes their paid work. The persistence of the gendered wage gap is due to occupational segregation, women's continued childrearing responsibilities, the lack of state programs (childcare, paid family leave, etc.) to offset this unequal responsibility, and the devaluation of women's paid and unpaid work, which deters men from pursuing these options. If only half the population alters their work-family commitments, and no policy changes facilitate it, the gender revolution will remain incomplete.

Significant changes have occurred, but not revolutionary ones. A recent Pew Research Center Study captured the changes in parental behaviors and attitudes. Among all parents with kids living at home in 1965, mothers did 8 hours of paid work, 32 hours of housework, and 10 hours of childcare per week.[15] Fathers did 42 hours of paid work, 4 hours of housework, and 2.5 hours of childcare per week. In 2015, moms' paid work increased to 25 hours, their housework declined to 18, and their childcare increased to 15. For dads, after a dip in paid work hours during the recession, they returned to 43 hours per week, and their time spent on housework and childcare increased to 9 and 7 hours, respectively.[16] Looking just at dual-earner couples, the numbers converge some and are much more equal than typical arrangements from decades ago, but a big gap remains. Parents are spending more time with kids, and fathers have nearly tripled the meager hours they spent 50 years ago.

Still, moms are spending about twice as much time as dads are with kids. Dual-income households divide labor more equally than ones where only one parent works, with total hours nearly identical. Breadwinning fathers' workloads are about 11 hours more than their non-working partners'. When moms serve as sole breadwinners, they put in 25 more hours of work per week. The disparity in housework and childcare between stay-at-home moms and stay-at-home dads is even more unequal. The former do 46 hours per week, three times as much as their breadwinning partners, while the latter do merely 6 more hours per week than women breadwinners. In terms of attitudes, both mothers and fathers are most likely to say young children are best served by a mother who works part-time (instead of full-time or not at all). Dueling work and family responsibilities are very or somewhat difficult to balance according to a majority of both working mothers and fathers.

Given the institutional contradictions that have only partially transformed gendered work-family arrangements and the unique impact of the Great Recession, I set out to study non-breadwinning men, both those who are able to choose to leave the paid labor force and those forced out. I focus on how these men and their families are affected by men's loss of breadwinner status and identity. Specifically, I seek to identify what conditions lead unemployed men and stay-at-home dads to either internalize and compensate for their loss of breadwinner status or reject this hegemonic ideal and redefine what it means to be a man.

The Non-breadwinners

I attended five job fairs, conducted 25 in-depth interviews with unemployed men and stay-at-home fathers, and gathered and analyzed data from dozens of online forums and diaries dedicated to unemployment and stay-at-home dads. The five job fairs I attended were held in Michigan (Dearborn and Detroit), Florida (Fort Lauderdale), and California (East Bay San Francisco and Sacramento).[17] My interview participants are diverse in numerous ways: how and why they became non-breadwinners, their length of unemployment, what kind of work they used to do and hope to do again, their marital status and number of dependents, where they live, and their age, social class, education, sexuality and, somewhat less so, race and ethnicity. Several are veterans. Two of the men were recently released from incarceration. My sample is similar to the population of stay-at-home dads in that they are older than other fathers and more likely to be white. My participants are more likely to have a college degree, which is less common among the population of stay-at-home dads. In two-parent, different-sex families, stay-at-home dads are rare. Only about 6% of fathers in these situations stay at home, compared to about 30% of similarly situated mothers.[18]

I made contact with prospective interview participants individually at job fairs, online (via unemployment and stay-at-home dad diaries, forums, and groups), and in a couple of cases, via personal contacts. Twelve of the non-breadwinning men are partnered stay-at-home dads by choice: Jamie, Don, Henry, Justin, Matthew, Mika, Nick, Peter, Ryan, Rob, Tim, and Zach. Their partners earn enough to allow these men to do unpaid work. Reflecting broader patterns of privilege and inequality, these men and their partners are mostly white, older, and highly formally educated. The other thirteen men unwillingly became non-breadwinners, losing their jobs right before, during, or in the wake of the recession. Anthony, Liam, and Marcus became stay-at-home dads to young children after losing their jobs, with their respective families relying on their wives' incomes. Four other unemployed men—Frank, Jonathan, T. J., Tyler—are either married with older kids who do not require much or any day-to-day care or are divorced, not living with their children, and only partially responsible for financial support. Phil is married with no children. Caleb, DeShawn, Dwayne, Jerry, and Jordan are all single with no children. These 25 non-breadwinners are situated differently based on their individual experiences, employment and family situations, and demographic characteristics. What influences their responses to being non-breadwinners and how they respond to their situations vary accordingly.

Expectations, Finances, Control, and Support

As with men who are unable or unwilling to fulfill body ideals, men who do not fulfill the breadwinner ideal respond in different ways. They internalize their socially unacceptable status, try to restore it via repair or compensation, or, in an increasing number of cases, reject the breadwinner standard and redefine what it means to be a man. The men I interview became non-breadwinners for a variety of personal, situational, and structural reasons. The four most important influences that affect how they respond to being non-breadwinners are their own and their partners' breadwinner expectations for them; their financial situation; their sense of control over their situation; and the support of their family and friends.

Breadwinner Expectations

Most of the unemployed men I interview are falling short of their own or their partner's work expectations. Conversely, most stay-at-home dads and their breadwinning partners like their arrangement. A man responds worst to being a non-breadwinner when *both* he and his partner are disappointed that

154 • The Breadwinner Dilemma

he is not the major income earner. Next worst is when *either* is disappointed in his job status. When neither partner is bothered by his unemployment or both prefer that he is the primary caretaker, negative feelings and reactions are significantly lessened. Rarely, though, are they entirely eliminated. Deviating from men's breadwinner ideal is challenging even for those couples who consciously reject it.

Frank is a white, 44-year-old former breadwinner who was laid off from his technology sector job two years before we speak, when U.S. unemployment peaked. His wife does not earn enough to support their middle-class life, in part because he had always earned more and they both expected him to do so. Frank does not blame himself for losing his job (his company downsized) or being unable to find one during the recession. Still, he says, "I consider this a temporary setback, so I would not want to change my definition of man as breadwinner." Two-plus years into his unemployment, he and his wife still view it as temporary. They were one of only a few different-sex couples I studied where both partners thought the husband should be the primary breadwinner.

Dwayne is a single African American man in his early 30s who has been inconsistently employed for many years. Despite what he identifies as a series of devastating economic recessions in his hometown of New York City, he says he feels responsible: "It's a man's job to find work and take care of myself." He stays up nights wondering why he can't find and keep a job. He feels additionally burdened to challenge negative racial portrayals and stereotypes. He says his childhood was filled with media images of black men as wealthy drug dealers, with expensive cars, gold chains, and beepers, which (other than the violence) attracted his peers. He committed himself to avoiding that trap and trying to share positive stories that he feels have been largely ignored—"the hardworking men and women who no one in America pays attention to. I feel these brothers and sisters are the real heroes of the community."

DeShawn, now in his 40s, experienced the consequences of violence firsthand when he was young. His father was murdered when DeShawn was in elementary school: "He always told me, 'If I'm not around, you're the man of the house.' And then [after my father was killed] my mother told me that—'You're the man of the house.' So that made me step up. But that's bad information, that you're the man of the house, because it puts responsibility on [a child's] shoulder; that puts a psychological responsibility in his mind, that he wants to live up to that and perform according to that standard. Because I was doing stuff [as a kid] I had no business doing." He resorted to crime to earn money and ended up incarcerated for most of his 20s and 30s. He still embraces the men-as-breadwinner model, in part because he remains single, but now has a career doing antiviolence work.

Disappointed spouses and partners heavily influence how men experience not being breadwinners. Jonathan, a white 50-year-old who has bounced around during many years of underemployment, and now unemployment, feels that burden. His wife always out-earned him but never desired to be the breadwinner. She always wanted him to earn enough so she could work part-time. "Each day, week, and month that goes by only adds to the disappointment," he says.

Zach, a white father of three in his mid-30s, chose to quit his career in social services to raise kids. His wife, Stacey, has always earned about double his income, so he was the obvious choice when they agreed that one of them should stay home. However, she would prefer to be the one to do so. She does what's best for the family, but he says, "She would quit her job tomorrow" if he could earn her salary. Stacey having to go to work while Zach spends time with the kids creates "a little resentment." His employment history and lifelong interest in fathering somewhat cushions her disappointment. He found his paid job rewarding, but other than the "gut check" of giving up a paycheck, his transition was easy. He always dreamed of a family above all. Zach feels he is "different than most men," that he was made to be a stay-at-home dad.

Most partners did not place sole or primary breadwinner expectations on the men I interview, and thus these partners did not feel let down when they became the sole provider. A few men still experience their unemployment as a failure despite their partner's support. Liam was forced into being a stay-at-home dad when he lost his financial services company. His wife's six-figure income provided for their family, and she was looking forward to Liam relieving her of the second shift of housework and childcare she had been largely shouldering when they both worked full-time. He says he was never hung up on the fact that she was earning more, but "I still felt that I wasn't quite living up to my role as a man, as the husband, as the father, to bring home something. I didn't really care if it was less than what my wife was making, but I wanted to contribute."

Mika, a 49-year-old father of Samoan descent, retired from the military in part to allow his new wife a chance to get her career started while he raised their baby. He thought the transition would be easy. It was not. He went from "having a position of responsibility and respect and, you know, ego building—you can add that in—" to staying home and putting all his focus and energies into caring for a baby: "I really didn't realize what I was getting into. I thought, 'Oh, this would be cool.'" Soon after, though, he had second thoughts: "I was still wanting to work and do something and feel needed," which he did not initially get from childrearing. Mika took great pride in his military work, and he was not quite ready to give up his career. After a year of being a stay-at-home parent, he returned to Iraq, working as a private contractor in a combat zone (which he described as "easier" than being a stay-at-home dad, given his extensive military training and experience, along with the shock of initially adjusting to being a primary caretaker). His wife supported his decision to retire and stay at home, as well as his decision to return to Iraq, and lastly, his return to being the at-home parent again.

About one-third of the men I interview are stay-at-home dads either because the couples wanted him in that role or they wanted one or the other to stay home. Importantly, they had the resources enough that losing his income didn't create financial distress. Peter is 48 and a stay-at-home dad for three former foster children whom he and his wife adopted. His wife, Regina, is an incredibly supportive partner who was recruited to run a hospital in the rural South. Peter lost his professional network when they left the West Coast, but he quickly found work after their move. Eventually, though, he found that his part-time career interfered with childcare, which led him to quit and stay home full-time. Regina laughed when he told her he quit his job. He, too, laughs as he shares the conversation with me:

> She goes, "I told you, you didn't have to [work]." And then she was like, "You know, I understand that you want to have a job and say you're contributing, but you being at home is what we need you to do to contribute to the family, not bringing in income." It was nice to hear your wife say "Hey, don't worry." But in the back of your head, you're thinking . . . and I've told her this, I said, "I know I hear you saying it. I see you. I see the words coming out of your mouth. I don't necessarily believe that you feel that way." And I've told her, I say, "I'm worried that you're going to come home one day and be like 'You lazy schmuck. Why aren't you working?'"

Peter and his wife have a strong marriage, and he is a proud and deeply fulfilled stay-at-home father. But he still can't quite silence the voice inside his head that questions whether he should be doing what he and his wife have explicitly agreed is best for them. Peter blames the generation and culture he grew up in for equating manhood with paid work. He actively resists this expectation while contending with its residue.

Many stay-at-home dads overcome these pressures. With their partners' support, they find ways to escape or accept leaving the paid labor force. Ryan, an early 30s white father of two, was laid off soon before he planned to quit working to take care of his kids. He beams: "I love [being a stay-at-home dad]. It's the job that I always wanted." He and his partner have made financial sacrifices, but they prefer that over using day care. They both wanted one parent at home, and both have been the working parent and the at-home parent.

Tim, white and a self-described feminist in his 30s, is married to a woman who usually earned more than him while he was working. He says, "I was never opposed to being a stay-at-home dad. I do whatever I have to do to help contribute. I didn't have that kind of 'I'm not a real man if I don't have a job' [attitude]. I honestly felt and feel that whoever stays home and whoever works, they're both a crucial part of the family, equally important, and both necessary." When he lost his job before his first child was born, "it was pretty much a no-brainer" that he would stay home, given his wife's high-income job. Other couples repeatedly made what they saw as the same pragmatic decision that so many couples do: the higher earner remains in the labor force and the lower earner, especially if much of that person's income will go to childcare, stays home. Setting aside gendered expectations and preferences for different-sex couples, the wage gap between women and men makes it more likely that *she* will stay home. Structural gender inequality plays out in the lives of individual families.

Phil and his wife, Cindy, are considering having kids, but for now, he is simply one more among the millions of long-term unemployed. They fled the harsh winters of northern Wisconsin for warmer weather, giving up two six-figure positions. Cindy quickly found a great job after their move, but Phil's unluckily timed break got engulfed by the recession. Cindy is open to any family arrangement and appreciates that Phil does all the work around the house. Phil is open to being a stay-at-home parent and is enjoying gardening and volunteering while trying to network and land a new job. He always expected that Cindy would earn more and embraced it. "I don't subscribe to the 'I'm the provider. I'm the big macho Neanderthal man. You, woman,'" he says. Phil thinks Cindy is smarter and always knew she would earn triple his income. He says he "couldn't give a shit" about men's stereotypical physical or financial expectations. Cindy's progressive ideology reduces pressure on Phil during his long-term unemployment. He's been out of work three years, much longer than the shocking peak national average of 40 weeks in 2011.[19]

Financial Situation

The unwillingly unemployed men I interview had to do what many singles and families do when an income is lost: accrue credit card and other debt, borrow money from friends and family, withdraw money from retirement funds, not pay all their bills on time, declare bankruptcy, skip doctor's visits and other basic health care, and more.

With only their own income to rely on, the single men I interview are generally the most financially insecure. None of them is a single parent and only one has a child for whom he is partially financially responsible. This contrasts sharply with many single women's experiences. One key reason women are overrepresented among those in poverty (i.e., the "feminization of poverty") is their much greater likelihood of being single parents.[20] Single mothers experience poverty because of little or no economic support from the children's fathers, a social safety net that alleviates far less poverty than comparable nations, occupational gender segregation, a gendered wage gap, and a general devaluation of women's work.[21] The 2012 poverty rate for families led by single mothers in the United States was 31%, nearly double that of single-father families.[22] In developing nations, girls' and women's denial of access to education, credit, inheritance, and more generally, social and political power further explains their comparatively worse circumstances. I did not have the opportunity to speak with families where no adults are employed, who deal with homeless or food insecurity or face dire poverty.

Jerry, T. J., and Dwayne are three single unemployed men severely constrained by their lack of income. Jerry was working part-time and caring for his dying mother before he moved to Nevada to find full-time work. He utilized the services of a homeless shelter for veterans before moving into a transitional housing facility. He says he should have earned a military pension but was kicked out for being gay well before the "Don't Ask, Don't Tell" policy. Despite being in his late 50s and having an inconsistent recent work history, he is optimistic that he will find enough work to meet his minimal needs. Meanwhile, he is buffered by local veterans' programs. T. J. is a divorced father of a high school graduate, white and in his late 40s, and has been unemployed for two years after a long period bouncing between the military, civilian jobs, and joblessness. He served for more than a decade but finds that civilian employers do not think those experiences translate. This is especially true for young returning veterans, ages 20–24, whom employers may stereotype as having PTSD symptoms and nontransferable skills such as being a sniper; their unemployment rate peaked at nearly one out of three, or double their same-aged nonmilitary peers.[23] T. J. says he would be homeless if not for help from his siblings over the years. He describes his situation as "still critical" even on his pension. He has to budget enough gas money to visit his adult son and attend community college classes. His child support responsibilities will end soon, but he will need that money to attend classes full-time. "I'd feel terrible if my son was living with me," he says. "I wouldn't be able to provide him with the things he needs. That really troubles me. I'm supposed to be able to support my family. I'm grateful my ex-wife and her husband are working."

Dwayne's years of unemployment and low-income jobs makes his situation tenuous. Family help out when they can, and because of them, he's unlikely to face homelessness, but money is extremely tight. He has tracked his spending to the penny at times: "On some occasions I had to make painful decisions like choosing between snacks and soap . . . I don't want to go back to being that way again. It's like living in a box. Everywhere I went, I ran into a wall." Even the job search process is a financial gamble, as he invests the little money he has in the resources needed to find work. It's a catch-22: "To look for a job, you need to have money. The bills are still coming in. Paper and toner for résumés, dry cleaning, and bus fare don't come cheap. Neither does information. And when you don't have money, you can't get to those job leads or the interview.

Unemployment is a race against the clock, trying to do as much as you can before your money runs out."

Some of the married unemployed men face serious short- and long-term financial challenges, if not the dollar-to-dollar constraints of T. J. and Dwayne. Frank's family had to declare bankruptcy to keep their home and they have depleted much of their retirement savings. Occasional financial support from parents ensures they do not suffer more serious consequences.

Marcus is an involuntarily unemployed stay-at-home father of one with a second child on the way. He is African American, in his early 30s, and despite his family's fiscal uncertainty, ebullient about the forthcoming birth of his second child. He lost several customer service jobs during recession cutbacks, but his wife earns enough to keep the family afloat. He picks up odd jobs here and there, while his mom watches his child, to cover grocery costs. Marcus remains resilient and mostly positive while still anxious about his situation: "I'm happy to be a father right now, but it's difficult knowing that you have another child on the way and trying to figure out, man, how am I going to provide for them? I'm going to need more room. I'm going to need—there's the pampers, the milk, you know—everything necessary to raise a child. I worry and I wonder, what am I going to do?" He is hopeful about finding work but scared it won't happen before the birth. Meanwhile, Marcus says he is "trying my damnedest not to spend money."

About half of the non-breadwinning men I interview are financially stable, usually thanks to their partner's income. Phil says he has "a lot of stress" from four years of lost salary, but Cindy's substantial income leaves them secure. Most of the men who are stay-at-home dads by choice made that decision with their partner because of their financial stability. Matthew, a mid-30s white father of one child, says he quit his career to stay home because his partner, David, earns more than twice as much as Matthew did—enough to sustain a comfortable existence in an expensive big city. Financial stability goes a long way toward alleviating non-breadwinning men's concerns about not fulfilling that ideal.

Sense of Control

Men's sense of control also influences their non-breadwinning experience. It is affected by whether they arrive there voluntarily, how it impacts their relationships, if they attribute job loss to personal or external reasons, and their emotions and sense of self and identity. Less control causes more problems.

Most unemployed men want to find jobs. Conversely, most of the stay-at-home dads do not. Anthony is one of the exceptions. He is an early 50s, unwillingly unemployed, white stay-at-home father of one tween daughter. He has been employed on and off for much of his adult life but has not held a full-time job for three years. "Even before the recession, I had a difficult time getting work," he says, blaming himself for his unemployment. "I don't think it's too much the recession. I think it's me." Anthony appreciates how staying at home positively affects his relationship with his daughter, and he enjoys cooking her meals and picking her up from school. However, he does not enjoy housework or other mundane childcare tasks. "You know, I love being a dad, but I would have no issue being the sole provider," he says. "It would do my ego a lot to make a decent living and to be coming and going." Anthony worries his unemployment is placing his marriage at risk, which reinforces his feeling of powerlessness. He says, "[My wife] does have an alpha personality. She really does, and I don't think I do. But I'm trying to change that only because it's going to give me a feeling of more control, you know. A feeling of more control, to be more involved with the family finances. And since I did get a rather nice inheritance . . . that's giving me a feeling that I'm, you know, in control of my finances. She has her finances with a job, and she has a lot of money put away. So I'm trying to get some control back."

Tyler, a 26-year-old white divorced father of two, is living in a halfway house after being released from prison. He has literally lost control over most aspects of his life since his incarceration. Several years ago, Tyler was living his dream. He was a rising star as a sales associate at a midsize tech company. He got married, had kids, and despite his lack of a college degree, he earned enough to buy a home in the suburbs. His wife was able to stay at home to raise their kids, which is what they both desired: "I felt great, because I felt I was unstoppable. Because my dad always instilled in me that you need to make six figures to be able to live a life, to be able to live not paycheck to paycheck. So because that was embedded in my mind at a young age, I had it in me that I had to make six figures." He worked hard and arrived at his goal. Tyler's life changed in an instant when he was hit by a car while crossing the street on his lunch break. His surgeries and degenerating condition led to a pain pill addiction, and because of his dependence, he illegally obtained prescriptions from multiple doctors. The judge gave him a harsh sentence. Tyler's life began to unravel as he headed to a county jail and then a state prison. Once there, he kicked his addiction and was a model inmate before completing rehab and moving into the halfway house.

Tyler now has little control over his financial situation or much else in his life. He faces numerous obstacles: a criminal record, a state-mandated requirement that employers report on his work status, mandatory counseling meetings, time-restricted leaves from the halfway house, confinement to public transportation, and limited cell phone minutes to manage his job search and personal life. "People lose their jobs like crazy because of the way this [halfway house is] ran," he says. The recession compounds his obstacles to employment. He has a large gap in his résumé, making him part of the less desirable long-term unemployed. And his earlier successful career makes him over-qualified for most of the positions available to people with a criminal record. Employers assume he will quickly leave for better opportunities. He is in a second catch-22: If he earns too much he loses his welfare and has to pay insurance to cover his treatment. He hopes to land a job, save money, and move into his own place, but feels hogtied: "[The] way this facility is ran . . . [all the restrictions] make you only reach for Toys R Us jobs, because you really couldn't have a full-time regular job here [because of outpatient drug and alcohol counseling requirements]. So it ain't like you can carry a nine-to-five job Monday through Friday." Tyler lost his career, marriage, independence, and freedom. In transition, he's struggling to restore all four and return to fulfilling his own and his family's breadwinner expectations.

The long-term unemployed who have been out of the labor market for more than a year are the slowest to reenter it. They represented nearly one-third of all unemployed workers during peak unemployment, and older (55-plus) long-term unemployed workers had the highest rates.[24] Frank's long-term unemployment and mounting financial troubles have affected him and his marriage. At his nadir, he says, "The rejections were really, really piling up, I mean the loss of control was like, 'I can't land a full-time job; bills are going to be difficult to pay.' So frustration kicked in, not depression right away but almost a sense of losing control and trying to protect my wife from the ugliness as far as you know the 'Did you look today?' 'Yes I did.' 'Did you get anything?' 'No, no, no I didn't.' And so that started to become a daily routine." Bankruptcy and the tight job market forced him to make compromises. He abandoned hope of restoring his career and simply sought whatever job he could find to alleviate his family's financial crunch. It was just "job searching," not a search for work he would find fulfilling or enjoyable. Any full-time gig would do. Frank does not feel personally responsible for his initial unemployment; he mostly views the recession as the source of his ongoing troubles. Still, his family's material reality and his scramble to find a paycheck have left him feeling as if he has little agency.

Marcus stays grounded during his bout with unemployment because of his wife's job and support and his love for his child. He says those things, along with prayer, help him stay positive in the face of the recession. He follows his mother's advice: "You can't control the world, but if you control the things that you're able to control, everything can work out for itself." He enthusiastically attends every job fair he can, constantly checks and applies for jobs, keeps his résumé up to date, and prepares himself for when an opportunity presents itself. He also has taken the extra time he has to lose weight and improve his health, which reduces his stress. "And that helps," he says, "But at the same time, I mean, when it boils down to it, you still want to be a breadwinner for your family, you still want to be the person your wife looks to and can count on, you know, saying, 'Hey, no matter what, I know my husband has my back,' and you know, telling her to calm down, and you know, 'We'll be OK.'" But he doesn't really know if that's true. Marcus is used to being self-reliant, a rock for himself and his family. Structural unemployment has him questioning himself as well as the concept of the American dream:

> All this is happening in the middle of the recession. And that's what makes it hard, you know, makes it difficult. I think everybody should have an opportunity. I mean, the American dream, it's not there anymore. I was raised [with this idea] from my parents [that] if you work hard and you save your money, you'll be able to get a home. You'll be able to take care of your kids, and you know, it's not that anymore. It's not that. That's not even . . . It's not anywhere close to that anymore.

Marcus gets frustrated when people assume he isn't working because he doesn't want to. "Take any job! Do anything!" doesn't account for being overqualified, as he has experienced.

Jerry also contemplates his situation in the context of the American economy and work-related values. He says there is "some mobility still" despite the country's problems. Staying optimistic eases his psychological burden. He admits, "It's easier said than done," but believes his difficult situation is temporary. "I'm doing what's necessary because of my own values of hard work, self-respect, and never giving up," he says. He's still angry about getting kicked out of the military for being gay and losing his pension; being discriminated against by his own country is "a factor that can't be ignored" in his having to utilize a homeless shelter. He was depending on that income: "It was just taken away, so it's like, all of a sudden, you're put in a different class; you're marginalized to a different class." His recent transition into his own subsidized apartment has him feeling not only upbeat but more autonomous "because I can control my environment a little more . . . If you can't control your environment, like in the shelter, there's always a sense of anxiety in the background."

Voluntary stay-at-home dads enjoy a much greater sense of control over their lives. Jamie, white and in his mid-30s, took some time to settle into his new role after stepping away from his career and adopting a child with his partner: "To go from being a working professional and just kind of feeling very comfortable in your job, and you know, kind of pushing things through, and you know, you get a phone call and you just deal with it, to . . . a defiant little child who doesn't want to do what you say—I mean, it's stressful." He still finds ways to challenge himself beyond being a parent and has found parenting much more manageable as his son ages. Stay-at-home dad Zach says that with three kids, "you're constantly being tested. There's always something going on. Somebody's fighting, something's happening, something's been spilling or getting damaged." His ability to calmly deal with the unexpected while still managing the household is what provides him with a sense of control. Zach says he "pretty much [does] everything." His wife "works and supports us and spends time with the kids. That's that. Everything else is me": bills, budgeting, cooking, cleaning, all work inside and outside of the house. Matthew says his husband's breadwinner status does not cause any gendered angst or sense of loss of control. His straight friends, though, have had a harder time giving up their careers: "I think it's a little different in my situation, because (a) it's a choice, [and] (b) it's a little different where I have some male friends that are stay-at-home dads who feel kind of weird about it 'cause their wives are the breadwinner and making more money."

Manhood is largely contingent on men's ability to control themselves, others, and their environment. For adult men, controlling their ability to provide for themselves and their families is the foremost measure of manhood. Losing that sense of control threatens their sense of self and identity, inviting an array of personal and social problems. Yet many stay-at-home dads interpret their nonfinancial contributions to their family as equivalent to their partner's breadwinning. They find a sense of control in being primary caretakers and home managers, and in other aspects of their lives.

Social Support

The social support unemployed men and stay-at-home dads receive also affects how they respond to being non-breadwinners. Partners first and foremost, and family, friends, and online and in-person support groups all matter. Unemployment and stay-at-home parenting can be particularly isolating. Men may be more susceptible to this isolation and all its consequences given their smaller friendship networks, the greater impact unemployment tends to have on their sense of self and identity, and for stay-at-home dads, the fewer peers they have and minimal socializing they do with stay-at-home moms. Being able to connect with others online and in person via online meet-up groups has expanded opportunities for unemployed people and stay-at-home parents to find extrafamilial support.

Several men worry about their marriages because of their long-term unemployment. Jonathan's extended non-breadwinning has endangered his relationship. He believes his wife, Suzy, is resentful of their financial situation, which undermines her support for Jonathan. His declining and now lack of contributions has culminated in her regularly commenting, "We're using my pay" or "my cash" for purchases. Instead of having free spending money or planning vacations to escape from and forget about work, her entire check goes to paying their bills, exacerbating her disappointment: "Perhaps the biggest casualty may be the fact that she has said she isn't sure if she is 'in love' with me, though she knows she loves me. The sooner I find work, the sooner I can begin to repair this part of our marriage." He says Suzy feels entitled to cutting back to part-time work, "having supported me all these years." Jonathan would like that but more realistically wants to land any paying job to stop the bleeding. Their multiyear ordeal has undermined their communication. Jonathan inquires about Suzy's day so that he "gets a taste of adult interaction," but they agreed not to discuss his unless he has good news.

Frank's involuntary unemployment has disappointed himself and his wife, caused them to declare bankruptcy, and left him feeling out of control. His joblessness, he says, "opened up a lot of frustration and resentment on her part for having to work full-time." Frank gained weight and began snoring loudly at night, interrupting his wife's sleep. She became angry and resentful, he says, "so the window of opportunity to have quiet, peaceful moments together was dwindling pretty rapidly at that point." Her anger was revealed at a friend's barbeque where "the drinks were really starting to flow" and "she was just saying a lot of hurtful, hateful things" about him. Frank has a source of support and escape in his elementary school–age daughter, who is shielded from much of her parents' problems. His parents also support him, both financially once in a while and emotionally during his troubles. Eventually, Frank channeled his frustrations into a blog that painstakingly documents his unemployment experiences. The blog was well received and led to a part-time writing position. It isn't generating much income, but his wife proudly shares his deeply personal and revealing published work with everyone she knows.

Anthony ponders whether his unemployment may lead to a divorce: "I don't know how much respect my wife has for me, I've got to be honest with you. I think she really feels [like] more of a caretaker with me than anything else. The sex life isn't there." His stress level has been reduced by his improved relationship with his daughter while being a stay-at-home dad and the inheritance he has to cushion him. And even though his marriage is not strong, Anthony says his wife has been "supportive and understanding" during his unemployment. "I'd have to say she's been very supportive," he says. "You know, she never laid any guilt upon me for the most part. Maybe one or two things were said here or there, but, really, you know, nothing out of the ordinary." He also attends local unemployment support meetings and is active in online forums, which provide him with "comfort" and help.

Henry is in the middle of a bitter divorce. He is white, in his late 40s, and a stay-at-home dad of one high schooler and one middle schooler. He quit his job when his older daughter was born because his wife's career was taking off and she had to move the family several times to follow promotions. Henry and his wife decided she earned enough and they wanted someone to be home with the kids, so he gladly accepted the responsibility. He says they were happy and all was well until their most recent move led his wife to work and spend time with wealthier "right-wing ex-military types" who take fancy vacations. Her mentality shifted from "it's our money" to "it['s] her money and she makes all the decisions, and all of a sudden money became an issue." He adds, "I guess the best way to describe it, she went from Mountain Girl, which would be like Jerry Garcia's wife, to Sarah Palin in about three years." He attributes some of this to their deteriorating relationship, but he still feels blindsided by her new attitude after years of being a stay-at-home dad:

> She seems to think that all her success is just because of her. All of a sudden, she's throwing that up in my face like, you know, "Be a real man." You know, she's throwing all this masculinity stuff in my face all of a sudden, "Oh, be a real man and go get a job," and, "I can't believe you've lived off your wife and you haven't done anything for 15 years." I think it's not even the access to the money that disturbs me. It's her unwillingness to acknowledge that, you know, I've sacrificed, too, and that . . . she would have never got this career if I wasn't home watching [our kids] all the time when they were sick, taking them to school, taking care of the house, taking care of the dogs, taking care of her [live-in] mother. It's like all of a sudden, everything I did doesn't matter, you know.

Henry has lost his partner's support, which he finds ironic and disturbing given their long-standing family arrangement. Now, with no paid work experience for years and a body that will no longer allow him to do the blue-collar work he did in his 20s, he must begin anew. He is fortunate to have strong financial and emotional support from his large family and friends. Henry is proud of the children he has raised and no longer looks to his soon-to-be ex-wife for support.

The single unemployed men I interview are mostly younger, in their 20s and 30s, and somewhat dependent on their families financially. They seem to rely more on their peers for social support. The recession's toll on youth unemployment means they all have friends who are underemployed or unemployed. In 2012, half of new college graduates were either underemployed (e.g., baristas and restaurant workers) or unemployed, not to mention drowning in more student debt than previous generations.[25] Parents and family often criticize younger people, not recognizing the unique circumstances this generation faces: high unemployment and fewer entry-level positions that provide opportunities for advancement, heavy school debt, lack of affordable housing.

Jordan, a white, 25-year-old recent graduate living with his parents, says his four-year degree has left him with nothing but debt. His parents wondered why he was pursuing unpaid internships instead of jobs, but he found even entry-level jobs require more work experience than he has: "To them getting a job is easy and I was simply being either lazy or holding out for the dream job." Overall, though, he is appreciative of his parents' support. They are paying down his debt, helping him pursue a physical therapy degree, and they have become more empathetic after his father briefly had to contend with the job market. Jordan relies on his friends, who "are sympathetic because many of them are living the same employment struggle as I am."

Tyler, fresh out of incarceration and living in the halfway house, says his parents have been supportive. They gave him money when he needed it in jail and help him now that he's out. But they remind him "pretty much every time" he talks to them that he screwed up and threw it all away: "That makes me feel like crap, [but then] they'll send me money." He also remains close with his ex-wife's family. Tyler has his young children and clings to the hope of restoring his marriage. Meanwhile, he relies on others' social support during his financially and emotionally difficult transition back into society and the workforce.

With the exception of Henry, whose wife has changed her mind about their breadwinner-caretaker arrangement, all the voluntary stay-at-home dads enjoy strong support from their partners and often their friends and close family as well. Nick, a white father of two young boys in his 30s, quit his middle school teaching job to raise his kids because his wife's law practice allows him to stay at home. Nick's wife has "always been good about saying 'we' or 'our,' as far as paychecks and money go," he says, and he actually pays the bills, which helps him deal with not earning his own paycheck. His parents and in-laws appreciate what he does. He says his friends are supportive, some even "jealous" but mostly out of ignorance, thinking "the grass is always greener on the other side." Nick says he occasionally calls on "some old buddies [who have kids] and I'll cry on their shoulders over the phone about some of the [difficulties of at-home parenting]. And they're pretty understanding, saying 'Yeah my wife went through a lot of that stuff, too,'" which makes him feel better.

When Peter finally quit his part-time job after his wife's career took them to a new state, he relied on her emotional support to navigate the transition. Regina, he believes, was trying to ease his fears of losing what was essentially his life: "I don't know how else to say it, but that was my life. That's who Peter was . . . [it's] what defines me." He gave up his career for her even better one. She in turn appreciates his sacrifice and raising of their children. Peter says his marriage is even stronger than before, although he suspects his insecurities can be tiresome.

Rob is taking a break from his highly specialized and well-compensated engineering work. He left a multinational corporation to join a fledgling start-up but "it went belly up." He and his wife decided Rob should raise their sons until they are school age before Rob returns to his career. He says everyone in his family is supportive, that their attitude is, "Hey, if you can't [work right now then], this is your next job; taking care of your family is job number one." He says even his "kind of old-school" 74-year-old father is supportive. Even though the area he lives in outside of D.C. has a culture where "men are always the breadwinners and the women always stay at home and have babies and all this other crap," he has found a large, active stay-at-home dads' group that has also been essential for his transition: "The support from that type of group really helped and kind of got my head refocused on what's important and what's not that important. Up to that time I was thinking, 'Oh, we've got to [earn] this much money, we've got to pay for this and all that,' and then after talking to [another stay-at-home dad] and thinking about it, I'm going like, 'You know, having my wife and kids [be] happy even if I'm not making money is fine; if we're OK financially then why not?' Basically the support from the group is what really, really helped."

Marcus's unplanned unemployment and turn as a stay-at-home dad is made easier by his wife, Angela: "The strength of my wife—she's my strongest supporter, so I have no regrets or qualms about that. Without my wife, I don't know how I'd make it sometimes." Marcus has shared his feelings of vulnerability with her as he struggles with unemployment. He says,

> Sometimes you have to show no weakness outside of your own door. But when you're inside your own door, you have to show actually some weakness, because you're an individual. Especially if you're married. I mean, you can't be tough all the time. You can't always be tough. You can't always have that same rocky exterior. Sometimes you have to show that you're soft as marshmallows on the inside. And it helps you. I mean, for a long . . . For a period of time, I bottled stuff up. And I learned to let it go now. I learned you can't keep it all in.

Angela has become the breadwinner, Marcus the primary caretaker, and they support each other as they prepare to welcome a second child into their family and Marcus tries to find work.

With a flourishing career, Cindy doesn't expect Phil to be the breadwinner, and he in turn does everything he can around the house so she is relieved of that work. "The traditional breadwinner, that was my role, and now it's 100% reversed," he says. "You know, she's been incredibly gracious in this whole thing. She understands. She's always trying to reinforce me because she said, 'Look, I work with people every day that are idiots.' She's like, 'I don't know how they have jobs and you don't.'" Phil describes his wife as his "rock" and wonders how single unemployed men endure the experience alone. He also regularly meets up with several other unemployed men to get out of the house, socialize, complain, and commiserate. There is a networking aspect to the group, but that's not its primary purpose. Phil says they go to a bar, have some food and a beer and speak their minds: "There's no airs that are put on. You know, you want to sit and cuss and say, 'I'm so fucking pissed off I can't believe what's happening,' go ahead. That's great, that's why we're there."

Outside of the group, Phil says, unemployment just isn't discussed. People find it depressing. The topic is hidden. "You know, it's almost the third rail of polite discussion," he says. "One is religion, two is politics and three is unemployment." For Phil and other non-breadwinners, the support of partners, family, friends, and online and in-person groups provides them with social and emotional connections that reduce the effects of their failing to live up to adult men's foremost ideal. Without such support, these men are more susceptible to enduring personal problems and contributing to social problems.

6

Unemployment Blues and Backlash

> In addition to sheer economic anxiety the [unemployed] man suffers from deep humiliation. He experiences a sense of deep frustration because in his own estimation he fails to fulfill what is the central duty of his life, the very touchstone of his manhood—the role of family provider. The man appears bewildered and humiliated. It is as if the ground had gone out from under his feet.
> —sociologist Mirra Komarovsky on unemployed men during the Great Depression[1]

By the summer of 2015, the U.S. unemployment rate finally appeared to be heading below 5%, back to prerecession levels. Recession and joblessness stories receded from the nation's news coverage. New narratives about income inequality and outsourcing captured headlines, prodded both by a decidedly mixed economic recovery and presidential campaign rhetoric. The unemployed, still disproportionately African American and Latinx, younger, and with lower levels of educational attainment, continued to suffer the psychological and social effects of joblessness. Those around them suffered as well.

Even for those no longer experiencing the primary symptom of jobless-ness, Great Recession–era malignancies proliferate: bankruptcies, mort-gage defaults, homelessness, a growing opioid addiction problem, and the amplification of decades-long trends of U.S. underemployment and loss of middle-class jobs. The so-called gig economy, where people cobble together an income doing freelance work (generally without health care or retirement benefits) now includes roughly one in three American workers, or about 53 million people. Perhaps the recovery's biggest asterisk is the preponderance of low-wage jobs it has produced, along with the seemingly permanent loss of better-paying jobs; as of 2014, in comparison to pre-Recession data, there were 2.3 million more of the former and 1.2 million fewer of the latter.[2] All of these troubling trends have contributed to a spike in suicide rates, driven mostly by big increases among the middle-aged, especially whites and women. Social iso-lation and lack of help-seeking foster hopelessness and untether some people from society. In 2014, nearly 43,000 Americans took their own lives, up from a recent low of just over 29,000 in the healthier economic times of 1999.[3]

Suicides and even potential media spectacles like murder-suicides of fami-lies by depressed failed breadwinners are less likely to capture national media attention since the Recession ended and the unemployment rate returned to historically normal levels. As I began writing this chapter in July of 2015, a quick online search revealed several under-the-radar recent cases of the most tragic lingering effects of the recession: loss of life. The Baltimore area had two murder-suicide cases within three months. One was 47-year-old Julian Roary, a father of 10- and 12-year-old boys living in the small town of Perry Hall, Maryland. Roary had just been let go from his 11-month temporary position as acting human resources manager at the Baltimore City Parking Authority and was facing another bout of unemployment. He could take no more after six years of temporary work, underemployment, and financial problems. A doctorate degree in organizational development apparently wasn't enough. Roary was angry, frustrated. He believed he was discriminated against because he was in his late 40s and simply felt he could not face another unemployment experience.[4] He is not alone. Researchers have found that suicide rates gener-ally climb during recessions and fall during expansions for people ages 25–64; the Great Recession correlates with a spike in suicides among people ages 40–64.[5] What was even more tragic and unusual, though not unheard of, was that he killed his two young sons before taking his own life. His girlfriend said he wanted his kids to be with him even in death.

Based on my interviews, the unemployed men who do worst are those who fail their own and/or their partner's breadwinner expectations, whose unem-ployment creates financial hardships, who are involuntarily unemployed and generally feel a lack of control over their lives, and who are criticized rather than supported by family and friends. They are more likely to feel emasculated and infantilized, and experience lower self-esteem, guilt, depression, social withdrawal, and weight gain. They sometimes compensate by exhibiting more anger, occasionally fantasize about escaping their situation, and try to find ways to reassert their manhood. They have more conflict with partners and families. In extreme cases not found among the men interview here, failed breadwinners commit deadly acts of violence against family, ex-bosses and coworkers, and even strangers.

All of the men I speak with struggle with the loss of a breadwinner identity and status, or at least an income, to some extent. They define or (as I discuss in chapter seven) redefine manhood so as to emphasize other ways they contribute to their families and communities, including as deeply involved primary caretakers of kids, partners who contribute more housework, money-savers due to their handy work or negotiating skills, and community role models because of their self-described moral behaviors. My research suggests that although some men—especially stay-at-home dads who receive strong support from partners—broaden their definition of manhood beyond being a breadwinner, it is still a key if not defining characteristic of men's identities.

Sweeping changes brought about by the women's movement and structural changes in the economy have reshaped gender, work, and family; most partnered men share breadwinning responsibility. But a cultural lag persists in men's definition of manhood. Being a man continues to be virtually inseparable from paid work, despite sweeping changes to the latter.[6] Most men who do little or no paid work suffer from the economic, emotional, psychological, and physical consequences of unfulfilled expectations and feelings of loss of control. So do their families and communities.

Internalizing: Down and Out

Sociologist Mirra Komarovsky's classic study of long-term unemployed men was published in 1940, just after the Great Depression concluded. The Depression was much deeper and lasted much longer than the Great Recession of 2007–2009, peaking at nearly 25% unemployment in 1933 and staying above 14% for a decade. Many of Komarovsky's findings (on her sample of native-born, mostly Protestant men forced to rely on social welfare) from eight decades ago are mirrored today. She found that unemployed men were humiliated by being failed providers and having to depend on others, and they experienced greater social isolation, less active sex lives, and in some cases, a loss of respect from their wives. Some turned to alcohol, some became unfaithful to their wives, and at least one man in her study became more physically violent with his children. Komarovsky describes one participant, "Mr. Patterson," as irritable, morose, disinterested in going out, and unable to sleep: "He feels that there is nothing to wake up for in the morning and nothing to live for."[7] He blamed himself for his unemployment, and he often thought about abandoning his family, imagining how much better off they would be without him.

Hobbies and interests were not enough to sustain men during their extended unemployment; their lives revolved around work. Without it, "they faced complete emptiness."[8] One woman among the many who lost respect for her husband said, "I still love him, but he doesn't seem as 'big' a man."[9] Many of the men, despite the scope and scale of the Depression, blamed themselves. Some blamed others, scapegoating working wives and "foreigners" for taking jobs that native-born white men felt entitled to: "The Italians, Irish, and colored people somehow get the preference," one unemployed man complained.[10]

After the recent Great Recession, one study found that about half of unemployed people say they had difficulty sleeping, 4 in 10 report strain in family relationships and loss of contact with friends, one-third say their self-respect had declined, 1 in 5 sought professional assistance due to anxiety or depression, and a small percentage had problems with alcohol or drugs.[11] African Americans and the long-term unemployed were most at risk of experiencing several of these problems simultaneously. My interviews with non-breadwinners produce results similar to Komarovsky's, with most unwillingly unemployed men feeling humiliated and emasculated by their situation. Many report depression, social withdrawal, and isolation. They also share how they feel infantilized by their economic dependence, reflecting their feelings of masculine incompetence. Eighty years of social change have not blunted the impact of men's internalization of their breadwinning failings.

Emasculated and Infantilized

"What do you do?" That's the first question strangers typically ask each other after exchanging names and a pleasantry. For men the only widely acceptable answer continues to be some kind of paid work. As the men I speak with repeatedly emphasize, they are judged as people and men based on what they do. When inquiries are met with "I'm unemployed," sympathy comes quickly, but it can be followed by a funereal silence.

Frank says some people avoid him as if his condition is contagious, "as if . . . they could catch unemployment through [a handshake] or something, or sitting on the same toilet seat." All of the unwillingly unemployed men and a few of the men who were stay-at-home dads by choice say they have felt emasculated or infantilized by their non-breadwinner status. Not earning an income leaves them feeling like economically dependent children who live off an allowance. A couple of men candidly express that they feel like women because of their joblessness. When masculinity is constructed in opposition to femininity and breadwinning is equated with masculinity, failed breadwinners may view themselves as the social antithesis of men. They casually equate the dependence inherent to childhood with womanhood.

Tyler's imprisonment and inability to support his family has undermined their middle-class life and his decision-making input. He sees that his wife needs help and feels guilty that he can't even support himself, that there's nothing he can do: "Like shit, when [she and her parents] are having a conversation about paying for my son's school, I'm . . . I stay quiet, because there's nothing I can say because I don't have a dollar to offer them, you know? So it definitely impacts me hard."

Jonathan's long-term unemployment strains his marriage with Suzy, as both expect him to be the breadwinner. He says, "I do not feel like a 50-year-old. I feel like a teenager who's trying to find himself and his place. In my head, I am disappointing and a disappointment to those around me." He does not feel like an adult, let alone a man: "It gets hard to look [my wife and kids] in the eyes, knowing that they are doing everything expected of them, by family and society, and I am not." Jonathan says that being jobless means that people discount his opinions, insights, and even values. They "do not see you as a whole person, someone on their level." He has to borrow money from family members, who provide it with no strings attached, but he keeps a running tally with the intent of paying them back. Despite the rising debt and his state of economic dependence on his wife and others, he says that other than his frustrating employment situation, he has become the man he wanted to become. Jonathan's sense of self is not entirely dependent on breadwinning.

Frank, 44, says it is "a really big gulf" between unemployment and acceptable manhood—to be in a position where you have no answer to the question, "What do you do?" He says that men's identities are mostly based on their work or hobbies, and right now, he has neither. It makes him feel "useless" as a father and a husband. His life revolves around food shopping, cooking, and meal scheduling, which he says make him feel like he has undergone a sex change. Frank's emasculation is symbolic: paid (masculine) work is replaced by devalued and unpaid (feminine) work. His feelings of being infantilized go further. His health has deteriorated since his unemployment, with one consequence being he twice lost control of his bowels. Frank wonders if he is figuratively and literally reverting to infancy.

Young, single, and defeated by the recession, Jordan is among the un/underemployed "boomerang kids," who return to live with their parents after college. He, too, feels like a child. He says he is a failure for not finding work and, at such a young age, having to give up his passion and his dream of being a forensic psychologist. Instead he has become pragmatic, as well as bitter, frustrated, angry, and depressed. He feels like a textbook definition of a failure, a "loser" who cannot support himself: "My view of a man, of manhood is an individual who is able to strike out and live on his own. Yes, he still maintains ties to those he loves, but he is his own person—financially, emotionally, and intellectually capable and independent. By those standards, I am not truly a man yet, and it drives me mad when I think about it." A lot of one's self-worth is tied to his or her job, he says, and "without a job, without the independence that the job will grant me, without the earning power, I am not really an adult. I am in a sort of hellish, prolonged junior-adult phase."[12] At 25, he is eager to have his own income and home, "to make my own way, to start my own family." Overwhelmed by it all, he says, "I often feel worthless." He avoids pursuing women because, right now, "there is nothing I can bring to the table." He mocks what might be his opening line: "Hey baby, I am unemployed, 25 years old, in school, and currently living with my parents. Do you want to go out?"

Liam and Marcus became involved stay-at-home fathers after losing their jobs. Both have supportive and understanding wives, but both men feel a loss of masculine identity due to their joblessness. Liam asks, "You ever see those girls that just have boyfriends that are unemployed and just hang out all day at the apartment? That's kind of what I felt like. It was just really, really depressing. Because I was raised in a family where the man needs to be the breadwinner, it really kind of takes a toll on you. You start feeling like you're not really a man anymore." Marcus feels more like a child than a woman. "In some ways, it's like being a kid again and having an allowance," he says, adding, "My wife by all means never makes me feel that way, but it may feel like that sometimes." He says it hurts to not be able to contribute financially and to put that pressure on his wife. He questions whether he is qualified for jobs similar to the ones he already held. Marcus's self-esteem has decreased, and he sees his future as uncertain. He experiences pain in not being able to buy his wife a birthday gift from money he earned. He can and does make sure the bills are paid, but it's his wife's income that pays them.

Most of those who have chosen to be stay-at-home dads have partners who provide strong financial and emotional support for their arrangement. Still, these men do not do paid work in a culture that says they should. Several say they feel slightly emasculated by their economic dependence. Peter, the adoptive father of three, exemplifies their contradictory experiences. He is grateful to be free to attend his kid's events and performances, but his ego and identity pay a price. There are days, he says, when he finds himself alone and "[caring] about daytime television more than you ever thought you would." Sometimes daytime grocery shopping spurs a crisis: "That conscious thought comes back to my head of 'Oh, my God, why am I not working?'" He says it's "an every day, every hour thing sometimes." Like Marcus, Peter "still can't get my head around" the fact he is not paying any family bills: "And I don't know if I'm ever going to get around that. I don't feel like it is my money to spend. I feel like I have to ask." He anticipated both identity and financial contribution anxieties before quitting his career, but they linger: "If you did

100% total, 51% was me giving up who I thought made me, me. And then 49% of it was 'How am I going to be able to be a husband and partner in this relationship [when] I'm not bringing in a check?' And 'Is my wife going to lose respect for me over time, and does that mean my wife will leave me?' I mean, yeah, it's a fear. And it's a fear that, even today, even after a year and a half of being a stay-at-home dad, I still deal with." Unemployment often produces stress and anxiety, both of which presage a decline in mental and physical health.

Depressed

Depression is common among people who are unemployed, regardless of gender. Indeed, many women may struggle more given their much greater likelihood of being single parents, shouldering all breadwinning and nurturing responsibilities. The masculine breadwinner ideal, though, generates particular feelings of gendered failure for men, even among men in economically secure families. Unemployed people have a 63% greater chance of dying than their employed peers. Unemployment increases men's mortality rates by more than a third over those of unemployed women, in part due to higher rates of heart attacks, alcohol and drug abuse, smoking, and unhealthy diets.[13] The involuntarily unemployed men I study deal with lowered and low self-esteem, frustration, guilt, shame, weight fluctuation, lethargy, irregular sleep patterns, decreased libido, worsening personal hygiene, and a general decline in mental and physical health, notably anxiety and depression. Stay-at-home dads who are not ideologically committed to being breadwinners experience fewer and much milder effects.

Frank's long-term unemployment experience has been crippling. He gained so much weight he feels imprisoned within his own body. He does not exercise and often wears his pajamas all day. He has to be reminded by his wife to shower regularly, which, he emphasizes, is "pretty disturbing." Frank is humiliated and anxious, lacks confidence and self-esteem, and is clinically depressed. He unsuccessfully tried to hide his deteriorating emotional state from family and friends. He says the "anxiety, depression, shame, embarrassment, and stuff" initially was too much to share with his wife: "I'm not one to do this, but I would almost find myself like in tears averaging once every three days [in] midafternoon, if my wife was at work, my daughter's at school. Just me alone in the house. Just the immensity of everything." He wears sunglasses to conceal his teary eyes, even on gray northern winter days. Sometimes his dreams consisted of manufactured humiliations, such as public firings and insults by ex-colleagues and bosses. Eventually he found a therapist, was prescribed antidepressants, and found outlets to ameliorate his joblessness. After our conversation, Frank writes me to share some follow-up thoughts:

Although I'm not an expert on suicide nor suicidal people, I did recall a very significant emotion I felt during my unemployment. When you mix anger, depression, despair, frustration and hopelessness together with feelings of loneliness, you reach a point of worthlessness. That's the nugget that many downtrodden people could relate to. When you mix in the myriad negative emotions to accompany that emptiness, you've hit bottom. I also mentioned feeling useless as both a husband and father. This would be the snapping point for many people. When they need to connect most with others they feel they can't for some reason or another. Some find religion (I did pray at times), strenuous exercise, therapy or just the comfort of family and home. I can say without a doubt that writing [my blog] helped save my life.

Others are not so fortunate. Men are several times more likely to commit suicide than women regardless of the state of the economy. In 2013, approximately 32,000 men and 9,000 women took their own lives.[14] This disparity is due to men's greater impulsivity, anger and aggression, and expectation for action; fewer emotional outlets; and unemployment's undermining of masculine selves. Also, men are more likely to use a gun. Joblessness reduces people's social ties, friendship networks, and adherence to social norms. Men, already less likely to maintain close attachments to others, are two to three times as likely to commit suicide after unexpectedly losing their jobs.[15] This kind of "economic suicide" is a literal escape from his own unacceptable sense of self. Researchers believe the recent global recession accounts for no fewer than 10,000 additional suicides in North America and Europe, nearly 5,000 in the United States alone. The pace of the increase was four times greater for men than women.[16] High unemployment and home foreclosures compound the stress and depression, helping push the suicide rate to 13 per 100,000 in 2013. The rate has been increasing, but it is well below its peak of 22 per 100,000 during the Great Depression.[17] Decades of U.S. economic changes have wrought greater insecurity and a weaker social safety net. Privatization and emphasis on market solutions also contribute to reduced social cohesion.[18] Men are more likely to internalize their inability to be breadwinners and view themselves as personally responsible for their perceived failure. Only a couple of the men I interview report feeling such despair that suicide crossed their minds; these thoughts were fleeting, though, and they were not seriously considered.

Jordan is one of these men. Living with his parents, with no job, no girlfriend, and seemingly no future, his depression morphed into hopelessness. He gave suicide a thought, but not much of one. He sees many of his fellow graduates landing jobs while he cannot find anything in a job market he calls "soul crushing." He finds it hard to enjoy life because he feels his has been a failure. Fellow twentysomething Tyler has not considered suicide, although he says, "Ever since I went to jail, I've had a lot of mental health problems."

He explains, "I get depressed, and I get anxiety real bad because . . . everything hit me, like, I don't got anything, I'm in a prison cell. I had no control over the outside world anymore[, over] what [my wife] did or what my kids did. I had no say in anything. So now that I'm out and can't find a job, it's hit me even harder." He's on medication and seeing a counselor, but the physical pain from his accident and the psychological pain from losing his idyllic life weigh heavily on him. He can't pick up his kids, and he let down his family: "I'm so damn young, and I was at such a pinnacle in my life. I was—I was somewhere where most people never are . . . I went from extremely high to extremely low. So it kind of pisses me off."

For Liam, the recession forced him to close his small business, which led to a deep and harmful depression before he recovered from it. Everything in his life, he says, slowly, almost imperceptibly deteriorated. Job searches in his field were fruitless. His libido decreased: "I wasn't initiating. It's so cliché but I just wasn't in the mood, you know?" If not for his wife's job, he says, his depression would have emerged much sooner. Looking back, thinking about how he was trying to return to work in a field he disliked, he observes, "It was a sad state of my life." At his nadir, a mid-40s involuntary stay-at-home dad wallowing in a sort of existential crisis, he questioned his past, present, and future life. Recalling those times, he says,

> I just walked around in these pajama pants all day. It was crazy. It was . . . I don't know . . . a slow, insidious kind of depression. My self-esteem was getting lower. I didn't recognize it at the time. I just thought this was just something that'll pass or is just a mood I was in or whatever. [Next thing I know,] I'm eight months into it. I was like, "This is something serious." I mean, it was affecting my relationship with my wife; it was affecting my relationship with my friends. It was just . . . I didn't want to do anything. I didn't care about anything. It's like you were dying very, very slowly, like a cancer or something. It's just . . . You can't really describe it. It's kind of creeping, just there, you know?

His failed attempts to land a job accelerated his downward spiral. "The depression just came on like a tidal wave," he says. He realized, "Oh, this is not going to be just a temporary little setback. This might be something a little bit more serious." This pushed him into an existential crisis. He was a failed breadwinner, blanketed by depression: "I was just getting lazy. I can see how housewives of the 1950s started drinking heavily. I can understand that now. It's pretty damn boring, and it's tedious, and it's monotonous; and [sad] to say, that's the way I was looking at it before I kind of woke up." Liam's awakening was realizing the greater importance of doing something that he loves and raising someone whom he loves over merely working a high-earning job. Before then, he says, "It never really even occurred to me that there were other things, more important things that will define you." Liam has embraced fatherhood and decided to pursue his dream of making music.

Marcus, too, was forced into being a stay-at-home dad after losing his job. "I've been there with the depression," he says, and "on that cycle where you kind of let yourself go." The job search is exhausting in all ways. "Sometimes you wake up and you don't want to do it," he says, asking himself, "'All right, what's today going to hold for me? What am I going to accomplish today? Am I going to get turned down for two or three more jobs today?,' you know, or 'Am I going to get a break today?'" A few temporary opportunities to make money a year ago helped him feel better. He also thinks about making sure he sets a good example for his young son. He promises himself he will stave off another bout of depression: "I can't go down that road. I've learned self-pity can . . . I mean, you can lose your relationship. You can lose yourself in self-pity if you're not careful."

Jerry saw a lot of that in the veteran's homeless shelter, where alcoholism and depression were common: "You start questioning yourself inside, and you start saying, 'Who am I? What did I do?'" He sees this as a universal issue, one that is magnified by failure: "I mean, even people who are working full-time in careers, it nags on them, you know—are they accomplishing what they need to accomplish in life? And when you get to the point where you get homeless, I guess it's like, yeah, you can really feel like you're losing yourself, losing your identity."

Socially Withdrawn

Depression, shame, social withdrawal, and isolation are mutually reinforcing— a sort of closed loop but one that impossibly only descends, like an Escher staircase. As with depression, unwilling non-breadwinners are more likely than voluntary stay-at-home dads to withdraw from social interactions, with a few exceptions in both groups. The shame and depression sometimes cause men to retreat from friends and family, avoid social events, and even conversations altogether. Fathers do not seem to stop interacting with their kids, who often provide relief from unemployment. Some men conceal their fears and anxieties from their partners, but most do not withdraw from them.

Stay-at-home dad Peter and long-term unemployed father Frank feel compelled to hide some of their anxieties and problems from their wives, knowing the consequences for themselves and their relationships. Regarding his transition out of the workforce, Peter says, "Over time I've been able to feel more comfortable expressing my frustrations to Regina without feeling like I'm demeaning myself." He still hesitates, though, to share with her his moments of emasculation and diminished self-worth. In his eyes, this would merely highlight and reconfirm his inadequacies as a husband and man. He says that even though he is in a great marriage, he's "still carrying that consciousness of

'I'm less of a man 'cause I'm not working.' And so do you really want to talk to your wife about not working?" Peter also does not feel he can talk to his employed friends, who tend to either tease him and joke about what they see as his cushy situation or, he senses, quietly assume something is wrong with him. "It's somewhat isolating because [you lose] your support network that you would normally have [if you were working]," he says.

Similarly, Frank says he has retreated within himself during his unemployment. He did not share his feelings with his wife "to protect her from a lot of the ugly stuff that was going on between the [lack of] job, the bills, the finances, the house situation, potential bankruptcy. Yeah, I was definitely trying to keep that on my shoulders and not hers." Withdrawing only bred resentment. Frank also noticed that some of his friends and family tended to call and check on him less frequently when times were toughest, further isolating him.

All of Liam's relationships were affected by his unemployment. "I didn't really like hanging out anymore," he says. "I just wanted to go to bed and go to sleep. I kind of came to accept it. And when you do that, when you accept that, it's a death sentence." Phil's move to the South leaves him partially dependent on his wife not just for income but for friendship networks as well. He says they mostly socialize with his wife's work colleagues, which means "there are always so many conversations about work and the job market and bosses, and it literally, I mean, I almost want to go, 'Hey I'm just going to go play with the dog while you all talk about that,' because I have nothing to give to those conversations." Phil says he doesn't feel ostracized—there's no malice in their conversation—but he "just [isn't] part of that world anymore." Cindy, ever supportive, declines some invitations that portend work-filled conversation. "I don't want anything to do with that," Phil says. It was women (mostly as a group) who felt excluded from this dinner-party career talk in decades past. Today, a mixed-gender gathering of professionals marks Phil as the sole outlier. He is not in touch with his friends as much either, which he attributes entirely to his unemployment: "Maybe that's a subconscious . . . my sense of worth has gone down or my sense of accomplishment, or I think I should be . . . I [should have] achieved more at this stage of my life, and therefore at some subconscious level, I'm ashamed. I don't know."

Most of the unemployed men have supportive partners who help them navigate their situations and keep them connected. Single men like Jordan and T. J. must actively seek support from others to stave off complete isolation. Jordan says he has done fairly well, but there have been moments when the shame causes him to avoid going out with and talking to employed friends ("I mean real talking, not Facebooking."). Withdrawing and staying in is a temporary escape, but do it too often and the consequences are severe. T. J., divorced and barely making ends meet, is isolated because he is single, recently retired from the military, and living in a state where he lacks a support network.

He says the first year of unemployment was the toughest. He was the most depressed then because he "kind of detached" from his ex-colleagues after retiring, was no longer active or keeping busy, and lacked other social groups. He is bipolar, prone to depression, and required physicians' assistance to manage his symptoms that first year. Today, T. J. still has trouble with depression and sits around a lot, tired and unmotivated. "Even to walk 10 feet to do dishes, let alone go outside . . ." he says, the thought trailing off as if it's too much to bear. He closes himself off in his home, often not speaking with people "because you're not on the same level as they are." Depressed, but not embittered or jealous, T. J. says, "I've gone through that pretty good: your first thoughts are [that] you're totally different because they're working, going on vacations, and you're growing gray hair and rotting. There's such a contrast. But I've learned not to be mad at them. That's their situation, and I'm happy for them. I don't wish this on anybody."

Unemployed men who perceive themselves (or are perceived by others) as failures are likely to experience social psychological and health consequences. A sense of emasculation, reduced self-esteem, and depression are common. Withdrawing from others provides a temporary cocoon from the pain, but ultimately only reinforces their isolation. For most men, other than some unintentional sabotaging of intimate relationships due to their social withdrawal, they confine their unemployment problems to themselves. They internalize their breadwinner failings.

Internalizing a sense of failure, feeling worthless, being moved to tears, and suffering from depression—these all threaten men's identities. However, in a sense, many of these men are doing what's expected of them when they conceal their pain and suffering from others. They are doing a manhood act when they "suck it up" and bottle up their (feminine-marked) emotions. This behavior is ultimately self-destructive. It is physically, psychologically, and relationally unhealthy; conforming to masculine ideals often is, especially so when men do masculinity under circumstances where they have limited or no access to economic power or control. Another set of situated manhood acts arise from positions of powerlessness: externalizing behaviors. These include compensating via anger, escape, and reassertion—and, all too often, violence.

Nonviolent Compensation

In 1983, actor Michael Keaton played Jack Butler in the film "Mr. Mom," a comedy about an auto industry engineer who loses his job during a recession. This forces his stay-at-home wife, Caroline, to return to the paid labor force and leaves Jack at home to take care of their kids and house. Working moms were unexceptional then, but the film's title and Keaton's over-the-top portrayal of an emasculated "househusband" betrays the gendered baggage attached to housework and childcare, as well as men's unemployment.

In a funny scene illustrating compensatory manhood, Ron, Caroline's boss, arrives at her and Jack's house in a limousine to pick her up for their work trip to California. Caroline excitedly runs upstairs, presumably to make herself more attractive for the fancy car service. Jack, looking disheveled and unmanly in his robe and aware that Ron might be a threat, scampers away from the window when he sees Ron confidently strolling toward the house in an expensive suit. Jack returns to greet Ron wearing overalls and protective goggles while revving a chainsaw. Jack and Ron begin posturing. Jack offers Ron a beer. Ron points out that it is seven o'clock in the morning. Jack waits a beat and offers a scotch. Ron, knowing Jack lost his job, says he cannot drink during working hours, then immediately and disingenuously apologizes for being insensitive about Jack's unemployment, patronizingly calling him "pal" and touching Jack's shoulder in a gesture of faux-consolation. Jack then guides Ron into the living room to tell Ron about his plans to use his time off from work to build an addition on the home. Jack says he is going to knock down some walls and do the rewiring himself. Ron asks him if he's going to use "220" for the wiring, the other option implicitly being 110 volts. Jack's complete lack of knowledge is exposed. But he's too deep into the lie and his masculine posturing to retreat, so he plunges ahead nonsensically, delivering one of the funniest lines in the movie: "Yeah, 220, 221. Whatever it takes."

Keaton's charisma and charm make Jack Butler's cringeworthy compensatory behaviors not only funny but accessible and understandable. We've all been or known the guy who, when feeling emasculated for some reason, only further embarrasses himself in some futile, failed attempt to reassert manhood. Some of these behaviors are sadly funny, especially the awkward cinematic versions. However, loss of face and loss of work can produce more serious compensatory manhood acts.[19] If men's sense of internalized failure lasts long enough and is difficult enough, if they are unable to repair what ails them, they resort to any number of nonviolent or violent actions in an attempt to restore their masculine selves.

A large and growing body of literature reveals how men, both individually and subculturally, attempt to compensate for various perceived shortcomings.[20] Researchers have found that men of all backgrounds use an array of compensatory manhood acts when they do not fulfill hegemonic masculine ideals, but gay men, female-to-male transmen, economically marginalized men, men of color, immigrants, and other systematically subordinated and marginalized men are structurally located in positions that elicit more of these responses. Men compensate by drinking heavily, posturing and getting in fights, bodybuilding, participating in sports and risk-taking activities, committing crimes, pursuing sexual conquests, practicing infidelity, doing less housework, segregating themselves from women, attacking and punishing other men's feminine displays, demeaning women when they are not around, and even verbally, sexually, and physically assaulting and abusing women, sometimes killing them. Merely referencing, describing, or bragging about some of the above sometimes suffices as a compensatory act.

Most often, men do these things because they feel discredited due to body or breadwinner failings. They attempt to restore their masculine selves—whether violently or nonviolently, depending on what resources they can usher—via actions that are intended to place them higher up the masculine hierarchy.[21] At minimum, they distinguish themselves from the subordinated status of woman and a feminine identity, thereby reproducing gender inequality. Note that women exist as objects of men's competition (and not unusually, bragging), even in the seemingly harmless, funny example portrayed by Keaton. In some cases, as when unemployed men use violence against woman partners to reclaim interpersonal power, the patriarchal agenda is conscious and explicit. Other times, as when gay men emphasize big bodies and muscles, the devaluation and subordination of women and femininity are merely implicit.

Expressions of anger, escape fantasies, and rhetorical reassertions are three nonphysically violent compensatory responses of the non-breadwinning men I interview. Stay-at-home dads may have even more reason than unemployed men to compensate given their doubly stigmatized roles as both unemployed and caregiving men. Negative feelings are usually offset, though, by those who choose this role and embrace an alternative definition of manhood.

Expressing Anger

Jack Butler's anxiety about the state of his marriage is an all-too-real experience for several unemployed men I interview. Anthony, emasculated by his so-called alpha wife and his long-term employment struggles, teeters between depression and anger. Along with the possibility his marriage may end in divorce, his dissatisfaction with not working causes him to "internalize depression and then explode with anger sometimes," he says. He is unable to relinquish control, perhaps especially to a woman. "Well, here I am, a man having to rely on a woman and it's not a good feeling at all, and it's a very helpless feeling," he says, labeling it unhealthy and paralyzing: "It affects how I feel as a man, and it affects my freedom of where I could go or what I could do in life."

Stay-at-home dad Henry's longtime arrangement with his wife broke down when, according to him, her progressive views shifted and she began to resent his unemployment. Before her change of heart, he had fully embraced his status and identity, but their impending divorce has led him to experience a lot of anger. He says, "I'm mad because, right now, I'm almost 50 and I have no stability. Economy sucks. All the jobs I used to do, I'm either physically not capable [of doing] them or those jobs are gone. You can't [work those jobs] and make $50,000 a year anymore, you know. Those jobs are all gone." Henry's wife accuses him of being angry, but he sees only depression.

Frank says "anger really rose to the top of the list" of his emotions at the peak of his unemployment and marital struggles: "I would say that's one of the biggest transformations: [I'm] very, very defensive. There's no such thing as a lighthearted remark. I took everything personal, and I responded to everything. If my wife said, 'I was just kidding' or [said] things I usually just let go or roll off my back, I was firing right back." He says that at times, he and his wife have been so flooded with emotions over his unemployment and their financial difficulties that they can't communicate. He, too, thinks his anger was a source of compensation and a way to disguise his depression. Given the fruitlessness of his job searches, he experiences his wife's regular, hopeful inquiries as demoralizing reminders of his failures. "She's just trying her best to stay [positive]," he says, "But within 20 minutes [of returning home from a busy day applying for jobs,] I can go from feeling relatively productive and good to just being squashed because, bottom line, I don't have a job." Frank's unemployment blog generated a lot of anonymous comments, mostly supportive and positive, though some criticized him for his physical and psychological deterioration, questioning his masculinity and resilience. He summarizes those criticisms: "Yeah, 'Man up, be the breadwinner, be the logical one, there's no time for depression or anxiety or anything like that. Just calm down and be the ruler of the house' was the basic message. Yeah, easy for you to say! If I could reply it would be 'OK, so, at the third year mark, are you allowed to feel a little angry or frustrated?' I mean, I don't know what the cutoff point is." Frank takes note of stories of unemployed men who escaped their circumstances by committing suicide, often leaving children and families behind. He says that although he sympathizes with their plights, he cannot imagine abandoning his daughter. His feelings of failure manifest themselves in depression and anger.

Long-term unemployed husband Phil more explicitly connects his anger to what amounts to a compensatory response to joblessness: "I'm tired of people saying, 'Oh, Phil, what are you doing these days?' I don't know. I can't say I'm working . . . and I can't say I got a promotion; I can't say I'm working on this great project." He has exceeded the limits of his patience: "I think I'm turning very much into an authoritarian. You know, 'Great, I'll listen to you, but at the end of the day, you know what? It's my decision. Get the hell away from me, I don't have time for this.' I don't know what it is, but I've become much more aggressive . . . in just making sure that the things I *can* control are controlled. You know, because maybe it's that I can't control my job aspect [of my life], I can't control my professional world, [but] I can control this. If I'm an asshole sitting in your office negotiating this, I don't have a problem with that. These are things that I can control to help save money, for me to contribute a little bit financially." When Phil was teased by a family member about being unemployed he says, "I didn't say it, but I felt [like saying], 'Screw you.'" He says it upsets him, but he blows it off if family members make jokes at his expense. "But I've gotten to the point where I would not let that go if it was just a casual acquaintance," he says, although he believes he would do so tactfully rather than confrontationally. "It all stems from a very kind of deep feeling of 'You know what? Just because I'm unemployed doesn't mean I'm useless,'" he says. Phil believes he proves his worth as a man in part by doing projects and work around the house, tapping into a blue-collar, physical masculinity to offset the loss of his white-collar breadwinner status.

Nonviolent anger bubbles up from the frustrations of long-term joblessness and a sense of loss of power and control. In Phil's case, he channels that anger into an aggression and assertiveness that provides him with more control over his environment. In Frank's case, the uncontrolled expression of anger is viscerally restorative. Both men restore their masculine identities, perhaps only briefly, by attempting to assert dominance using their feelings of anger.

Fantasizing about Escaping

Another nonviolent compensatory behavior is to have fantasies of temporarily escaping the harsh reality of unfulfilled masculine ideals. Recall that some Gentlemen's Fighting Club members fantasize about possessing superhero powers and enjoying unlimited control over their all-too-normal bodies and physical abilities. The fantasies of depressed non-breadwinning men are circuitously restorative; instead of fantasizing about newfound wealth and success, some men imagine leaving their families and simply eliminating their familial breadwinner responsibilities. None actually do so, but that the thought occurs to several of them is revealing. The daily, even hourly reminders and pressures of not fulfilling the most fundamental responsibility our society assigns to fathers can be unbearable. No person can occupy that space long term without enduring severe consequences. If men cannot eliminate that feeling of failure by either finding work or uncoupling breadwinning and ideal manhood, they may consider alleviating it by escaping the situation. This was common during the Great Depression, when many men abandoned their families. Some committed suicide. The national rate spiked to more than 22 per 100,000 in 1932.[22] Others just walked away. A 1940 poll found that 1.5 million married women had been abandoned by their husbands.[23] Younger and older men alike have been fleeing from breadwinner expectations ever since.[24]

For several non-breadwinning men, including Frank, Liam, and Anthony, the job market and their situations were so bleak at times that they considered mentally and physically checking out. They entertained several possibilities: taking a permanent one-way trip, entering a psychiatric facility, or committing suicide. These fantasies contrast sharply with those of emasculated GFC members, who envision playing superhero in the streets. It begs the question why Frank, Liam, and Anthony don't slip into comparable economic fantasies where they are rich and accomplished, their status and identity repaired and restored. This seems even more surprising given that, as prevalent as superhero culture is, it is dwarfed by Americans' dreamy obsessions with wealth and success.

Depression is the most likely reason these unemployed men don't escape into heroic breadwinning fantasies. Frank, Liam, and Anthony's fantasies of escaping their breadwinner responsibilities coincide with paralyzing depression and a sense of hopelessness. Perhaps some GFC members felt a similar paralysis during their boyhood or young adulthood because of their lack of physical agency, but their feelings were likely less grave and more isolated. Other people were not depending on them to embody manhood.

Liam's forced unemployment and involuntary role as stay-at-home dad sent him into a tailspin. Deeply depressed at his lowest point, he says,

I don't think I had suicidal thoughts but I thought about just walking away from everything; just walking away, just going somewhere. I didn't have a place to go, didn't have a destination, but I really didn't want to be where I was at. It popped in my head. And once it pops in your head, you bring it around and around again, almost like a merry-go-round. It goes away for a little bit but it comes right back around. Thank God I knew it for what it was. I was like, "This is not an option; you just can't walk away from your problems. That's not a way to solve problems. Is that the way you want your [son] to see you solve problems—that you walk away from them? No. You have to persevere and push through." I kind of just stuck it out. Talking about walking away, that was . . . When I look back, that just sounds so childish and immature. I mean, how could you even entertain a thought like that, just walking away? It's crazy.

In part, Liam's familial support and a growing love and appreciation for being a parent prevented him from acting upon his fantasy. If his unemployment lasted many years, as was common during the Depression, perhaps he and others would more seriously entertain an escape.

Anthony says he sometimes fantasized about "getting on a bus with a load of money and taking off to someplace I've never been to before. But of course, I never really would do that. It's crossed my mind, but I wouldn't do that. It's just a fantasy, you know, an escape from the everyday ho-hum of life." He identifies other ways he psychologically escapes, namely, his increased viewing of pornography. Drugs and alcohol are also commonly used to dull unemployed men's pain and help them psychologically escape feeling worthless and depressed.[25]

The only non-breadwinner who literally, if temporarily, escaped his situation was Mika. He was retired military turned stay-at-home father. The transition was difficult. His wife's budding career meant they had to move soon after he retired, so he lacked friends in his new community, let alone other stay-at-home dads with whom to connect: "Everybody else in the neighborhood who stayed home were women. So I think there was like a big sense of isolation. It was my first time having to deal with that, with not having a support group. And I think I did it for nine months and then, you know, I went off to Iraq for a year to be a contractor. And it put our daughter into day care. Being a stay-at-home dad was really tough. So maybe it was an escape for me." I ask him if living on a base while retired also left him on the outside of the soldier and warrior culture and community and if he desired to reclaim that position. "Wow, yeah, you hit the nail on the head. That's exactly how I felt," he says. "I've always had an adventuresome spirit, you know, to go places, see places. And you know, being around these people, hearing their war stories, they just added to it. It was like, 'Man, I got to go!'" Mika's literal escape from being the primary caretaker of an infant and not doing paid labor was a decision he arrived at with his wife. Upon his return, he resumed his new role as the at-home parent but enjoyed more support from other family and newfound friends. He felt compelled to prove himself one more time in a war zone, in no small part because of the lack of masculine rewards he received from caring for his child.

Reasserting Manhood

Another way to nonviolently attempt to restore a sense of control is to reassert manhood via claims or actions. Responses to American racism provide many examples. African Americans have countered their experiences of dehumanization and accompanying atrocities and oppression by whites—from slavery to Jim Crow segregation and lynchings to racial profiling, mass incarceration, and police brutality—by collectively and individually asserting their dignity and humanity. Sometimes this was gendered, as when black men responded to whites calling them "boys" by asserting "I Am a Man" before and during the Civil Rights era or when Sojourner Truth famously delivered her "Ain't I a Woman?" abolitionist challenge to an audience of mostly white women suffragists. The Black Lives Matter movement that emerged in response to police violence shines light on a long-standing problem of police violence that activists emphasize has been ignored because of the United States' indifference to the plight of African Americans.

Another example is how people respond to being made to feel invisible. Ralph Ellison's nameless narrator and protagonist in his 1953 novel *Invisible Man* symbolically confronts the phenomenon of black men's experiences of invisibility.[26] Today, ours is a culture where wealth is publicized and celebrated, individual identity is sacred, and the importance of visibility can be observed in everything from the commodification of fame to the ubiquity of selfies. Being made invisible because of your race or ethnicity, social class standing, or both invites the unseen to loudly and publicly reassert themselves. This helps explain why flashy cars, nice clothes, loud jewelry, and a "look at me" attitude and lifestyle are common among those with the fewest resources and low status. And let's face it: it's mostly men who gravitate to these kinds of displays. Success, accomplishment, status, and control are inextricably linked with manhood. When billionaires publicly joust with each other over their respective fortunes (as did Mark Cuban and Donald Trump during Trump's campaign), it should come as no surprise that people with little money try to make claims to high status and assert that they are worthy of not only acknowledgment but respect and dignity.[27]

Non-breadwinning men sometimes feel and are made to feel like less than men. So they reassert themselves by making various claims to manhood. Sometimes these men simply want to verbally challenge those who think their employment status undermines their manhood. Stay-at-home dad Ryan uses avoidance, sarcasm, and direct challenges to combat others' ignorance or negative assumptions. When people "roll their eyes" at him when he tells them he's a stay-at-home dad, he says, "There's many times where I've wanted to sort of fight against that, like I wanted to stand up for myself and just sort of fight these assumptions." Other times, he thinks, "You don't have to get it. It doesn't matter to me if you get it because my wife does and, you know, me being a stay-at-home dad doesn't mean everything that you think it means."

Anthony and Marcus are involuntarily unemployed at-home parents. Anthony finds himself asserting his status to his daughter: "I'm afraid that she's going to see men as weak or as not being providers, and that worries me. And I had to tell her [when she made an innocent comment or inquiry], you know, I work around the house. I do the dishes, the laundry, I cut the lawn, I take out the garbage, I pick you up, you know. It's not like I'm not doing anything around here. And I had to patiently tell her that. So that worries me." Anthony would prefer to be the breadwinner, but he finds value and importance in his role as stay-at-home father. Marcus is even more intent on returning to paid work: "The way things are now, it's not normal, and it's not OK, and it sometimes doesn't feel OK. Sometimes you feel you have to kind of, well, you want to assert yourself, like, 'Hey, I'm still a father, I'm still a man. I still live and breathe.' And you feel sometimes that you're less than other people."

Jamie is a white, gay, partnered 34-year-old father of two young kids. He left his career to be the full-time stay-at-home parent but did so with trepidation. Gay stereotypes and prejudices have "always been an issue for me," he says. They have obstructed his sense of gender identity. When he was in his early

20s, he provided customer service phone support. Callers would sometimes mistake him for a woman because of his name and feminine-sounding voice, so he took up smoking to deepen his voice and began going by "J. P." instead of Jamie. Eventually, with counseling, he realized, "I needed to be OK with who I was" as a first step, before expecting others to accept him. Quitting his career to raise kids—"doing a very nontypical male role"—brought judgment from others and reopened old identity wounds. Jamie compensates for his perceived feminine, devalued, unpaid work by emphasizing its masculine characteristics, as well as highlighting and focusing on his education. "I'm still a leader," he says, "I'm just a leader of the household. I'm still very aggressive because I still set goals [for] myself, regardless of if it's with the kids, or it's something we need to do for the family, or if it's something with myself [educationally], I still am aggressive in reaching my goals." He immediately returned to school after quitting his job, which has bridged his transition out of his career and buffeted him as he grapples with childcare. He says,

> I think if I didn't [take classes], I probably would go crazy. I mean, it originally started as having something on my résumé [for] when I went back into the workforce, but it really became—it's really become something that I really feel that I need. I need [it] in order to have that other outlet, you know, to take these different classes and learn new things and kind of be thinking in a different mind-set, versus you know, "Did I wash the bottles? Did I put the sippy cup out? Do I need to go to the store to buy baby food? Do I have diapers?"

Jamie says he is a lot more comfortable with where he's at in his life now that he is so heavily invested in his education. He has also weathered some challenging parenting problems, which has made him appreciate fatherhood more. But it's clear that Jamie feels compelled to reassert his masculine identity due to his unemployment.

Without a breadwinner's income, status, or identity, some men use their bodies to reassert their masculinity. This strategy has become more common in a postindustrial American economy populated by a roughly equal number of women and men.[28] Men's work has become a more tenuous source of manhood. Men can signify manhood by wielding and leveraging their bodies in various ways: building them up; using them for competition, sport, and violence; talking about their bodies as sexual tools that are used to control others; consuming excessive amounts of food and alcohol; and practicing stoicism by not complaining about pain or injuries.[29] Aggressive posturing and discourse can also substitute for feeling disempowered. Unemployed father Anthony says he occasionally resorts to anger and shouting to compensate for his non-breadwinner status, explaining,

Sometimes I feel I have to assert myself, but you know, it usually just causes an explosive confrontation, and I really don't like to play the macho role. It kind of goes against my nature. I don't think I should have to. It's not who I am, and when I do try to assert myself, it just . . . the results were nothing that I would want to keep. You know, it would only be bad feelings. Because, really, basically, I'd just be overcompensating for feeling bad at someone else's expense, so it's not worth it. I just try to be who I am.

There are more indirect approaches to reasserting masculinity via bodies, including secretly cheating on partners and avoiding or refusing to do housework.[30] Long-term unemployed married men Jonathan and Phil take the opposite tacks on these respective issues, seeking greater intimacy and taking on more housework. Jonathan says, "My libido has in fact increased, as I seek to be 'satisfying' [sexually] since I have not been in my employment and ability to provide." His wife's libido, though, has decreased as his unemployment has dragged on.

Phil has been using his free time to work on the fixer-upper house he and Cindy bought. He is intent on making some sort of contribution to the household, motivated both by a need to assert himself and an unhealthy amount of guilt. He says Cindy's positive attitude reinforces his desire not to let her down. When they met and married, he was "financially stable" and she "never bargained for" him being unemployed, "so maybe it's just simply that these are things I can do; I have control over this so I need to keep the yard looking good, I need to work on the house, I need to have a big flower garden. I need to do that." Jonathan and Phil try to use their bodies to reassert a sense of control, channeling their economic emasculation into being more attentive partners. Conversely, Anthony sometimes uses anger to reassert his status.

Although compensatory manhood acts are adaptive behaviors—they are, after all, attempts to restore what men feel they've lost—these actions can also be self-destructive. A third type of response proves corrosive solely or primarily for the boys and men engaging in it. Putting on a "cool pose" or conforming to a "code of the street" that revolves around fearless toughness may undermine young (disproportionately poorer, African American and Latino) men's commitment to and progress in school.[31] Similarly, joining gangs and committing crimes are ultimately self-destructive actions sometimes done in response to feeling emasculated. Many men also try to reassert their threatened masculinity by engaging in various risk-taking activities. They jeopardize their health and well-being by drinking excessively, drinking and driving, engaging in extreme sports, avoiding health care, and many other ways in which they can use their bodies to prove their toughness and, however provisionally, gain a sense of control. There are a range of adverse health effects for being non-breadwinning men that vary by social location. One study found that men with the highest incomes are most adversely affected by being secondary earners.[32]

Men's attempts to reassert their masculinity by using and controlling their bodies or situations, fantasizing about escaping, and expressing anger result in various outcomes. Some of these attempts are merely rhetorical, others actually can benefit men and their relationships, and still others, for the most part, only negatively impact men themselves. The most pernicious and devastating compensatory manhood acts are various forms of interpersonal violence. Controlling and dominating others' bodies is a distressingly common means of reasserting masculinity.

Compensatory Masculine Violence

Men commit more than 8 out of 10 violent crimes, including nearly 9 out of 10 murders and almost all rapes.[33] Their motivations for doing so are as diverse as the men themselves. However, a large and growing number of studies have found that men's violence is often compensatory—a response to feeling disempowered, shamed, the victim of an injustice.[34] The most common sources of adult men's feelings of disempowerment and shame are threats to their breadwinner status and identity. Research on economically marginalized men of various racial and ethnic groups find that beyond relying on sports or sexual conquests, fighting and violence are common ways to signify and attempt to restore, to realign themselves with, ideal manhood.[35]

Compensatory masculine violence knows no bounds. The targets and victims may be strangers, acquaintances, or intimates of any gender, one person or as many as the perpetrator can victimize. The types of violence include physical and sexual, from bar fights and street violence to intimate partner violence, rape, and sexual assault, and even mass shootings and acts of terrorism. The human toll is costly. It, too, takes many forms—physical, psychological, lethal.

Whether men are individually or collectively unable to fulfill breadwinner expectations, one all-too-common response is to use violence against women to reassert their authority. Issei, or first-generation Japanese Americans, lost not only their possessions and freedoms when the U.S. government interred them during World War II but also their status and authority within their families.[36] Their American-born children, the Nisei (second) generation, lost respect for the Issei. Some Issei men gave up on maintaining power and control in the family, internalizing a sense of failure and becoming lethargic and hopeless. Others compensated by using violence against their woman partners.

Contemporary research on violence in intimate relationships finds that men often use violence to compensate for their failed breadwinner status, whether due to being unemployed, doing "women's work," or simply earning much less than woman partners.[37] Revealingly, the opposite phenomenon does not seem to occur: there is no compensatory feminine violence. Women who earn much less than men partners, who work in gender-non-conforming jobs, or who are unemployed do not attempt to assert their status by using violence against men. They have no need to as either they are not violating gendered norms (when they earn less or do not do paid work) or the masculine-typed work they do is more highly valued. Either way, control is not an essential expectation for womanhood, and violence is neither expected nor rewarded.

Sometimes men's violence is directed at targets outside of the home, whether specific individuals or groups are identified as sources of grievance. The slang term *going postal*, which was coined following a string of post office shootings in the 1980s and '90s, is now used generically for workplace shootings by disgruntled former employees.[38] Workplace homicides have increased from only 15 in 1982 to around 800 per year. Men commit well over 9 out of 10 murder-suicides in the United States, an even higher proportion than homicides.[39] Many murder-suicides follow severe financial stress, usually unemployment, with the perpetrators most often killing family members or workplace colleagues before taking their own lives.[40] Masculine identity crises are common among school shooters (due partly to failed bodies) and domestic terrorists (usually older, motivated more by failed breadwinning). They often exhibit a masculine rage that they attempt to resolve through violent behavior; a fetish for guns and weapons compounds their violent potential.[41]

In 2009, 22-year-old Richard Poplawski became a domestic terrorist. He shot and killed three Pittsburgh police officers and seriously wounded two others. Poplawski and his mother had gotten into an argument at home about a pet dog urinating on the carpet, one of many shouting matches between them. She called 9-1-1 to have him removed from her home. The responding officers had no idea Poplawski was heavily armed and had donned a bulletproof vest in anticipation of their arrival. He'd also been following and falling further down the right-wing rabbit hole of government conspiracy theories, anti-Semitism, and racism. Poplawski was expecting—eagerly anticipating, really—a race war: "If a total collapse is what it takes to wake our brethren and guarantee future generations of white children walk this continent, if that is what it takes to restore our freedoms and recapture our land: let it begin this very second and not a moment later."[42] As is all too common, Poplawski's virulent racist fears and anxieties, along with his belief that the government was conspiring to remove citizens' first and second amendment rights, were stoked by extremist websites and organizations. His personal failures and frustrations likely acted as an accelerant for the fire. He grew up in a violent, deeply troubled home, ultimately living with his grandparents, including a racist grandfather who abused his mom and grandmother and fired off guns in their home on more than one occasion. As an adult, Poplawski was issued and violated a legal order to stay away from an ex-girlfriend (after going to her place of work and unsuccessfully proposing to her).

Just a few years out of high school, he had failed to fulfill multiple career goals he'd set. He was discharged from the marines after three weeks. He moved away, to Florida, and then had to return home to Pittsburgh. Poplawski's father said his son told him he moved back because he "was tired of just working to live. He talked to me like a man who was like, 'Dad, I'm going to make some money, I'm going to make a lot of money, I'm going to find a way to succeed.' And with his intelligence, I thought he would. I knew he would." A year later, further removed from his aspirations and even deeper into antigovernment, gun-confiscation paranoia, Poplawski's failures and fears culminated in deadly violence. Ever so temporarily—and with the ultimate cost to others (and eventually, himself, as he later was sentenced to death)—he restored a sense of control. Poplawski is somewhat atypical in that he was young when he committed his violent act. It has been mostly older and middle-aged white men, those who feel most entitled to viable careers and breadwinner status, who have externalized their feelings of being threatened by women and people of color taking "their" jobs. Economic recessions and bouts of unemployment can be an explosive combination.[43]

The biographies of Oklahoma City bomber Timothy McVeigh and many of the terrorists involved in the September 11 attacks were marked by rage, entitlement, and emasculation, fueled in part by economic and professional failures. McVeigh received several medals for his army service in the Persian Gulf War but had to drop out of Special Forces training. His antigovernment ideology was later fed by underemployment, debt, and a strong distaste for federal taxes.

One of the 9/11 terrorist attack leaders and hijackers, Mohamed Atta, was also motivated in part by a lack of career success. He grew up in a modern Egyptian family, the younger brother of two older sisters who would go on to become a medical doctor and a professor. Atta's father "was the disciplinarian, grumbling that his wife spoiled their bright, if timid, son, who continued to sit on her lap until enrolling at Cairo University. 'I used to tell her that she is raising him as a girl, and that I have three girls, but she never stopped pampering him,'" he told a reporter after 9/11. He explained that he told his son he "needed to hear the word 'doctor' in front of his name . . . We told him your sisters are doctors and their husbands are doctors and you are the man of the family."[44] Humiliation and emasculation marked the biographies of multiple 9/11 terrorists and many others around the world. Just as the forces of globalization create instability, chip away at patriarchal arrangements, and generally threaten the current social order in the United States, they do so with greater effects abroad. Wars and Western occupations compound the impact of globalization, often experienced by non-Western countries as the literal or symbolic destruction of their cultures and beliefs. Western military, political, economic, and cultural forces push some men in these countries to embrace radical theologies and take up arms against the sources of these threats.[45] For example, the Taliban's efforts to reinstitute patriarchal authority in Afghanistan consists of imposing a rigid separation of spheres whereby not only feminism and gender equality are rolled back but all gendered roles and activities are strictly bifurcated. Violations are often met with violent enforcement.

Interviews with religious-based terrorists around the world reveal that many are animated by a sense of wounded masculinity, often for economic reasons.[46] Terrorism is often a response to humiliation, whether economic, political, religious, or ideological.[47] Compensatory violence restores a sense of manhood; it physically cleanses the feminizing emotion of shame.

Failed breadwinners often internalize or externalize their diminished status, symbolically and literally punishing themselves and others. As the Great Recession receded and job opportunities reemerged, many men returned to the paid labor force. Reclaiming their status as breadwinners, or at least members of the workforce, is a source of repair, closing and healing the wounds of unemployment. Alternatively, some men who were pushed or simply moved out of their breadwinner roles and into those of stay-at-home father come to embrace their new identity. They find greater value in raising and connecting with their kids, whom they tended to neglect some before their transition out of the workforce. Along with it, they transition into different ways of conceptualizing and modeling manhood. They redefine their responsibility, from providing economically to spending quality time with and meeting their children's basic needs. Ideas and language revolving around being a provider, making sacrifices, and being career-oriented for the benefit of the family are supplanted by a depth of commitment to emotional intimacy, being present, and sacrificing one's ego and career for the well-being of their partners and families. These men redefine not only their roles but their beliefs about enactments of manhood.

7

Redefining Manhood

Stay-at-Home Dads
as Real Men

Jenny and Ryan are in their 30s and raising two young boys, Evan and Grayson. After years of swapping breadwinner and primary caretaker roles while navigating an unsteady labor market, they have settled into the respective positions they find most fulfilling and feel suit them best. Being a stay-at-home dad is his "dream job," Ryan says. "I mean, cargo shorts full of dirty diapers and trash, you know, that shows that it has been a good day." Whereas Jenny felt isolated and trapped as the stay-at-home parent, Ryan prefers it over paid work.

Still, neither is immune to moments of reservation. Just as Ryan occasionally questions his masculinity when finances are tight, he says Jenny sometimes struggles with a "sort of maternal guilt" for choosing to be the breadwinner, "like she is somehow not doing enough. And that's something I fight by encouraging her and letting her know what [she's doing brings] value to our family." Their mutual support and appreciation steady them during these times of unease. So do their parents, all four of whom are supportive.

Others' reactions to their arrangement are not so consistently positive. Ryan says,

We've had people who were like, "Oh, I see," and you know immediately what they are thinking—that I am somehow lazy or that I'm not really a man, that I am, you know, whatever, insert [some] sort of derogatory [name]. They think

that my wife is—"Oh, so she's like the man of the household." I have that interacting with neighbors, you know, just explaining what I do:

"Oh, is it Daddy's day off?"

"No, I'm actually a stay-at-home dad."

"Oh, so you work at night?"

"No, this is what I do. I'm a stay-at-home dad. I work, you know, like a
stay-at-home mom but with a penis. Like if you picture that, but not a mom."

"Oh, so you're like the mom?"

"No, I'm their dad."

I'm still their dad, you know. I'm still the one that is putting them in
slightly dangerous situations to see how they are going to react. But I'm
also changing the diapers and responsible for coming up with a nutritious
and exciting lunch every day. And a lot of times [I have] that conversation
sort of over and over again, especially with this one [much older] neighbor,
and I don't think he knows what I do yet, even though on a weekly basis
he's like,

"Oh, are you home from work?"

"No! No! We had this conversation . . . never mind."

Ryan's sarcastic, humorous account of his experiences reflects the reality
that breadwinning mothers partnered with stay-at-home fathers are, statistically speaking, a new and unusual phenomenon. Ryan's older neighbor, like
many from that generation, can't wrap their minds around it. How can men
possibly do what (many assume) comes naturally to women? How can
men *mother*?

As with all social behaviors, what our culture determines to be proper nurturing and caretaking behaviors are learned. If they are not acquired earlier in
life, they can be done so later. This means that parents with enough resources
can decide what's best for their individual and familial needs, and everyone can
adjust accordingly, regardless of their sex or gender. Families without enough
resources may be forced into new and unexpected work-family roles. Sometimes this is a widespread phenomenon, as when the economic circumstances
of working-class men in Mexico City compelled them to make significant day
care contributions. This structural change meant these men's statuses weren't
threatened by doing what was previously seen as women's work.[1] The recession
hasn't had that effect here. Even with each other's support, along with families'
and friends', it isn't easy for those who buck the stereotypes. Jenny's and Ryan's
gendered identities are challenged by their atypical arrangement. But it feels
right, and it's working for them, so they conquer any obstacles—financial,
social, or otherwise. For Ryan, this requires staving off feminine attributions
while simultaneously redefining what it means to be a man. He asserts a broad
definition of responsible fatherhood instead of the breadwinner ideal.

Family Men

In a postindustrialized, post-second-wave feminist society, the men-as-breadwinner ideal is as antiquated as the women-as-homemaker ideal. Sole-breadwinning men are anachronisms: most women want to and do work, most families need two incomes, and 40% of women out-earn their husbands.[2] Much of the sole-breadwinner ideal is also based on an exaggerated history of its prevalence and longevity.

The experiences of long-term unemployed men during the Great Depression revealed that they and their families' economic and psychological suffering did not result in monolithic outcomes. Some men did not blame themselves, and many received strong support from their wives. As the Depression dragged on, it became clearer that men did not shoulder much responsibility for their unemployment. Half as many men's personalities changed for the better as did for the worse, according to their families. They became more pleasant, attentive, agreeable, and conflict avoidant. Some became less authoritarian, knowing they could not maintain that status if they were not the breadwinner. Although stay-at-home fathers were not a documented phenomenon during the Depression, unemployed men who were more committed to being fathers and husbands (and not just breadwinners) suffered less from their unemployment. Some unemployed men continued to view housework as women's work, but others contributed more. In one "equalitarian" family, "the husband assumed part of the housework duties because he loves to cook, enjoys housework, and likes to finish work together with his wife so that they may enjoy their leisure together. He makes fun of the husband whose pride is hurt by housework. His notion is that marriage is a partnership, and whatever needs to be done must be done by both."[3] The husband used to work as a truck driver, but even then, he tried not to work too much so that he could be around his family more, which his wife preferred. They had simple needs, didn't spend much money, and had close friends who were also disinterested in climbing economic or social ladders.

Mid-20th-century America was widely romanticized in 1950s sitcoms and U.S. popular culture as a time of innocence, prosperity, and *Ozzie and Harriet*–style domestic bliss.[4] In truth, the so-called traditional family from this era, with Dad as breadwinner and Mom as homemaker, was a historical artifact. It was a blip on the radar screen of American family types past and present, brought about by various economic, social, and political forces.

Engaging in 1950s nostalgia whitewashes that era's institutional racism and inequality, not just in the Jim Crow South but nationwide. Racism increased African American men's unemployment rates and reduced their incomes, which propelled a disproportionate number of African American women into the labor force. It is not a coincidence that mythic representations of the ideal 1950s family exclude black families. Nostalgic images of smiling moms similarly erase structural gender inequality. Although World War II brought record numbers of all women into the labor force, including married women, they were widely purged from or demoted to lower paid "female jobs" when men returned from war.[5] Women were also confined to separate and unequal roles within their marriages. This attempted separation of spheres by legislators, employers, unions, physicians, religious leaders, cultural critics, scholars, and husbands led many suburban housewives to feel trapped. They were isolated, bored, unfulfilled, depressed, and more.

It was "the problem that has no name," as Betty Friedan identified it in *The Feminine Mystique*.[6] More and more women desired all the benefits that accompany paid work, and more were enacting these desires. Women's labor force participation rose throughout the 1950s, climbing to 4 out of 10 (among women ages 16 and older) at the close of the decade.[7] One-third of these women workers had minor children at home. They and their families strayed from the neatly constructed narrative for that era and thus their existence gets clouded out. So do the many other family types that existed then, including single parents, stepfamilies, and extended families composed of various members and relationships.

Diversity of family types has been the norm throughout American history. Today, single dads account for more than 1 out of 12 households with minor children, or 2.6 million households. That is an eightfold increase since 1960, up from the rarely recalled 300,000 single fathers then. This half century or so of changes in family patterns has included a fourfold increase in the number of single mother–led households as well, reaching 8.6 million.[8] The increasing array of family types also now includes a growing number of families that have turned the breadwinner-husband, homemaker-wife model on its head.

By all measures, stay-at-home dads have been on the rise for several decades. They now comprise 16% of all at-home parents. Today's stay-at-home dads are four times as likely as their father's generation to report choosing this role as opposed to ending up in it because they lost their jobs or are ill or disabled, in school, or retired.[9] Depending on what criteria one uses to determine who qualifies as a stay-at-home dad, they number anywhere from fewer than 200,000 to around 2 million.[10] The numbers peaked during the Great Recession and have dipped slightly since, but the multidecade trend leaves no doubt that stay-at-home dads are here to stay.

The predecessor to this new generation of committed stay-at-home dads was the involved father. The earlier predecessor was the so-called househusband—the stigmatized, emasculated equivalent of "housewife." As gendered norms changed and the economy shifted, highlighted by more women working more hours outside the home, men slowly began to respond by increasing the number of hours they spent with their children and on doing housework. There was and has been a cultural lag, though; many men did this family work unwillingly. Still, in 1965, men averaged fewer than seven total hours per week of childcare and housework. Father norms caught up some by the 1990s, when most different-sex couples were dual-income and fatherhood began to include more engaged parenting expectations and practices. By 2015, fathers were doing seven hours per week of childcare and another nine hours of housework, about two and a half times as much family work as they did in 1965.[11] Expectations for fathers to be nurturing emerged in the 1970s and took hold over the next two decades. This new "family man" departed significantly from his father: "American fathers are increasingly likely to be nurturing family men rather than the distant providers and protectors that they once were."[12] And how could 1990s fathers remain distant, given that only one out of five of them were sole breadwinners?

The decades of cultural and economic changes that have resulted in men spending more time interacting with and caring for their kids has had a rather unsurprising effect: many enjoy it! Nearly half of fathers in dual-earner couples report a desire to spend more time with their children.[13] They are also more likely to recognize and appreciate the value of childrearing. Fathers today are unquestionably more engaged parents than were their fathers and grandfathers. For stay-at-home dads, even many who did not choose to exit the labor force, the experience leads them to add engaged, responsible fatherhood to their definition of manhood.

This has had a significant effect on families and society. However, critics rightly point out that progress toward gender equality has been slow and may have even stalled; the revolution is incomplete.[14] Women are still doing much more unpaid work, and men are doing more paid work. Many men—even in dual-earner households—still resist doing what they see as "women's work" at home. Unemployed fathers mostly still do not embrace being at-home parents. Whereas nearly three out of four stay-at-home moms say they do that work by choice, only about one out of five stay-at-home dads do so.[15] In other words, most men who are stay-at-home dads would rather not be, and if afforded the opportunity to exit that role, they will do so. Part of this is explained by these men's higher rates of disability as well as their relatively lower education levels and corresponding work opportunities; many have been pushed out of the paid labor force.[16] Even among younger men who profess a desire to be more equal, their practices trail their attitudes.[17]

Men's increased childcare hours may be misleading. Some research suggests that fathers are not as engaged and as involved as mothers, whether because men's parenting consists of more play time or it exhibits a certain detachment.[18] Critics question whether widely used time use survey research tools accurately capture the full range of parenting responsibilities.[19] Time spent and tasks completed are easily quantified; less so are more subtle, virtually around-the-clock parenting responsibilities such as being emotionally attuned, available, and supportive. Sharing this kind of parenting work poses another obstacle beyond women's and men's distribution of hours and tasks.

Survey research finds that public attitudes are also far from egalitarian. A recent survey found that half of respondents supported the idea of mothers staying home to raise children, but fewer than 1 out of 12 respondents said the same for fathers.[20] Qualitative studies continue to find that at least a proportion of men who fully embrace carework are subject to jokes and snarky comments from friends and strangers. The "Mr. Mom" comments haven't fully abated.

And why would they? Why should we expect them to in a society that continues to place such little value on parenting? U.S. federal policy provides a maximum of 12 weeks of leave per year—unpaid—when parents welcome a child into their family or they must care for a seriously ill child. This contrasts sharply with other highly developed nations. Our lack of a national childcare policy or program does not even allow for a fair comparison with countries that help parents' with infants and toddlers to transition back to work. The meager benefits accorded to American parents indicate our collective lack of appreciation for and value assigned to carework.

It is also indicative of how we continue to devalue feminine-marked work. Many actual and prospective fathers may find attractive the intrinsic rewards of at-home parenting: deeper and better relationships with children, being able to attend all their activities, relishing in and contributing to kids' development, and much more. But the structural obstacles our society erects (or, at minimum, accepts) undermine any chance that men will embrace at-home parenting as frequently or enthusiastically as women. The cultural obstacles are just as significant. Egalitarianism is not possible when two unequal groups have been providing distinct, essential contributions to a society and only one is motivated to significantly alter its behavior.

Expectations for men to be breadwinners, or at least income earners, make it difficult for them to distance themselves from that role. Some men, though, do seek alternative meanings of manhood. This is true for nearly all the stay-at-home dads I interview. Unsurprisingly, my solicitation for interviews yielded mostly voluntary stay-at-home dads—men who embrace the identity. Some, though, were forced into it, primarily due to job loss. Similar to other studies of stay-at-home fathers, my sample lacks the racial and economic diversity that survey research finds exists among this population. The predominantly white, middle-class, enthusiastic group of stay-at-home dads (SAHDs) I speak with betrays the reality that the larger population is decidedly less enthusiastic, less likely to be middle class, and disproportionately African American.[21] I follow the calls of gender scholars who emphasize that there is "a need to study both individual and collective resistance to manhood acts, no matter who performs them, presuming an enduring concern with understanding the social processes through which gender inequality can be overcome."[22]

(Mostly) Happy SA(H)Ds

A small but significant proportion of men are reconstructing or abandoning the breadwinner ideal. They are redefining manhood and making it more attainable. They can do so by prioritizing aspects of their masculine identity that they are currently more able to achieve. For example, some men change how they measure success by focusing on "couple self-sufficiency." This allows them to reframe being dependent on their partners' income as succeeding as a couple, rather than being an individual failure.[23] They also can focus on the importance of active fatherhood, emphasizing their intimate connections with their children and their children's development. This new family man is still a provider, only now he's not solely or even primarily an economic one. He is also, sometimes solely or primarily, responsible for his children's emotional and social well-being. In these ways, stay-at-home fathers can highlight what they can achieve as caretakers rather than conforming to the breadwinner ideal.

Peter: Proud as a Peacock

When Regina received a dream job offer in the South, she, Peter, and their three children relocated from the West Coast. Peter had to give up his professional network and later chose to quit his career altogether when it interfered with his ability to be there for his kids. Regina invited and welcomed that decision. She earns more than enough to support the family, and she loves that Peter is home for their children. It has taken him some time to acclimate to his new identity as a stay-at-home dad, and he still sometimes struggles with the insecurities that accompany not earning an income, but he has developed an appreciation for the meaning and value of his unpaid work. His relationships with Regina and their kids have grown to the point of being not only unbreakable but unbendable. Nothing comes between Peter and his family—not friends who tease or don't accept him, not his isolation from stay-at-home moms, and not the broader culture that still expects men to get paid.

For Peter, his decision was about being unselfish: "Finally I realized I had to check my ego at the door and do what I had to do for my kids." The couple's stable financial situation, Regina's strong support of Peter's belated decision to stay home, and Peter's recognition of the importance of involved parenting all outweigh outside critics and Peter's past and present difficulties letting go of his professional identity.

At social events, other men are often left speechless when Peter tells them he's a stay-at-home dad. Their anxieties are eased when they find out he used to have a career. He encounters the same surprised reactions when he meets other fathers at Jack and Jill, a national organization of mothers that seeks to enrich African American children so they can be tomorrow's leaders. "I mean, the looks on their face[s are] just hilarious. People can't . . . 'You're what?'" is all they manage to mutter, he says.

If you peel back the social veneer, Peter says, many men are at home raising their children, even in the South, for one reason or another. However, he says, the expectations and perceptions have not caught up with economic realities. This produces "kind of a double whammy on you" where men, he says, have to deal with their own personal hang-ups as well as everyone else's: "No one wants to have a group session at Starbucks and talk [about it] because it's weird, right? I mean, it's just not the way we're programmed as men." Peter thinks his generation may be the last one with these hang-ups because they were the last to mostly be raised in breadwinner-father, stay-at-home-mother homes. When he volunteers at his children's school, what's novel about him is not that he is a man but that he looks so different than his children. "The race issue still perplexes some of the kids," he says, "but the gender role doesn't seem to perplex them at all; just Charity's dad in the class." Of course, as hopeful as Peter is about the attitudes of his children's generation, he has to deal with the views of his own and earlier generations. He says, "I'm thinking for older dudes, quite frankly, they have to think I'm like a kept man. I'm sure what they think [is] 'Oh, look, he's got it easy. Found himself a [rich woman] and now he's a kept man.'" Conservative views of gendered roles make the small number of stay-at-home dads even less visible in the South, which makes it difficult for Peter to find other at-home parents for socialization and playdates. He says he's often ignored by stay-at-home moms. The times he wasn't, playdates were awkward. They "made everyone feel uncomfortable" because strangers assumed they were a single family.

Peter's assumptions about older men's views arise in part from some of his friends' judgmental comments about his choices and situation. It has cost him some friendships:

> I had a friend tell me, "I can't believe you're throwing it all away to follow [Regina] there. Why would you do that?" I had other friends joke like—to this day, I mean, it's those lifelong friends—"Well, how's that apron fit?" Like, "Excuse me?" "Well, I'm just joking with you about being a stay-at-home dad. How's that apron fit?" But now, after a year and a half, of course, those jokes have kind of died down because [they get] stale after a while.

He says the friends who don't talk to him anymore are the same ones who had a problem when Regina didn't take his last name. They aren't able to deal with how our society is changing, Peter says, "And that's not my problem. I'm not a shrink . . . if they can't handle it, that's on them. Wish them a good life."

202 • The Breadwinner Dilemma

If it sounds like there's an edgy defiance to Peter, there is. He is uncompromising in placing his family first. Negative comments from strangers and tired and tiresome jokes from friends only reinforce his unwavering commitment to his family and role. "As long as my wife and kids are OK with me," he says, "I could really, quite frankly, [not] give a damn what anybody else thinks." He attributes some of his imperviousness to gendered judgment and criticism to his more visible violation of Southern racial boundaries: "Part of it, too, when you're in an interracial marriage and you're living [in the South], you'd better [grow] a thick skin quick and deal with your comfort level [in] being who you are," he says.

Peter's experience has made him realize how unappreciative our society, including our government, is of at-home parents. This feminist critique of patriarchy, whereby much of men's paid work has been made possible by women's unpaid work at home, does not escape Peter, though he only seems to have thought about it after being placed in the position mostly occupied by women: "You start to realize as a guy how effed up it is the way we treat women in our society, the way we treat those that provide for our children. I mean, it's just crazy." He thinks stay-at-home parents should be able to file a W-2 with what their projected income would be, "just to recognize that what we do at home is worthy." He emphasizes, "It's real work. It's not the greatest work. Doing laundry gets old after a while, but someone has to do it . . . [we're not] just sitting around watching daytime television and eating bonbons."

That hypothetical W-2 could easily reach six figures. Imagine how much a single-parent CEO forced to hire parenting services (day care, transportation, food preparation, housekeeping, scheduling, etc.) would spend. Peter says he is also made a "second-class citizen" by needing his spouse to cosign for a loan or credit card. The parallels to the decades of experiences among stay-at-home mothers are obvious. The lack of societal recognition and compensation contribute to feelings of being dependent and infantilized—all of this for doing the unpaid work that is essential for families and society, freeing up others to do paid work.

Regina's income and support, and the meaning Peter derives from his new role, have helped him mostly overcome the difficult transition from thriving professional to at-home parent. When he's feeling vulnerable, he is now in a place where he can discuss it with Regina: "I'm fortunate that my wife is my best friend, so I'm able to talk openly about it." He says his marriage is stronger than ever: "And I'm sure I drive my wife crazy with my insecurities to a certain extent, but, like I said, I've got a great spouse[;] I'm lucky that she doesn't fall into the stereotype of women [who think men should be earning a paycheck]." If the government doesn't do it through formal recognition, Peter and some other stay-at-home dads need their partners to help soothe their wounded masculine egos.

Most important, Peter sees daily the positive impact being a stay-at-home dad has had on his marriage and his kids, their improved grades and well-being. He appreciates how engaged he is with his family now that his career isn't a distraction. Even on his bad days, he says "this dad thing is great," that "it's a blast to be able to do stuff and see them grow." Peter describes himself as "really close with the kids." He feels sorry for parents who choose or are stuck working instead of being home with their kids: "I mean, you do what you have to do in American society, but it's . . . to miss the things that people miss, those are once-in-a-lifetime opportunities with your kids. And you miss them and for what, a job that doesn't respect you anyway? Come on." He understands people have to pay their bills, but "it's a wonderful thing" being with his kids all the time. He says he values family more than ever before: "I was very symbolic of a lot of men. You know, you get married and you have a kid, but it's still about you. It's still an ego thing. The life I was living, when I died, so what? I mean, what, they're going to build a statue of me? And even if they did, so what? The real legacy of your life, of what type of person you are, is your children. They're that living monument to who and what you and your family believed in." He wants to be judged by his kids' lives, by "what success-ful, functional human beings they are." I ask Peter how he thinks he would have responded to a question about stay-at-home fathers before he had kids: "Oh, this person's out of their mind, and they're just trying to justify being at home." But now, he says,

> My daughter got straight A's this year. I'm a proud dad now. I'm like the peacock showing all his feathers walking around. You can't top that. I don't care what you do at your job, you can't top my kid getting straight A's. You can't top my son being able to read. He's going into kindergarten, and he's reading at a second-grade level. Beat that.

When Peter and I discuss what he now finds to be the most fulfilling part of his life and how he would have answered that question while he was excelling in his career, he says, "[If you asked me a couple years ago] I would say my job probably. Then I would give some BS answer of how I'm setting a great example to my kids and fighting for what's right. The answer would have been solely focused on me. Even though I would have been talking about everybody else, it would have been focused on what I'm doing in my life." However, today, he beams at his son's swimming lesson progress, from not being able to swim a few months ago to seeming to be "part dolphin," and says that he feels most fulfilled "being a dad. I really do."

Peter's time as a stay-at-home dad has shifted his views on the value of paid work and parenting, as well as gendered social norms. He says, "It's changed me. It's like real men can be stay-at-home dads. Real men can have a wife that earns—I have some friends who could never handle their wife making more money than them. It's almost absurd that men put themselves in these boxes that don't exist in this modern economy." Peter rejects those boxes in a way that does not challenge the necessity of manhood but rather how it is defined: "I still consider myself a man—I'm strong, I'm married, I provide for my family. But all those have different characteristics now to me in the sense that providing for my family doesn't necessarily mean I have a job and income. Providing for my family means that I was willing to accept a better economic opportunity for my wife, and I'm willing to provide for my family by doing what I'm doing as a stay-at-home dad."

Just as the 1990s' emergence of the family man was a significant departure from generations past—with the new expectation to fold a more intimate, engaged style of parenting into the provider and protector ethos—contemporary stay-at-home dads like Peter reflect another evolutionary step. Their progression has them rejecting not only the breadwinner ideal but the expectation that fathers are financial providers at all. Instead they redefine manhood to include a broader kind of responsible fatherhood that in some ways strips away gendered expectations and roles: fathers should place the well-being of their partners and families ahead of themselves. That may require them to sacrifice successful careers and become financially dependent on more successful woman partners. It may also involve having their manhood questioned. A healthy streak of masculine American individualism helps ward off those social pressures and stigmas. And indeed, Peter and some of the other stay-at-home dads I interview frame their decision to abandon careers and a paycheck for the benefit of their families as "real" displays of manhood. They reject the tired, anachronistic breadwinner ideal, but they do so in a way that rejects not the idea of manhood but rather only that iteration of it. In other words, they still stake a claim to a highly masculine identity instead of abandoning altogether the pursuit of manhood, however it's defined.

That latter project is what scholars have referred to as gender vertigo, degendering, or undoing gender, whereby not only can people choose whatever careers, interests, partners, and lives they desire; they can to do without any gendered cultural baggage.[24] Gender as we know it—the identity, social category, cultural expectations, and social structure—will be dismantled. None of the fathers I interview believe that gender is a meaningless social construct that ought to be rejected outright. What I suspect is these men are a bridge generation to a more deeply reworked version of ideal manhood. They still grapple with rigid manhood ideals even as they reject aspects of them. Eschewing gender altogether is a qualitatively different undertaking than trying to stake claim to a redefined manhood, regardless of how much softer or kinder it may be. By attempting to establish a new ideal, these men implicitly place other men who are unwilling or unable to fulfill this new ideal lower on the masculine hierarchy.[25]

However, because our society still expects men to be financial providers, Peter's assertion of still being a "real man" is accompanied by lingering identity struggles. "That's why I was saying it'd be nice if I got a pay stub every couple weeks even if I didn't get any money," he says, "just so I could associate that what I'm doing has [an] economic value. If all the other men see that there's a dollar value, then [it's easier to see] I'm worthy of what I'm doing." Peter's desire to monetize his familial contributions is filtered through a lens of dominant cultural expectations: men are supposed to be breadwinners. The unpaid work that has been and continues to be associated with women is devalued. Peter does not distance himself from this work (although he hates doing some of it, especially laundry and cleaning bathrooms). He just wishes it would be assigned value in accordance with paid work. Perhaps he would appreciate Regina surprising him with "at-home dad" business cards, as one breadwinning wife in another study did for her stay-at-home husband.[26]

Peter tries to shield his kids from his dissonance, expecting that the world they will inherit to look much different than the one he grew up in. He does not want his kids, especially his son, to be a living anachronism. He explains, "I don't want my son to grow up—and I don't think any boy in this day and age should grow up—thinking that the world revolves around him." He thinks that's setting them up for failure given young women's better college and professional school graduation rates. "It's going to be a woman-dominated world," he says, "so if you raise your son to be what's been a 'traditional man,' I don't know how your son functions in a healthy relationship. I don't even think he'll ever get married because you're going to have all these women that have been told for generations now that they can have it all and they can do it all." Without this progress, he thinks people—women and men alike in different-sex couples—will make outdated, "stupid decisions" based on men being leaders of the family, prioritizing *his* career regardless of whether he earns more than his partner: "I mean, that's just asinine. To me, it's . . . I would do a real disservice to my son if I am portraying what I'm doing as a problem. So I try, especially in front of my—and in front of my daughters too—but especially in front of my son, I try not to have [dissonant] dad moments 'cause when he grows up and he has to deal with it, have flexibility to adapt to the world that he's living, I don't want to put that burden on him that he's not a man if he's not [a breadwinner]."

Jamie: Acclimating and Appreciating

Like Peter, Jamie left an upwardly mobile career to be a stay-at-home dad. He was able to do so because his partner, Thomas, earns enough to support their family. They would have preferred Jamie be the breadwinner and Thomas stay home, but Jamie's income would not allow it. They were faced with two difficult decisions when they decided they wanted to adopt: whether it was worth it for Jamie to keep working, only to have much of that income gobbled up by day care expenses, and whether they should move back to Jamie's home state of Iowa, where they could get married and both secure full custody of any kids they adopted. They chose to make the move, uprooting their lives to ensure they received the same legal rights accorded to other parents. Many adoption agencies were not interested in working with a gay couple, though, so they began the more difficult path of fostering kids in hopes that they would retain permanent custody. Eventually they were awarded custody of a preschooler they fostered and later a newborn. Jamie became the stay-at-home parent, which, given the exorbitant day care costs for two kids, was an even more rational decision after the second child joined their family.

The couple's stable financial situation and their long-standing arrangement of combining and sharing their money eliminated that potential anxiety for new stay-at-home dad Jamie. What he has struggled with most are the loss of work-based status and identity, social isolation, and the day-to-day difficulties and tediousness of parenting. He says,

> I did go through some down times. I sort of questioned my self-worth, like, when I would tell some people that I stayed at home with the kids, it sort of stopped the conversation. [Like] who was I if I wasn't working [as an office manager for a not-for-profit]? I worked through that, but for a while there, it was just really . . . it was a big struggle for me. The day that it all hit me [was when] I dropped the six-year-old off at summer camp, and then I'm driving clear out [of town] to go pick up a prescription and then go get that filled. You know, it's like, I'm just like the errand boy, really, with all this running back and forth.

He and Thomas knew few people nearby because Jaime had been away for many years, and they were less likely to encounter other gay dads. Jamie's encouraging and helpful mother was a buoy, but he needed more support. Raising an unusually defiant child mostly by himself during the week (Thomas often traveled for work) made Jamie feel even more isolated. He was like other stay-at-home fathers, who as a group have been found to be more isolated than stay-at-home mothers.[27] Being gay can make this even more acute. Jamie says, "One of the biggest struggles that I had was having this whole sense of feeling very alone." Initially he couldn't find any other gay dads. There was nobody in his life he could relate to, which "was really a struggle" for him. Finally he found an online group for gay fathers and made some connections. Jamie now interacts with a couple dozen gay dads across the country. They swap advice about parenting in general and being a gay parent specifically. "That's been very helpful for me," he says.

Thomas and Jamie have not closely connected with other parents nearby, but neither have they encountered discrimination. When Jamie met and told his son's teacher that he was a stay-at-home dad, she didn't blink, responding, "Oh, that's great. We have volunteer opportunities right over here." Likewise, he was welcomed into a local stay-at-home moms' group and introduced to an LGBTQ parents' group through their church, but there were no gay dads. He says he never sees any dads when they visit the local children's museum, let alone any gay dads. "I wish there were people that were actually closer, that we could actually maybe go on playdates with," he says, "because for me it's important [for] the kids. I want the kids to see other families like ours."

LGBTQ stay-at-home parents face an array of unique or heightened challenges, including fewer or no nearby peer families; the possibility that family will withdraw contact or support; a history of marginalization and discrimination; a sense of being judged about how they raise their kids, particularly regarding issues tied to gender and sexuality; and the social and emotional isolation that accompanies these experiences. Jamie has endured all of these to a greater or lesser extent. Thomas's conservative Christian sister and brother-in-law, who "believe very strongly that marriage is between a man and a woman," have been a problem: "They point-blank told us that our kids were probably in a better situation with us than what they could have been in or what they were probably previously in, but they thought it was a real shame that our kids were only going to be raised seeing one lifestyle. Which we found very offensive. If I can protect our kids from hate and people that I feel are really judging us unfairly, then I will." This includes keeping those family members away from his kids. His in-laws' prejudicial comment is unintentionally partially true: statistically speaking, the kids *are* better off with Jamie and Thomas as their parents since, regardless of sexuality, "families headed by (at least) two committed, compatible parents are generally best for children."[28]

Jamie's confident resolve in the face of family prejudice succeeds a long history of adolescent and teenage struggles with his sexuality. Just as a counselor helped steer him through that process, he relied on one when he was at his low point as a new stay-at-home dad. She helped him set personal goals beyond parenting so that he could find more balance in his life. He found a gym with day care service so he could work out, began a video diary site documenting his parenting experiences, and enthusiastically enrolled in online courses to finish his degree.

College coursework was an important bridge when he struggled with not having a career, not finding satisfaction in parenting, and lacking outside sources of intellectual stimulation and challenge. He hates housework,

208 • The Breadwinner Dilemma

finding it monotonous and unfulfilling. In his own words, coursework kept him sane. Jamie's difficult transition into his new role was made easier by their financial stability, by his partner's and both their mothers' support, and because he wasn't forced into it. Eventually, his defiant son became less defiant, and parenting became a source of pride and reward. He no longer feels like he is straddling two identities: "[Previously I would say to people I met] 'I'm a stay-at-home dad, but I'm working on my bachelor's degree online.' And I've sort of dropped that. I talk more about, 'Yes, I'm a stay-at-home dad, and we have a six-year-old, and he's getting ready to go into kindergarten, and he's been working all summer on [the] alphabet, and trying to learn numbers.'" Jamie has noticed that others' reactions have been more positive since he has enthusiastically embraced being a stay-at-home dad. Whereas before he felt like it was a conversation stopper, now the response tends to be, "Oh, that's great. That's awesome. What's that like for you?" Today, he finds most fulfilling the time he gets to spend with his kids. "It's amazing to watch [the baby] grow and then to help him figure out [how the world works]," he says, "but it's also been a lot of fun with [my son] too, because he is so, so smart." Jamie finds fulfillment in watching his kids grow and learn and now recognizes his own growth from being the primary caretaker. He has learned to be patient and flexible, two things his career did not foster.

LGBTQ parents often feel like they are under a microscope, with good reason. "I feel very judged at times," Jamie says. When his son told Jamie he wanted to have a Barbie-themed birthday party, Jamie's mind immediately went to the time he was visiting his family and his sister-in-law openly criticized him. His son wanted to play Ken and Barbie and chose to be Barbie, which prompted Jamie's sister-in-law to comment, "That's wrong." That earlier judgment caused Jamie to reflexively reject his son's birthday party request: "'No, you're not going to have a Barbie party,' [I told him] because I immediately felt uncomfortable, and I felt I would be judged, because people would think that I was making him do that."

After speaking with Thomas and thinking it over, they decided their son should be able to have whatever party theme he wanted, regardless of how others might judge them. Eventually they arrived at a compromise: a two-themed party, Barbie and Toy Story, which his son also loves, so that other parents wouldn't flinch at sending their boys to the party. "The more I thought about it, the more I thought, 'You know, I'm not going to let these people rule my life,'" Jaime says. "That's not fair to me, and that's not fair to these kids for me to always be worried, 'What are these people thinking of us? Or me?'"

The same issue has arisen on other occasions, including when their son attended a summer camp intended for girls, complete with makeovers and princess costumes, and a couple of Halloweens where he chose costumes meant for girls. "And so I'm a little bit nervous about that, just because of other kids," Jamie says. He thinks he will continue to worry about those things because boys can be so mean. But he goes along with Thomas's firm belief that their son should do as he pleases, recalling, "As a kid, I had my Cabbage Patch Kids, and played with He-Man, and you know, I had boy and girl things. And I played with My Little Pony. I didn't do the dress up stuff, but if that's what he wants to do, I mean . . . I don't know, I—we'll just have to cross that bridge when we get to it." Preparing for and worrying about how others might view and judge them, particularly regarding their kids' gender and sexuality, is a common response to the unique pressures faced by LGBTQ parents.[29]

Similar to Peter, Jamie's experiences as a stay-at-home father have shifted his views on manhood. Previously, he would have put more emphasis on being a breadwinner. "I think in some ways, it's changed in that I'm doing a role that probably I would have considered more of a female role," he says. Being a stay-at-home dad and sometimes being judged for it by others has occasionally exacerbated his lifelong gender identity issues. He continues to identify and highlight what he sees as the more masculine aspects of his role, including being "goal-oriented" and a "leader" of the family: "As far as being a breadwinner, that doesn't really bother me as much as it might bother others" because Thomas always earned so much more and they enjoy a comfortable living.

Mika: Mr. Big Shot to Dad

"The transition from senior-ranking enlisted person to being a stay-at-home dad, watching an infant, caring for an infant, was really, really tough on me," 49-year-old Mika says. He retired early from the military because he and his wife, Celia, preferred one of them stay home with their new baby. He thought it would be fairest not to interfere with her blossoming career after his 20 years in the military. He was so overwhelmed, he briefly returned to the workforce as a private contractor in Iraq.

In a short couple of years, he went from being a competent and respected military officer ("I was pretty much the boss.") to an overwhelmed and not-so-competent stay-at-home dad ("I didn't know what I was getting into. I thought it was going to be easy.") to a private contractor in Iraq ("It was pretty rough [then] in Iraq, but I thought being a stay-at-home dad was even tougher."), and finally back to being the primary caretaker with the arrival of their second baby. Relative financial stability, personal autonomy, his wife's support for each transition he made, and their family and friends' childcare contributions all allowed Mika to more easily navigate these disparate and sometimes contradictory roles and responsibilities. His one-year stint in Iraq, which was motivated in part by a desire to be in a combat zone with friends who also were risking their lives, led to an epiphany: "I got paid well when I was there, but I realized, probably really for the first time in my life, that money was not that important. That family was even more important. Money, you know, sort of went down to the bottom as far as my priorities." He returned home, but quickly invested much of his time and energy into various nonmilitary training and educational pursuits, still leaning heavily on day care and others to care for his infant daughter. Like Jamie, Mika has a strong inner drive for success and desire to improve himself however he can, whether physically, emotionally, or cognitively.

It took the birth of his son, a growing comfort level caring for his kids, and finding a group of stay-at-home dads to socialize and commiserate with before Mika embraced his new identity. Although there were other stay-at-home dads at his old base, they flew under the radar. He was aware of only a couple of "out" stay-at-home husbands of military wives: "The rest seem to be incognito. Because I would hear from other people when I say, 'Yeah, I'm a stay-at-home dad.' They're like, 'Oh, yeah. This guy's a stay-at-home dad. [That] guy's a stay-at-home dad.' And I was like, 'Really? They live close to me. I never knew that.'" Mika wonders, "Where are they, are they hiding?" He thinks they are because they are younger and "they're afraid, they don't want to admit" that they don't have jobs.

Mika says he never felt welcomed by stay-at-home moms on or off of military bases. He says there were instances when he and his daughter would be ignored at the playground—or worse. "Sometimes they would just, they would see me coming with my children, and it was like instinctual or something," he says, half-jokingly, "but they would take off. You know, it was like, 'Adult male at the playground: Warning, warning!'" The dad's group he eventually found and joined reduced his social isolation and allowed him to bond with others in a similar situation and blow off some steam on kid-free, dads' social nights. Fellow military retirees have also been supportive, Mika says, lauding him for landing in an admirable position after a long career: "Man, I wish I was in that situation. You know, that's a great situation to be in," they tell him.

Mika suspects his in-laws might think he is sponging off of his wife because they have not commented on his at-home status. And he also assumes some of his friends from Samoa think he's not being a real man because he is no longer the breadwinner. Overall, though, he has not taken any grief. I ask him if others sometimes think he is just unemployed and can't find a job. "No, I haven't come across that," he says, "maybe because of the way I carry myself. You know, I still have sort of like a military bearing even though I'm real patient and calm now." Others' reactions are usually more surprised than judgmental. I ask him how these interactions begin. "I'm like, 'I'm a stay-at-home dad.' And then I say, 'Oh, yeah, I'm retired military, too.'" I ask him how quickly the second sentence follows the first. "It follows it, almost always. But I've noticed that [lately] I just say, 'I'm a stay-at-home dad.' But at the beginning, you know, it would come quickly. Sometimes it would be like, 'Oh, I'm retired so I stay at home and watch my kids now.'" Although Mika is simultaneously working on a graduate degree while being the primary caretaker, he feels less compelled to highlight his former or current educational or occupational statuses or accomplishments. He admits his ego partially fuels his graduate work, but he embraces his stay-at-home father identity. He recognizes and appreciates all the positive ways his kids and his parenting experiences have changed him.

Mika worries less about projecting a tough, masculine self. He's calmer, more patient, less self-absorbed. He has lost interest in watching sports. ("It used to sort of be my life.") Most important, he says, he is more in tune with his kids and how they see and experience the world. "Going from the military, a very machismo, tough environment to a stay-at-home dad is ego busting," he says. But he explains,

> I was able to view life again through [my daughter's] eyes. I think as adults, we take life for granted. Like, say, flowers and rainbows and that sort of thing. That excited my daughter, you know, as a little child. And I was able to look at it and get excited, too. It's like, wow, you know, I would just walk by these nice-looking plants where she would stop and smell it and be happy. I sort of learned to do that, too. So it helped get me in tune, more back in tune with nature and looking at life through a different perspective.

He describes it "an awakening experience." He was so focused on money and material possessions that he was missing out on life: "I'm a more spiritual-thinking person now, because of my daughter's excitement about the little things in life, or the magical things that she thinks. You know, I see things as magical now." Mika's daughter also reawakened his childhood memories of being in nature.

Mika no longer has an edge or alertness about him. "When your kid's screaming and throwing a fit or just crying, you learn to deal with it and have patience," he says. "Some things really don't matter that mattered before, while I was a military guy. I don't have to walk around, you know, thinking, 'I'm Mr. Big Shot.' I'm just a dad now. I'm fine with that . . . And I see [other dads on the base], you know, the way they hold themselves in that confident, cocky—you know, the persona that they portray. I don't have to do that anymore. Being a stay-at-home dad, it changes you. It changed me. Like, you know, 'Hey, I'm here for my children, my family, but not for myself.'" He grew up in a household he describes as having "a lot of physical, emotional, and mental abuse," so when his daughter reacted poorly to getting spanked as a form of discipline, he stopped the practice: "I guess the older I got, the more I realized violence really doesn't solve anything; it just makes more problems.

I remember thinking, 'Man, I don't want my kids to grow up in a situation where there's constant fear.' That's crazy. I can't imagine treating children like the way I was treated."

Virtually all Mika's views have been altered since he committed to being a stay-at-home dad. Among them are those on manhood and gendered expectations for kids and adults. When I ask him what it means to be a man, he says,

> Wow. That should be an easy question, but it's not. What it means to be a man? That's a tough question. You know what, if you had asked me this while I was in the military, I would be able to spout off, but now I can't. I guess as a stay-at-home parent and a stay-at-home dad, you know, you look at the genders differently. There's . . . maybe it's blurry. Gender becomes blurred, you know, sexual orientation becomes blurred. It's how you care for your kids. I guess being a man is just looking at the world with a sense of justice, equality. Just because you're a man doesn't mean you're entitled to certain things. So that's what I want my son to follow—[the idea that] people are equal. Gender[s] should be treated equally. [There] shouldn't be differences; although there's physical differences, in your mind, we should be equal. So it doesn't matter if you're a man or a woman.

Mika's evolving views on gender, work-family roles, and equality arise from his personal experiences as a breadwinner, partner, and at-home parent. Not even a nearly lifelong commitment to perhaps the most segregated social institution in American society prevents him from bonding with his kids and eventually embracing a non-breadwinner identity.

Ryan: Living the Dream (Sort Of)

Ryan is one of several stay-at-home fathers I interview who share with me stories of being abused as a child. His parents' alcohol abuse and accompanying physical violence colored much of his childhood. He found himself doing whatever he could to shield his siblings and cousins from the violence. I hesitate to draw any sweeping conclusions, but it is notable that Ryan's experience of trying to protect other children from abuse is a common thread among the voluntary stay-at-home fathers I interview. Desiring to protect and parent kids came naturally to them as adults after being forced into those situations as kids.

Ryan's partner, Jenny, and their two young sons have helped Ryan overcome a violent, difficult childhood. For a couple of years, Ryan and Jenny rotated in and out of the workforce, swapping roles as caretaker and breadwinner. Ultimately, though, they were trying to figure out how to get Jenny back into the workforce full-time and have Ryan, the self-described "more nurturing one," be the stay-at-home parent, while still being able to pay their bills. Then Ryan was laid off from his job, and the decision was made for them. Ryan likens it to being pushed off a cliff from which they were trying to figure out how to climb down; it took months for them to land softly and upright. During that time Jenny could not secure a full-time position, while Ryan turned down multiple offers. He felt guilty, as if he was being derelict in his duties as a man. Eventually Jenny landed a good job, and they were able to accomplish their goal. They live quite modestly and are far from financially secure, which continues to cause Ryan some masculinity anxiety, but they make it work. Jenny feels challenged and fulfilled by her work; Ryan describes being a stay-at-home dad as his "dream job."

The financial and social pressures they face are relieved by their mutual commitment to their family arrangement, appreciation for each other's work, and supportive parents. All of these help steel their resolve. Ryan has also connected with other stay-at-home parents, both in person and via online groups. He says other moms at school tend to be standoffish until they meet Jenny. He has fallen into a group of moms whom he describes as "sort of like the alternative moms, you know, the tattoo moms or the lesbian couple. They are cool with me. We can hang out. I am somehow accepted, and I don't know what that is or what that says about anything bigger, but those are the ones who tend to invite me do things." He has also connected with other dads online, some who live nearby and others far away. They commiserate about their situation, whether it is being "treated like a pariah" at a playground filled with moms or just general parenting issues.

However, some of their extended family question Ryan and Jenny's arrangement on conservative religious grounds, "like it is somehow unbiblical or heretical that I would be the one at home," Ryan says. Acquaintances, neighbors, and strangers have provided mixed feedback on their arrangement, as Ryan describes in the introduction to this chapter. Some people just can't wrap their minds around Ryan being home full-time. Their young boys even sometimes have to help explain, "This is what my daddy does. He takes care of us; he's a stay-at-home dad." The eye-rolling and other explicit or subtle negative reactions come frequently enough that they have generated different responses from Ryan, as well as introspection. Now he mostly just blows them off, knowing that people's judgments are based on lack of information; his family know best what he does and why it's valuable.

Ryan and Jenny often find humor in the gendered norms from which they deviate. They joke about Ryan being the one who does the laundry and takes care of the kids and house, but it reflects negatively on Jenny if someone visits and the house is unkempt. Vice versa, if the yard is a mess, Ryan says it reflects on him. Even their boys mirror some of the mommy versus daddy stereotypes: "It is funny, whenever they are taking care of each other, they still say that they are the mommy. So if my five-year-old is taking care of my three-year-old, he goes, 'It is OK, Mommy's here.' I am like, 'Hey, what's up? I'm the one!

214 • The Breadwinner Dilemma

It's Daddy that takes care of you!' And they just laugh. So there is still that association, you know, even with our boys, who have mostly known me being at home; there is still that association with the mom being the real nurturing one." Their parents' division of labor has had some effect, though, on the boys' gendered views. The younger one, Ryan says, recently proclaimed, "'Mommy is a boss because girls are bosses and boys cut down trees.' And it's like, I don't know exactly what that means; it seems like he's getting at something pretty profound there, but I can't get it out."

Ryan's own thoughts and identity have become more concrete. He considers himself manly for doing the unpaid work he does, which he describes as much tougher than any white- or blue-collar job he's ever held. And being there for his family is so much more fulfilling. He pushes back against those who accuse stay-at-home dads of being feminine. Caretaking is not essentially feminine and earning a paycheck is not essential to manhood, he says, noting the sacrifices he and Jenny have made. He says that Jenny sees him as strong not only because of his physical strength but because of his ability to comfort their children. When I ask him directly what it means to be a man, Ryan responds,

I think of the *Big Lebowski* quote of "being a man is doing what needs to be done in whatever situation. You know, that and [a pair of testicles]." . . . These ideas about being a man, I don't know, I've kind of laid out and then reexamined a lot. You know, like there are times when I'm saying, "I can't lose being strong and reliable" and these masculine qualities like being this sort of John Wayne character. And then, I don't know, these seem sort of limiting, this almost archaic look at being a man. For me, [being a man] also means not just changing a diaper, but not being a wuss about it. Or like, I don't need a gold star because I changed a diaper. Like that's just what I do. Or teaching my kids how to be loving and caring, while also teaching them to be adventurous. And I guess a lot of times when I think of what it means to be a man, I think of what is it that I would like my boys to look like when they're older. You know, that I want them to be creative, I want them to be self-assured, I want them to be adventurous, I want them to look after, you know, be protectors of people that are smaller or picked on or that sort of thing.

Ryan's ideas about parenting, socialization, and manhood both stray from and conform to hegemonic masculine ideals. He is atypical in many ways: his assertion that men can nurture as well as women, his desire to inculcate that behavior in his boys, his decision to leave the paid labor force, and his strong support of his wife's breadwinner status. Yet Ryan also believes that girls and boys have inherent differences, and he sees his parenting style as distinctly masculine. He says he "doesn't totally buy into" the idea of gender-neutral parenting. His boys gravitate to cars and dirt piles. While he doesn't think those are uniquely masculine interests, these preferences seem "part of who they are and not as much socialized." The boys also are "nurturing with dolls and animals [but] that's not what they go to first; that's more of something that we tried to add on." Reflecting broader societal views, Ryan labels some traits and interests masculine and others feminine. As the dad—not a gender-less parent—he says his parenting style includes an emphasis on adventurousness and intentionally placing his kids "in slightly dangerous situations to see how they are going to react." Ryan does not want to degender his kids or our society. Rather he proposes a redefinition of manhood that is broader, less rigid. Like other stay-at-home dads, he believes that sacrificing a career and paycheck for the benefit of the family is as manly as it gets, asking what better illustration is there of a provider and protector.

Zach: Impressed with His "Feminine Side"

Zach and Laura have three kids, ages eight, six, and four. He describes their home life as "controlled chaos." It has taken him years to figure out how to manage the "24/7, nonstop" onslaught. A self-described neat-freak, Zach finds his kids' messy, dirty ways both impressive and wearying: "They can trash a bathroom in one day. I mean, they pee all over the place, they make messes on the sink, stuff falls on the floor and they leave it there." Being the at-home parent has forced him into being the "enforcer" with the kids: "My wife's the good cop; I'm the bad cop. I will lay down the law on this stuff all day long, and I'll nail my kids [making messes] left and right, trying to make them clean up after themselves."

Zach quit his non-breadwinning job when their second child arrived because, like so many other parents, working simply to pay for day care made little sense to them. Also, he always wanted to stay at home. He ascribes some of this to a lonely childhood marked by bullying and isolation from other kids. He dreamed of having a big, tight-knit family that spent most of their time together. That wish has come true.

Zach was marginalized and targeted as a kid because, like so many boys, he did not fit into the tiny box of acceptable masculinity. He thinks his childhood gender identity both foreshadowed and made easier his decision to become a stay-at-home dad:

> I'm not your guy's guy. I've always had more women and girls as friends. So it's . . . let's put it this way: my friends that know me well would tell you that I'm impressed with my feminine side. So in a way, it's helped me be able to do what I do. Every day I'm doing a load of laundry. Every day I'm doing a load of dishes, I'm getting kids out of bed and getting them dressed. I make breakfast, lunch,

and dinner every day. So you have to have a different mind-set to be able to do all that. You're not your normal "man's man."

Like Ryan, Zach uses terminology tied to culture (man, not male), but culture and biology are so often conflated. It is easy to read his reference to a feminine mind-set as something that is hardwired, part of our essential natures.

Even though Zach prefers and was able to make the decision to stay at home, abandoning a paycheck and closing his private bank account was "a gut check" and "not an easy thing to swallow," he says. "It just came down to, now that I didn't have a salary coming in, it was stupid to have my own bank account. Now her money is my money, and . . . you know, I'm not making any money." The loss of an income, exiting the paid labor force, and being financially dependent on someone else—even his partner and the mother of his children—sometimes overwhelms Zach's choice to stay at home. "I'm doing this so that our family can live and be happy," he says, "and that basically [means] my wife's salary is my salary, so it is challenging." Laura earns enough to support them, but they have made some cutbacks, mostly in leisure activities and vacations. He plans to "look for something that'll bring in some more salary" when his youngest goes to school.

Laura also wanted to be the at-home parent, but hers has always been the breadwinning career. "She went to work because it was what was best for the family," he says. "She would quit her job tomorrow" if Zach could earn a family wage. This is not possible, so she supports his staying home. Similar to several other stay-at-home dads I interview, though, Zach feels as if his wife is not immune to taking his unpaid work for granted. He recalls commiserating with a close friend who stays at home with her kids: "You know, stay-at-home parents, they have the most unappreciated jobs ever. Because the other parent doesn't see the big picture of the stay-at-home parent, doesn't understand what it's like, and they don't appreciate it. Because I definitely don't feel appreciated. It's hard to feel fulfilled about something [when] it is not appreciated."

The popularity of the *Mad Men* series has given Betty Friedan's "problem that has no name" an updated moniker: "Betty Draper disease."[30] The long list of dissatisfactions of 1950s suburban housewives included feeling unappreciated (especially by partners and kids), being on call 24-7, being isolated (stuck at home, while their partners work/travel too much), being bored and lacking cognitive stimulation, feeling fatigued by tedious housework and endless errands, feeling like they are spinning their wheels and not accomplishing anything, feeling trapped, and feeling economically dependent and vulnerable.[31]

Zach and the other stay-at-home dads check off most of these boxes. They, and all of today's at-home parents, also often have to reconcile with being forced into staying at home because of job loss or unaffordable day care. Uniquely, stay-at-home dads confront some additional challenges: they often feel isolated from stay-at-home moms (the vast majority of at-home parents), they are socially isolated and less accepted because they are atypical and seen as unmanly, they depart from what their fathers did, and they are more likely to have a resentful partner who would prefer to stay home. Men have been expected to break free of the confinement of the feminized "domestic sphere" not only for work reasons but also for other embodied enactments of manhood: hiking, fishing, hunting, drinking, golfing, exercising, and so forth. However, men enjoy some unique benefits as at-home parents: they are often disproportionately rewarded for being involved dads, they are very rarely single parents and less likely to have to rely on welfare, and when they do paid work, they are not subject to gendered discrimination and inequality.

Zach's wife's support and appreciation are mixed, in his mind. His parents (especially his mother) are strongly supportive, reveling in spending time with Zach and the kids. Other family members have not voiced their opinions. Overall, he says, "I don't think I've been viewed differently by family and friends. In fact, I've probably earned more respect." Like other dads, Zach says he regularly hears wearisome comments from strangers when he's out with his kids, especially from older women: "The funniest comment we always joke about with other stay-at-home dads is [when] we get the 'Oh, it's Daddy's day out?' or, 'Oh, you're giving Mommy the day off?' or something like that. And you kind of turn around and look at them and go, 'Daddy's day is every day,' and you try not to make a smart comment back." He says these unwelcome comments have decreased over the last eight years, attributing the reduction to broader changes in work-gender stereotypes and patterns. Zach thinks both the growth of stay-at-home dads and women's success at work has helped uncouple gender and work-family roles. These have fueled progress, whether that means fewer stay-at-home moms at the playground who "look at you as if you could be a pedophile" or the positive comments the majority of people offer him. He says most people have a positive reaction, and many dads will say, "Oh, man, that's a cool job, I wish I could do that." Although some think "you get to sit home and watch movies and whatever," which, "if you're a crappy stay-at-home dad, that's what you do. You play video games, you don't regard your kids." Zach says they don't understand how he always has to be energetic with a good demeanor because "[kids are] always going to be emotionally challenging."

As with most of the other stay-at-home dads, he never fully connected with stay-at-home moms. Zach says he "never got that warm, fuzzy feeling" during group playdates. Gatherings he tried to host were sparsely attended. He took the hint and eventually found a nearby stay-at-home dads' group populated by several dozen fathers. They organize playdates, exchange parenting tips, watch each other's kids in a pinch, and go out once a month without the kids. Many men have stayed in the group even after their kids reached high school age.

The camaraderie and support have been essential to Zach. Their experiences are his, and his are theirs.

Zach feels as if the dad's group has had a bigger impact on his gendered identity than becoming a stay-at-home dad, because he always expected to be an involved father. "I think I'm different than most men," he says. "I think almost to a point that what I do as a stay-at-home dad—I was kind of always made to be this way. I wasn't career-oriented." (His language slips between biology and culture again—do we read it as his essential nature when he suggests he was "made to be" a nurturer?) He acknowledges that society's view of him as a man is still mixed at best, but becoming a stay-at-home dad is "the best thing I could have done." His definition of manhood never conformed to others': "A lot of guys probably would not view me as a man because I'm a stay-at-home dad, and I do the laundry, and I change the poopy diapers and, you know, I wipe my kids' butts all the time and all that stuff. I don't think a lot of guys would say that's being a man. I've never really agreed with the [stereotype] of what a man's man is." Zach's version of manhood revolves around responsible fatherhood and putting family first. He is so attached to his kids, he no longer looks forward to or even much enjoys time away from them. Men's weekends have lost their appeal. Even driving to his alma mater to attend an all-day tailgate and football game with his college buddies is no longer enticing: "I missed my kids. I kept thinking, 'Damn, I wish I was at home watching this football game on TV just with them.'"

Marcus and Anthony: Reluctant Primary Caretakers

Unlike the fathers previously discussed, Marcus and Anthony never wanted to be stay-at-home dads. Joblessness and underemployment forced them to take on primary caretaking responsibilities. They do so reluctantly because they believe men should do paid word, if not be the primary breadwinners. Their sense of familial responsibility and deep love for their kids, though, trump the potentially paralyzing effect of being failed breadwinners. They are engaged, loving parents who do not hesitate to meet all of their children's needs.

Marcus has a partner, Angela, and family who recognize that the recession caused his unemployment and that he's doing everything he can to find a new job. He embraces what he expects will be a temporary stint as stay-at-home dad. He says it is "not normal" for a man not to work. Being jobless has caused him self-esteem issues and bouts of depression. A second child on the way amplifies their financial uncertainty and his anxiety. However, his son keeps him grounded: "I remember that I'm a father first and foremost. And that I have somebody that looks up to me, and cares about me, and only knows me as 'Dad.' So that part of it makes it easier—makes it a little bit easier. The best thing I have is when I'm picking my son up. He doesn't know what's going on.

He just wants to go to sleep, wake up, and play. And eat something when he's hungry. And you know, the innocence of my son makes it a little easier."

With Angela working full-time and also taking evening classes toward a graduate degree, Marcus is almost the sole caretaker of their preschool-age son. He describes his daily caretaking routine:

> I get up at 6:30 in the morning. I get him ready for school, make his breakfast, make sure he has an outfit, has his uniform out. I take him to class. I find out what's going on with his classes. I pick him up every day from school. I'm here for his aftercare. I make sure he has dinner. I make sure he's progressing in school, and I just pretty much take care of him. I take that role from my wife, so I make sure he has a bath and he's put in bed also by the time she gets home.

He understands that their situation is tough on Angela, so he tries to free her to just enjoy the precious little time she's able to spend with their child. Previously she did more of the caretaking work when she and Marcus were both working and she wasn't in school.

When I ask Marcus if being unemployed or being a stay-at-home father has altered his views on manhood, he says they have not. However, his response to this question and other related questions is filtered through his experiences as an involuntarily unemployed stay-at-home dad who identifies as the head of his family's household. He says, "With a family, you're only as strong as your weakest member. If the head of the family isn't strong, what are you going to do?" Success and failure are the leader's responsibility, dependent upon decisions he makes that should put family first, he says: "Are you going to be [up] for the moment to make the [best] decision, or are you going to be too wrapped up in like, 'Hey, I [got a job] and I've got my balls back.'" Marcus expresses views on manhood that might appear contradictory. He believes paid work is essential for "normal" manhood but also says that doing what is best for the family is the responsible, manly thing to do. Men, he says, should be the heads of the household, yet he defers to his wife's desire to get a graduate degree before considering pursuing his own education. He also questions cultural stereotypes and expectations placed on men: "I would change, definitely, that a man shouldn't cook and clean, that it would offend his masculinity. I think you still can be a man and be a good father, still be a loving father. [Men] can still be tough, but actually showing emotions occasionally does help."

Marcus's views reflect the contradictions of the moment: decades of economic and cultural forces have undermined men's breadwinner status and identity. They have challenged gendered work-family arrangements and inequalities and increased men's involvement in childcare. The meanings of responsible fatherhood and manhood have broadened. Marcus is like so many fathers today, grappling with their identity, roles, and responsibilities as the ground shifts beneath them. Under these circumstances, it is easy to appear to be in two places at once. Manhood ideals are cultural ideals; there are no universals, not even breadwinning.[32] Norms vary endlessly from one place to another. Change is possible.

Fellow involuntarily unemployed dad Anthony is of two minds as well. "I love it," he says when I ask him about being a stay-at-home dad. "You know, I would get frustrated at first, but I'm really enjoying watching my daughter grow up [and] spending this precious time with her." However, "I'm embracing being a stay at home dad because, really, it's either embrace it, or go insane, or get depressed," he says. Anthony, too, thinks men should be breadwinners and has battled unemployment, accompanied by depression, for decades, including on and off during his 10-year marriage. His wife has been supportive, and he has found additional support online in various forums, but Anthony mostly isolates himself from others and channels his energy into his daughter: "Someone told me—who I met [looking for] a job once—'You're a stay-at-home dad. You have a very important role in life. It's important. So screw 'em if they don't want you. What you're doing now is more important.' And that's given me great comfort, and that's opened my eyes, too. You don't want to hire me? Screw you. I'll raise my child. This is more important. I'm not going to devalue myself because you don't want to hire me. I'm not going to allow you to make me feel worse about myself."

Anthony has had to redefine the value of primary caretaking to alleviate some of his perceived failings and stave off depression: "Well, at first I was very depressed about it. But I'm trying to focus and trying to make it like a job with the cleaning, the laundry, the dishes." He now tries to treat housework like any other job he's had in an effort to gain some satisfaction out of doing it well. That's the difficult part, he says, whereas "being a dad—that just speaks to everything. It's, you know, I love it." He now recognizes just how important parenting is, and how much more value he places on his relationship with his daughter than he used to, when he was solely focused on work and unemployment.

Men who identify joblessness as the reason they are at-home parents are more likely to cling to the breadwinner ideal and suffer from failing to fulfill it. They do not embrace being stay-at-home dads as enthusiastically as do men who choose this role, but they do value their improved relationships with their kids. Other research has found that conservative working-class men's orthodox gender ideologies were unshaken by disruptions to their employment, largely preventing a degendering of housework.[33] Those who choose to be stay-at-home dads, generally with their partners' support and the financial ability to do so, struggle less with the breadwinner ideal. As a group, they are more highly educated and more likely to be middle/upper class. Their families have enough resources to soften the gendered identity blow that accompanies doing "women's work." This also fosters their inclination to redefine manhood, because embracing involved parenting means being open to being changed, to seeing the world through children's eyes and reveling in their growth and development. They enjoy strong bonds with their partners and children and think of themselves as better men than they were before.

A Dad Revolution?

There has been what can fairly be described as a seismic shift in gendered work and family arrangements since the 1950s. Compulsory homemaker roles for women are a distant memory. Detached, breadwinner-only roles for men have become more of a punch line than the norm. Women breadwinners are more common not only because there are more families led by single mothers but because a growing number of married women earn more than their partners. In turn, men are more engaged parents, highlighted by the statistical and cultural phenomenon of stay-at-home fathers. By all accounts, these men think and behave in many ways that would have been unrecognizable to their fathers and grandfathers when they had young children.

What I and other researchers find is that voluntary stay-at-home dads look a lot like voluntary stay-at-home moms. They choose to stay at home with their partners' support, often because they agree that one parent should stay home and he is better suited for it and/or earns less money. These dads are deeply committed parents, closely connected with their children. Like stay-at-home moms, they do the bulk of if not all of the housework. Doing this culturally undervalued job makes them respect and appreciate what at-home moms have done for decades—what these men sometimes describe as the profession of parenting. Raising children and giving up paid work helps stay-at-home dads develop patience and selflessness. It makes them less materialistic and more attuned to emotions and nature; they become nurturers, if they weren't already. Children benefit academically, behaviorally, and emotionally from the closeness and attention.[34] These men often receive strong support from family, friends, and parenting groups, and positive attention from strangers.

When their choice is met with disapproval, they defiantly assert the importance of their family above all else, whether their own success, a breadwinner identity, or what they see as outdated masculine ideals. They turn critics' questions around, rhetorically asking how other men can succumb to the mindless and meaningless breadwinner ideal, prioritizing their careers and egos over their families. Voluntary stay-at-home dads are more likely to question broader gender inequalities and intentionally raise their kids to avoid falling into old patterns. They describe their decision to stay home as not only a sacrifice but the responsible and manly thing to do. They redefine manhood in ways that accommodate their gender nonconformity.[35] Even involuntary stay-at-home dads are changed by the experience of raising their children, depending on their ideology.[36] They, too, often become more nurturing and attuned to their kids, take on more of the housework, incorporate involved fatherhood into their identities, and ultimately contribute to greater gender equality in their parenting.[37]

Despite these changes and progress toward gender equality, we are not on the cusp of a dad revolution. Voluntary stay-at-home fathers are likely to remain small in numbers. So long as childcare and housework remain unpaid, devalued, and considered "women's work," it is unlikely that more than a small minority of fathers will exit the paid labor force. So long as a gender wage gap remains, different-sex parents will have the decision made for them when they determine which one should stay home to raise kids. So long as men's identities are inextricably tied to the breadwinner ideal above all others, we cannot expect them to risk their sense of self by staying at home. So long as the economy continues to produce mostly low-paying jobs, the option to stay at home will remain beyond reach for most parents. As we have already seen with the post-Recession dip in the number of stay-at-home dads, few entirely buy in, and many who do will eventually opt out.[38] It has become clear that women's work-family changes are not enough to finish the revolution. Men must change, too.

What *will* lead to a dad revolution? What can close the gap? There are two main pathways: First, find ways to uncouple gender—including inequality, expectations, identity, desires, and so on—from paid and unpaid work. Second, assign much more value to parenting, beginning with work-family policies that subsidize and support parents (to be discussed in more detail in the conclusion). There is a chicken-and-egg dilemma here: Will greater respect and more generous benefits for parenting be achieved only after we have redone manhood or undone gender entirely—that is, after we have created a society where there are no feminine- or masculine-marked characteristics, work, attitudes, behaviors, and identities? Or, is it only possible to untether gender from work if we transform workplaces and families to encourage and allow for a 50-50 split in breadwinners and at-home fathers and mothers, regardless of their economic and social resources?

Sociologist Judith Lorber, while appreciating the undeniable progress that has resulted from feminists' efforts to mainstream women into the workforce and allow them to acquire greater economic, social, and political power, thinks the "change families first" approach is fatally flawed. Implied in her view is that it will take another gender revolution to produce a dad revolution: "Feminism as a movement, in the fight for equal treatment within the present gender structure, has lost sight of the revolutionary goal of dismantling gender divisions. The present drive toward gender balance or mainstreaming gender continues the attempts to undo the effects of gender divisions, but it is these divisions that perpetuate gender inequality."[39] Only a gender-free world, she argues, can produce a gender-equal one. Separate will always be unequal. Gender differences are arbitrary artifacts of culture; they can and do change and, in theory, could be eliminated.

Conversely, we must ask if redoing or undoing gender can only be achieved by deploying the power of the institution of government—perhaps in response to grassroots activism—to undermine gender inequality in the institutions of work and family. If social policy and accompanying cultural shifts can produce a world where women and men are just as likely to be in the workforce or at home raising children—or rotating back and forth between the two—will this not eventually lead to the reconfiguring or possibly dismantling of gendered differences? Would stay-at-home dads no longer be stigmatized, struggle with the loss of breadwinner identity, and attempt to assert a new definition of "real manhood?" Will the children of these parents create a gender-free world?

Although it is unclear whether changes in gender ideology or changes in family structure must come first, they are not contradictory. Calls to undo gender are persuasive—they reflect the arbitrary nature of gender differences and seek gender equality and justice. Achieving this lofty goal seems daunting and, at best, will take many decades. Meanwhile, we should use every tool available to combat the oppression, depression, inequality, suffering, and violence that are symptoms of men's pursuit of hegemonic masculine ideals. Redoing manhood is a laudable interim goal for undoing gender. Substituting responsibility for power and control, we can make manhood possible and diminish its toxic effects.

Part III

**The Future of the
Manhood Dilemma**

Conclusion

Making Manhood Possible

> I don't know that I can separate out being
> a man from being a good person.
> —Gentlemen's Fighting Club member
> Jason

> I wouldn't put up with somebody think-
> ing I was less of a man because I'm a
> stay-at-home dad.
> —stay-at-home dad Rob

If men benefit from gender inequality, how can they be persuaded to help oppose it, especially if it requires them to change their behavior? I take it as a given that virtually all women and transgender people support changes to current manhood ideals and gender arrangements, which are all too often sources of their discrimination, violence, and oppression. Speaking with and listening to the men in this book, it is clear that they, too, would largely welcome change. Most men don't feel particularly privileged or powerful in their daily lives. The tensions, conflicts, and insecurities that accompany capitalism, postindustrialization, and declining patriarchal relations invite fundamental changes. Many men would prefer a more egalitarian society.

Contemporary American culture assigns boys and men an impossible mission: to ceaselessly maintain control of themselves and not be controlled by others or the circumstances they face. They are expected to stifle the full range of basic human emotions and to physically dominate and not be dominated by others. Later, they are expected to sexually attract and masterfully perform for women and establish themselves as reliable breadwinners. These body and breadwinner ideals are beyond even the reach of Tom Cruise and a 100-million-dollar budget. No man can possibly complete this mission.

Marginalized and subordinated men face structural and cultural obstacles that make achieving manhood even less possible for them. The privileges of patriarchal arrangements are enjoyed by all men but are not equally distributed. Queer men, men of color, resource-poor men, men with disabilities, undocumented men, and others enjoy fewer of these benefits.

I find that when men fail to fulfill hegemonic manhood ideals, they internalize their failures and endlessly try to repair them or compensate for them. These responses to failure pose dangers to the men themselves, others in their lives—especially women—and society at large. And many men know it. Most of the men in this book view these ideals as unattainable, onerous, sometimes undesirable, and often costly. They have felt and often continue to feel the burdens of fitting into a tiny box, of endlessly having to prove their manhood while avoiding all things feminine. They express feeling trapped and constrained by our narrow definition of masculinity. They see and suffer the consequences of pursuing body and breadwinner ideals, the costs of privilege that accompany successful and unsuccessful attempts to fulfill these ideals.[1] A lifetime of suppressing emotions, competing with others, and not taking proper care of one's body, both inside and out, takes its toll. The physical, interpersonal, and psychological consequences are considerable.

Men live shorter, more dangerous, and less healthy lives because the expectation for them to be dominant and in control produces greater levels of violence, risk-taking, economic stress, substance abuse, and social isolation and leads them more often toward the avoidance of health care and suicide. Just as marginalized and subordinated men enjoy fewer of the privileges of manhood, they disproportionately endure the costs of its pursuit. Many men would embrace being unburdened of this impossible mission.

Most important, a growing number of men are open to change for more selfless reasons: because they empathize with girls and women. The culmination of decades upon decades of feminist activism coupled with dramatic economic changes have opened up a window of opportunity whereby a growing number of men view the pursuit of orthodox manhood ideals as anachronistic and unrealistic—a fool's errand. We now live in a more gender equality–minded society. Most men agree that women should not be excluded from any areas of life—whether social, economic, or political—or subject to discrimination, harassment, or violence.[2] Industrialization led to a dominant model of fatherhood: good fathers were good breadwinners. Maybe deindustrialization, greater workplace gender parity, and the introduction of progressive work-family policies will lead to a new dominant model: responsible and engaged fatherhood.

Today more than ever, there is the possibility of redefining manhood in such a way as to make it attainable and feminist, as a subset of the men in this book attempt to do. Establishing and maintaining power and control come into conflict with the growing expectation of engaged fatherhood. The provider and protector ethic, many men report, is outdated. Men's long-standing expectation to be responsible is the thread that connects yesterday's emotionally distant provider-protectors to today's responsible fathers. This emerging ideal expects dads to be far more involved and engaged parents than in generations past. Our roller coaster economy of bubbles and busts, made excruciatingly clear by the Great Recession, highlights how fragile are men's breadwinner identities and how little control over them men wield. A more realistic, obtainable set of manhood ideals should attract more and more men and would be beneficial to all.

We might be on the cusp of a significant redefining of manhood, but changes to it are not inevitable. Researchers have documented how progress toward gender inequality has slowed or even stalled. And as joblessness recedes along with the most devastating impacts of the Great Recession, we face a return to the status quo, including involuntary stay-at-home fathers hightailing it back to paid work. It will take significant grassroots efforts, systemic changes to work-family laws and policies, and perhaps American families' mounting struggles and dissatisfaction to spur these changes. Womanhood has been transformed. Now manhood must be as well. The new dominant version of manhood must be equitable and attainable. We can create manhood ideals that are neither unachievable nor destructive. It can be just a mission, not an impossible one.

Signs of Progress

Progress toward gender equality is evident in all areas of American life. The last century of activism and social change has resulted in widespread legal, political, and social advancements for women.[3] Highlights include women's suffrage; greater access to and participation in the paid labor force; access to birth control and abortion rights; the prohibition of discrimination in education (Title IX); less gender segregation in fields of study; higher rates of college graduation (which now exceed those of men); greater access to political power; an antiviolence movement that has transformed laws, policies, and attitudes regarding sexual harassment and intimate violence; a culture that increasingly celebrates women athletes and artists; more gender-egalitarian attitudes regarding work-family arrangements; and the nomination of the first woman to lead a major party's presidential ticket, as well as her near victory.

These changes were hard fought, and as I discuss in the following section, they are uneven and far from complete. The breaks from the past are revealing, though, in that they expose gender as an arbitrary cultural artifact that is malleable, not a biological inevitability to which we are condemned. What it means to be a woman today looks quite different than it did a century ago in the United States. Men and manhood have been slower to change.

Yet progress can be seen in men's changing attitudes and practices on many of the issues identified here. Survey research since the 1950s reveals that public attitudes have become much more supportive of women's rights and opposed to confining women to lower status roles.[4] For example, nearly all Americans say they would vote for a woman president today, but that figure didn't even reach 50% until after World War II.[5] Americans, especially younger ones, now support and desire a greater balance between work and family. Single young adults envision egalitarian relationships as the ideal, if workplaces and work laws and policies allowed for this arrangement.[6] Recent survey research also suggests that Americans largely support women working. This includes mothers of young children if the family depends on her income.[7] There remains a gap, with respondents more likely to endorse men working to support families. But the gap is smaller between gender groups than it is within when analyzing questions about women and men in an array of work-family scenarios. In short, attitudes about women's and men's work-family balance is influenced more by family situations than gender. To address these work-family challenges, more Americans now support federal and state policies that would and do provide paid family leave and higher wages and continued expansion of more affordable health care.[8]

Of course, attitudes are one thing; actions are another. Men have already chosen or been forced to change their work-family practices. Recall that fathers in 2015 were doing 16 hours per week of childcare and housework, up from only 7 hours in 1965.[9] And long-term, voluntary stay-at-home fathers are a growing demographic. Further, public attitudes about sexuality have undergone rapid and seismic shifts. Only conservative Republicans remain strongly opposed to same-sex marriage and "acceptance" of homosexuality.[10] Recent cohorts of younger men are those most likely to embrace gender and sexuality equality and to reject homophobia. Millennials find it difficult to believe that we only recently established marriage equality or stopped using sexuality to gatekeep military service. Might evidence of antihomophobic and equality-minded young men in homosocial, historically hypermasculine contexts such as sports teams and fraternities suggest a new "inclusive masculinity" that challenges hegemonic masculinity?[11] Out athletes and fraternity members who receive strong support from teammates and friends certainly indicate social progress. Younger men view gender and sexuality as much more fluid, and their actions reflect their beliefs. They are more emotionally and physically intimate with other men, platonically and sexually. They are more likely to become familiar with the experiences of women, which leads them to becoming less sexist.

I think, at least as far as the United States is concerned, we would be going too far to argue that there are now dueling dominant masculinities, one orthodox and the other inclusive. Locating and studying inclusive masculinities is essential; indeed, I hope that my own research on stay-at-home fathers contributes to this literature. However, my data suggest that men who adopt antisexist and antihomophobic attitudes and practices still view orthodox masculinity (i.e., hegemonic masculine ideals) as the standard to which they and other men are held. They know that they are swimming against the tide. It doesn't force them to change course, but they are well aware theirs is not the dominant mode of thinking or acting. Inclusive masculinities may be becoming more prevalent; there may even be pockets where they are the locally prevailing standard. Culturally speaking, though, orthodox masculinity is still dominant. Men continue to believe that there are natural, immutable gender differences, which are used to justify not only difference but inequality.[12] Nevertheless, these cracks in the façade of manhood indicate that inclusive masculinities could one day replace the orthodox kind.

There is no reason to continue to assign men an impossible mission, one that is so destructive for all. These manhood ideals are as artificial as the movie sets that serve as the backdrop to Tom Cruise's missions: The sets look real. The actors persuasively play the roles they are given. The audience, in turn, suspends its disbelief and accepts that world as real. Though our own reality isn't quite as flimsy as an action movie set, it too is sustained by our willingness to buy into and play roles, and put on believable performances for audiences. Doing what is expected of us as men—pursuing manhood ideals—doesn't necessarily lead to Hollywood-level wealth and fame, but it does offer rewards. Ultimately, though, it is an act that fewer and fewer men embrace. To mix movie hero metaphors, the impossible body and breadwinner mission assigned to men is to be Supermen in the streets, sheets, and suites. Some of the men I interview may occasionally fantasize about being heroes and superheroes, but most simply desire to set and meet more realistic expectations for ideal manhood. They are a captive audience; many are hungry for new models of manhood.

When I ask them what it means to be a man, many identify characteristics and behaviors that they associate generically with responsible adulthood. Stay-at-home dad Jamie says, "I don't think there should be so much of this, you know, 'Men do this, women don't do this.' I think that if I could change the definition, I would try to make them more synonymous." Gentlemen's

Fighting Club participant Stuart thinks expectations have shifted since his parents grew up, and today, "I really do find it difficult to consider the roles of a man as different than the roles of a woman." Fellow fighter Barry says, "I guess there's a part of me that wants to answer that question and knows where you're coming from. But then there's another part of me that's like, you know, that's just another bullshit label. I don't have to aspire to anything because I have a penis, right? I mean, I'm not a man, I just am who I am."

Many of my interviewees also reject orthodox masculinity; it never reflected their experiences or interests. Jonathan, one of the long-term unemployed, says he rejected his parents' approach and determined early on in his relationship, "I will be affectionate to my wife and kids and that I [will] equally share all parts of my life and responsibilities in married life." Stay-at-home father Tim says, "I'm not into the machismo kind of thing," using language that reflects stereotypes of Latin American men as hypermasculine. "Men need to be role models for boys and girls, and raise them to be good people and to care about people in the world."

GFC fighter Jackson's rejection of orthodox masculinity sometimes elicited verbal or physical bullying. Today, he says, "I'm just more concerned about just doing me, whatever makes me happy. And I've heard it from people before, like, 'You're not masculine or manly enough.' I'm like, 'I . . . it's just not an interest of mine,' you know? 'Sorry, can't do it.' It has its consequences. You know, I've had people call me a faggot." When Penis Health Club member Stephen was a kid, he faced bullying for not being like the other boys. He says he was the "loser kid in elementary school that everybody picked on," which makes him particularly attuned and prone to interceding today when he sees similar behavior.

Just a few of the men I interview believe that physical strength or toughness are important features of manhood. Similarly, most do not emphasize the importance of heterosexual virility, although this is widespread on Club forum posts. Many men, especially the unwillingly unemployed, support the breadwinner ideal. Much more frequently, though, when men begin describing manhood, they talk about responsibility. And when doing so, they refer to being accountable for one's actions, being a source of love and support for partners and children, standing up against bullies, being an asset to the community, and leaving the world a better place than how they found it. Men in each of the four groups, but especially stay-at-home dads, talk specifically about setting their egos aside for the benefit of others.

PHC member Larry says, "There are guys who tie their feelings of being a man to their ability to inflict their will on others. And to me that's being a bully; that's not being a man." GFC fighter Darren is surprised "at how many guys are still pumped up about, 'Yeah, my wife works at home and that's the way it should be,' and 'I make all the financial decisions in the family.'" As far as Club member Ed is concerned, "the whole virility, macho, beer-slogging image" needs to go: "It has so many negative connotations. It's abusive, and rude ... obnoxious and disrespectful. It disrespects men and women. It's a bullying attitude."

My question about the meaning of manhood elicits a methodical, thoughtful response from PHC member Travis. He says,

> A man is fully accountable for all of his actions. And he cares for his spouse and loved ones. He does everything he can to support them, not only by working to the best of his capability to provide for their temporal needs, but also by providing the love, the care, the tenderness, and the emotional support that each family member requires of him.

Travis also emphasizes that actions have consequences and men must take responsibility for these as well. A man "who wantonly nails anything with two legs, with complete disregard for consequences afterwards—is that a man, or is that just a guy who's getting his rocks off on someone?" he asks rhetorically. It's not about being or even trying to be perfect, he says, but rather "when you screw up, you also own up."

Notably, when describing manhood, men in the three groups that are not stay-at-home dads consistently talk about the importance of being a committed and engaged father. GFC fighter Freddy says he would be "a kick-ass stay-at-home dad" if he was in that position. He is insulted by the "dopey father" stereotype so widely depicted in popular culture. Although he and his wife agree that she is the primary caretaker, when she travels, he says he meets his kids' basic needs; he doesn't need to be told which folder his kids' homework goes in or what day it's due. Ed uses the example of presidential masculinities to illustrate what he believes has changed over the last half century: "Lyndon Johnson was a bullying SOB, and he was a 'real man,' you know, a Texan man. And Barack Obama is a caring family man who does not exhibit any of those characteristics, as far as I can tell." (Our interview precedes the 2016 election.)

According to voluntary stay-at-home dad Zach, "To be a man is to be a good dad, to be a good husband, to be a good person, and try to take good care of my family and giving back to my community." His peer, Justin, gets "frustrated with crappy dads [who] spend a lot of time watching football" instead of enjoying family time: "It's like, man, you're really missing out." Justin believes the standard is "so low" that men are considered good dads if they play ball with their kid every couple of weeks:

> [Actually] being a good dad is a daily thing; [it's] being a good parent. I guess my pet peeve or whatever is even saying "mother" or "father." I try to refer to myself

as a parent. That's a non-gender-specific kind of term. It's like, parent, that means you do it all. My brother-in-law, he never changed a diaper. Can you believe that—never changed a diaper?

Justin thinks only a small minority of men, regardless of whether they are at-home parents, do the kind of intensive parenting expected of and done mostly by mothers. His preference for gender-neutral terms reveals his belief that men can and should do this work just as well. He implicitly seeks to redefine manhood.

Ryan says he used language he's not proud of when he was younger. His feminist wife and his feelings of responsibility for his two young kids have led him to interrogate his earlier use of "that's so gay" and has prevented him from telling his boys to "man up, or sack up": "I think a lot of times, it means don't cry, don't whine, do what needs to be done. It is like, stop being a sissy, some-thing like that—like stop being in any way feminine, stop being weak. And it is another one of those things where this phrase that I've always used—[am I now going to be] saying it in front of my kids? Like, what does this mean? What do I think it means? What does society mean by it? And is this what I want to teach my kids?" When his prekindergarten son falls and scrapes his knee and, at the sight of his own blood, "loses it like he has just been shot," Ryan resists the cultural temptation to tell him to man up. He says he might tell his son to toughen up if he's reacting only to the blood rather than pain and believes he would do the same if he had a daughter. His parenting is gendered, but (by his own account) not sexist. Previously, he admits, he was casually homophobic and sexist. As a husband and a father, he finally began examining the meanings of his words. He found that he couldn't reconcile saying "that's so gay" with his earlier belief that it had nothing to do with sexuality, especially after putting himself in the shoes of his gay friends. Now he says he recognizes "the power of language and words and the way words are used to put people down."

When I ask men what they might like to change about expectations placed on them as a group, they consistently identify the expectation to stifle many of their emotions and to put on a front of invulnerability. It turns out that big boys do cry—or at least they want and need to and wish they wouldn't be ridi-culed or considered weak for doing so. Many also want to stop being told to "man up" when displaying emotional vulnerability or doing anything else per-ceived as even the slightest bit feminine. And for most of the voluntary stay-at-home dads, manhood is inseparable from responsible, engaged fatherhood.

Signs of Stalled Progress

Despite all the progress made since what has been called the 1960s gender revolution, scholars have concluded it was always uneven, is unfinished, has stalled, and is unlikely to be completed.[13] Much of the progress plateaued in the mid-1990s and hasn't budged much since. The uneven nature of the progress is depressing, if unsurprising—many of the accrued rights and privileges have been enjoyed mostly by middle-class, white, and straight-identified women.

There remains a sizeable gendered gap in resources and power. Women, especially less formally educated women, continue to do less paid work and more unpaid carework than men.[14] The gender pay gap remains stubbornly wide. Unpaid family leave laws and policies offer little support to all but the most economically secure families. At the top of the hierarchy, power is even more concentrated among men. Only 22 of the Fortune 500 CEOs are women, and only 3 are women of color.[15] Persistent barriers and biases continue to undermine women's access to leadership positions.[16] Only one woman of color made the list of the 400 wealthiest Americans in 2016; among these billionaires, just over 10% are white women. Even in the not-for-profit sector, there is a large gap: women are the CEOs of a paltry 18% of these organizations. The numbers are only slightly better in higher education, where just over a quarter of colleges and universities have women leaders. Gender inequality within the realm of politics is just as dismal. Only 20 out of 100 U.S. senators are women, along with a slightly lower percentage of U.S. House members. Only 33 of 535 members of Congress are women of color. At the state level, there are only six women governors. The power gaps are repeated in other arenas, including unions and religious institutions.

As many have noted and I document in this book, changes in intimate relationships have been even slower. Gender inequality has been most persistent in interpersonal expressions of power, where various gendered double standards have progressed less than women's material gains.[17] Research confirms what we have observed for some time: men continue to take the initiator role in heterosexual dating, sex, and marriage proposals; women continue to be expected to play the gatekeeper role and are often judged and stigmatized for their sexual desires and behavior, especially outside of committed relationships; men are supposed to be taller and older in different-sex couples, indicating their greater social power; and large majorities of all groups of women still take their new husband's surname, with children usually assigned the same name.

These subtle and sometimes less-than-subtle arrangements and practices reveal how little progress has been made on how we do gender in our intimate relationships. Another example is the fervent pressure placed on women to practice "intensive mothering," which emerged on the heels of women's mass entrée into the paid labor force.[18] This fueled, in part, the contentious debate about professional women opting out of their careers to raise children. No such pressures or debates revolve around fathers and fathering. Manhood continues to be narrowly defined, while motherhood has been expanded to accommodate the "supermoms" who do it all, only to then later get chastised for not being good enough moms. Boys and men's pursuit of manhood ideals still all too often takes the form of violence against girls and women. Despite declining rates of sexual assault, rape, and all forms of intimate violence against women, the rates remain high. These continue to be social problems, not individual ones.

There are many explanations for why the revolution may have stalled. They include men's lack of change, due largely to the continued devaluation of anything marked feminine; essentialist and individualistic attributions to gendered behaviors; lack of work-family policies that would provide institutional support; unconscious gender bias; and antifeminist backlash. Boys and men enjoy many gendered privileges. Our society more explicitly values and rewards masculine-marked characteristics and behaviors. Doing masculinity—being tough, strong, competitive, independent, successful, a leader—brings symbolic, psychological, social, and material rewards. Men often benefit simply from attempting to do and be these things or attaining them ever so briefly. Conversely, feminine-marked characteristics and behaviors are devalued. Boys and men must distance themselves from femininity if they are to avoid being ridiculed, ostracized, bullied, socially and economically marginalized, and more. This has produced a flood of women into fields and careers that men dominated but very little of the reverse. And when women choose careers or paths that allow them to be primary caretakers, observers often attribute this to their essential natures rather than the gender pay gap or the lack of work-family policies that would allow women to more fairly share carework. There has also been a robust antifeminist backlash movement, which turned feminism into "the other F-word."

Among the men I interview, a sizeable minority attribute social differences to girls'/women's and boys'/men's essential natures, as they've done historically. It was men, after all—scientists, politicians, preachers, employers, and judges—who created and enforced (and still do) ideologies that deemed women and men so essentially different and, inevitably and essentially, women so inferior.[19] Some of my interviewees simply support the social separation of these groups on some tasks and roles. Overall, these men think that to be a man means being a protector and provider. They also think that the man should be in charge, the head and leader of the household, the family's rock, and generally, able to "handle their business." As might be expected, men in the fighting club and the online penis enlargement club are more invested in an essentialist, orthodox masculinity that views women and men as binary beings. Whether this is due to self-selection into these groups, the influence of the respective clubs, or some combination, a higher proportion of these men use language that refers to an essential physicality and a need to control their own and others' bodies.

The overall progressive politics of the stay-at-home dads precludes most from slipping into essentialist explanations for their kids' behavior, but some do. Nick says, "Boys are different creatures than girls, you know. We're the hunters, and they're the gatherers. They're delicate creatures. My mom told me a long time ago, when I was 17, 'Don't try to figure them out.'" As flawed as they are, these 100,000-year-old explanations for subtle differences in contemporary gendered behavior are seductive. They are simple, categorical: caveman versus cavewoman, Mars versus Venus, X versus Y, testosterone versus estrogen. They provide easy-to-digest understandings of (what amount to fairly small) group average differences in behavior. What Nick and most of us are liable to do is fall victim to confirmation bias, whereby we take note of and highlight kids' gender-appropriate behavior and ignore or dismiss the rest.

According to a handful of GFC members, men are or should be programmed differently. "When you ask, 'What does it mean to be a man?'" Freddy says, "I almost want to say, to fight. And maybe metaphorically and literally. I just think we're built for it. I really think we're built to fight." His occasional fighting partner, George, says, "My dad always said, 'Boys don't cry, you get up,' all this sort of stuff. And I do a little of that to [my son], but he beat me to the punch. He beat me to that. He does it himself." Darren says he was raised to believe in gender equality and that there aren't important gender differences. However, he says, "As I get older and reality sets in, [I've learned] I actually really do enjoy the role of being the caretaker or the role of being [physically] dominant." Thanks to GFC, he says, "You're cognizant more of your power and your ability to, you know, how you can pin people and hold people and, you know, things like that. I think there's a difference between fighting a guy and winning versus maybe expressing your physical dominance over a woman." He embraces the former—it meets one of his midlife desires—but rejects the latter as misogynist. When his girlfriend "kicked my butt" on a mountain hike, set up camp, started a fire, dug a snow cave, and took care of him while he was freezing and barely functioning, he found it "a pretty powerless, humiliating experience." Yet when I ask him if it negatively impacted his relationship or if he resented her, he responds, "No, no, it's all positive, and it just makes me want to be better. Makes me want to hang around her." He desires strength and also finds it attractive in women.

A minority of men across the four groups continue to embrace orthodox masculinity. PHC lurker Isaiah provides an exhaustive answer when I ask him what it means to be a man. He says,

> I think it means that you are someone who's supposed to be a protector and a provider for other people. You're supposed to be a leader. You're supposed to embody positive qualities, kind of a positive attitude. You're not supposed to display your emotions unnecessarily. You can display your emotions for certain things, but not all things. Having a firm handshake I think is one of the [bases of] being a man—not too strong, not too soft. Know how to control your temper. And being well-rounded in a lot of stuff but having one thing in particular that you're good at.

This young man has internalized a long list of expected behaviors that even with constant effort and self-monitoring, no man can possibly achieve. He is set up for failure and all of the harsh consequences that follow.

Jonathan, a long-term unwillingly unemployed father, says he "reluctantly still follow[s] the old adage" that men should be stoic. He feels compelled to be the rock for his family. He says he has cried only once in nearly 20 years, after the death of his brother. Even then, he held it in until he was home alone, the only place he will allow himself to express emotions. It is no secret that suppressing human emotions is physically unhealthy and may herald an explosive and dangerous release of those emotions when they can no longer be contained.

Tyler's view of a man, which he hasn't been able to fulfill since he was incarcerated, is fairly orthodox: "Somebody that definitely supports the family financially—if not the breadwinner, definitely works. I definitely don't agree with being a 'stay-at-home dad.' Definitely work, definitely take care of the house in terms of fixing stuff and taking out the trash and stuff like that. You know, being in equal partnership with your significant other, whether you're married or not. Take care of the kids, make sure the kids are at school, or doing their thing. Disciplinary actions toward your kids if needed. You know, taking care of the bills, making sure everything's paid." His and the preceding men's views reflect the hegemonic masculine ideals that continue to serve as the dominant American model. As these men can personally attest, this model is unattainable. It leaves them feeling unfulfilled and often rather powerless. And it relegates women to secondary status.

Among all the interview participants, GFC regular George was the only one to vociferously reject feminist views on gender equality. He says his beliefs, which he labels "equalist or humanist," support gender equality more than feminists' because "feminism is essentially female supremacy." He initially deflects my question about what it means to be a man but, after thinking about it some more, decides to respond:

What do men do better? What does it mean to be a man? Better inventors, better at building hierarchies, better at industrialization, better at building societies. Absolutely necessary to have a family. A woman and children is not a family. That's just a woman and her children. For a family structure, you need to have a man and woman with their children . . . Some [characteristics] overlap with women but certainly a sense of selflessness. A sense of overcoming the odds, risk, aggression—both social and some physical aggression. I kind of see those as intertwined more so than [for] women. Mercy, kindness, and compassion but from a masculine expression.

George views feminism as an ideology that deems women superior, but his own views align with men's rights and antifeminist groups that deem men superior. He is an outlier among the men I interview but representative of a minority of American men who feel that men are the victims of gender inequality thanks to feminist activism.

Signs of Manhood in Flux

Decades of cultural and structural change have upset, if not upended, gender ideologies and arrangements. Change generates competing responses: conflict, pushback and backlash, and growth. Gendered work-family conflicts and tensions highlight the instabilities. Further change, one way or another, seems inevitable. The men in this study—collectively and, in some cases, individually—reflect these contradictions, offering a range of views on gender and manhood. This is perhaps illustrated best in their responses to my asking them the meaning of the expression "man up."

The participant most resistant to redefining manhood and embracing feminist-led gender equality, George, hates the expression because he thinks it's sexist against men: "When it comes from a woman, [it means] 'Do stuff for me. Do the stuff that I don't want to do. Sacrifice your life on the first date or you're a coward' kind of a thing. 'Give me money, buy me stuff, make me comfortable, provide for me for life, man up.'" George asks why we don't ever hear "woman up" and suggests it should be used for "traditional woman stuff" like "man up" is used for things associated with men. For example, he says, "Don't take any drugs when you're delivering the baby. That's your job, all right." Or unemployed wives should always cook meals that satisfy the breadwinning husband.

No other men respond similarly to my prompt, but nearly half say "man up" is used by others, mostly men, to challenge men to stop acting feminine. They say it means "Suck it up," "Stop whining," "Don't be a pussy," "Stop being a girl," "Stop acting like a little bitch," "Put your big-boy pants on," and "Get your balls back." Most do not see this as a problem, reflecting the casual sexism that remains so prevalent. Some men are put off by this, but they recognize that these expressions are widely used. This suggests that the dominant cultural standard remains something far from an inclusive masculinity. Most interpret the expression as "be a man, don't be a woman," but some suggest it means "don't be a boy." Whereas *manhood* was a term used to demarcate adult men from boys and boyhood in preindustrial America, after the forces of industrialization, capitalism, and feminism left many men economically insecure and feeling threatened, the term *masculinity* largely supplanted manhood and was contrasted with femininity.[20]

Isaiah says "man up" means "don't be a woman," rather than a boy "because women are supposed to be full of emotion. They're allowed to cry [or] be angry. But [for men,] there's no need for that, for something as simple as getting hurt on the field; just man up and leave that stuff at home." GFC fighter Sammy says, "I think my interpretation is more encouragement. It's to toughen up. I mean, be a man. Don't cry, right? Don't be a sissy." Dwayne, who has long been struggling with unemployment and underemployment, says, "'Man up' means for a man to be brave and stand up for himself. It's usually used when a male is acting soft, weak, or is afraid to do something." He says men say it to other men "when a guy is acting whiny about approaching a girl or hesitant to do something they know they want to do." He sees it as "a positive expression meant to encourage men to stand up, take charge of their lives, and go for what they want." Sammy, Isaiah, and Dwayne view the expression positively, as one that helps men learn to be better men—rather than, more generically, better people. Stay-at-home dad Zach thinks it means "grow a set of balls." He adds, "You know, don't be a puss, don't be a wuss." He says a man might say this to another if he's "whining about it being cold outside."

Several men say "man up" is used to get men to reclaim their independence and identity from women. For Darren, "man up" is about overcoming challenges, but he thinks most other men use it to mean "don't let your wife run the house. You know—get some balls, wear the pants." Involuntary stay-at-home dad, Liam, says, "When I've heard it, it means get your balls back from your wife. Sometimes I've heard it [as], 'Go to the freezer, get your balls out, put 'em back on, and let's go out and get a drink. Man up.' I think it just means like 'have some balls.' 'Have some conviction.'" Conviction, apparently, resides within men's reproductive genitalia. Liam says he used the expression once to help his friend get over a relationship that ended: "After a while, this whining and complaining that he would do—I was just like, 'Dude, you need to shut the fuck up and man up.' I think it kind of shocked him because I was a very supportive friend up to that point. But how much are you going to wallow in your grief? Wallow for a while, get it out, and then move on, because there are plenty of other chicks out there. Yeah, take your panties off and put your big boy pants on."

GFC fighter Jackson, who says he is "just not into" being masculine and has been called a fag for his gender nonconformity, seems to embrace the expression as a tool to get men to stop acting effeminate. He says, "Well, dude, 'man up' is real. Everybody, no matter what flavor of man you are, everybody needs to man up. That is, grow a pair. I would say it means [to] get back to your core, be a man. Suck it up, don't be effeminate, don't cry. Don't bitch, don't whine about it. Just . . . put on your stone face, and push through. I hear it, and the direct translation I get is like, 'Stop being a bitch.' Yeah. 'Stop being a bitch. Man up.'" These interpretations are the most explicitly sexist among the subset of men whom, in other ways (such as their physical appearance or their parenting styles and practices), challenge gender binaries.

Several men believe the expression's power is intensified if it's uttered by a woman. Club member Colin says he would interpret it as being told he was inadequately masculine compared to other men; his long-standing concerns about his penis size helps explain this interpretation. Fellow Club member Travis agrees that it would be "a poke in the eye" if it comes from a woman, whereas it's more likely to be used jokingly between men. Given how fragile men's egos are, he is not surprised to see the sad and desperate posts on the Club forum:

> Men don't know how to handle [threats to their ego]. There's guys on there that, after they asked [their girlfriends if they'd ever had sex with a man with a bigger penis] and got an answer that they didn't like, you know, they developed a drug habit, they became alcoholic. They lost everything. They went into a catatonic depressed state for a week. That's why I say the male ego is really fragile, because something as trivial as that can make a male do all kinds of silly things. But like anyone else, my ego drives me to do stuff that a sensible person would probably think twice before doing.

I ask for an example, and he says when running laps on a track, he tries to beat the person next to him: "My ego says, 'I need to outrun him.' Now if that person happens to be a 'her,' I *have* to outrun her." He can accept being beat by a man, but "if there's a girl in the other lane and she outruns me, I'm not very happy with myself or with the rest of the day. And to be honest, it is very immature. But it's there. And I'd be lying to myself if I pretended it wasn't."

Ed says the expression could be used positively, to encourage men to "get your head on, be strong, show some courage . . . Courage, smartness, common sense, strength, leadership, those are all positive ways of using that term," he says, but "the way it's used primarily, it's derisive." These derisive attacks leave men psychically wounded and women castigated as inferior—often as "girls" (not adults), not deserving of respect. The same mentality within the military resulted in World War I soldiers suffering from combat stress and PTSD (as we now recognize it). They had their manhood questioned and were thrown back into combat with the idea it would help them get over their "shell shock." Psychiatrists attributed these men's visceral reactions to the horrors of trench warfare (paralysis, uncontrollable shaking and crying, nightmares) not as the consequences of the atrocities they witnessed and participated in but as individual character flaws.[21] All too often, historically and contemporarily, when men fall short of the cultural ideal, they are told to double down by "manning up." We question individuals, not the unrealistic and unhealthy ideals to which they are held.

A couple of men say the phrase could be used positively to encourage men to be responsible fathers. PHC member Brandon says he used it to pressure a friend to take care of the baby he accidentally fathered, especially because he didn't use protection. Stay-at-home father Peter, who quit his career to follow his wife out of state, says he gets "nosebleed pissed" when men father kids and promptly abandon them:

> If you're married or even if you're not married, [if] you have kids, "man up" means "put the needs of everybody else in front of [yours]." To me, that's manning up—that you can't allow yourself to be self-consumed with woe-is-me-isms, or "poor me," or what-I-want-isms over what's best for your children or your family. I see these dudes that aren't taking care of their kids—I'll be honest with you, they're a bunch of bitches, if you ask me. That's the worst type of man. If my son grew up like that, I'd be so disappointed. You father these children and you don't take care of them—no way, that's not being a man. I'm comfortable saying that's being a bitch. I'm sorry, it just is.

By all accounts, Peter has been transformed by his transition from career man to stay-at-home dad. He has begun redefining manhood to prioritize the well-being of his partner and kids over his ego-fueled career and income. He aspires to raise empowered and antisexist kids, regardless of their genders. However, when enforcing this ideology, he can't help but slip into language that conveys the inferiority of women. Peter's use of the term *bitches* is not meant to be equivalent to the group, women, to whom this term is derisively applied. It makes no sense in this context—women mostly do take care of their kids! Instead, he uses it for men who are irresponsible, who have failed his litmus test for manhood. A man who is called a "bitch"—whether because he cries too much, is too dependent on his wife, or fails to take care of his kids—is no man at all. He is the opposite: a woman. Ironic in this context.

Some men critique the sexist basis and consequences of the expression, indicating a desire to abandon it and perhaps the ideals it represents. "Yeah, I fucking hate that expression," GFC member Asher says when I ask him about

the phrase. "It's basically saying, 'Be a straight—be this American, macho, predominantly straight [man]' . . . or it's like saying, 'If you're not a man, you're
a pussy.'" Another GFC participant, Barry, thinks the expression is so outra-
geous it invites mockery: "I love that expression. Well, I mean, it's a funny
expression. To me, it's like an anachronism. I don't think somehow that as a
sex, we're better able to handle certain things or rise to certain occasions. To
me, it's like this giant cosmic sort of joke. I think that a four-year-old girl can
man up just as easily as John Wayne." Barry says the expression is about recognizing what we can and can't change and trying our best regardless. He says
someone might think, "I'm absolutely doomed to failure if [I'm] to be judged
by my ability to achieve perfection," but if they still press on, they are manning up. Then he deconstructs it: "If a four-year-old does that, that's manning
[up]—and it's not even fair to say that's manning up, because what, am I claiming that those are traits that are somehow unique to men? I don't think that.
And that's why I think it's fun to say 'man up'—because it's so ridiculous."

Other men worry the expression is not to be taken lightly because of its
serious consequences. Travis and several others believe men use "man up" to
humiliate other men. He says it is used in the military, especially during training, to get individuals to stop complaining and fall into line—that is, to conform to the group and set aside their individual concerns. Perhaps civilian men
use it similarly as a means of punishing men who stray from hegemonic ideals
to help ensure group cohesion and a (privileged) collective identity. One man's
failures might be seen and responded to as a threat to all.

PHC member Tomás has felt that sting many times, such as when he cries
watching films. Other men have told him, "'You've got to man up. You can't
cry, because you cry like a woman,' or, 'You cry like a baby.'" Tomás thinks
"man up" is used as "a big putdown, [such as when] somebody is dressed differently. So you know, they need to man up, and they [need to] start to look more
like a man. It's like, come on, get over this stuff."

Another Club member, Bryan, thinks it can be used to get someone to
mindlessly conform to prove his manhood: "It's kind of used as a way to get
people to follow the pack. In my adolescent days, any number of things any
day, you know, [other boys would say] 'Come on, pussy,' you know, 'Chicken,'
whatever." He says that if you conformed, you "might kind of gain respect in
the eyes of your buddies, but at the end of the day, it's like, really, does it matter
that I jumped over the ravine or not?" In adolescence the challenge might be
innocuous, but as boys turn to young men, the stakes are often raised. Jumping
ravines might later become "man up, drink these 12 beers," says Travis, describing this as "emotional blackmail" and a "manipulative tool." I ask him why he
thinks it's such an effective tool. He explains, "Because it questions your very
manhood. The person that's saying 'man up' is asserting that 'you are not a man
if you don't do what I just said.' I disagree with the precept because I feel that a

man clearly is the master of his own actions, not dependent on the approval or disapproval of anyone else."

Travis, Tomás, and Bryan reject the practice of wielding as a weapon the threat of emasculation. Most voluntary stay-at-home dads, and many other men I interview, largely reject the ideals altogether. They propose to redefine manhood so as to make responsible and engaged fatherhood its centerpiece. Periods of change and flux create tensions and contradictions. We must ask ourselves how such conflict and uncertainty can be leveraged to foster progress.

Ways to Move Forward

Fully realized feminist change should bring a "crumbling of gender divisions and statuses," and if viewed in historical terms, it's possible it isn't far off.[22] The only path to gender equality, many feminist scholars argue, is to elimi- nate gender as a category of difference associated with sex. Anthropological, sociological, psychological, historical, and other evidence supports this pos- sibility; our biology does not constrain us from doing gender in any way we prefer. It is possible to shed all of the gendered cultural baggage that weighs us down. However, long-standing structural and cultural constraints—despite some changes and progress—are formidable obstacles to a utopian gender-free society. We must create bold visions before we can transform societies. This is a vision I share. In the immediate future, though, that mission seems as impos- sible as current manhood ideals.

I propose we build a bridge to this potential revolutionary future by attempting to fundamentally reform manhood, along with the institutional and cultural scaffolding that maintains the toxic current ideals. Perhaps this is the only viable bridge to the gender-free goal, as we have no contempo- rary society to look to for a road map. This is still a daunting task; systemic social change always is. It will require redefining manhood in such a way as to make the new dominant version nonhegemonic—that is, it cannot be based on power differences among men and between women and men. I propose we pursue "equality masculinities," which "legitimate an egalitarian relation- ship between men and women, between masculinity and femininity, and among men."[23]

Woman feminists have long led this effort. They have also long argued that men must be active participants, or "comrades in struggle," as feminist scholar and author bell hooks referred to men doing antisexist work more than three decades ago. She critiques the view among a subset of radical "bourgeoisie white feminists" who view all men as oppressors. This view ignores the rela- tive lack of power enjoyed by many men of color and other men and turns off women who partner with them and share their racial and class struggles.

hooks opposes separatist agendas, instead arguing that we should recognize the costs of masculinity while still holding men accountable to sexism. Ultimately, hooks says, "Since men are the primary agents maintaining and supporting sexism and sexist oppression, they can only be eradicated if men are compelled to assume responsibility for transforming their consciousness and the consciousness of society as a whole. . . . This does not mean that they are better equipped to lead feminist movement; it does mean that they should share equally in resistance struggle."[24]

I believe appeals for a new version of manhood that are most likely to resonate with men, and all Americans, are those that borrow from, extend, and redirect entrenched ideals. Also, I expect that men are more likely to gravitate to new models of manhood that are more attainable than the current one. We can construct an egalitarian, achievable dominant version of manhood if we strip out the pursuit of power and control. We can redirect the expectation for men to be responsible away from requiring that they be financial providers and physical protectors and toward an all-encompassing definition of being a provider, with an emphasis on caretaking. Responsible fatherhood means contributing to parenting to ensure all of the children's needs are met: financial, physical, emotional, developmental, and more. Love is not a scarce resource.

Many men already fully embrace nonhegemonic masculinities. Many others desire to and partially do; they just need greater cultural and institutional support to help them traverse the obstacles that stall their progress. Ryan is one of these men; a little more support would help get him over the hump. He now critically reflects upon sexist and homophobic language and doesn't use it. But he is caught between two worlds:

> I think even in sort of addressing these things with language and stuff like that, there are times when I am feeling down and feeling this sort of—feeling depressed and down—and I feel like I am not being a man. That I'm like—that there is still this feeling of being weak or letting emotions dictate how I react. And then sort of examining that and wondering if that's, you know, if that's true. But there are times when I feel like I'm sort of caught between this still evolving, not fully formed idea of what being a man is and this cultural sort of norm that I've grown up with, and you know, [feeling that I've] sort of fallen short of both of them.

Ryan could be relieved of his masculine insecurities if we broadened and redefined manhood to allow men to feel vulnerable and express more emotions. Others just need a push, too. PHC member Andre rejects "shallow" definitions of manhood that include physical and sexual prowess or penis size, but he says, "I have my weak moments where I feel like less of a man for not being hung." By his own report, his size is actually well above average, but distorted pornographic images combined with stereotypes of African American men leave him susceptible to some orthodox ideals he consciously opposes.

Men want a new mission—a doable one. "I think that it's absolutely true that no man could live up to these things all the time," Barry says. Jason implicitly critiques George and some others at GFC: "[They] simply react against what they see as effeminate definitions of modern masculinity versus personal fulfillment. We can be whatever we want to be. We don't have to wholly reject modernity. We don't have to wholly absorb being metrosexuals either. We can do anything that we want to do. It doesn't have to be automatically, 'This is OK for guys,' 'This is not OK for guys.' We're not necessarily limited to old, worn conceptions of masculinity, or we shouldn't be." As one stay-at-home father put it, "This ain't the 20th century. There are 300 million people in the U.S., so there are 150 million ways to be a man."[25]

A plea to men's individuality would resonate with many in our culture. This would merge men's expectation to be independent with American culture's individualistic focus. But social norms and dominant-culture ideals are not about to be replaced with 150 million individual agendas. A structure will remain in place. What if we could construct a new version of ideal manhood that eliminates the shame and humiliation men feel for not fulfilling current ideals? Stay-at-home dad Matthew is more or less already there. He says he feels "more manly in a way" because intensive parenting has provided him with "more a sense of self." His peer, Tim, agrees, saying, "It's made me a better man, and a better husband, easily. I'm just more in tune to kind of the needs of the family." He says being at home "makes you look differently at life" and that "having a daughter, I'm much more cognizant of how women are treated, you know, media depictions of women." Being an engaged parent to a daughter—being attuned to her experiences, needs, and desires—has given him a depth of intimacy and empathy that marks too few father-daughter relationships. He now recoils at the toy store aisles that are gender segregated: "I think that's just crazy. I think we're still trying to pigeonhole men to be—[to] fit into this box, [which] makes it hard to raise good men who aren't abusers to women and who respect women. You know—boys don't cry, boys shouldn't be crying. Boys have to be tough, not show their emotions."

What men have not yet quite figured out is that if they humanize women, they will also more deeply humanize themselves. Men have always had women in their lives—as mothers, daughters, sisters, wives, girlfriends, and more—but historically, these relationships included or were defined by a power dynamic that compelled men's emotional distance from women. At-home fathers and working mothers might reduce gender inequality by reducing couple's gendered parenting differences.[26] Further, at-home fathers who return to the workforce may make personal and professional choices to allow them to remain deeply engaged parents, may challenge stereotypes about women and men workers, and for those who end up in positions of power, might create policies and practices that facilitate a better work-family balance and chip away at the "mommy track" and general "motherhood penalty" experienced by working moms. Some research has found that male judges and CEOs who have daughters are more supportive of women's rights and more likely to close the gender pay gap.[27]

Of course, not every man wants to or will father children, let alone raise a daughter specifically. Establishing new ideals that are similarly inaccessible poses some of the same problems. There are many other avenues to establishing equality masculinities. Responsibility to family could be defined as being responsible in part for the well-being of all friends and family, which would leave men more deeply connected to others, staving off their greater social and emotional isolation and getting them to see the world through others' eyes. The movement to transform our culture is well under way. Many agents of change have been challenging sexism and hegemonic masculine ideals for decades, whether they be feminists or profeminists, antiviolence activists, gender benders, or the more recent phenomena of breadwinning moms and stay-at-home dads. The biggest missing piece, to date, probably has been the lack of institutional support for these efforts.

Change here, too, seems more possible within the next generation given the current political and social climate. After decades dismantling of the social safety net, there is now political momentum for an array of policy changes that would allow families greater flexibility and support. Many changes have already been adopted by cities and states and, unilaterally, by private employers. The populist appeal that arguably colored both major parties' 2016 presidential primary seasons suggests in part that people need and want more help. The lingering effects of the Great Recession and the irreversible changes wrought by technology and globalization have created instability, stagnant wages for working- and middle-class employees, and many home foreclosures. Health care, housing, and student loan debt have skyrocketed. The mental health consequences are visible everywhere, from an epidemic of opioid addiction to a spike in suicides. Government policies can and do move the needle. For example, research reveals that generous unemployment benefits can reduce suicide rates.[28]

We need look no further than Scandinavia to find models that would promote more gender equality while simultaneously reducing an array of accompanying social problems.[29] Let's be clear: None of these countries has eradicated gender inequality. But combinations of more progressive gender ideologies and a series of national policies and programs leave them way ahead of the United States.[30] For years, U.S. activists, scholars, and even some politicians have proposed a series of modest policy changes—ones widely enacted among virtually all other developed nations—that could fundamentally alter gender arrangements and make our lives not only more equitable but generally healthier. These policies include pay equity, lengthier and paid family and medical leave (including separate "use it or lose it" benefits for two-parent families), subsidized and expanded day care and before/after-school care, Social Security credits for at-home caretakers, higher minimum and median wages, shorter work weeks, flexible work schedules, and universal health insurance. These would help address gender, race, class, and other inequities that constrain people's and family's choices to do what they prefer and perhaps what suits them and their children best: "Achieving these goals means creating policies that provide equal opportunities for women at work, for men in caregiving, and for families to weather unpredictable changes in their economic fortunes and household composition. As a package, such policies provide greater economic security, lessen work-care conflicts, and constrain inequality within and between families. They also begin to redress the imbalance that places a higher social and economic value on market work than on caregiving in its many forms."[31]

Systemic, structural inequities and problems need systemic, structural solutions. It is unrealistic to expect the gender revolution to be finished or to expect manhood ideals to be transformed solely by individuals and families. It requires institutional support to enable them to make such changes. Addressing these problems will not entirely eliminate toxic masculinities, and eliminating toxic masculinities won't eliminate all social problems. However, with cultural and institutional support, we can redefine manhood to be nonhierarchical and less destructive. We can undermine gender inequality by creating an ideal version of manhood that is both more possible and more equitable.

Appendix

Studying Men and Manhood

This project arose out of my ongoing interests in how American men respond when they perceive that their status or identities are threatened. Previously, I have used national survey data to reveal that men whose breadwinner status and identities are threatened are more likely to use violence against woman partners.[1] Later, I conducted a broad study of the NRA, arguing that the gun rights movement is a conservative, reactionary men's movement responding not only to perceived threats to gun rights but also to late 20th-century liberal group rights movements.[2] I launched the current project in 2011, in the aftermath of the Great Recession, with a particular interest in compensatory manhood acts. Recently, masculinity scholars have encouraged researchers to focus more on what men do, particularly what they do "individually and collectively, such that women as a group are subordinated to men as a group and such that some men are subordinated to others."[3] The call to study men's practices and the processes by which they establish and maintain power and control reflects established social theory that "sees gender not as an attribute of individuals but as the name we give to cultural practices that construct women and men as different and that advantage men at the expense of women."[4]

Heeding that call, I set out to study situations and contexts most likely to spark men's actions—those where they find themselves unwilling or unable to fulfill body and breadwinner ideals. Empirical possibilities abound, but I settled on studying members of a fight club, an online penis health club, unemployed men, and stay-at-home dads. The first two groups, in part, are composed of men responding to their perceived body failures. The latter two groups offered the promise of studying men's reactions to not fulfilling the breadwinner ideal.

As my research reveals, men react to perceived failure in varied and multiple ways. I use a modified grounded theory method to code and analyze data collected using in-depth interviews with members of the four case study groups, which are complemented and supplemented by participant observation and document analysis.[5] Grounded theory's emphasis on action dovetails with my project's focus on manhood acts and calls from scholars to study what men do.

Four Case Study Groups

I learned about the first group, the Gentlemen's Fighting Club, through national media stories. I contacted one of GFC's organizers and he generously allowed me to arrange a visit so I could observe some training and begin interviewing members. In total, I interviewed 13 members individually, conducted a group interview with three members, and participated in a fighting event.

The second group I studied, the pseudonymous "Penis Health Club," is composed of two online sites dedicated to penis exercises and health. I first encountered one of these websites early on in my research, while doing random online searches related to compensatory masculinity. Other sociologists had written on erectile dysfunction and pick-up artists, but to my knowledge, none had studied members of these online penis enlargement sites. Both sites have online message boards containing hundreds of thousands of posts by thousands of members on anything related to penises, as well as many other topics. Obtaining interview participants proved difficult, though, given that virtually all members conceal their identities behind an online pseudonym. I was able to interview 14 PHC members after joining the respective sites, sending countless invitations via internal messaging systems, using snowball sampling, and being granted permission to post a solicitation for participants on one of the sites. I chose not to study another fairly heavily trafficked third site (and various smaller, less-trafficked websites dedicated to similar issues). The third site differed in two key ways. First, unlike the other two sites, it is much more of a profit-making endeavor led by a single proprietor rather than a community of members seeking to expand and share knowledge. Second, it appears to be visited mostly by much younger men who are attracted to the proprietor's and other posters' misogynistic views of women and sex. In that sense, it is a worthy group to study, ripe for critical feminist analysis. However, its comparatively smaller membership and significantly different approach and politics led me to exclude it from the current research. All of these online groups invite much more study and analysis, as I have examined them only with the intent of furthering an understanding of men's unfulfilled body ideals. There is much more to be learned from these groups.

The Great Recession, unfortunately, provided many sources of data on the third group, unemployed men. I collected data via unemployment blogs, diaries, social media sites, and news stories, and attended several job fairs and interviewed unemployed men whom I originally contacted online or met in person. Men in the fourth group, stay-at-home dads, often author blogs and participate in multiple formal and informal national and local groups. They were easy to locate and, when they were able to find time in their busy child-care schedules, enthusiastically agreed to participate in my research. There is some overlap between the third and fourth case study groups. Many men willingly and unwillingly navigate back and forth between the labor market and caretaking responsibilities. I interviewed 25 unemployed men and stay-at-home dads, once again using snowball sampling to obtain some of the interview participants. To diversify my sample, mutual friends introduced me to three participants with no online presence.

Interviews and Participants

I conducted open-ended, in-depth, semistructured interviews with 55 participants. The participants include men living in 23 U.S. states in all regions of the country, and one military member stationed in Iraq. Of the participants, 15 are men of color, more than half of them African American, with several Asian American/Pacific Islander men, one multiracial participant, and despite my best efforts, only one Latino man. Five of the men identified as gay, and two as bisexual, mostly among the stay-at-home dads and PHC members. Participants range in age from 18 to their early 60s.

Interviews lasted between 45 and 145 minutes, with most about 75–90 minutes. A handful of these interviews were conducted in person with GFC members and unemployed men, but most were completed via phone conversations. I chose to use phone rather than video calls because of the sensitive and sometimes potentially embarrassing topics of discussion. I believe that not having to reveal their faces or make eye contact with me (along with my guaranteeing confidentiality and assigning them pseudonyms) made it easier for some participants to share their deeply personal thoughts and experiences. For better or worse, several mentioned they felt more comfortable speaking with me because I am a man and have more of an insider's (and presumably more sympathetic) view of their experiences.

I used a series of interview guides for the four groups. These guides had much in common, with sections addressing participants' boyhood and adult experiences, their views on manhood, and how their current and earlier life experiences have shaped their views. Interviews were conversational and open-ended, allowing participants to answer questions and raise topics that they identified as important. Most of the interviews were digitally audio-recorded and transcribed by a professional, which I then checked for accuracy. A small minority of participants declined to be recorded, instead agreeing to participate only via email interviews or allowing me to take notes during our phone conversation. I randomly assigned pseudonyms for all participants.[6] I then coded all interviews using a modified grounded theory method, whereby I did an initial coding followed by focused coding. The first pass is broader, coding line by line to ensure that all potential codes are captured. Some examples of these for unemployed men include: changing careers, questioning choices, being supported, and facing criticism. I then winnowed down the initial codes into focused codes, which better capture commonalities and patterns often represented by multiple initial codes. Some examples include: asserting identity, negotiating roles, internalizing failure. From there, I used a spreadsheet program to organize quotes thematically, arranging them by subtopic and participant. Grounded theory method has researchers simultaneously collecting, coding, analyzing, and writing memos about their data from beginning to end. Doing so facilitates theoretical sampling, which requires the researcher to intentionally seek data that challenge preliminary findings. If none can be found, the researcher is more confident in the findings. I adhered to this method as best I could, given some limitations, including access to members of some of my groups and some resource constraints. In sum, I systematically collected, coded, and analyzed interview (and other) data in an effort to identify patterns and exceptions to these patterns.

Qualitative research is constrained by small samples and thus does not typically lend itself to generalizable findings. My research is no different, despite my commitment to obtaining a diverse set of American men. That I am studying American manhood precludes me from making sweeping generalizations based solely on my interview and other data. However, in conjunction with the robust scholarly literature on manhood generally and some of my case study groups and issues specifically, I am confident that most of what I have found would be replicated by other researchers studying the same phenomena.

I offer the additional caveat that, early on in my research, I learned that potential interviewees whom I contacted online or who had some basic internet research skills sought more information about me prior to agreeing to participate. The result may be a sample that was not scared off by summaries of my earlier scholarship and my overall digital footprint. (I suspect my previous research scared off some gun rights supporters or conservatives who distrust academics.) The information contained in the informed consent form, which I provided to all participants, was consistent with what prospective participants were likely to discover online. Noting this pattern, though, I sought to locate participants offline whenever possible. I found it challenging to get men of color to agree to speak with me, which my sample somewhat reflects. They were understandably skeptical of how a white researcher might use information about their gendered practices and views. I broached topics of race and sexuality with men of color and gay or bisexual men by acknowledging and addressing stereotypes and prejudices. This built trust and resulted in more honest conversations.

I did not compensate nor promise any benefits to the participants, but many told me immediately afterward that they enjoyed our conversation. Some reported it to be eye-opening, helpful for getting them to reflect on important issues in their lives that perhaps they had not thought so deeply about. A few participants described it as therapeutic. One stay-at-home dad, for example, ended our conversation appreciatively, saying, "[This has made] me think a lot more about where I'm at, and . . . I'm actually feeling a lot better than I had previously." This was not unusual. Participants often genuinely thanked me at the conclusion of our conversations and inquired to learn more about my project and what I was finding when I interviewed other men.

Participant Observation

In addition to interview data, I also collected field notes while participating in and observing fight club activities and job fairs. Participant observation is essential for research on boxing and similar activities; researchers must immerse themselves in the action to comprehend the feelings and experiences of participants.[7] I observed a lunchtime workout attended by some GFC participants, which included some grappling and moderate hitting. Later, I participated in a fighting event that was organized at my behest. In both cases, I took extensive notes immediately after the event and later coded these notes as I did my interviews. Participating in fights and using my brother's attendance to help recall and verify events and interactions helped me accurately recollect what happened.

As part of my research on unemployed men, I attended two job fairs in the Detroit, Michigan, area and one each in Fort Lauderdale, Florida; Sacramento, California; and the San Francisco Bay Area. The first four were held at hotels and the last at a community college. Countless national and local websites advertised these types of events weeks and months in advance. Virtually all were free and open to the public. At the five fairs I attended, I interacted mostly with job-seekers, approached many of them outside of the fair to solicit participation in my research, and generally observed and took notes on all aspects of the fairs. I dressed semiprofessionally to fit in with the majority of attendees and was inauspicious, carrying a leather notepad folio in which I periodically took notes, something other attendees occasionally did. In most cases, I lined up with job-seekers prior to the event, eavesdropping on and sometimes participating in their conversations as we entered buildings, signed in, and waited for the job fair doors to open. During the events, I entered and exited multiple times, moving back and forth between the fair, the informal waiting areas immediately adjacent, and parking lots outside to try to speak with people before they left. I collected materials provided by the fairs and individual employers, and I listened in on conversations but did not present myself as a job-seeker. As far as I could tell, I went unnoticed in the large, fluid crowds. No job fair officials or hotel security approached me, even as I continuously approached exiting job-seekers to secure participants for my research. Much more conspicuous were the prospective employers making their own parking lot pitches, trying to recruit job-seekers while avoiding the steep job fair table fees.

Document Analysis

The third and final sources of data are digital and physical documents. These include data collected via searches of hundreds of online conversation threads and thousands of online forum posts by Penis Health Club members (amounting to only a fraction of the hundreds of thousands of posts authored and viewed by tens of thousands of members), as well as longer articles published by PHC administrators and profiles of dozens and dozens of PHC members. I copied and pasted relevant information into a word processing document and then followed the same coding procedures as outlined previously. Even though the posts are publicly accessible and members almost universally use a pseudonym, I follow emerging ethical practices regarding online data by assigning new pseudonyms and slightly altering quotes to make them search engine–proof. I have not altered the general content or meaning of any of the quotes.

I supplemented interview data for unemployed men and stay-at-home dads by analyzing numerous online blogs, diaries, and news stories by and about these men. The unemployed men's online data were more useful, as they consistently addressed and reflected upon many of the core issues in my interviews. Stay-at-home dads' blogs and diaries sometimes did as well but tended to focus much more on the minutiae of raising children. When I could collect relevant data, as I did with interview and field note data, I coded and then organized them in a spreadsheet program.

Acknowledgments

First and foremost, I thank all of the interview participants, each of whom was so generous and candid as I probed their inner worlds. I hope you find your truths throughout this book and take from it as much I did from our conversations. Special thanks to those whose generosity included access to other participants and entrée into new social realms.

From start to finish, my brother, friend, and mentor, Dan Melzer, provided invaluable feedback, skillful and exhaustive editing, emotional support, and many doses of grounding humor. Unflinching, lifelong support from my mother, Hindy Melzer, has made every part of my life immeasurably better and easier. And whatever abilities I possess to connect and have sincere conversations with people from all walks of life surely originate from her own humility and sense of humanity.

There are too many family and friends to thank for their support throughout this unexpectedly long process. My deepest gratitude to Tina Fields, Bonnie and Bill Fields, Asher and Shiloh Levos and their parents, Toni Szot, Linda and Al Coppersmith, Richard and Alana Waldorf, and Marilyn Cohen. Many thanks to Todd and Hope Migliaccio, Brad Chase and Jill Shaw, Holger Elischberger and Mike Laber, Lynn Verduzco-Baker, Allison Harnish, Trisha Franzen, Michael Dixon and Stacy Levin, Helena Mesa, Ron Mourad, Rick Keith, Ryan Flaherty and family, the LeBanks, Adam and Patience Stern, Brian Hall and family, and Laura Gibbons.

This book benefitted from invaluable feedback from numerous friends and colleagues. Trisha, Todd, Yi-Li Wu, Elizabeth Ben-Ishai, Michael Kimmel, James Messerschmidt, Michael Messner, Douglas Schrock, and Michael Armato offered helpful comments on various iterations of the project proposal. Tina, Mike, Shea Krajewski, and John Thiels provided sharp suggestions for various chapter drafts. Thank you to Arlene Stein, Jodi O'Brien, and the anonymous reviewers and staff at *Contexts*. My sincere thanks to the many anonymous reviewers, and most effusive praise to Kristen Barber and Matthew Ezzell: please accept my heartfelt gratitude for your laborious, instrumental feedback, along with my apologies for any of the book's outstanding shortcomings. Jennifer Flores, Tom Gerschick, and a handful of Albion College students—especially Alice Coyne, along with Zack Koshorek, Tim Billings, Johanna Schulte, and Amanda Bedker—offered much needed research assistance and other contributions.

The Rutgers University Press team has been exceptional to work with. Peter Mickulas, Alissa Zarro, and their staffs deserve a ton of praise and credit. This work was supported by grant money from the Hewlett-Mellon Fund for Faculty Development at Albion College, Albion, MI. Finally, thanks to my yoda, Eileen Bond.

Notes

Introduction

1 Some material from this and the following two chapters originally appeared in Scott Melzer, "Ritual Violence in a Two-Car Garage," *Contexts* 12.3 (2013): 26–31.

2 Michael A. Messner, *Politics of Masculinities: Men in Movements* (Thousand Oaks, Calif.: Sage, 2007), 6.

3 Michael S. Kimmel, *Manhood in America: A Cultural History*, 2nd ed. (New York: Oxford University Press, 2006); Michael Schwalbe, *Manhood Acts: Gender and the Practices of Domination* (Boulder, Colo.: Paradigm, 2014).

4 Roger Daniels, *Coming to America: A History of Immigration and Ethnicity in American Life* (Princeton, N.J.: Harper Perennial, 2002).

5 Stephanie Coontz, *The Way We Never Were: American Families and the Nostalgia Trap* (New York: Basic Books, 1992).

6 Mirra Komarovsky, *The Unemployed Man and His Family: The Effects of Unemployment upon the Status of the Men in Fifty-Nine Families* (New York: Dryden Press, 1940).

7 Kimmel, *Manhood*.

8 Stephen Whitehead, Anissa Talahite, and Roy Moodley, *Gender and Identity: Key Themes and New Directions* (New York: Oxford University Press, 2013).

9 Barbara J. Berg, *Sexism in America: Alive and Well* (Chicago: Lawrence Hill Books, 2008).

10 I loosely follow the approach in R. W. Connell, *Masculinities* (Berkeley: University of California Press, 1995), as I have done previously (see Scott Melzer, *Gun Crusaders: The NRA's Culture War* [New York: New York University Press, 2009]).

11 Douglas Schrock and Michael Schwalbe, "Men, Masculinity, and Manhood Acts," *Annual Review of Sociology* 35 (2009): 277–295 (284).

12 Sara L. Crawley, Lara J. Foley, and Constance L. Shehan, *Gendering Bodies* (Lanham, Md.: Rowman & Littlefield, 2008).

13 There is overlap between these last two groups. A diverse set of circumstances and choices caused these men to be non-breadwinners: some were forced to be the primary caretakers of their children after losing their jobs.

14 Drew Desilver, "For Young Americans, Employment Returns to Pre-Recession Levels," Washington, D.C., Pew Research Center, May 8, 2015, http://www.pewresearch.org/fact-tank/2015/05/08/for-young-americans-unemployment-returns-to-pre-recession-levels/.

15 Thomas J. Gerschick and Adam S. Miller found that men came to terms with their physical disabilities three ways: they continued to *rely* on hegemonic (dominant) masculine body ideals, which stigmatize physically dependent men as unmanly, and therefore they attempted to do everything for themselves; they *reformulated* the ideals to match their physical limitations while still fulfilling generic masculine ideals (e.g., they framed their ability to provide instructions to their caretakers as masculine displays of independence and decision-making power); and they *rejected* hegemonic body ideals, embracing identities and subcultures that value intellect and humanity above physical control and dominance. Thomas J. Gerschick and Adam S. Miller, "Coming to Terms: Masculinity and Physical Disability," *Masculinities* 2 (1994): 262–275.

16 T. M. Achenbach and C. S. Edelbrock, "The Classification of Child Psychopathology: A Review and Analysis of Empirical Efforts," *Psychological Bulletin* 85 (1978): 1275–1301.

17 Jodi A. O'Brien, *The Production of Reality: Essays and Readings on Social Interaction*, 5th ed. (Thousand Oaks, Calif.: Pine Forge Press, 2011).

18 The terms *compensating*, *overcompensating*, and *compensatory masculinity* have been used inconsistently in the psychological and sociological literatures. The concept arises from psychoanalytic theory, especially the work of Alfred Adler and Sigmund Freud (for a brief summary, see Robb Willer, Christabel L. Rogalin, Bridget Conlon, and Michael T. Wojnowicz, "Overdoing Gender: A Test of the Masculine Overcompensation Thesis," *American Journal of Sociology* 118.4 [2013]: 980–1022). According to this approach, men judged to possess a feminine trait will register their protest by immoderately and indiscreetly demonstrating its masculine counterpart. Psychoanalytic theories make the mistake of attributing behavior to innate traits or inaccurately assumed universal experiences (such as all boys being raised by mothers), ignoring social influences or diverse childrearing arrangements. More contemporarily, the term *overcompensation* is widely used popularly and by scholars, yet "over" seems an unnecessary addition given that compensatory acts also arise from reactions to failure and their ubiquity isn't disputed. Also, the term rings more of judgment than analysis.

19 James Gilligan, *Violence: Reflections on a National Epidemic* (New York: Putnam, 1996), 77.

20 Schwalbe, *Manhood Acts*.

21 Paula England, "The Gender Revolution: Uneven and Stalled," *Gender & Society* 24 (2010): 149–166.

22 Anne Fausto-Sterling, *Sexing the Body: Gender Politics and the Construction of Sexuality* (New York: Basic Books, 2000).

23 Judith Butler, *Gender Trouble: Feminism and the Subversion of Identity* (New York: Routledge, 1990); Candace West and Don H. Zimmerman, "Doing Gender," *Gender & Society* 1 (1987): 125–151.

24 West and Zimmerman, "Doing Gender," 146.

25 Serena Nanda, *Gender Diversity, Crosscultural Variations*, 2nd ed. (Long Grove, Ill.: Waveland Press, 2014).

26 Judith Lorber, "Believing Is Seeing: Biology as Ideology," *Gender & Society* 7 (1993): 568–581.

27 Victor Gecas and Peter J. Burke, "Self and Identity," in *Sociological Perspectives on Social Psychology*, ed. Karen S. Cook, Gary Alan Fine, and James S. House (Boston: Allyn & Bacon, 1995), 41–67.

28 Jan E. Stets and Peter J. Burke, "Identity Theory and Social Identity Theory," *Social Psychology Quarterly* 63 (2000): 224–237; Sheldon Stryker, *Symbolic Interactionism: A Social Structural Version* (Menlo Park, Calif.: Cummings, 1980).

29 Willer, Rogalin, Conlon, and Wojnowicz, "Overdoing."

30 Catherine Connell, "Doing, Undoing, or Redoing Gender? Learning from the Workplace Experiences of Transpeople," *Gender & Society* 24.1 (2010): 31–55; Kristen Schilt and Laurel Westbrook, "Doing Gender, Doing Heteronormativity: 'Gender Normals,' Transgender People, and the Social Maintenance of Heterosexuality," *Gender & Society* 23.4 (2009): 440–464; Candace West and Don H. Zimmerman, "Accounting for Doing Gender," *Gender & Society* 23.1 (2009): 11–122.

31 Joan Acker, "Hierarchies, Jobs, Bodies: A Theory of Gendered Organizations," *Gender & Society* 4.2 (1990): 139–158; Barbara J. Risman, *Gender Vertigo* (New Haven, Conn.: Yale University Press, 1999).

32 Meika Loe, "Working for Men: At the Intersection of Power, Gender, and Sexuality," *Sociological Inquiry* 66.4 (1996): 399–422; Mimi Schippers, "Recovering the Feminine Other: Masculinity, Femininity, and Gender Hegemony," *Theory and Society* 36.1 (2007): 85–102; Mary Neil Trautner, "Doing Gender, Doing Class: The Performance of Sexuality in Exotic Dance Clubs," *Gender & Society* 19.6 (2005): 771–788.

33 Ola W. Barnett, Cindy L. Miller-Perrin, and Robin D. Perrin, *Family Violence across the Lifespan: An Introduction*, 3rd ed. (Thousand Oaks, Calif.: Sage, 2011).

34 Laura Kramer and Ann Beutel, *The Sociology of Gender: A Brief Introduction* (New York: Oxford University Press, 2014).

35 Arlie Russell Hochschild and Anne Machung, *The Second Shift* (New York: Penguin, 2012).

36 Maxine Baca Zinn and Bonnie Thornton Dill, "Theorizing Difference from Multiracial Feminism," *Feminist Studies* 22 (1996): 321–331; Patricia Hill Collins, *Black Feminist Thought: Knowledge Consciousness, and the Politics of Empowerment* (New York: Routledge, 1990); Kimberley Crenshaw, "Demarginalizing the Intersection of Race and Sex: A Black Feminist Critique of Antidiscrimination Doctrine," *Feminist Theory and Antiracist Politics* 139 (1991): 139–167.

37 Michael Kaufman, "The Seven P's of Men's Violence," Michael Kaufman (website), 1999, 2–3, accessed July 18, 2016, http://michaelkaufman.com/articles-2.

38 Connell, *Masculinities*; Don Sabo, "Masculinities and Men's Health: Moving toward Post-Superman Era Prevention," in *Men's Lives*, ed. Michael S. Kimmel and Michael A. Messner, 8th ed. (Boston: Allyn & Bacon, 2010), 243–260.

39 Sabo, "Masculinities."

40 Judith Halberstam, *Female Masculinity* (Durham, N.C.: Duke University Press, 1998); James Messerschmidt, "'Doing Gender': The Impact and Future of a Salient Sociological Concept," *Gender & Society* 23.1 (2009): 125–151.

41 Halberstam, *Female Masculinity*; C. J. Pascoe, *Dude, You're a Fag: Masculinity and Sexuality in High School* (Berkeley: University of California Press, 2007); Schippers, "Recovering the Feminine Other."

42 Schrock and Schwalbe, "Men, Masculinity, Manhood Acts."

43 Sharon R. Bird, "Welcome to the Men's Club: Homosociality and the Maintenance of Hegemonic Masculinity," *Gender & Society* 10.2 (1996): 120–132; Paul Kivel,

"The Act-Like-a-Man Box," in *Men's Lives*, ed. Michael S. Kimmel and Michael A. Messner, 8th ed. (Boston: Allyn & Bacon, 2010), 83–85.

44 Kimmel, *Manhood*; Pascoe, *Dude*.

45 Peter E. Murphy, *Studs, Tools, and the Family Jewels: Metaphors Men Live By* (Madison: University of Wisconsin Press, 2001); Pascoe, *Dude*.

46 Suzanne Pharr, *Homophobia: A Weapon of Sexism* (Berkeley, Calif.: Chardon Press, 1997); Crawley, Foley, and Shehan, *Gendering Bodies*.

47 Schippers, "Recovering the Feminine Other."

48 Kristen Schilt, *Just One of the Guys: Transgender Men and the Persistent of Gender Inequality* (Chicago: University of Chicago Press, 2011); Barrie Thorne, *Gender Play: Girls and Boys at School* (New Brunswick, N.J.: Rutgers University Press, 1993).

49 Crawley, Foley, and Shehan, *Gendering Bodies*; Kimmel, *Manhood*.

50 England, "The Gender Revolution."

51 Emily W. Kane, *The Gender Trap: Parents and the Pitfalls of Raising Boys and Girls* (New York: New York University Press, 2012).

52 David D. Gilmore, *Manhood in the Making: Cultural Concepts of Masculinity* (New Haven, Conn.: Yale University Press, 1990).

53 See Connell, *Masculinities*; R. W. Connell and James W. Messerschmidt, "Hegemonic Masculinity: Rethinking the Concept," *Gender & Society* 19 (2005): 829–859 (832).

54 Antonio Gramsci, *Selections from the Prison Notebooks* (New York: International Publishers, 1971).

55 Connell and Messerschmidt, "Hegemonic Masculinity."

56 West and Zimmerman, "Doing Gender," 126.

57 Some of the criticism is directed at how others have interpreted and implemented the concept, and some of it relates to problems with the concept itself. Scholars have spent three decades doing research on a wide diversity of masculinities (gay, Chicano, disabled, Southern, older, black, etc.), leading many to reify these as static categories. What gets lost in their analyses is masculinity as ideology and hegemony as a configuration of practices that produce gender inequalities. Another problem is the difficulty of pinpointing what hegemonic masculinity is and who enacts and benefits from it, given so much cultural variation in masculinity by location, region, and group. Are there distinct local, regional (i.e., cultural), and global hegemonic masculinities? See Christine Beasley, "Rethinking Hegemonic Masculinity in a Globalizing World," *Men and Masculinities* 11.1 (2008): 86–103; D. Z. Demetriou, "Connell's Concept of Hegemonic Masculinity: A Critique," *Theory and Society* 30.3 (2001): 337–361; Mike Donaldson, "What Is Hegemonic Masculinity?," *Theory and Society* 22 (1993): 643–657; Jeff Hearn, "From Hegemonic Masculinity to the Hegemony of Men," *Feminist Theory* 5 (2004): 49–72; Richard Howson, *Challenging Hegemonic Masculinity* (New York: Routledge, 2012); Patricia Yancey Martin, "Why Can't a Man Be More like a Woman? Reflections on Connell's *Masculinities*," *Gender & Society* 12.4 (1998): 472–474; Schwalbe, *Manhood Acts*.

58 Schrock and Schwalbe, "Men, Masculinity, Manhood Acts," 278. Importantly, males must "signify possession of a masculine self" to be deemed legitimate men and gain access to manhood's privileges (280).

59 Schrock and Schwalbe, 281.

60 Maxine P. Atkinson, Theodore N. Greenstein, and Molly Monahan Lang, "For Women, Breadwinning Can Be Dangerous: Gendered Resource Theory and Wife Abuse," *Journal of Marriage and Family* 67.5 (2005): 1137–1148; Kate Cavanagh,

R. Emerson Dobash, Russell P. Dobash, and Ruth Lewis, "Remedial Work: Men's Strategic Responses to Their Violence against Intimate Female Partners," *Sociology* 35 (2001): 695–714; James Ptacek, "The Tactics and Strategies of Men Who Batter: Testimonies from Women Seeking Restraining Orders," in *Violence between Intimate Partners*, ed. Albert P. Cardarelli (Boston: Allyn & Bacon, 1997), 104–123.

61 Pascoe, *Dude*; David Grazian, "The Girl Hunt: Urban Nightlife and the Performance of Masculinity as Collective Activity," *Symbolic Interactionism* 30 (2007): 221–243; James Messerschmidt, *Nine Lives: Adolescent Masculinities, the Body and Violence* (Boulder, Colo.: Westview Press, 1999); Robert L. Peralta, "College Alcohol Use and the Embodiment of Hegemonic Masculinity among European American Men," *Sex Roles* 56 (2007): 741–756.

62 Schwalbe, *Manhood Acts*.

63 Messerschmidt, *Nine Lives*.

64 Along these lines, I argue that if hegemony requires both dominant and subordinate groups, as well as the mix of domination and consent that is built into our institutions, then there cannot be various local *hegemonic* masculinities. Hegemonic masculinity must exist at no smaller than a societal or national cultural level (or "regional," per Connell, *Masculinities*). I am not suggesting there aren't different local or situational expectations for how to do masculinity appropriately—there are—but they should be thought of as locally dominant masculinities rather than hegemonic. They must, by definition, not be hegemonic if they do not conform to the current American patriarchal system of gender relations.

65 Not all culturally dominant versions of manhood must be hegemonic. A new, gender egalitarian standard of masculinity would not be hegemonic in the Gramscian sense because it would not involve the domination and control of a subordinate group. It would not legitimize men's power and might not entail the pursuit of power and control at all.

66 Messerschmidt, *Nine Lives*.

67 Nanda, *Gender Diversity*.

68 Eric Anderson, *Inclusive Masculinity: The Changing Nature of Masculinities* (New York: Routledge, 2009); Hannah Fingerhut, "Support Steady for Same-Sex Marriage and Acceptance of Homosexuality," Washington, D.C., Pew Research Center, May 12, 2016, http://www.pewresearch.org/fact-tank/2016/05/12/support-steady -for-same-sex-marriage-and-acceptance-of-homosexuality/; Mark McCormack, *The Declining Significance of Homophobia: How Teenage Boys Are Redefining Masculinity and Heterosexuality* (New York: Oxford University Press, 2012).

69 For examples, see Allan G. Johnson, *The Gender Knot: Unraveling Our Patriarchal Legacy*, 2nd ed. (Philadelphia: Temple University Press, 2005); Kimmel, *Manhood*; Richard Majors and Janet Mancini Billson, *Cool Pose: The Dilemmas of Black Manhood in America* (New York: Lexington Books, 1993); West and Zimmerman, "Doing Gender."

Chapter 1   Ritual Violence in a Two-Car Garage

1 Martha McCaughey, *The Caveman Mystique: Pop-Darwinism and the Debates over Sex, Violence, and Science* (New York: Taylor & Francis, 2008).

2 Loïc Wacquant, *Body & Soul: Notebooks of an Apprentice Boxer* (New York: Oxford University Press, 2004); Steven Hoffman, "How to Punch Someone and Still Be Friends," *Sociological Theory* 24.2 (2006): 170–193.

3 Kris Paap, *Working Construction: Why White Working-Class Men Put Themselves—and the Labor Movement—in Harm's Way* (Ithaca, N.Y.: Cornell University Press, 2006).

4 Because most know each other and they received widespread media coverage, I more closely guard GFC fighters' identities than I do men in the other three groups I study.

5 Christian Alexander Vaccaro, "Male Bodies in Manhood Acts: The Role of Body-Talk and Embodied Practice in Signifying Culturally Dominant Notions of Manhood," *Sociology Compass* 5.1 (2011): 65–76.

6 Michael S. Kimmel, *Manhood in America: A Cultural History*, 2nd ed. (New York: Oxford University Press, 2006).

7 Michael S. Kimmel and Matthew Mahler, "Adolescent Masculinity, Homophobia, and Violence: Random School Shootings, 1982–2001," *American Behavioral Scientist* 46.10 (2003): 1439–1458 (1450).

8 Gary T. Barker, *Dying to Be Men: Youth, Masculinities, and Social Exclusion* (New York: Routledge, 2005).

9 Susan Bordo, *Unbearable Weight: Feminism, Western Culture, and the Body* (Berkeley: University of California Press, 1994).

10 Kimmel, *Manhood*; William Pollack, *Real Boys: Rescuing Our Sons from the Myths of Boyhood* (New York: Henry Holt, 1998); E. Anthony Rotundo, *American Manhood: Transformations in Masculinity from the Revolution to the Modern Era* (New York: Basic Books, 1994).

11 Michael S. Kimmel, *Guyland: The Perilous World Where Boys Become Men* (New York: HarperCollins, 2008).

12 Ann Arnett Ferguson, *Bad Boys: Public Schools in the Making of Black Masculinity* (Ann Arbor, Mich.: University of Michigan Press, 2000).

13 Meda Chesney-Lind and Nikki Jones, eds., *Fighting for Girls: New Perspectives on Gender and Violence* (Albany, N.Y.: SUNY Press, 2010).

14 Kimmel, *Manhood*.

15 Arlie Hochschild, *The Managed Heart: Commercialization of Human Feeling* (Berkeley: University of California Press, 1983).

16 Christian A. Vaccaro, Douglas P. Schrock, and Janice M. McCaber, "Managing Emotional Manhood: Fighting and Fostering Fear in Mixed Martial Arts," *Social Psychology Quarterly* 74.4 (2011): 414–437.

17 R. W. Connell, *Masculinities* (Berkeley: University of California Press, 1995); Kimmel, *Manhood*; Michael A. Messner, *Power at Play: Sports and the Problem of Masculinity* (Boston: Beacon Press, 1992).

18 Hoffman, "How to Punch Someone."

19 Michael Gottfredson and Travis Hirschi, *A General Theory of Crime* (Palo Alto, Calif.: Stanford University Press, 1990).

Chapter 2 Fighting Back

1 Michael A. Messner, *Politics of Masculinities: Men in Movements* (Thousand Oaks, Calif.: Sage, 2007); Kris Paap, *Working Construction: Why White Working-Class Men Put Themselves—and the Labor Movement—in Harm's Way* (Ithaca, N.Y.: Cornell University Press, 2006); Michael Schwalbe, *Unlocking the Iron Cage: The Men's Movement, Gender Politics, and American Culture* (New York: Oxford University Press, 1996).

2 Michael A. Messner, *Power at Play: Sports and the Problem of Masculinity* (Boston: Beacon Press, 1992).

3 Debby Phillips, "Punking and Bullying: Strategies in Middle School, High School, and Beyond," *Journal of Interpersonal Violence* 22.2 (2007): 158–178.

4 Frank D. Adams and Gloria J. Lawrence, "Bullying Victims: The Effects Last into College," *American Secondary Education* 40 (2011): 4–13; Anne Williford, Aaron Boulton, Brian Noland, Todd D. Little, Antti Kärnä, and Christina Salmivalli, "Effects of the KiVa Anti-bullying Program on Adolescents' Depression, Anxiety, and Perception of Peers," *Journal of Abnormal Child Psychology* 40 (2012): 289–300.

5 Elijah Anderson, *Code of the Street: Decency, Violence, and the Moral Life of the Inner City* (New York: W. W. Norton, 1999); Geoffrey Canada, *Fist Stick Knife Gun: A Personal History of Violence* (Boston: Beacon Press, 1995); Andre Dubus III, *Townie: A Memoir* (New York: W. W. Norton, 2011).

6 Ann Arnett Ferguson, *Bad Boys: Public Schools in the Making of Black Masculinity* (Ann Arbor: University of Michigan Press, 2000).

7 Anderson, *Code of the Street*; Victor M. Rios, *Punished: Policing the Lives of Black and Latino Boys* (New York: New York University Press, 2011).

8 William Pollack, *Real Boys: Rescuing Our Sons from the Myths of Boyhood* (New York: Henry Holt, 1998); Michael S. Kimmel, *Manhood in America: A Cultural History*, 2nd ed. (New York: Oxford University Press, 2006).

9 Christina Salmivalli and Tiia Helteenvuori, "Reactive, but Not Proactive Aggression Predicts Victimization among Boys," *Aggressive Behavior* 33.3 (2007): 198–206.

10 Michael Kaufman, "The Seven P's of Men's Violence," Michael Kaufman (website), 1999, 1, accessed July 18, 2016, http://michaelkaufman.com/articles-2.

11 James Garbarino, *Lost Boys: Why Our Sons Turn Violent and How We Can Save Them* (New York: Free Press, 1999).

12 Garbarino, 63.

13 James Gilligan, *Violence: Reflections on a National Epidemic* (New York: Putnam, 1996). Violence is a "masculinity resource" here, as described in James Messerschmidt, *Nine Lives: Adolescent Masculinities, the Body and Violence* (Boulder, Colo.: Westview Press, 1999), 12.

14 Sara L. Crawley, Lara J. Foley, and Constance L. Shehan, *Gendering Bodies* (Lanham, Md.: Rowman & Littlefield, 2008), 59.

15 For a summary, see Douglas Schrock and Michael Schwalbe, "Men, Masculinity, and Manhood Acts," *Annual Review of Sociology* 35 (2009): 277–295 (284).

16 Maxine P. Atkinson, Theodore N. Greenstein, and Molly Monahan Lang, "For Women, Breadwinning Can Be Dangerous: Gendered Resource Theory and Wife Abuse," *Journal of Marriage and Family* 67.5 (2005): 1137–1148; Scott Melzer, "Gender, Work, and Intimate Violence: Men's Occupational Violence Spillover and Compensatory Violence," *Journal of Marriage and Family* 64.4 (2002): 820–832.

17 Thomas J. Gerschick and Adam S. Miller, "Coming to Terms: Masculinity and Physical Disability," *Masculinities* 2 (1994): 262–275.

18 Schrock and Schwalbe, "Men, Masculinity, Manhood Acts."

19 Messerschmidt, *Nine Lives*.

20 Anderson, *Code of the Street*.

21 Kristen Barber, *Styling Masculinity: Gender, Class, and Inequality in the Men's Grooming Industry* (New Brunswick, N.J.: Rutgers University Press, 2016); Maxine Leeds Craig, *Sorry I Don't Dance: Why Men Refuse to Move* (London: Oxford University Press, 2013); Kimmel, *Manhood*; Messner, *Politics of Masculinities*.

22 Judith Lorber, "Believing Is Seeing: Biology as Ideology," *Gender & Society* 7 (1993): 568–581.
23 David M. Buss, "Psychological Sex Differences: Origins through Sexual Selection," *American Psychologist* 50.3 (1995): 164–168; Steven Pinker, *The Blank Slate: The Modern Denial of Human Nature* (New York: Penguin, 2003).
24 Janet Shibley Hyde, "The Gender Similarities Hypothesis," *American Psychologist* 65 (2005): 373–398; Janet Shibley Hyde, "Gender Similarities and Differences," *Annual Review of Psychology* 60.6 (2014): 581–592.
25 Allan G. Johnson, *The Gender Knot: Unraveling Our Patriarchal Legacy*, 2nd ed. (Philadelphia: Temple University Press, 2005); Laura Kramer and Ann Beutel, *The Sociology of Gender: A Brief Introduction* (New York: Oxford University Press, 2014); Lorber, "Believing Is Seeing"; Serena Nanda, *Gender Diversity, Crosscultural Variations*, 2nd ed. (Long Grove, Ill.: Waveland Press, 2014).
26 Kimmel, *Manhood.*
27 Melanie Heath, *One Marriage under God: The Campaign to Promote Marriage in America* (New York: New York University Press, 2012); Messner, *Politics of Masculinities*; Schwalbe, *Unlocking the Iron Cage.*
28 Christian A. Vaccaro, Douglas P. Schrock, and Janice M. McCaber, "Managing Emotional Manhood: Fighting and Fostering Fear in Mixed Martial Arts," *Social Psychology Quarterly* 74.4 (2011): 414–437.
29 Loic Wacquant, *Body & Soul: Notebooks of an Apprentice Boxer* (New York: Oxford University Press, 2004).
30 Marlow Stern, "The Rise of 'Rowdy' Ronda Rousey: The 14-Second Assassin," accessed March 12, 2015, https://www.thedailybeast.com/the-rise-of-rowdy-ronda-rousey-the-14-second-assassin.
31 "Fight Club," *E:60* (Bristol, Conn.: Entertainment & Sports Programming Network, September 17, 2011), https://www.youtube.com/watch?v=SNwITprJo-A.
32 H. P. van der Ploeg, T. Chey, R. J. Korda, E. Banks, and A. Bauman, "Sitting Time and All-Cause Mortality Risk in 222,497 Australian Adults," *Archives of Internal Medicine* 172.6 (2012): 494–500.

Chapter 3   Seeking Growth

1 Don Kulick, "No," *Language and Communication* 23 (2003): 139–151.
2 Lynne Luciano, *Looking Good: Male Body Image in Modern America* (New York: Hill and Wang, 2001).
3 Michael S. Kimmel, *Guyland: The Perilous World Where Boys Become Men* (New York: HarperCollins, 2008), 208.
4 Office of Justice Programs, "Sexual Violence," National Crime Victimization Rights Week, 2015, accessed June 8, 2016, http://victimsofcrime.org/docs/default-source/ncvrw2015/2015ncvrw_stats_sexualviolence.pdf?sfvrsn=2.
5 Luciano, *Looking Good.*
6 Susan Bordo, *The Male Body: A New Look at Men in Public and in Private* (New York: Farrar, Straus and Giroux, 2000), 32.
7 Janet Lever, David A. Frederick, and Letitia Anne Peplau, "Does Size Matter? Men's and Women's Views on Penis Size across the Lifespan," *Psychology of Men & Masculinity* 7.3 (2006): 129–143.
8 Meika Loe, *The Rise of Viagra: How the Little Blue Pill Changed Sex in America* (New York: New York University Press, 2004), 78.

9   Michael Kaufman, "Men, Feminism, and Men's Contradictory Experiences of Power," in *Theorizing Masculinities*, ed. Michael Kaufman and Harry Brod (Thousand Oaks, Calif.: Sage, 1994), 142–164.

10 The Penis Health Club is the name I have chosen to represent the pair of online forums I studied. To maintain their anonymity, I use pseudonyms for all members, including forum posters who almost universally have pseudonymous usernames, and I have altered quotes taken from forum posts. Pseudonyms of forum posters (but not interview participants) are italicized.

11 No one mentioned the sight of their father's penis causing any psychological harm, although Freud would argue those experiences precede our conscious recollections; in other words, his thesis is essentially untestable.

12 Kevan R. Wylie and Ian Eardley, "Penile Size and the 'Small Penis Syndrome,'" *BJU International* 9 (2007): 1449–1455.

13 On street socialization, see James Diego Vigil, *A Rainbow of Gangs: Street Cultures in the Mega-City* (Austin: University of Texas Press, 2002). On the sex-equivalent version, see Kimmel, *Guyland*.

14 Sharon R. Bird, "Welcome to the Men's Club: Homosociality and the Maintenance of Hegemonic Masculinity," *Gender & Society* 10.2 (1996): 120–132; David Grazian, "The Girl Hunt: Urban Nightlife and the Performance of Masculinity as Collective Activity," *Symbolic Interactionism* 30 (2007): 221–243; Michael S. Kimmel, *Manhood in America: A Cultural History*, 2nd ed. (New York: Oxford University Press, 2006); C. J. Pascoe, *Dude, You're a Fag: Masculinity and Sexuality in High School* (Berkeley: University of California Press, 2007).

15 Debby Herbenick, Michael Reece, Vanessa Schick, and Stephanie A. Sanders, "Erect Penile Length and Circumference Dimensions of 1,661 Sexually Active Men in the United States," *Journal of Sexual Medicine* 11 (2014): 93–101.

16 David Veale, Sarah Miles, Sally Bramley, Gordon Muir, and John Hodsoll, "Am I Normal? A Systematic Review and Construction of Nomograms for Flaccid and Erect Penis Length and Circumference in up to 15521 Men," *BJU International* 115.6 (2015): 978–986.

17 Peter A. Lee, "Survey Report: Concept of Penis Size," *Journal of Sex & Marital Therapy* 22.2 (1996): 131–135.

18 Pascoe, *Dude*.

19 Angela Y. Davis, *Women, Race, & Class* (New York: Vintage Books, 1983); Manning Marable, "The Black Male: Searching beyond Stereotypes," in *Gender through the Prism of Difference*, ed. Maxine Baca Zinn, Pierrette Hondagneu-Sotelo, and Michael A. Messner, 2nd ed. (Boston: Allyn & Bacon, 2000), 251–257.

20 Wesley Morris, "Last Taboo: Why Pop Culture Just Can't Deal with Black Male Sexuality," *New York Times*, October 27, 2016, http://www.nytimes.com/interactive/2016/10/30/magazine/black-male-sexuality-last-taboo.html.

21 Lever, Frederick, and Peplau, "Does Size Matter?"

22 Loe, *The Rise of Viagra*.

23 Jane Ward, "Average Frustrated Chumps: The Nexus of Misogyny and Male Suffering in the Global Pickup Artist Industry" Chicago: American Sociological Association Annual Meetings, August 23, 2015. On violence, see Diana Scully and Joseph Marolla, "'Riding the Bull at Gilley's': Convicted Rapists Describe the Rewards of Rape," *Social Problems* 32.3 (1985): 251–263.

24 Allan G. Johnson, *The Gender Knot: Unraveling Our Patriarchal Legacy*, 2nd ed. (Philadelphia: Temple University Press, 2005), 52.

25 Michelle Marie Johns, Emily Pingel, Anna Eisenberg, Matthew Leslie Santana, and José Bauermeister, "Butch Tops and Femme Bottoms? Sexual Positioning, Sexual Decision Making, and Gender Roles among Young Gay Men," *American Journal of Men's Health* 6.6 (2012): 505–518; David A. Moskowitz and Trevor A. Hart, "The Influence of Physical Body Traits and Masculinity on Anal Sex Roles in Gay and Bisexual Men," *Archives of Sexual Behavior* 40.4 (2011): 835–841; Chongyi Wei and H. Fisher Raymond, "Preference for and Maintenance of Anal Sex Roles among Men Who Have Sex with Men: Sociodemographic and Behavioral Correlates," *Archives of Sexual Behavior* 40.4 (2011): 829–834.

26 Alfredo Mirandé, *Hombres y Machos: Masculinity and Latino Culture* (Boulder, Colo.: Westview Press, 1997); Don Sabo, Terry A. Kupers, and Willie London, eds., *Prison Masculinities* (Philadelphia: Temple University Press, 2001).

27 Toni Calasanti, "Firming the Floppy Penis: Age, Class, and Gender Relations in the Lives of Old Men," *Men and Masculinities* 8 (2005): 3–23.

28 Bordo, *The Male Body*, 77.

29 Lever, Frederick, and Peplau, "Does Size Matter?"

30 Kimmel, *Guyland*.

31 Bordo, *The Male Body*.

32 Jocelyn A. Hollander, "Vulnerability and Dangerousness: The Construction of Gender through Conversation about Violence," *Gender & Society* 15.1 (2001): 83–109; Michael Kaufman, "The Seven P's of Men's Violence," Michael Kaufman (website), 1999, accessed July 18, 2016, http://michaelkaufman.com/articles-2; Peter M. Nardi, ed., *Men's Friendships* (Thousand Oaks, Calif.: Sage, 1992).

33 Wylie and Eardley, "Penile Size," 1449.

34 Loe, *The Rise of Viagra*.

35 Loe.

36 The high proportion of "big gainers" is almost certainly due to this subset of Club members being more willing to speak with me.

Chapter 4 Compensating for Body Failures

1 Matthew B. Ezzell, "'I'm in Control': Compensatory Manhood in a Therapeutic Community," *Gender & Society* 26.2 (2012): 190–215.

2 Kate Cavanagh, R. Emerson Dobash, Russell P. Dobash, and Ruth Lewis, "Remedial Work: Men's Strategic Responses to Their Violence against Intimate Female Partners," *Sociology* 35 (2001): 695–714; David A. Collinson, *Managing the Shopfloor: Subjectivity, Masculinity and Workplace Culture* (New York: Walter de Gruyter, 1992); Peter Hennen, "Bear Bodies, Bear Masculinity: Recuperation, Resistance, or Retreat?," *Gender & Society* 19 (2005): 25–43.

3 James Messerschmidt, *Nine Lives: Adolescent Masculinities, the Body and Violence* (Boulder, Colo.: Westview Press, 1999), 12.

4 Susan Faludi, *Stiffed: The Betrayal of the American Man* (New York: William Morrow, 1999), 445.

5 One member of GFC, with his wife's approval, doesn't hold her hand in public so his hands are free to quickly take action against any threats. He acknowledges that this is highly unlikely given his class and location privileges.

6 James William Gibson, *Warrior Dreams: Paramilitary Culture in Post-Vietnam America* (New York: Hill and Wang, 1994).

7   These behaviors have also been documented in experimental research. For example, see Sapna Cheryan, Jessica Schwartz Cameron, Zach Katagiri, and Benoît Monin, "Manning Up: Threatened Men Compensate by Disavowing Feminine Preferences and Embracing Masculine Attributes," *Social Psychology* 46 (2015): 218–227.
8   R. W. Connell, *Masculinities* (Berkeley: University of California Press, 1995).
9   See C. J. Pascoe, *Dude, You're a Fag: Masculinity and Sexuality in High School* (Berkeley: University of California Press, 2007), 61.
10 Susan Bordo, *The Male Body: A New Look at Men in Public and in Private* (New York: Farrar, Straus and Giroux, 2000); Mels van Driel, *Manhood: The Rise and Fall of the Penis*, trans. Paul Vincent (London: Reaktion Books, 2009).
11 *The Butch Factor*, directed by Christopher Hines (Los Angeles: Rogue Culture Productions, 2009).
12 Eric Anderson, *Inclusive Masculinity: The Changing Nature of Masculinities* (New York: Routledge, 2009); Hennen, "Bear Bodies, Bear Masculinity"; *The Butch Factor*.
13 Maeve Nolan, "Masculinity Lost: A Systematic Review of Qualitative Research on Men with Spinal Cord Injury," *Spinal Cord* 51 (2013): 588–595.
14 Thomas J. Gerschick and Adam S. Miller, "Coming to Terms: Masculinity and Physical Disability," *Masculinities* 2 (1994): 262–275.
15 Bordo, *The Male Body*, 57.
16 Patricia A. Adler and Peter Adler, *The Tender Cut: Inside the Hidden World of Self-Injury* (New York: New York University Press, 2011).
17 Greg Perry, "Hung like a Hamster," in *Wingspan: Inside the Men's Movement*, ed. Christopher Harding (New York: St. Martin's Press, 1992), 41–42.
18 Perry, 42.
19 George Lakoff and Mark Johnson, *Metaphors We Live By* (Chicago: University of Chicago Press, 1980); Peter F. Murphy, *Studs, Tools, and the Family Jewels: Metaphors Men Live By* (Madison: University of Wisconsin Press, 2001).
20 Margaret Atwood, "Ch. 50—Writing the Male Character," in *Second Words: Selected Critical Prose* (Toronto, Canada: O. W. Toad, 2004), 412–432 (413).
21 James Gilligan, *Violence: Reflections on a National Epidemic* (New York: Putnam, 1996), 110.
22 Michael Kaufman, "The Construction of Masculinity and the Triad of Men's Violence," in *Beyond Patriarchy: Essays on Pleasure, Power, and Change*, ed. Michael Kaufman (Toronto: Oxford University Press, 1987).
23 Jessie Klein, *The Bully Society: School Shootings and the Crisis of Bullying in America's Schools* (New York: New York University Press, 2012); Messerschmidt, *Nine Lives*; Debby Phillips, "Punking and Bullying: Strategies in Middle School, High School, and Beyond," *Journal of Interpersonal Violence* 22.2 (2007): 158–178.
24 Victor M. Rios, *Punished: Policing the Lives of Black and Latino Boys* (New York: New York University Press, 2011).
25 Klein, *The Bully Society*; Katherine S. Newman, *Rampage: The Social Roots of School Shootings* (New York: Basic Books, 2005).
26 Klein, *The Bully Society*, 3.
27 Michael S. Kimmel, *Misframing Men: The Politics of Contemporary Masculinities* (Piscataway, N.J.: Rutgers University Press, 2010), 125.
28 Michael S. Kimmel and Matthew Mahler, "Adolescent Masculinity, Homophobia, and Violence: Random School Shootings, 1982–2001," *American Behavioral Scientist* 46.10 (2003): 1439–1458 (1450).

29 Douglas Kellner, *Guys and Guns Amok: Domestic Terrorism and School Shootings from the Oklahoma City Bombing to the Virginia Tech Massacre* (Boulder, Colo.: Paradigm, 2008).

30 Near the end, he wrote about refusing to take an antipsychotic drug his psychiatrist prescribed following a night of drunken violence (most of which Rodger was on the receiving end of). The drug is prescribed for treatment of schizophrenia, symptoms of bipolar disorder, and people with autism suffering from irritability. It is important to note that people with mental health disorders are not more likely to engage in violence, including mass shootings; quite the opposite, those with serious disorders are more likely to be targets of other people's violence. See Gilligan, *Violence*; James Garbarino, *Lost Boys: Why Our Sons Turn Violent and How We Can Save Them* (New York: Free Press, 1999).

31 Richard Slotkin, *Regeneration through Violence: The Mythology of the American Frontier, 1600–1860* (Norman: University of Oklahoma Press, 1973).

Chapter 5 Non-breadwinners

1 Michael S. Kimmel, *Manhood in America: A Cultural History*, 2nd ed. (New York: Oxford University Press, 2006).

2 Stephanie Coontz, *The Way We Never Were: American Families and the Nostalgia Trap* (New York: Basic Books, 1992).

3 Kim Parker and Wendy Wang, "Modern Parenthood: Roles of Moms and Dads Converge as They Balance Work and Family," Washington, D.C., Pew Research Center, March 14, 2013, http://assets.pewresearch.org/wp-content/uploads/sites/3/2013/03/FINAL_modern_parenthood_03-2013.pdf/.

4 D'Vera Cohn, Gretchen Livingston, and Wendy Wang, "After Decades of Decline, a Rise in Stay-at-Home Mothers," Washington, D.C., Pew Research Center, April 8, 2014, http://www.pewsocialtrends.org/2014/04/08/after-decades-of-decline-a-rise-in-stay-at-home-mothers.

5 Brigid Schulte, "Nearly 40 Percent of Mothers Are Now the Family Breadwinners, Report Says," *Washington Post*, May 29, 2013, http://www.washingtonpost.com/local/nearly-40-percent-of-mothers-are-now-the-family-breadwinners-report-says/2013/05/28/8de03ec8-c7bb-11e2-9245-773c0123c027_story.html.

6 Bureau of Labor Statistics, "Labor Force Statistics from the Current Population Survey: Unemployment Rate," accessed June 10, 2016, http://data.bls.gov/timeseries/LNS14000000.

7 Josh Mitchell, "Who Are the Long-Term Unemployed?," Washington, D.C., Urban Institute, July 2013, http://www.urban.org/sites/default/files/publication/23911/412885-Who-Are-the-Long-Term-Unemployed-.PDF.

8 Andrew Sum, Ishwar Khatiwada, Joseph McLaughlin and Sheila Palma, "The Great Recession of 2008–2009 and the Blue-Collar Depression," *Challenge* 53.4 (2010): 6–24.

9 National Women's Law Center, "Unemployment: Stronger Recovery Reaching Women," Washington, D.C., May 2013, accessed July 20, 2016, https://nwlc.org/wp-content/uploads/2015/08/mayrecoveryfactsheet.pdf.

10 Michael Schwalbe, *Manhood Acts: Gender and the Practices of Domination* (Boulder, Colo.: Paradigm, 2014).

11 Schulte, "Mothers Are Now the Family Breadwinners."

12 Noelle Chesley, "Stay-at-Home Fathers and Breadwinning Mothers: Gender, Couple Dynamics, and Social Change," *Gender & Society* 25.5 (2011): 642–664;

Beth A. Latshaw, "Is Fatherhood a Full-Time Job? Mixed Method Insights into Measuring Stay-at-Home Fatherhood," *Fathering* 9.2 (2011): 125–149; Gretchen Livingston, "Growing Number of Dads Home with the Kids," Washington, D.C., Pew Research Center, June 5, 2014, http://www.pewsocialtrends.org/2014/06/05/growing-number-of-dads-home-with-the-kids/.

13 Paula England, "The Gender Revolution: Uneven and Stalled," *Gender & Society* 24 (2010): 149–166; Kathleen Gerson, *Unfinished Revolution: How a New Generation Is Reshaping Family, Work, and Gender in America* (New York: Oxford University Press, 2010).

14 Kathleen Gerson, "Gender Politics in Intimate Relationships," New York, American Sociological Association Annual Meetings, August 11, 2013.

15 Parker and Wang, "Modern Parenthood."

16 Kim Parker and Gretchen Livingston, "6 Facts about American Fathers," Washington, D.C., Pew Research Center, June 15, 2017, http://www.pewresearch.org/fact-tank/2017/06/15/fathers-day-facts/.

17 Collecting job fair data from three states in three U.S. regions furthered my goal of studying American manhood's general features, as did interviewing a fairly diverse group of men dispersed throughout the country. However, this predictably resulted in research sites and samples that are non-representative (they were chosen in part out of convenience), and data and analyses that do not exhaustively include some important contextual factors (e.g., local job markets, subcultural norms).

18 Parker and Wang, "Modern Parenthood," 45.

19 Joyce Jacobsen, "The Great Recession's Impact on Men" (working paper, Wesleyan Economic, Wesleyan University, May 2012), accessed August 1, 2016, http://repec.wesleyan.edu/pdf/jjacobsen/2012009_jacobsen.pdf.

20 D. M. Pearce, "The Feminization of Poverty: Women, Work and Welfare," *Urban and Social Change Review* (February 1978): 28–36.

21 England, "The Gender Revolution."

22 Carmen DeNavas-Walt, Bernadette D. Proctor, and Jessica C. Smith, "Income, Poverty, and Health Insurance Coverage in the United States: 2012," *United States Census Current Population Reports*, September 2013, https://www.census.gov/prod/2013pubs/p60-245.pdf.

23 Shaila Dewan, "As Wars End, Young Veterans Return to Scant Jobs," *New York Times*, December 17, 2011, http://www.nytimes.com/2011/12/18/business/for-youngest-veterans-the-bleakest-of-job-prospects.html.

24 Alexander Eichler, "Nearly Half of Oldest Unemployed Have Been Jobless for over a Year," *Huffington Post*, January 2, 2012, http://www.huffingtonpost.com/2011/11/02/long-term-unemployment_n_1071851.html?ref=business&mid=52159.

25 Hope Yen, "1 in 2 New Graduates Are Jobless or Underemployed," *Associated Press*, April 23, 2012, http://finance.yahoo.com/news/1-2-graduates-jobless-underemployed-140300522.html.

Chapter 6   Unemployment Blues and Backlash

1 Mirra Komarovsky, *The Unemployed Man and His Family: The Effects of Unemployment upon the Status of the Men in Fifty-Nine Families* (New York: Dryden Press, 1940), 74.

2 Kate Rogers, "In Economic Address, Hillary Clinton Calls Out 'Gig' Economy," *CNBC*, July 13, 2015, http://www.cnbc.com/2015/07/13/in-economic-address-hillary-clinton-calls-out-gig-economy.html.

3 Sabrina Tavernise, "U.S. Suicide Rate Surges to a 30-Year High," *New York Times*, April 22, 2016, http://www.nytimes.com/2016/04/22/health/us-suicide-rate-surges-to-a-30-year-high.html.

4 Alex Lemieux, "Murder-Suicide Claims Life of Father and Two Sons Due to Unemployment," *Guardian Liberty Voice*, July 18, 2015, http://guardianlv.com/2015/07/murder-suicide-claims-life-of-father-and-two-sons-due-to-unemployment.

5 K. A. Hempstead and J. A. Phillips, "Rising Suicide among Adults Aged 40–64 Years: The Role of Job and Financial Circumstances," *American Journal of Preventive Medicine* 48.5 (2015): 491–500; Feijun Luo, Curtis S. Florence, Myriam Quispe-Agnoli, Lijing Ouyang, and Alexander E. Crosby, "Impact of Business Cycles on US Suicide Rates, 1928–2007," *American Journal of Public Health* 101.6 (2011): 1139–1146.

6 Michael S. Kimmel, *Manhood in America: A Cultural History*, 2nd ed. (New York: Oxford University Press, 2006).

7 Komarovsky, *The Unemployed Man*, 27.

8 Komarovsky, 81.

9 Komarovsky, 23.

10 Komarovsky, 119.

11 Rich Morin and Rakesh Kochhar, "The Impact of Long-term Unemployment: Lost Income, Lost Friends—and Loss of Self-Respect," Washington, D.C., Pew Research Center, July 22, 2010, http://www.pewsocialtrends.org/files/2010/11/760-recession.pdf.

12 Jordan is suffering from the more challenging path to adulthood documented in Michael S. Kimmel, *Guyland: The Perilous World Where Boys Become Men* (New York: HarperCollins, 2008).

13 Matthew E. Dupre, Linda K. George, Guangya Liu, and Eric D. Peterson, "The Cumulative Effect of Unemployment on Risks for Acute Myocardial Infarction," *Archives of Internal Medicine* 172.22 (2012): 1731–1737; David J. Roelfs, Eran Shor, Karina W. Davidson, and Joseph E. Schwartz, "Losing Life and Livelihood: A Systematic Review and Meta-analysis of Unemployment and All-Cause Mortality," *Social Science & Medicine* 72.6 (2011): 840–854.

14 Jiaquan Xu, Sherry L. Murphy, Kenneth D. Kochanek, and Brigham A. Bastian, "Deaths: Final Data for 2013," *National Vital Statistics Report* 64.2 (February 16, 2016), http://www.cdc.gov/nchs/data/nvsr/nvsr64/nvsr64_02.pdf.

15 Daniel Coleman, Mark S. Kaplan, John T. Casey, "The Social Nature of Male Suicide: A New Analytic Model," *International Journal of Men's Health* 10.3 (2011): 240–252.

16 Aaron Reeves, Martin McKee, and David Stuckler, "Economic Suicides in the Great Recession in Europe and North America," *British Journal of Psychiatry* 205.3 (2014): 246–247.

17 Luo et al., "Impact of Business Cycles."

18 Robert DeFina and Lance Hannon, "The Changing Relationship between Unemployment and Suicide," *Suicide and Life-Threatening Behavior* 45.2 (2015): 217–229.

19 Erving Goffman, "On Face-Work," in *Interaction Ritual: Essays on Face-to-Face Behavior* (New York: Pantheon Books), 5–46.

20 For summaries, see Matthew B. Ezzell, "'I'm in Control': Compensatory Manhood in a Therapeutic Community," *Gender & Society* 26.2 (2012): 190–215; Douglas Schrock and Michael Schwalbe, "Men, Masculinity, and Manhood Acts," *Annual Review of Sociology* 35 (2009): 277–295; J. Edward Sumerau, "'That's What a Man Is

Supposed to Do': Compensatory Manhood Acts in an LGBT Christian Church," *Gender & Society* 26 (2012): 461–487.

21 James Messerschmidt, *Nine Lives: Adolescent Masculinities, the Body and Violence* (Boulder, Colo.: Westview Press, 1999).

22 Tavernise, "U.S. Suicide Rate Surges."

23 Frederick L. Allen, *Since Yesterday: The 1930's in America* (New York: Harper and Row, 1986).

24 In Kimmel's *Guyland*, he suggests that today, a large swath of boys and young men escape the elusive and tenuous chase of manhood by avoiding relationships altogether, as well immersing themselves in fantasies via video games and porn. Barbara Ehrenreich documents men's rebellious flights from family commitments and breadwinner responsibilities beginning in the 1950s. Barbara Ehrenreich, *The Hearts of Men: American Dreams and the Flight from Commitment* (New York: Anchor Books, 1983).

25 Ilana Demantas and Kristen Myers, "Step Up and Be a Man in a Different Manner: Unemployed Men Reframing Masculinity," *Sociological Quarterly* 56 (2015): 640–664.

26 Ralph Ellison, *Invisible Man* (New York: Random House, 1952).

27 Allan Smith, "'He Doesn't Have the Cash': Mark Cuban Questions Whether Trump Is 'as Rich' as He Claims after FEC Report," *Business Insider*, June 21, 2016, http://www.businessinsider.com/mark-cuban-donald-trump-wealth-fec-report-2016-6.

28 Kimmel, *Manhood*.

29 Christian Alexander Vaccaro, "Male Bodies in Manhood Acts: The Role of Body-Talk and Embodied Practice in Signifying Culturally Dominant Notions of Manhood," *Sociology Compass* 5.1 (2011): 65–76.

30 Arlie Russell Hochschild and Anne Machung, *The Second Shift* (New York: Penguin, 2012); Elizabeth Miklya Legerski and Marie Cornwall, "Working-Class Job Loss, Gender, and the Negotiation of Household Labor," *Gender & Society* 24 (2010): 447–474; Christin L. Munsch, "Her Support, His Support: Money, Masculinity, & Infidelity," *American Sociological Review* 80 (2015): 469–495.

31 Elijah Anderson, *Code of the Street: Decency, Violence, and the Moral Life of the Inner City* (New York: W. W. Norton, 1999); Richard Majors and Janet Mancini Billson, *Cool Pose: The Dilemmas of Black Manhood in America* (New York: Lexington Books, 1993).

32 Kristen W. Springer, "Economic Dependence in Marriage and Husbands' Midlife Health: Testing Three Possible Mechanisms," *Gender & Society* 24.3 (2010): 378–401.

33 FBI Uniform Crime Reports, "2014 Crime in the United States: Persons Arrested," accessed November 2, 2015, https://ucr.fbi.gov/crime-in-the-u.s/2014/crime-in-the-u.s.-2014/persons-arrested/main.

34 Ezzell, "Compensatory Manhood"; Schrock and Schwalbe, "Men, Masculinity, Manhood Acts."

35 Anderson, *Code of the Street*; Jason T. Eastman, "Rebel Manhood: The Hegemonic Masculinity of the Southern Rock Music Revival," *Journal of Contemporary Ethnography* 41.2 (2012): 189–219; Loic Wacquant, *Body & Soul: Notebooks of an Apprentice Boxer* (New York: Oxford University Press, 2004).

36 Yen Le Espiritu, "All Men Are *Not* Created Equal: Asian Men in U.S. History," in *Men's Lives*, ed. Michael S. Kimmel and Michael A. Messner, 8th ed. (Boston: Allyn & Bacon, 2010), 17–25.

37 Maxine P. Atkinson, Theodore N. Greenstein, and Molly Monahan Lang, "For Women, Breadwinning Can Be Dangerous: Gendered Resource Theory and Wife Abuse," *Journal of Marriage and Family* 67.5 (2005): 1137–1148; Scott Melzer, "Gender, Work, and Intimate Violence: Men's Occupational Violence Spillover and Compensatory Violence," *Journal of Marriage and Family* 64.4 (2002): 820–832.

38 Ronald D. Brown, *Dying on the Job: Murder and Mayhem in the American Workplace* (Lanham, Md.: Rowman & Littlefield, 2013).

39 James Alan Fox and Jack Levin, *Extreme Killing: Understanding Serial and Mass Murder* (Thousand Oaks, Calif.: Sage, 2012).

40 John L. Oliffe, Christina S. E. Han, Murray Drummond, Estephanie Sta. Maria, Joan L. Bottorff, and Genevieve Creighton, "Men, Masculinities, and Murder-Suicide," *American Journal of Men's Health* 9 (2015): 473–485.

41 Douglas Kellner, *Guys and Guns Amok: Domestic Terrorism and School Shootings from the Oklahoma City Bombing to the Virginia Tech Massacre* (Boulder, Colo.: Paradigm, 2008).

42 Quoted in Rich Lord and Paula Reed Ward, "A Portrait of Contrasts Emerges from Those Who Knew Poplawski," *Pittsburgh Post-Gazette*, April 12, 2009, http://www.post-gazette.com/local/city/2009/04/12/A-portrait-of-contrasts-emerges-from-those-who-knew-Poplawski/stories/200904120213; Bill Martin, "Racist Pittsburgh Triple Cop-Killer Gets Death," *Southern Poverty Law Center*, June 29, 2011, https://www.splcenter.org/hatewatch/2011/06/29/racist-pittsburgh-triple-cop-killer-gets-death; Dennis B. Roddy, "Suspect in Officers' Shooting Was Into Conspiracy Theories," *Pittsburgh Post-Gazette*, April 5, 2009, http://web.archive.org/web/20090406070123/http://www.post-gazette.com/pg/09095/960750-53.stm.

43 Fox and Levin, *Extreme Killing*.

44 Jim Yardley, "A Portrait of the Terrorist: From Shy Child to Single-Minded Killer," *New York Times*, October 10, 2001, http://www.nytimes.com/2001/10/10/world/nation-challenged-mastermind-portrait-terrorist-shy-child-single-minded-killer.html.

45 Michael S. Kimmel, *Misframing Men: The Politics of Contemporary Masculinities* (Piscataway, N.J.: Rutgers University Press, 2010); Jessica Stern, *Terror in the Name of God: Why Religious Militants Kill* (New York: HarperCollins, 2003).

46 Stern, *Terror*.

47 See Kimmel, *Misframing Men*.

Chapter 7   Redefining Manhood

1 However, upper-class men continued to hold those orthodox views and stigmatize men who did childcare. See Matthew C. Gutmann, *The Meanings of Macho: Being a Man in Mexico City* (Berkeley: University of California Press, 1996).

2 Alex Williams, "Just Wait until Your Mother Gets Home," *New York Times*, August 12, 2012, http://www.nytimes.com/2012/08/12/fashion/dads-are-taking-over-as-full-time-parents.html?pagewanted=3&_r=1&hp.

3 Mirra Komarovsky, *The Unemployed Man and His Family: The Effects of Unemployment upon the Status of the Men in Fifty-Nine Families* (New York: Dryden Press, 1940), 61.

4 Stephanie Coontz, *The Way We Never Were: American Families and the Nostalgia Trap* (New York: Basic Books, 1992).

5 Coontz, 31.

6 Betty Friedan, *The Feminine Mystique* (New York: W. W. Norton, 1963).

7 Coontz, *The Way We Never Were.*

8 Compared to single mothers, single fathers are two and a half times as likely to cohabitate with a partner, many of whom are likely to be doing some or even most of the domestic work. Gretchen Livingston, "The Rise of Single Fathers: A Ninefold Increase since 1960," Washington, D.C., Pew Research Center, July 2, 2013, http://www.pewsocialtrends.org/2013/07/02/the-rise-of-single-fathers/.

9 Gretchen Livingston, "Growing Number of Dads Home with the Kids," Washington, D.C., Pew Research Center, June 5, 2014, http://www.pewsocialtrends.org/2014/06/05/growing-number-of-dads-home-with-the-kids/.

10 Debated criteria include whether a stay-at-home dad should be counted if he is unmarried, works some or not at all, works from home, cohabitates with someone other than his child/children's other biological parent, and actually identifies as a stay-at-home father. See Noelle Chesley, "Stay-at-Home Fathers and Breadwinning Mothers: Gender, Couple Dynamics, and Social Change," *Gender & Society* 25.5 (2011): 642–664; Livingston, "Dads Home with the Kids."

11 Kim Parker and Gretchen Livingston, "6 Facts about American Fathers," Washington, D.C., Pew Research Center, June 15, 2017, http://www.pewresearch.org/fact-tank/2017/06/15/fathers-day-facts/.

12 Scott Coltrane, *Family Man: Fatherhood, Housework, and Gender Equity* (New York: Oxford University Press, 1996), 5.

13 Kim Parker and Wendy Wang, "Modern Parenthood: Roles of Moms and Dads Converge as They Balance Work and Family," Washington, D.C., Pew Research Center, March 14, 2013, http://assets.pewresearch.org/wp-content/uploads/sites/3/2013/03/FINAL_modern_parenthood_03-2013.pdf.

14 Paula England, "The Gender Revolution: Uneven and Stalled," *Gender & Society* 24 (2010): 149–166; Kathleen Gerson, *Unfinished Revolution: How a New Generation Is Reshaping Family, Work, and Gender in America* (New York: Oxford University Press, 2010).

15 Livingston, "Dads Home with the Kids."

16 Chesley, "Stay-at-Home Fathers."

17 Gerson, *Unfinished Revolution*; Kathleen Gerson, "Gender Politics in Intimate Relationships," New York: American Sociological Association Annual Meetings, August 11, 2013.

18 W. Jean Yeung, John F. Sandberg, Pamela E. Davis-Kean, and Sandra F. Hofferth, "Children's Time with Fathers in Intact Families," *Journal of Marriage and Family* 63 (2001): 136–154.

19 Andrea Doucet, "Parental Responsibilities: Dilemmas of Measurement and Gender Equality," *Journal of Marriage and Family* 77 (2015): 224–242.

20 Wendy Wang, Kim Parker, and Paul Taylor, "Breadwinner Moms: Mothers Are the Sole or Primary Provider in Four-in-Ten Households with Children," Washington, D.C., Pew Research Center, May 29, 2013, http://www.pewsocialtrends.org/2013/05/29/breadwinner-moms/.

21 Livingston, "Dads Home with the Kids."

22 Douglas Schrock and Michael Schwalbe, "Men, Masculinity, and Manhood Acts," *Annual Review of Sociology* 35 (2009): 277–295 (290).

23 Carrie M. Lane, "Man Enough to Let My Wife Support Me: How Changing Models of Career and Gender Are Reshaping the Experiences of Unemployment," *American Ethnologist* 36.4 (2009): 681–692.

24 Judith Butler, *Undoing Gender* (New York: Routledge, 2004); Francine M. Deutsch, "Undoing Gender," *Gender & Society* 21.1 (2007): 106–127; Judith Lorber, *Breaking the Bowls: Degendering and Feminist Change* (New York: W. W. Norton, 2005); Barbara J. Risman, *Gender Vertigo* (New Haven, Conn.: Yale University Press, 1999).
25 Michael Armato, private communication.
26 Brad Harrington, Fred Van Deusen, and Iyar Mazar, "The New Dad: Right at Home" (Center for Work and Family, Boston College, 2012).
27 Harrington, Deusen, and Mazar; Aaron B. Rochlen, Ryan A. McKelley, Marie-Anne Suizzo, and Vanessa Scaringi, "Predictors of Relationship Satisfaction, Psychological Well-Being, and Life Satisfaction among Stay-at-Home Fathers," *Psychology of Men & Masculinity* 9.1 (2008): 17–28.
28 Timothy J. Biblarz and Judith Stacey, "How Does the Gender of Parents Matter?," *Journal of Marriage and Family* 72.1 (2010): 3–22 (17).
29 Emily W. Kane, *The Gender Trap: Parents and the Pitfalls of Raising Boys and Girls* (New York: New York University Press, 2012).
30 Williams, "Just Wait until Your Mother Gets Home."
31 Friedan, *The Feminine Mystique.*
32 David D. Gilmore, *Manhood in the Making: Cultural Concepts of Masculinity* (New Haven, Conn.: Yale University Press, 1990).
33 Elizabeth Miklya Legerski and Marie Cornwall, "Working-Class Job Loss, Gender, and the Negotiation of Household Labor," *Gender & Society* 24 (2010): 447–474.
34 Harrington, Deusen, and Mazar, "The New Dad."
35 Aaron B. Rochlen, Marie-Anne Suizzo, and Ryan A. McKelley, "'I'm Just Providing for My Family': A Qualitative Study of Stay-at-Home Fathers," *Psychology of Men & Masculinity* 9.4 (2008): 193–206.
36 For exceptions, see Legerski and Cornwall, "Working-Class Job Loss"; Jennifer Sherman, *Those Who Work, Those Who Don't: Poverty, Morality, and Family in Rural America* (Minneapolis: University of Minnesota Press, 2009).
37 Chesley, "Stay-at-Home Fathers"; Sherman, *Those Who Work.*
38 Beth A. Latshaw, "Is Fatherhood a Full-Time Job? Mixed Method Insights into Measuring Stay-at-Home Fatherhood," *Fathering* 9.2 (2011): 125–149.
39 Lorber, *Breaking the Bowls,* 157.

Conclusion

1 R. W. Connell, *Masculinities* (Berkeley: University of California Press, 1995).
2 David A. Cotter, Joan M. Hermsen, and Reeve Vanneman, "The End of the Gender Revolution? Gender Role Attitudes from 1977 to 2008," *American Journal of Sociology* 117.1 (2011): 259–289.
3 See Paula England, "The Gender Revolution: Uneven and Stalled," *Gender & Society* 24 (2010): 149–166.
4 Cotter, Hermsen, and Vanneman, "The End of the Gender Revolution?"
5 Clare Malone, "From 1927 to Hillary Clinton, How Americans Have Felt about a Woman President," FiveThirtyEight, June 9, 2016, https://fivethirtyeight.com/features/from-1937-to-hillary-clinton-how-americans-have-felt-about-a-female-president/.
6 David Pedulla and Sarah Thebaud, "Can We Finish the Revolution? Gender, Work-Family Ideals, and Institutional Constraint," *American Sociological Review* 80.1 (2015): 116–139.

7 Jerry A. Jacobs and Kathleen Gerson, "Unpacking Americans' Views of the Employment of Mothers and Fathers Using National Vignette Survey Data: SWS Presidential Address," *Gender & Society* 30.3 (2016): 1–29.

8 Kathleen Gerson, "Different Ways of *Not* Having It All: Work, Care, and Shifting Gender Arrangements in the New Economy," in *Beyond the Cubicle: Insecurity Culture and the Flexible Self*, ed. Allison Pugh (New York: Oxford University Press, 2016), 155–178.

9 Kim Parker and Gretchen Livingston, "6 Facts about American Fathers," Washington, D.C., Pew Research Center, June 15, 2017, http://www.pewresearch.org/fact-tank/2017/06/15/fathers-day-facts/.

10 Hannah Fingerhut, "Support Steady for Same-Sex Marriage and Acceptance of Homosexuality," Washington, D.C., Pew Research Center, May 12, 2016, http://www.pewresearch.org/fact-tank/2016/05/12/support-steady-for-same-sex-marriage-and-acceptance-of-homosexuality/.

11 Eric Anderson, *Inclusive Masculinity: The Changing Nature of Masculinities* (New York: Routledge, 2009).

12 England, "The Gender Revolution"; Cecilia L. Ridgeway, "Framed before We Know It: How Gender Shapes Social Relations," *Gender & Society* 23 (2009): 145–160.

13 Cotter, Hermsen, and Vanneman, "The End of the Gender Revolution?"; England, "The Gender Revolution"; Kathleen Gerson, *Unfinished Revolution: How a New Generation Is Reshaping Family, Work, and Gender in America* (New York: Oxford University Press, 2010); Judith Lorber, *Breaking the Bowls: Degendering and Feminist Change* (New York: W. W. Norton, 2005).

14 England, "The Gender Revolution."

15 Catalyst, Pyramid: Women in S&P 500 Companies, New York: Catalyst, accessed July 26, 2016, www.catalyst.org/.

16 Catherine Hill, "Barriers and Bias: The Status of Women in Leadership," American Association of University Women, March 30, 2016, accessed July 25, 2017, http://www.aauw.org/research/barriers-and-bias/.

17 England, "The Gender Revolution."

18 Sharon Hays, *The Cultural Contradictions of Motherhood* (New Haven, Conn.: Yale University Press, 1996).

19 Michael S. Kimmel, *Manhood in America: A Cultural History*, 2nd ed. (New York: Oxford University Press, 2006).

20 Kimmel.

21 Kimmel.

22 Lorber, *Breaking the Bowls*, 165.

23 James W. Messerschmidt, "Engendering Gendered Knowledge: Assessing the Academic Appropriation of Hegemonic Masculinity," *Men and Masculinities* 15.1 (2012): 56–76 (73).

24 bell hooks, *Feminist Theory: From Margin to Center*, 3rd ed. (New York: Routledge, 2015), 83.

25 Alex Williams, "Just Wait until Your Mother Gets Home," *New York Times*, August 12, 2012, http://www.nytimes.com/2012/08/12/fashion/dads-are-taking-over-as-full-time-parents.html?pagewanted=3&_r=1&hp.

26 Noelle Chesley, "Stay-at-Home Fathers and Breadwinning Mothers: Gender, Couple Dynamics, and Social Change," *Gender & Society* 25.5 (2011): 642–664.

27 Adam Glynn and Maya Sen, "Identifying Judicial Empathy: Does Having Daughters Cause Judges to Rule for Women's Issues?," *American Journal of Political Science* 59.1 (2015): 37–54.

28 Jonathan Cylus, M. Maria Glymour, and Mauricio Avendano, "Do Generous Unemployment Benefit Programs Reduce Suicide Rates? A State Fixed-Effect Analysis Covering 1968–2008," *American Journal of Epidemiology* 180.1 (2014): 45–52.

29 Gerson, *Unfinished Revolution*; Jennifer L. Hook, "Care in Context: Men's Unpaid Work in 20 Countries, 1965–2003," *American Sociological Review* 71.4 (2006): 639–660; Pedulla and Thebaud, "Can We Finish the Revolution?"

30 Sarah Thébaud and David S. Pedulla, "Masculinity and the Stalled Revolution: How Gender Ideologies and Norms Shape Young Men's Responses to Work–Family Policies," *Gender & Society* 30.4 (2016): 590–617.

31 Gerson, "Different Ways of *Not* Having It All," 173.

Appendix

1 Scott Melzer, "Gender, Work, and Intimate Violence: Men's Occupational Violence Spillover and Compensatory Violence," *Journal of Marriage and Family* 64.4 (2002): 820–832.

2 Scott Melzer, *Gun Crusaders: The NRA's Culture War* (New York: New York University Press, 2009).

3 Douglas Schrock and Michael Schwalbe, "Men, Masculinity, and Manhood Acts," *Annual Review of Sociology* 35 (2009): 277–295 (278).

4 Schrock and Schwalbe.

5 Kathy Charmaz, *Constructing Grounded Theory: A Practical Guide through Qualitative Analysis* (Thousand Oaks, Calif.: Sage, 2006); Barney G. Glaser and Anselm L. Strauss, *The Discovery of Grounded Theory* (Chicago: Aldine, 1967).

6 For the Gentlemen's Fighting Club, I have assigned pseudonyms that do not always reflect their cultural heritage. I do so because of the small, tight-knit nature of the group, which would allow some members to easily identify others if they knew their ethnicity and other identifying information.

7 Loic Wacquant, *Body & Soul: Notebooks of an Apprentice Boxer* (New York: Oxford University Press, 2004).

Index

205–209; and military, 158, 162; as stay-
at-home dads, 205–209; stereotypes, 92;
subordination of, 21–22, 121–122
gender: as arbitrary, 230; conformity, 41, 56;
definitions of, 13–14; equality, 229, 244;
identity, 14–15, 187–188, 209; nonconformity, 222, 241; as performance, 13–15; as
social construct, 13–14. *See also* degendering; doing gender; redoing gender
gender-appropriateness, 14, 20, 55
gender vertigo. *See* degendering
genitalia: female, 94, 104; as symbol of manhood, 18, 102. *See also* penis
Gentlemen's Fighting Club (GFC): experience of, 1–3, 29–36, 42–45; and fantasies,
118; as fraternal, 71–73; history of, 36;
introduction to, 23–24; member benefits,
67; reactions to, 64–65
Gilligan, James, 124–125
girls: and body control, 122–123; and fighting, 40–41
globalization, 192–193, 247
Great Depression, 171–172, 184, 196
Great Recession, 8, 149–150, 161–162, 229;
aftereffects, 169–170, 193, 247; and suicide, 176

health, 17, 172, 173, 175, 189–190, 228;
mental, 106–108, 118, 171, 175–178, 180,
268n30
hegemony, 41, 64, 261n64; cultural, 20;
diminishing of, 31, 229–232; rejection of,
232. *See also* ideals: hegemonic; masculinity: hegemonic
heteronormativity, 97
heterosexism, 22
heterosexuality, 18, 86, 97
hierarchy, 61, 92, 235; of masculinities, 21, 41,
103, 205; in schools, 126
homophobia, 57–58, 89, 122, 234
homosociality, 70–71, 73, 89
hooks, bell, 244–245
humanization, 246
humiliation, 55, 58, 103, 126, 193
humor, 75–76, 78, 181, 213–214

ideals: attainable, 229; cultural, 20–21, 101;
as destructive, 84, 228; hegemonic, 64,
100, 118, 122, 125, 231, 238; manhood, 101,

106, 108, 113, 117–118, 204. *See also* body
ideal; breadwinner ideal
identity: gendered, 117; loss of, 178; multi-
plicity of, 16; reclaiming, 55, 84; threats
to, 117
ideology, 20–21, 220, 223, 236, 239, 242
impotence, 83–84, 102. *See also* erectile dysfunction (ED)
inappropriateness, 65
independence, 122, 173–174, 240
individualism, 204
individuality, 40, 246
industrialization, 6, 39, 149, 228
inequality: gender, 14, 151, 182, 239; income,
169; as natural, 231, 236–237; reduction
of, 246–247
infantilizing, 172–174
injuries, 44–45, 76–78
injustice, 126, 133–134, 135–136
insecurity, 96, 100–101, 101, 118
insults, 18, 45–46, 92, 121–122, 165, 242–243
internalizing, 10–11, 16–17, 24, 54–58,
87–103, 108, 176, 180
internet, 163, 164, 183, 191, 206–207, 213
intersectionality, 16
intimacy, 36, 84, 86, 84, 106, 189, 246
invisibility, 186–187
isolation, 106, 163, 178–180, 186, 206, 217, 247

job fairs, 144–148

Kaufman, Michael, 16
Komarovsky, Mirra, 171–172

Latinos, 98–99, 232
LGBTQ parents, 207–209
libido, 177, 189
locker-room syndrome. *See* small-penis
syndrome
Lorber, Judith, 222–223
losing, of fights, 71, 79–80

manhood: attainable, 229; claims to, 187;
concepts of, 6–8; construction of, 62, 80;
and control, 163; definitions of, 17, 171,
204, 231–234; essential, 64; as fatherhood, 234; models of, 64; questioning of,
243–244; as responsibility, 232–233; as
restrictive, 17–20; as tenuous, 40, 71, 96;
threats to, 19–20; visceral, 71

About the Author

SCOTT MELZER is professor of sociology and chair of the women's, gender, and sexuality studies program at Albion College in Michigan. He is the author of *Gun Crusaders: The NRA's Culture War.*